AF836625

COMPARATIVE LAW IN ASIA

This book includes essays in honour of Professor Andrew Harding, a leading scholar in the fields of Asian legal studies and comparative constitutional law.

Written by his colleagues and friends, the essays deal with important themes in comparative law in Asia, including comparative law methodology and theory; comparative constitutional law; legal transplants and development; comparative law and society. The essays cover Malaysia, Singapore, Thailand, Myanmar, Southeast Asia and Commonwealth Asia.

Comparative Law in Asia

Essays in Honour of Andrew Harding

Edited by
Ngoc Son Bui
and
Munin Pongsapan

•HART•
OXFORD • LONDON • NEW YORK • NEW DELHI • SYDNEY

HART PUBLISHING

Bloomsbury Publishing Plc

Kemp House, Chawley Park, Cumnor Hill, Oxford, OX2 9PH, UK

1385 Broadway, New York, NY 10018, USA

Bloomsbury Publishing Ireland Limited, 29 Earlsfort Terrace, Dublin 2, D02 AY28, Ireland

HART PUBLISHING, the Hart/Stag logo, BLOOMSBURY and the Diana logo are trademarks of Bloomsbury Publishing Plc

First published in Great Britain 2025

Copyright © Ngoc Son Bui and Munin Pongsapan, and Contributors 2025

Ngoc Son Bui and Munin Pongsapan, and Contributors have asserted their right under the Copyright, Designs and Patents Act 1988 to be identified as Authors of this work.

All rights reserved. No part of this publication may be: i) reproduced or transmitted in any form, electronic or mechanical, including photocopying, recording or by means of any information storage or retrieval system without prior permission in writing from the publishers; or ii) used or reproduced in any way for the training, development or operation of artificial intelligence (AI) technologies, including generative AI technologies. The rights holders expressly reserve this publication from the text and data mining exception as per Article 4(3) of the Digital Single Market Directive (EU) 2019/790.

While every care has been taken to ensure the accuracy of this work, no responsibility for loss or damage occasioned to any person acting or refraining from action as a result of any statement in it can be accepted by the authors, editors or publishers.

All UK Government legislation and other public sector information used in the work is Crown Copyright ©. All House of Lords and House of Commons information used in the work is Parliamentary Copyright ©. This information is reused under the terms of the Open Government Licence v3.0 (http://www.nationalarchives.gov.uk/doc/open-government-licence/version/3) except where otherwise stated.

All Eur-lex material used in the work is © European Union, http://eur-lex.europa.eu/, 1998–2025.

A catalogue record for this book is available from the British Library.

A catalogue record for this book is available from the Library of Congress.

Library of Congress Control Number: 2025945899

ISBN: HB: 978-1-50998-654-5
ePDF: 978-1-50998-656-9
ePub: 978-1-50998-655-2

Typeset by Compuscript Ltd, Shannon

For product safety related questions contact productsafety@bloomsbury.com

To find out more about our authors and books visit www.hartpublishing.co.uk. Here you will find extracts, author information, details of forthcoming events and the option to sign up for our newsletters.

PREFACE

I wish first of all to thank very sincerely Professor Bui Ngoc Son and Dr Munin Pongsapan for organising and editing this book, and in so doing to mark my own contribution, such as it is, to Asian comparative law studies. Secondly, of course, I wish to give heartfelt thanks to all of the contributors, all of whom are personal friends as well as extraordinarily talented scholars. I feel deeply honoured, privileged, humbled, astonished, and of course also delighted by this book and the conference that led to it.

The experience of attending the conference, with its fascinating themes and responses, has prompted me to think again about my own experience of the evolving landscape of Asian comparative law.

I was a relatively late comer to the subject, having during my first 15 years as an academic studied comparative constitutional law with special reference to Malaysia and Singapore. In the mid-1990s I began teaching law in Southeast Asia, which required me to broaden my horizons to law in several sub-disciplinary areas, especially legal history and law and society. This teaching commitment also required me to acquire knowledge of several countries.

At that time the subject was relatively underdeveloped, certainly compared with the present. It was difficult to find suitable, even purely descriptive let alone analytical, material to give to students to read that would excite their interest and imaginations. In some areas I found that the only way forward was to write or commission the material myself in an attempt to frame the subject and link it to comparative law in general. My focus was consistently on constitutional law, a subject which required an expansion of knowledge into history, culture and politics, and one to which I returned constantly. This trajectory led me in due course to work on more general subjects, such as law and development and legal history.

Around the millennium a very clear shift took place in comparative law, which had tended to focus on doctrinal issues and on common law/civil law comparison, especially within a European/North American compass. In a series of notable publications around the year 2000, comparative law scholars shifted their ground towards the discussion of legal traditions and systems other than those derived from Europe, and on the European legal traditions as transplanted across the world. A necessary consequence of this development was to pay attention to societal contexts as well as substantive contents. Context became more important than content. The understanding appeared to be that any general propositions about law, including the definition of law itself, could not be made without paying attention to Asia, with its teeming diversity of legal traditions. Yet scholars were unsure of their assumptions and even their precise questions. This was the cue to the developing Asian law scholarly community to seize its moment, and it did so with relish.

However, there was still a gap in orientation between 'Asian law' and 'comparative law'. Asian law scholars have developed their work because they considered it intrinsically important, not especially because it reinforced or undermined any general assumptions about the nature or trajectory of law as such. This is a tension that I think is still in the process of being resolved. My library contains a large number of books that I have collected together as constituting a genre: their titles nearly all involve the words 'in Asia' or the like. Some of these I have edited myself. Yet I now question why this appendix 'in Asia' is apparently so often required. Any good discussion of law is surely of both specific and general value, irrespective of its locus. We do not usually add geographical reference to the titles of general works about law, unless we are writing purely doctrinal or professional works that depend on specific jurisdictions.

Yet, as this volume strongly attests, discussion of law in Asia is at its root discussion of matters of general purport, not simply that which appears exotic. Yet I must confess that it is because Asia presents diversity and contrariness that I have always been excited to study it. The challenges are irresistible. Why has Thailand had 20 constitutions? How and why do 'Westminster' conventions work differently in Malaysia? How do socialist and Confucian legal traditions jive together in Vietnam? How was civil law changed when transplanted to Japan? These are the kinds of question that have excited Asian law scholars. The challenges are irresistible, but the rewards are also great.

In my experience and observation, comparative law scholars generally start by specialising in a doctrinal area of law and in a particular legal system. This is hardly surprising, because clearly one has to start somewhere. This has certainly been my own experience. The scholars who have contributed to this book have astonished me with the speed with which they have both acquired such expertise and expanded both their theoretical insights and the empirical scope of their work. I am not being modest when I say that all of them – I mean those younger than myself – are far ahead of where I was at their age. It would be ego-boosting to think that this was a case of dwarves standing on the shoulders of giants. To the contrary, it actually resembles to me the exactly opposite configuration. Working with and learning from both my contemporaries and, increasingly, from those 20, or 30, and in some cases even 40 years younger than myself has been one of the true joys of my own work. This has been the case with the book series Constitutional Systems of the World, with Hart Publishing, of which I am co-founding editor with Professor Peter Leyland, and which has spawned 40 books, most Asian countries being covered. It has been the case also with teaching Asian law subjects; with journal articles and special issues; with conferences and edited books; and so on. Another enormously pleasurable consequence of these opportunities has been to be able to discuss comparative law with scholars and students across many countries on several continents.

Looking back over 47 years in academia, I have been extremely fortunate in ways too countless to list, but mainly in the people I have had the pleasure of working with. I am still motivated and fascinated by the diversity and profound consequentiality of Asian comparative law. Once again, I thank the publishers (I have worked with Hart Publishing continuously for 20 years), editors and contributors, and express the hope and the expectation that this book will in its own way add depth and lustre to our great subject.

Andrew Harding
Johor Bahru
April 2025

TABLE OF CONTENTS

PART III
LEGAL TRANSPLANTS, LAW AND DEVELOPMENT

PART IV
COMPARATIVE LAW AND SOCIETY

LIST OF CONTRIBUTORS

Editors

Ngoc Son Bui, Professor of Asian Laws, Faculty of Law, University of Oxford

Munin Pongsapan, Associate Professor, Thammasat University

Contributors

Benjamin L Berger, Professor and York Research Chair in Pluralism and Public Law, Osgoode Hall Law School, York University

Albert HY Chen, Cheng Chan Lan Yue Professor and Chair of Constitutional Law, University of Hong Kong

David M Engel, Suny Distinguished Service Professor of Law Emeritus, The State University of New York at Buffalo

Justin O Frosini, Associate Professor of Comparative Public Law, Bocconi University and Robert J Abernethy Adjunct Professor of Constitutional Law, Johns Hopkins University SAIS Europe

Tom Ginsburg, Leo Spitz Distinguished Service Professor of International Law, University of Chicago

Andrew Harding, Professor of Law, University of Reading Malaysia

Arif A Jamal, Associate Professor, Faculty of Law, National University of Singapore

Rawin Leelapatana, Assistant Professor, Chulalongkorn University

Peter Leyland, Professor of Public Law, SOAS, University of London

Mara Malagodi, Reader, School of Law, University of Warwick

Jan Michiel Otto, Professor Emeritus Law and Governance in Developing Countries, Leiden University

Victor V Ramraj, Professor, University of Victoria

Adam Reekie, Assistant Professor, Faculty of Law, Thammasat University

Surutchada Reekie, Assistant Professor, Faculty of Law, Thammasat University

Lasse Schuldt, Assistant Professor, Faculty of Law, Thammasat University

Dian AH Shah, Assistant Professor, Faculty of Law, National University of Singapore

Kevin YL Tan, Adjunct Professor, Faculty of Law, National University of Singapore

Bryan Dennis G Tiojanco, Project Associate Professor, University of Tokyo

Khemthong Tonsakulrungruang, Lecturer, Faculty of Political Science, Chulalongkorn University

Introduction

NGOC SON BUI AND MUNIN PONGSAPAN

Comparative law in Asia has expanded significantly in the last decades. Professor Andrew Harding is a leading scholar in the field of Asian comparative law. Written by his colleagues and friends, essays in this book deal with important themes in comparative law in Asia that feature Harding's scholarship. We group these essays into four categories: comparative law methodology and theory; comparative constitutional law; legal transplants, law and development; and comparative law and society. The essays were presented and discussed at a workshop organised on Harding's birthday, 30 June 2024, in Oxford by the Oxford Programme in Asian Laws, Faculty of Law, University of Oxford.

I. Harding in Asian Comparative Law

A. Comparative Law Methodology and Theory

Comparative law scholarship has for many years explored methodological questions.[1] Mathias Siems's recent book deals with various traditional methods (typology of legal systems, functionalism, universalism) and extended methods (eg, jurisprudential, socio-logical, quantitative, empirical) of comparative law.[2]

Harding's scholarship explores aspects of comparative law methodology. The book *Comparative Law in the 21st Century*, which Harding coedits with Professor Esin Örücü, raises ontological questions about the nature and purposes of comparative law.[3] Harding cofounded Hart Publishing's book series 'Constitutional Systems of the World', which seeks to offer contextual analysis of constitutional systems.[4] This series is informed by contextualism in comparative constitutional law which

[1] Jaakko Husa, *Introduction to Comparative Law* (Hart, 2023); Geoffrey Samuel, *An Introduction to Comparative Law Theory and Method* (Hart, 2014); Mark Van Hoecke (ed), *Epistemology and Methodology of Comparative Law* (Hart, 2004).

[2] Mathias Siems, *Comparative Law*, 3rd edn (Cambridge University Press, 2022).

[3] Andrew Harding and Esin Örücü (eds), *Comparative Law in the 21st Century* (Kluwer Law International, 2002).

[4] Constitutional Systems of the World, www.bloomsbury.com/uk/series/constitutional-systems-of-the-world.

moves beyond the formal constitutional texts to consider social and political contexts under which constitutional systems operate.[5] Harding's books on Malaysia and Thailand in that series well illustrate the contextual approach to comparative constitutional law in Asia.[6]

Harding's scholarship is strongly concerned with local contexts and their relations with global doctrines. In the article 'Global Doctrine and Local Knowledge: Law in South East Asia', Harding demonstrates that the interaction between the global and the local is important in comparative law.[7] He puts forward many questions for comparative law methodology:

> For the comparative legal theorist the kinds of issues illustrated here present many frustrating, intractable, problems: what exactly is law? what is it for? what is its relation with society, culture, and religion? where does it come from? where is it going to? can law reform society? can law drawn from foreign models be successfully applied? can law be harmonised across areas where there is a high degree of pluralism and different degrees of development? More problematically: how do we even conceptualise justice in these matters where global doctrine and local knowledge seem to conflict? Do we study these questions as legal technicians, as social scientists, or as intellectual historians? We start with overwhelming questions, and despite our heroic efforts we generally also finish up with those same questions still being asked.[8]

Harding contributes to Asian comparative law methodology by moving beyond doctrinal analysis of legal rules to consider contextual factors of legal development in the region.

B. Comparative Constitutional Law

Comparative law traditionally focuses on private law, but the last decades have witnessed the continued expansion of comparative constitutional law.[9] Harding has made important contributions to comparative constitutional law scholarship with a focus on Asia, particularly his comparative writings on constitutional questions on Malaysia, Thailand and Myanmar.[10] His scholarship on Asian comparative

[5] Vicki Jackson, 'Comparative Constitutional Law: Methodologies' in Michel Rosenfeld and András Sajó (eds), *The Oxford Handbook of Comparative Constitutional Law* (Oxford University Press, 2012) 66–67; David S Law (ed), *Constitutionalism in Context* (Cambridge University Press, 2022).

[6] Andrew Harding, *The Constitution of Malaysia: A Contextual Analysis*, 2nd edn (Hart Publishing, 2022); Andrew Harding (author) and Peter Leyland (eds), *The Constitutional System of Thailand: A Contextual Analysis* (Hart Publishing, 2011).

[7] Andrew Harding, 'Global Doctrine and Local Knowledge: Law in South East Asia' (2002) 51 *The International and Comparative Law Quarterly* 35, www.jstor.org/stable/3663271.

[8] ibid, 46–47.

[9] Ming-Sung Kuo, 'Four Matters of Interpretation: The Constitutional Phenomenon in Comparative Studies' (2025) XX *Oxford Journal of Legal Studies* 1 (advance article).

[10] Andrew Harding (ed) (with the assistance of Khin Khin Oo), *Constitutionalism and Legal Change in Myanmar* (Hart, 2019).

constitutional law features, among other things, the Westminster Constitution,[11] the monarchy,[12] constitutional courts[13] and central–local relations.[14] On the latter, his recent book explores territorial governance of five Southeast Asian countries: Indonesia, Malaysia, Myanmar, the Philippines and Thailand.[15]

Harding contributes to the expansion of jurisdictions covered in Asian comparative constitutional law. His scholarship explored underrepresented jurisdictions, particularly Thailand and Myanmar. Harding also contributes to the expansion of the substantive contents of Asian comparative constitutional studies. Beyond courts, his scholarship deals with a wide range of institutional questions, particularly monarchy and territorial governance.

C. Legal Transplants, Law and Development

An important theme in comparative law is legal transplants or the movement of law from one jurisdiction to another.[16] Alan Watson argues that legal transplants are the main mechanism of legal development as legal innovations are rare.[17] In contrast, Pierre Legrand contends that legal transplants are impossible because the meaning of legal rule is historically and culturally conditioned and hence cannot travel across jurisdictions.[18] Harding engages in the legal transplants debate. He argues that legal transplants are possible in both private law and public law, although process is not easy, and further underlines that 'they are fundamentally related to the society of the donee, but not necessarily that of the donor'.[19]

Legal transplants are closely connected to another theme in comparative law: law and development. Law and development comprises external efforts to promote domestic legal reforms to support social-economic development in the

[11] Andrew Harding, 'The "Westminster Model" Constitution Overseas: Transplantation, Adaptation and Development in Commonwealth States' (2004) 4 *Oxford University Commonwealth Law Journal* 143, /doi.org/10.1080/14729342.2004.11421442.

[12] Andrew Harding and Harshan Kumarasingham. 'The Malay Monarchies in Constitutional and Social Conception' (2022) 9 *Asian Journal of Law and Society* 399, doi.org/10.1017/als.2022.32.

[13] Albert HY Chen and Andrew Harding (eds), *Constitutional Courts in Asia: A Comparative Perspective.* of *Comparative Constitutional Law and Policy* (Cambridge University Press, 2018).

[14] Andrew Harding and Mark Sidel (eds), *Central-Local Relations in Asian Constitutional Systems* (Hart, 2015).

[15] Andrew Harding, 'Territorial Governance in Southeast Asia' (Hart, 2025).

[16] Mindy Chen-Wishart, 'Legal Transplant And Undue Influence: Lost In Translation Or A Working Misunderstanding?' (2013) 62 *The International and Comparative Law Quarterly* 1; Daniel Berkowitz, Katharina Pistor and Jean-Francois Richard, 'The Transplant Effect' (2003) 51 *The American Journal of Comparative Law* 163.

[17] Alan Watson, *Legal Transplants: An Approach to Comparative Law*, 2nd edn (University of Georgia Press, 1993).

[18] Pierre Legrand, 'The Impossibility of "Legal Transplants"' (1997) 4 *Maastricht Journal of European and Comparative Law* 111, 114.

[19] Andrew Harding, 'The Legal Transplants Debate: Getting Beyond the Impasse?' in Vito Breda (ed), *Legal Transplants in East Asia and Oceania* (Cambridge University Press, 2019) 13–33, 31.

developing world, and ideas underpinning these efforts.[20] Law and development normally involve the transplantation of law from developed countries into developing countries.[21] Harding has explored the external aspects of law and development: efforts of external actors to promote law reforms in other countries. He explores external efforts to promote law reform in Myanmar.[22] While law and development scholarship largely focuses on Western providers, Harding investigates Singapore law and development, or its external efforts to promote law reforms in ASEAN countries.[23] Harding's scholarship also deals with the internal logic of the relationship between law (including constitutional law) and social-economic development.[24]

D. Comparative Law and Society

The growing scholarship of comparative law and society or socio-legal comparative law is characterised by the replacement of the formal understanding of law by the concept of legal culture and the consideration of the causal link between law and society.[25] Harding's comparative law scholarship deals with social-legal aspects, particularly evident in his emphasis on the existence of different layers of legal culture in Southeast Asia, which are rooted in local customs, Hinduism, Islam, Buddhism, among others. He writes:

> First there was the custom or 'native' law of the aboriginal inhabitants, which is still recognised by the courts as positive law in several parts of the region. Then came several strata of transplanted law: adat (Malay custom), which was based on the rumah gadang (long house); in adat perpatih, the customary law of the Minangkabau matrilineal society, property passed along the female line; Hindu and Buddhist law from South Asia, uniquely amalgamated, and operating at the rarified level of the kraton (court); Islamic law from the Middle East, which mingled with adat and formed the basis of personal law in maritime South East Asia; and Chinese law via immigration and imitation. All these not only had great influence but influenced each other in interesting ways.[26]

The arrival of western colonial powers in the twentieth century adds layers of common law and civil law to the Asian legal systems.[27] These systems have been

[20] Yong-Shik Lee and Andrew Harding, 'Law and Development' in Mathias Siems and Po Jen Yap (eds), *The Cambridge Handbook of Comparative Law* (Cambridge University Press, 2024) 510.

[21] John Gillespie and Pip Nicholson (eds), *Law and Development and the Global Discourses of Legal Transfers* (Cambridge University Press, 2012).

[22] Andrew Harding, *Theories of Law and Development: Asian Trajectories and the Salience of Judicial Reform in Myanmar* (2018) 46 *Asian Journal of Social Science* 421.

[23] Andrew Harding, *Multi-Level, Recursive Law and Development: Singapore's Legal Role in ASEAN* (2018) 5 *Asian Journal of Law and Society* 251.

[24] Andrew Harding, 'Constitutionalism and Development: A Mismatch or a Dream-Team?' (2019) 12 *Law and Development Review* 647.

[25] Siems (n 1) 174.

[26] Harding (n 7) 42 (internal citations omitted).

[27] MB Hooker (ed), *The Laws of South-East Asia: European laws in South-East Asia* (Butterworths, 1988).

further supplemented by layers of global and transnational laws in the context of twenty-first century legal globalisation.[28] Different layers of legal cultures can exist, interact and compete in one jurisdiction, which generates a complexity of laws. This complexity of legal culture is also evident in other parts of Asia. For example, different layers of legal culture (customary, Confucian, socialist, etc) exist in the Chinese legal system.

II. Contributions to this Book

Essays in this book are organised according to the four themes above.

Part one deals with questions of comparative law methodology. Arif A Jamal underlines building blocks for a grammar of comparative law understandings of Southeast Asia, including the consideration of local contexts, and the departure from Euro-/Western-centric points of reference to consider Asian jurisdictions and other non-western jurisdictions, dynamic forces of legal change and thick description. Victor V Ramraj's essay indicates how legal pluralism offers a distinct way of thinking about complex global problems. Justin O Frosini's essay indicates that comparative public law is no longer a neglected discipline.

Part two explores Asian comparative constitutional law. Kevin Tan considers the development of comparative constitutional law in Asia over the past six decades. He suggests that 'we want to take Asia on its own terms and consider how constitutions and constitutional laws are used in a variety of ways to respond to problems in each society'. Other essays deal with specific constitutional questions. Peter Leyland explores the multilayered character of the Westminster constitutional systems. Drawing on ideas of constitutional political economy, Tom Ginsburg provides a framework for thinking about the relative power of monarchy vis-à-vis civilian powerholders, and illustrates it with the case of Malaysia. Dian AH Shah explores religious federalism defined as 'the devolution of power to sub-national governments on religious policy- and law-making' in Malaysia. Mara Malagodi investigates gender constitutionalism and reproductive politics in the Asian contexts, particularly Nepal. Rawin Leelapatana investigates how and to what extent the *lèse-majesté* campaign decision affects the development of liberal constitutionalism in Thailand. Khemthong Tonsakulrungruang explores certain aspects of independent accountability agencies (IAA) in Thailand, ascertaining what exactly IAA is, what it means to be independent, and what has gone wrong with it. He argues that an independent watchdog is a commendable idea implemented amidst an illiberal environment, leading to its independence being captured.

[28] John Gillespie, 'Localizing Global Competition Law in Vietnam: A Bottom-Up Perspective' (2015) 64 *International and Comparative Law Quarterly* 935.

Part three deals with legal transplants, law and development. Based on Andrew Harding's argument in his seminal article 'Global Doctrine and Local Knowledge' that universal social problems invariably provoke local solutions, Lasse Schuldt's paper examines how the war on fake news has been localised in Malaysia, Singapore and Thailand. Surutchada Reekie and Adam Reekie challenge a narrative that Thailand's Civil and Commercial Code of 1923 Code is generally considered as a mere historical footnote; an abject failure, decades in the making, that was never genuinely adopted by the country. Bryan Dennis G Tiojanco argues that the 1987 Philippine Constitution and the 1991 Local Government Code illustrate that constitutionally enforcing people empowerment boosts development. Jan Michiel Otto examines a nascent practice of local lawmaking and urban planning in late-colonial Bandung, Indonesia. He demonstrates that the Ethical Policy of the Indies Government 'provided some extra space and support for those who genuinely wanted to improve the social and economic conditions and the political participation of the subjugated Indonesian people'.

Part four explores topics of social-legal comparative law. Through a case study of a small Thai town Ban Sai, David M Engel seeks to prove that transplanted law in village Thailand grows in a cultural soil that is inhospitable in many ways yet is also experiencing shifts and stress. Benjamin L Berger contextualises the concept of semi-autonomous social fields in the study of constitutional law. Engaging with Harding's work on religion in Southeast Asian constitutionalism, Berger argues that 'religion, the semi-autonomous social field *par excellence*, has a special capacity to point us to the patterns of mutual influence and dependence – of non-isolation – that characterize the relation between these normative orders and the state'. Albert HY Chen critically discusses recent scholarship that seeks to apply the concept of 'dual state' or 'authoritarian rule of law' to the case of China. His chapter indicates that there are different, interactive forms (normative and prerogative) of legality in China.

III. Conclusion: The Future of Asian Comparative Law

Harding and authors of essays in this volume have made significant contributions to comparative law in Asia. The future of the field requires continued expansion of methodology, jurisdictions and the contents of comparative study of Asian laws.

The continued expansion of methodology of comparative law in Asia is important for its future development. Moving beyond doctrinal studies, essays in this book situate formal laws in Asia within the dynamics of politics, society, economy and religion. Contributors in the book approach comparative legal questions from various perspectives: doctrinal, economic, socio-legal, etc. The field can explore other approaches. For example, comparative jurisprudence in Asia is a promising approach to look at the philosophical foundations (eg Confucianism, Legalism, Buddhism, Hinduism) of Asian laws.

Second, the future of the field requires the expansions of jurisdictions. Comparative law has conventionally focused on western jurisdictions. This book adds to global comparative law scholarship by a focus on Asia. The Asian jurisdictions covered are diverse, including both common law and civil law jurisdictions, big and small jurisdictions, and jurisdictions in different parts of Asia. Scholarship on comparative law in Asia, however, tend to focus on big and developed countries, such as Japan, China, Singapore and India. Knowledge of comparative law in Asia can be further enriched by the expansion to understudied jurisdictions in Southeast Asia (eg Laos and East Timor), South Asia (eg Bhutan and Sri Lanka) and Central Asia.

Third, the expansion of substances of comparative law in Asia is necessary. Moving beyond private law, this book covers private law, public law and village law. The future of the field requires more attention to indigenous law, dynamic law, religious law and colonial law. In addition, given recent trend of regionalisation and internationalisation, regional law (eg ASEAN law) and comparative international law in Asia require further studies.

PART I

Comparative Law Methodology and Theory

1

The Grammars of Comparative Law Discourse

ARIF A JAMAL*

I. Introduction

In his one of his well-known works, Andrew Harding identified a significant challenge for comparative law, at least when it comes to addressing Southeast Asia. Harding said:

> The fundamental conceptual problem confronting those working on law in South East Asia is that the conventions of comparative law are often inadequate to convey South East Asian legal reality; what comparative law therefore lacks, to my mind, is *a suitably flexible and sophisticated grammar of discourse*.[1]

Indeed, 'it could be seriously questioned whether comparative work on law in South East Asia could ever actually fit even into the broadest current notions of what comparative law can be expected to do.'[2]

This chapter seeks to take up Harding's challenge and develop, drawing on Harding's own work, a grammar of discourse for comparative law understandings of Southeast Asia and more generally. The chapter will discuss the terms of the grammar – that is, how the grammar should be framed – beginning by critically examining existing frameworks for doing comparative law. Second, the chapter will move on to develop the grammar beginning with 'grammatical rules' derived from the insights developed by Harding's own past work. This will emphasise the need to be comparative in a highly contextual way. Finally, by incorporating other theoretical materials, the chapter will seek to show that suitably broader conventions of comparative law can indeed fit Southeast Asia (and beyond) if we move

* My thanks to Don Loke (BA, LLB (NUS)) for his excellent and thoughtful research assistance in the preparation of this chapter. Any errors are my own.

[1] Andrew Harding, 'Comparative Law and Legal Transplantation in South East Asia: Making Sense of the "Nomic Din"' in David Nelken and Johannes Feest (eds), *Adapting Legal Cultures* (Hart Publishing, 2001) 203, dx.doi.org/10.5040/9781472559166. Emphasis added.

[2] ibid, 203.

from attempting to find a grammar to embracing the use of *grammars* for the different discourses an appropriate comparative law will need to have.

II. Framing a Grammar for Comparative Law

To begin with, we can take a reminder from Jaako Husa's work about what motivated comparative law. Husa tells us that 'the scholarly fountains of current comparative law are rooted in the past project of developing comparative law into a genuine science' and that while the 'spirit of 'scientification' has waned … Because no dominating paradigm has emerged, the earlier layers of scholarship still exist.'[3]

It is thus that comparative law has often sought to develop a 'scientific' rubric to classify and compare legal orders – a sort of legal taxonomy. In this respect, we can draw a distinction between comparative law adopting a micro- vs macro-comparative focus. Here, Husa's other writing in a book that he says provides an introduction to comparative law helps us sketch out the terrain. In micro-comparison, the object of study is either individual legal rules or individual legal institutions. For instance, one may compare the institution of marriage between two jurisdictions.[4] In macro-comparison, comparison takes place between legal systems or even between legal families/cultures.[5]

Macro-comparison does not concentrate on individual legal rules, institutions or concrete problems and the ways in which to solve them; instead, the abstraction level of the topics compared is higher. Comparison could, for example, be aimed at issues that concern legislative methods, the style of writing provisions, the doctrine of legal sources or even the style of entire legal systems.[6]

We can thus call out some of the 'usual suspects' of the macro-comparative perspective enumerated by Husa.

A. Legal Families

The legal families approach was an early macro-comparative perspective. Traditionally, legal families were simplified groups like 'common law countries', 'civil law countries', 'mixed legal systems', 'religious-traditional' systems and

[3] Jaakko Husa, 'Comparative law's pyrrhic victory?' (2023) 30 *Maastricht Journal of European and Comparative Law*, 680, 682.

[4] Jaakko Husa, *A New Introduction to Comparative Law*, 1st edn (Bloomsbury Publishing, 2015) 101, retrieved from www.perlego.com/book/394428/a-new-introduction-to-comparative-law-pdf (original work published 2015).

[5] ibid, 102.

[6] ibid.

'socialist' systems.[7] This structure is now considered rather outdated and misleading inasmuch as it might obscure and obfuscate as much as it enlightens. Nonetheless, Husa notes the metaphorical importance in the term 'family':

> The family metaphor makes it possible to speak of family members, like sisters and brothers and also of the father and the mother. Legal historians too have been fond of the family metaphor because it brings up the significance of legal history. Secondly it makes possible the use of a more extensive family concept, i.e., the fact that it is meaningful to speak of legal families belonging to the same family. Legal systems can be more or less related. We can also talk about a close relative or a distant relative.[8]

B. Legal Culture(s)

A second approach emphasises the importance of cultural factors. The concept of legal culture can be used in at least two ways. First, 'it refers to a group of factors (e.g., language, mentality, politics and history) that are outside the formal legal system but are connected to the actual operation of the legal system in a broad sense'.[9] For instance, one may compare the litigious American legal culture with what it sees as litigious Japanese legal culture.[10] Second, 'in comparative law literature legal culture is used as a macro-level concept with which reference is made to entities larger than one system, such as Western legal culture, Asian legal culture or Islamic legal culture'.[11]

Sibling legal systems from the families approach might be situated in different legal cultures and hence operate differently. Mindy Chen-Wishart's study of the issue of undue influence in contract in the law of England and Singapore is a case in point. Chen-Wishart notes that: 'Since English contract and commercial law has been transplanted into the Singaporean legal system largely wholesale, I rashly expected to likewise, within limits, be able to largely transplant the substance of my contract law lectures from England.'[12] That assumption was incorrect, however, because

> the treatment of undue influence in family guarantees threw up an unexpected divergence. Unexpected because Singaporean courts professed to be applying the very same law; yet they interpreted and applied this law in such a way as to reach apparently opposite conclusions from the English decisions.[13]

[7] ibid, 211–20.
[8] ibid, 227.
[9] ibid, 229.
[10] ibid.
[11] ibid.
[12] Mindy Chen-Wishart, 'Legal Transplant and Undue Influence: Lost in Translation or a Working Misunderstanding?' (2013) 62 *The International and Comparative Law Quarterly* 1, 3
[13] ibid.

What Chen-Wishart found was, for instance, that: 'It is evident that Singaporean courts are averse to finding undue influence against the husband/father in the family business guarantee situation and this has twisted the interpretation of the doctrine from the way it is applied in English cases.'[14] In her more detailed analysis, Chen-Wishart points to a number of cultural factors – including, inter alia, the influence of Confucian traditions – that make the Singaporean approach different from the English approach, notwithstanding their common 'legal family'.

The larger point to take from this analysis is the impact of cultural factors – and of differing legal cultures – in the shaping legal outcomes.[15]

C. Functional Approach

Another contender for a taxonomy of legal systems comes from Ugo Mattei's functional approach in which the classification criteria are based on the role or purpose served by laws. This approach is supposed to be culturally neutral. According to Mattei, 'In the classification three basic types of legal system were separated: (1) professional law; (2) political law; and (3) traditional law.'

Professional law is the field of law controlled by trained specialists (jurists, lawyers, judges). This might be otherwise seen as formal or hard law. Political law is law that is greatly defined by political relations, and so a 'softer' law. Traditional law included legal systems in which law and religion, or some other philosophic-religious tradition, have not been separated, ie the secularisation that has passed through legal systems has not occurred as in political law and professional law. This might in other schemas be called 'customary' law.[16]

D. Legal Traditions

H Patrick Glenn developed the concept of legal tradition. Law, he said, 'is essentially a tradition, that is to say something that has come down to us from the past'.[17]

Emphasising the historicity of legal systems, or, invoking TS Eliot, their 'pastness', as well as their broader social context and grounding, the legal traditions approach casts law as being deeply linked to its sociological and anthropological contexts. Thus, though traditions may have come from the past they certainly have a present-ness too. In Glenn's schema the major legal traditions are the Talmudic,

[14] ibid, 9.

[15] For a discussion of Confucian norms in constitutional law, see Bui Ngoc Son, *Confucian Constitutionalism in East Asia* (Routledge, 2016).

[16] Husa (n 4) 232–33.

[17] HP Glenn, 'A Concept of Legal Tradition' (2008–2009) 34 *Queen's Law Journal* 427, 431 (citing AWB Simpson).

civil law, Islamic, common law, Hindu and Confucian, and the traditions of Indigenous peoples (chthonic legal traditions).

E. Macro Comparisons for Southeast Asia

As noble as the aspirations, and inspirations, of macro-comparative approaches might be, in Harding's view they are a poor fit especially for Southeast Asia. Certainly, Harding laments the use of legal families, saying: 'Legal families tell us nothing about legal systems except as to their general style and method and the idea makes no sense whatsoever amid the nomic din of South East Asia.'[18] But he goes further and casts doubt on all macro-comparative ventures: 'We are not obliged to embrace the entire globe with some kind of neat doctrine.' Rather: 'we need to shed our jurists' cloaks, equip ourselves with thick notebooks, immerse ourselves in context, and acquire as much local knowledge as possible'.[19] But then what of the needed grammar? First of all, Harding rejects taxonomy as a suitable grammar here, critiquing Ugo Mattei who proposes taxonomy as the grammar for legal discourse. 'On the contrary', Harding says, 'taxonomy is reductionism: it is what we have *instead of* legal discourse.'[20]

Thinking about languages might help us here. When we turn to a grammar for a language it tells us the structure that is used, and that we should use, to express the language: verb here, preposition there, definite articles or not, etc. Grammars provide structure both by being descriptive as well as – at least in minds of some – being prescriptive and normative. Thus, we might say: 'such poor writing; full of grammatical errors!'. Of course, sometimes grammatical rules appear more respected in the breach, such as the idea that, in English, one should not split the infinite – an oft-ignored convention if there ever was one. That said, as anyone who has ever tried using word-by-word translation software will know, a failure to capture that part of grammar which we call syntax, as well as to adopt appropriate idiomatic expressions, makes for clunky and poorly received translations. A good translation captures the different grammatical structure of the other language in syntax, and style. However, it is also the case that grammars can be very particular and localised *within* a language. For instance, it is not unusual in South Asian English to talk about '*pre*poning' (that is, bringing forward; the opposite of *post*-poning) a meeting and, in Singapore, it would be perfectly normal to say that an item costs '20 over dollars' (for more than 20 and as opposed to 'over 20 dollars'). These expressions make sense according to the localised English grammars notwithstanding that they would sound odd and maybe confusing to speakers of English in other parts of the world.

[18] Andrew Harding, 'Global Doctrine and Local Knowledge: Law in South East Asia' (2002) 51 *The International and Comparative Law Quarterly* 35, 49.

[19] ibid.

[20] ibid. Emphasis in original.

III. Constructing a Grammar I: Harding's Grammatical Insights

Thus far, we have identified both attempts to do comparative law properly, as well as, following Harding, some of the inadequacies of these attempts. In order not to throw out the baby with the bathwater, however, we should note that there are at least elements in some of the approaches which could be useful aspects of a better grammar of comparative law discourse.

In this respect, Glenn's emphasis on history and the social, cultural and philosophical context of tradition appears agreeable since these factors would seemingly highlight the intricacies and diversities when looking across different legal realities. However, the macro-comparative perspective of a grand tradition may lose a lot of relevant, comparative colour. Consider the tradition of Islamic law that Glenn identifies. While Islamic law is indeed grounded in a rich history, this history evidences a great deal of difference due to a number of varying influences. For example, consider briefly Indonesia, Malaysia and Singapore in Southeast Asia. Although the majority of Muslims in all three of these countries share a fairly common heritage of Malay culture and by and large adherence to the Shafi'i school of Sunni Islam, salient social and political differences account for much variation in the way in which the Islamic legal tradition functions in the different countries. For instance, Malaysia and Indonesia are Muslim majority environments, while Muslims are a minority in Singapore. Singapore and Malysia, however, shared the experience of being British colonies and having received English Common Law, but Indonesia was a Dutch colony and received Civil Law. Indonesia and Malaysia have federal structures (states in Malaysia; provinces in Indonesia), but Singapore does not. Islam is the religion of the federation according to the Constitution of Malaysia, while Singapore's Constitution makes no declaration of religious affiliation, and the Preamble to Indonesia's Constitution – notwithstanding its Muslim majority – refers to Almighty God and, as one of its five basic principles (Pancasila), the One and Only God. Even without delving deeper into the local contexts, just these few factors make it clear that seeing Malysia, Singapore and Indonesia as participating – albeit in varying degrees – as part of an Islamic tradition may be to paint with too broad a brushstroke as experiences legally will vary considerably due to localised factors.

How then can we build a grammar for comparative law discourse? I suggest that Harding himself provides us a number of 'grammatical building blocks' to which can be added additional blocks from other works, and it is to a discussion of the first part of this that I now turn.

A. Local and Contextual

The first building block comes from what we have just noted and from Harding's appeal to develop our thick notebooks. Any grammar that we develop must be well informed and attuned to the local context. Thus, larger generalisations that cut across local contexts – as they almost all will probably do – will not provide the right means for discourse. On the contrary, they will tend to obscure by agglomerating. Hence, a grammar for all of Southeast Asia or all of Islamic law will not serve us very well since these could skip much detail. Concomitantly, we should be aware of how this detail is derived from contextual factors, including history, demographics and geography, of the role of the state and the articulation of the constitutional order, of cultural forces, etc. Of course, it is not just Harding who makes this point, but it would surely be an important part of his grammar.

B. The Independent Importance of Asia (and Other Locales)

A second building block of the grammar is to move away from a Euro- or Western-centric focus as the paradigm for analysis. Just as Chen-Wishart came to realise, perhaps to her surprise, that it was not appropriate to transpose English approaches to Singapore notwithstanding facially similar doctrine, we should not see Southeast Asia, Asia, or indeed other parts of the world as derivatives of European and Western experiences. These days, this perspective is well captured by the moves to decolonise comparative law, which emphasise the need to move away from Euro-/Western-centric points of reference.[21] In such a perspective, Asia (and others) must be taken on their own terms as fully independent objects of study. Naturally, there may be influences between locations in Asia or elsewhere and the West. And of course, colonialism was one of the powerful forces that spread Western legal forms – in particular, English Common Law and Continental European Civil Law systems – to many parts of the world and fundamentally remade many legal regimes outside of the West along Western lines. Additionally, there may be linkages amongst the non-Western contexts of various types and forms, such as, for example, through the influence of Confucian ideas in East Asia or of Islam across North Africa, and Central, South and Southeast Asia. But in instances such as this what is important is to see local developments on their own terms and in their own light and context, rather than (only) with a comparison to the West.

A reflection drawn from how Islam as a religion is discussed is illustrative. It is usually estimated that around 80–85 per cent of the world's Muslims identify as belonging to the Sunni tradition of Islam, with 10–15 per cent adhering to the Shia tradition and perhaps five per cent or less to the Ibadi tradition. The categories of orthodox and heterodox, which were drawn principally from Christianity,

[21] Edward Said's books, *Orientalism* (Routledge and Keegan Paul, 1978) and *Culture and Imperialism* (Vintage Books, 1993) are classical and powerful works in this genre. In legal scholarship, one can also see, for example, Antony Anghie, *Imperialism, Sovereignty and Making of International Law* (Cambridge University Press, 2005); Lena Salaymeh and Ralf Michaels, 'Decolonial Comparative Law: A Conceptual Beginning' (2022) 86 *Rabels Zeitschrift für ausländisches und internationales Privatrecht* 166; and Sherally Munshi, 'Comparative Law and Decolonizing Critique' (2017) 65 *American Journal of Comparative Law* 207.

make little sense in the context of Islam where there is not and has never really been an institution or body that could claim to propound the *ortho doxa* of Islam in the way that the Catholic or other churches may purport to do for Christianity. But since the paradigm of analysis in Western scholarship had been Christianity, Sunni Islam as the majoritarian tradition was routinely referred to as 'orthodox' Islam, while the Shia and other traditions were called 'heterodox'. What this example shows is the problem of casting a phenomenon in terms which are unsuitable or ill-fitting: the result is an analysis that misinterprets and misrepresents. The lesson to be taken is that to understand properly we should adopt an appropriate framework, which, in Asia and other parts of the world, will be a framework independently grounded in local experience without the local being seen as derivative of – or being forced to fit into – a framework that applies to a different context.

C. The Shape of the Comparative Lens(es)

We have already explored some of Harding's scepticism about meta narratives and the deployment of macro-comparative viewpoints in noting his comments about the uselessness of the legal families approach for understanding Southeast Asia. To this, we can add the need to be locally aware and to find contextually appropriate rubrics for understanding and analysis. Do these perspectives inexorably lead us to abandon any form of understanding beyond the micro level, beyond a single jurisdiction? Harding seems to suggest not, or at least not exactly when we consider Southeast Asia.

To this end, Harding remarks that, within the region, the diverse cultures and contexts inhibit a stable definition of a macro concept like 'South East Asian law'.[22] Notwithstanding, Harding argues that there exists a creative and syncretic 'South East Asian law'.[23] Hence, a form of macro-comparative framework for Southeast Asia may be possible. However, this macro-comparison is likely to take a 'regionalist' approach where jurisdictions within Southeast Asia are compared with each other.[24] To be clear, this is in contrast to the prevailing macro-comparative methods that are 'microscopic, Eurocentric, rule-based, concerned with private rather than public law, is legislative and integrative in purpose, and assumes a degree of commonality and convergence in that which is compared'.[25] In the alternative, Harding's approach calls for more comparison of the contexts of rules, both public and private, in a non-technical, sociological way, from a global perspective, for broad intellectual as well as legislative purposes. Therefore, a reformed comparative law approach should take, as mentioned, a regional approach that would capture these elements.[26]

[22] Harding (n 1) 209.
[23] ibid.
[24] Harding (n 18) 48.
[25] Harding (n 1) 204.
[26] Harding (n 18) 51.

D. Family Resemblance

Building on the above, the concept of family resemblance developed by Wittgenstein may be a useful heuristic for us to employ. Although developed in the context of understanding language and the concept of a game, the notion of family resemblance appears to provide a way to find relationality without similarity and so a sense of a regional outlook. As Craig Fox writes:

> Wittgenstein speaks of concepts having or lacking frontiers [*Grenzen*]. He suggests that one may use a concept (perhaps my example of 'biological mother') in such a way that it has very clear, rigid limits … But 'game', according to Wittgenstein, is not like this: its applications are not closed by a frontier.[27]

It is thus that Biletzki and Matar write:

> He [Wittgenstein] points to 'family resemblance' as the more suitable analogy for the means of connecting particular uses of the same word. There is no reason to look, as we have done traditionally – and dogmatically – for one, essential core in which the meaning of a word is located and which is, therefore, common to all uses of that word. We should, instead, travel with the word's uses through 'a complicated network of similarities overlapping and criss-crossing' (*Philosophical Investigations*, 66). Family resemblance also serves to exhibit the lack of boundaries and the distance from exactness that characterize different uses of the same concept.[28]

Since family resemblance is not looking for essential cores or attributes but to 'network(s) of similarities overlapping and criss-crossing', it can provide the analytical rubric for legal systems which share features but whose boundaries are porous. Law in Southeast Asian jurisdictions, and in other parts of the world, may thus exhibit family resemblances – having likenesses without being alike – which makes a regional approach sensible without it being delimiting.

Family resemblance is also much different from legal families. While the legal families framework suggested something essential, the family resemblance rubric, as we have said, sees family connection not as constituted by an essential core but by a broader, more diffuse and more plural form of connection. I am thus suggesting that we can include the concept of family resemblance in a Harding-esque grammar of comparative law discourse.

E. Discourse as Organic and Dynamic

As a corollary to all of the above, a further element to our grammar is that it must be seen as both dynamic and organic. It will have to be dynamic to account for the

[27] Craig Fox, 'Wittgenstein on Family Resemblance' in Kelley Dean Jolley (ed), *Wittgenstein: Key Concepts* (Routledge, 2010).

[28] Anat Biletzki and Anat Matar, 'Ludwig Wittgenstein' in Edward N Zalta and Uri Nodelman (eds), *The Stanford Encyclopedia of Philosophy*, Fall 2023 edn, plato.stanford.edu/archives/fall2023/entries/wittgenstein.

impact of changes and evolutions across a number of vectors. Geopolitical changes will be one such vector. And indeed the arrival, and then departure, of colonial presence and the way such presence impacted pre-existing legal systems, probably speaks enough about the influence of geopolitical power on a legal order. Regional associations or blocks that may seek forms of legal harmonisation, or flounder in such attempts, are another pertinent example of this phenomenon. The impact of power shifts and the forging of new alliances is another example. In this respect, we need only consider what is happening to dilute the mantra of globalisation today, a mantra that was so ascendent until recently, and how new configurations of alliance are unravelling or at least recasting globalisation. Dynamism is also part of deliberate choices and social shifts. For example, it would have been a bold pundit who at the turn of the millennium would have ventured the prediction that by 2010 India would have repealed the colonial-era section 377 of its Penal Code, which criminalised sexual relations between men, and that, by 2022, Singapore would have done the same with its Penal Code counterpart of section 377A. Shifting attitudes and policy appetites which engendered these moves evidence the internal socio-political dynamics in these societies. A grammar of comparative law that fits these locales must recognise these dynamic forces.

The grammar must also account for shifts happening organically from the 'social soil' as it were. Social mobilisation, changing leaders, as well as responses to new challenges generating their own social movements (awareness about climate change and sustainability, for instance, or changing understandings of family). Simply put, and obviously, societies change and just in the same way as a language grammar must account for new words or expressions – perhaps by blessing as grammatically correct what was in the past grammatically incorrect due to social changes[29] – so too must a grammar of comparative law be open to organic social changes that alter legal outlooks and legal norms. Hence, Glenn's legal traditions framework is quite correct to emphasise the 'past-ness' of traditions to which we can add that there is no end to their history so even the heritage of a tradition will necessarily look different in the future than it does today because of organic changes and dynamism.

F. Grammar as Thick Description

In his work, *A Realistic Theory of Law*,[30] Brian Tamanaha states that:

> Law is rooted in the history of a society, continuously remade in relation to social factors. Law is an integral aspect of society and society infuses law, their interaction mutually constitutive and bidirectional in cause and effect. Law assumes different forms and functions in connection with levels of social complexity and surrounding economic, political, cultural, technological, ecological, and social factors.

[29] eg, 'Kinda' is now an entry in the *Oxford English Dictionary*. It is defined as meaning 'kind of' but, by its inclusion in the 'authoritative' OED, might now be said to be part of the standard vocabulary of English.

[30] Brian Z Tamanaha, *A Realistic Theory of Law* (Cambridge University Press, 2017),1.

Citing Eugene Ehrlich's *Fundamental Principles of the Sociology of Law*, Tamanah also says that we must find the real 'centre of gravity' for the law not in the state but in society.[31]

These perspectives can be married to Clifford Geertz's famous development of a 'thick description' methodology in his classical work, *The Interpretation of Cultures*.[32] In looking at social phenomena, the methodology of thick description seeks to include the context, meaning and intentions behind it. In other words, it interprets the social and cultural significance of the behaviour. For instance, understanding that a wink (to use the example of a behaviour that Geertz employs) might be a signal in a certain social interaction, of a joke, or a form of communication within a specific cultural setting. Now, if following Tamanaha (and Ehrlich) we are to see law as a fundamentally a social phenomenon, then, following Geertz, we should look at it from a thick description vantage point. Thick description is apposite to the development of a grammar for discourses of comparative law in the Harding-type line we have been discussing. What this means for such a grammar is that it should explain – or guide – our understanding of a legal system in the manner of unpacking the deeper understanding of the law's culture(s) and specific contexts. Thick description thus offers up a grammar not of simplification but of richness and complexity. Comparatively, it also helps us see that what appears similar can – like a wink – have different meanings in different social and cultural contexts and help us to understand why this can be so. Harding's outlook would thus (at least implicitly) align with the methodology of thick description.

IV. Constructing a Grammar II: The Contribution of New Legal Realism

Andrew Harding would probably happily align himself to the law and society movement. In this perspective:

> Law is created and put into practice through societal processes. Simultaneously law effects and affects social change. Beyond a causal relationship, law is further understood to constitute social institutions such as the polity, family, property, corporation, crime, even the individual.[33]

One developing trend of law and society studies may be found in the New Legal Realism (NLR) movement. NLR aims to be 'empirically grounded, philosophically pragmatist, institutionally cognizant, and critically ambitious'.[34]

[31] ibid, 2.

[32] Clifford Geertz, *The Interpretation of Cultures: Selected Essays* (Basic Books, 1973) 3 ff.

[33] Joachim J Savelsberg and Lara L Cleveland (2013) 'Law and Society', Oxford Bibliographies, 'Sociology',. doi: 10.1093/obo/9780199756384-0113.

[34] Victoria Nourse and Gregory Shaffer, 'Varieties of New Legal Realism: Can a New World Order Prompt a New Legal Theory' (2009) 95 *Cornell Law Review* 61, 136, scholarship.law.cornell.edu/clr/vol95/iss1/8.

> This new paradigm entails a recursive understanding of law, of how law both responds to and shapes individual and political behaviour, and of how law and social and institutional structures reciprocally interact. In this effort, new forms of analysis will emerge that will reconstruct law's concepts in their participatory, human, and vulnerable forms. This analysis will 'discover' new values and concepts from the world in 'emergent analytics', rather than pre-packaged statistical programs or canned histories. Law will once more take a lead in its self-understanding; it will not bow simply to other disciplines but will help to transform them.[35]

Moreover, when done appropriately, NLR is also self-consciously aware of even its own social context and position. Thus:

> This new legal realism emphasizes the importance of empirical engagement, including the bottom-up emergent analytics we have highlighted, but it does not accept that social science is ever impartial. All social science is partial and cannot help but be so; that is social science's dilemma. Such a new realism nonetheless embraces empirical study because (again) there is no choice if we wish to make more informed decisions. Such a new realism thus makes two additional moves: it turns its critical gaze on itself (including the risks in its empirical work), and it is fundamentally pragmatic, stressing the importance of revisability and learning. It accepts neither the head-in-the clouds empiric-free reasoning of much of legal scholarship nor the hollow hopelessness of some in social science. It is ultimately optimistic, maintaining that law is a world of action and our responsibility is to participate in it.[36]

What is particularly interesting in NLR for our grammatical endeavour is the empirically informed, analytics driven context it can provide. NLR seems to promise empirical *content* to fit the socio-legal context, illuminating both. Thus, NLR can perhaps put flesh on the bones of the concerns we have been dealing with about law as a social phenomenon.

Indeed, in some of his works Harding has remarked on precisely the type of empirical differences, or 'differences in fact', that are important to understand in looking at different legal orders. For instance, in 'Monarchical Constitutional Guardianship and Legal Métissage in Asia',[37] Harding and De Visser emphasised the need 'to examine Asian monarchies through both constitutional analysis as well as a careful study of their surrounding society and culture'.[38] Considering the *empirical accounts* provided in the accompanying case studies, it is clear that 'the study of monarchies requires more than a legal-doctrinal approach to do justice to their multifaceted and multi-functional nature'.[39]

[35] ibid.

[36] ibid, 137. For examples of comparative law empirical scholarship see Holger Spamann, 'Large-Sample, Quantitative Research Designs for Comparative Law?' (2009) 57 *American Journal of Comparative Law* 787; and Holger Spamann, 'Empirical Comparative Law' (2015) 11 *Annual Review of Law and Social Science* 131.

[37] Andrew Harding and Martje De Visser, 'Monarchical Constitutional Guardianship and Legal Métissage in Asia' (2022) 9 *Asian Journal of Law and Society* 345.

[38] ibid, 360.

[39] ibid. Emphasis added.

In 'Decentralisation and Local Government Autonomy in Southeast Asia',[40] Harding examines decentralisation trends in five Southeast Asian states: Indonesia, Philippines, Thailand, Malaysia and Myanmar. Harding observes that 'we see three instances of operation of decentralisation over 20–30 years; one stable decentralised system that has changed little during that period; and one process of decentralisation that has not yet occurred'. And in 'Conventions and practical interpretation in Westminster type constitutional systems',[41] Harding notes that 'if we consider the importance and the impact of constitutional practice, and especially of conventions, we see that practical interpretation (i.e, constitutional interpretations given by the executive or legislative branch) is at least as important as judicial interpretation, and in fact more important in some areas of constitutional law.'[42]

These observations made in Harding's own work display a concern to examine actual, practical, developments and to employ these in comparison. Such empirical observations enhance our comparative understandings by bringing into sharper relief distinctions that might otherwise be occluded. So, a grammar that draws in the data of empirical examination, while still being critical about its empirical processes, can give us clearer, more precise and more insightful view of legal regimes.

V. Grammar/Grammars

> One important outcome of the diversification of comparative law is an accompanying realization that there is a world outside the old cultural and epistemic boundaries, beyond common law and civil law, and beyond private law. One further concretization is the considerable expansion of comparative law scholarship focused on Asian systems.[43]

This essay has taken its inspiration from Harding's call for 'a suitably flexible and sophisticated grammar of discourse'. This call was made in the context of Harding's examination of and reflections about Southeast Asia. I think it is fair to say – and fair to say that Harding would agree – that what applies for Southeast Asia would also apply in other locations, *mutatis mutandis*. Indeed, that is why, in this discussion, I have cast Harding's call more generally and not just as a something that he would say, or that we should think about, in relation only to Southeast Asia. But if this is the case, then the question arises whether we can speak about a

[40] Andrew Harding, 'Decentralisation And Local Government Autonomy In Southeast Asia' in 8th Asian Constitutional Law Forum (Conference Proceedings), *Asian Constitutional Law: Recent Developments and Trends* (Vietnam National University, 2020) 420, 431.

[41] Andrew Harding, 'Conventions and practical interpretation in Westminster type constitutional systems' (2022) 20 *I-CON* 1914.

[42] ibid, 1936.

[43] Husa (n 3) 685.

needed grammar or if we must understand that the grammars themselves must be developed in context and therefore be different. In fact, if one of the insights to be gained by seeking to take steps towards answering Harding's call for a grammar for Southeast Asia is that a Southeast Asian grammar must fit its *local* milieu and not be derivative of Euro- or Western-centric perspectives, then, *ipso facto*, a comparative law grammar for other parts of the world would also need to fit those, different, local milieux. And indeed why not? We readily accept that grammars must vary for different languages and indeed might also vary *within* languages (recall the prepone/postpone discussion). So, why not different grammars for comparative law in different parts of the world?

In this respect, while the nomic din of Southeast Asia may be particularly loud, it can hardly be said to be unique. Hence, embracing grammatical plurality to properly compare legal systems should not cause us any disquiet. Indeed, this may be the best lesson that can be taken from Harding's corpus of thoughtful and sympathetic scholarship. If you want to understand a region's legal regime(s) and understand them comparatively, then you must commit to learning its context in all its complexity. 'The relationship between the global and the local is one of critical importance to all regions of the world', Harding tells us, and surely he is right in saying so. Furthermore, his challenge to develop an appropriate grammar to situate this relationship for Southeast Asia, when projected globally, inspires us to think not just of a grammar for comparative law discourses, but rather of the several grammars we may need.

2

Confronting Global Complexity and Crisis: Lessons from the 'Nomic Din' in Southeast Asia

VICTOR V RAMRAJ*

> [O]ur lack of real knowledge and understanding of law and society in South East Asia … has been hampered by … the 'nomic din' of South East Asia's legal pluralism …[1]
>
> It is appropriate to think of law in South East Asia geologically, as a series of layers each of which overlays the previous layers without actually replacing them, so that in places, due to tectonic shifts, the lower layers are still visible, although not perfectly distinguishable from each other.[2]

Perhaps the most elusive goal for public law scholars today is understanding how, through law, humanity can respond to the most profound global challenges of our time, from pandemics to the climate crisis to the emergence and possibly existential threat posed by artificial intelligence (AI). While governments can respond to these challenges by using the instruments of domestic public law at their disposal or by working with other states through international law, these state-centred legal instruments do not always appear up to the task. There is a deep misalignment between contemporary global challenges and the formal legal tools typically used

* Victor V Ramraj is Professor of Law and Chair in Asia-Pacific Legal Relations (previously held by Professor Andrew Harding) at the University of Victoria in British Columbia, Canada. Since 2017, he has served as Director of the Centre for Asia-Pacific Initiatives. Before returning to Canada in 2014, he spent 16 years at the National University of Singapore and was twice seconded to the Centre for Transnational Legal Studies in London. He also teaches regularly at Chulalongkorn University in Bangkok. His research interests and publications span comparative constitutional law, transnational regulation, emergency powers, and law, complexity and crisis. An earlier version of this chapter was presented at the 21st ASLI Conference at Chulalongkorn University in Bangkok, on 29 May 2024. I am grateful to the participants in that conference, including Andrew Harding, for stimulating exchanges.

[1] Andrew Harding, 'Comparative Law and Legal Transplantation in South East Asia: Making Sense of the Nomic Din' in David Nelken and Johannes Feest (eds), *Adapting Legal Cultures* (Hart, 2001) 199–222, 203.

[2] ibid, 205.

to address them.[3] In the face of these challenges, a historical, comparative and legal pluralist inquiry into what Andrew Harding, following Clifford Geertz, has called the 'nomic din' of Southeast Asia – and the layering of legal orders he draws out – offers a promising response. Specifically, by challenging law's insularity and drawing attention to its multi-scalar nature, Harding prompts us to reflect on law holistically and helps us to see that the complexity of global problems need not leave us paralysed. Rather, by drawing on the lessons of legal scholarship in Southeast Asia – and the ways that law has operated in Southeast Asia in diverse forms, at multiple levels, and in more and less formal ways – we can plot a course for responding creatively to global complexity and crisis. The chapter begins by showing how complex global problems, particularly those amounting to crises, and the global institutional architecture are fundamentally misaligned. It then shows how other disciplines have developed theories both to describe and help develop responses to complex problems. Finally, it shows how legal pluralism – amid the nomic din of Southeast Asia – offers a distinct way of thinking about law, one that supports in theoretical and practical ways the development of innovative approaches to law and governance in response to global complexity and crisis.

I. Global Challenges and Misalignment

SARS, MERS, and the COVID-19 pandemic. Rising sea levels. Microplastic pollution. Global financial crises. AI. Global inequality. Food insecurity. These and other global challenges exceed the capacity of law to address on its own. They do not sit easily with the legal architecture of the modern state, traditional ideas of state sovereignty, or even some approaches to transnational law. Domestic law is obviously problematic precisely because global problems defy territorial borders, as the COVID-19 pandemic and the climate crisis make clear. The complexities of contemporary geopolitics and the formal, state-centric and geopolitically contentious nature of international law reduce its efficacy. And while transnational law allows for legal innovation beyond the state and on a global scale, it typically focuses on specific industries or sectors. Recent attempts to pluralise international climate law show some hope. But as traditionally conceived within a statist imaginary, international law and its formal institutions are ill-suited to handle global complexity and crisis.

Let us start by defining key terms and concepts. First, it is important to distinguish complicated problems or systems from *complex* ones. Some of the recent writing on complexity uses some version of a modern aircraft or jet engine to

[3] See, for example, Julia Kreienkamp and Tom Pegram. 'Governing Complexity: Design Principles for the Governance of Complex Global Catastrophic Risks' (2021) 23 *International Studies Review* 779, 785; Brian Chaffin, Hannah Gosnell and Barbara Cosens, 'A decade of adaptive governance scholarship: synthesis and future directions' (2014) 19 *Ecology and Society* 56 (unpaginated open access PDF, 7).

illustrate the difference between a system that is complicated – but one that can ultimately be understood (and built or serviced) in a linear, systematic way – and one that is complex, such as an ecosystem, the human body or the global political economy, in which the constituent parts interact with each other and the external environment in ways that often defy scientific methods of analysis. To understand these complex systems, we need a more holistic approach. Defining complexity can be especially challenging because it is used by researchers in different ways. Some use it to refer to systems or clusters of systems that interact with one another in multiple, unpredictable ways. Others use it to refer to theories *about* such systems or clusters of systems – or theories of how to model or respond to such systems. Consider this formulation from the *Harvard Business Review*:

> Complex organizations are far more difficult to manage than merely complicated ones. It's harder to predict what will happen, because complex systems interact in unexpected ways. It's harder to make sense of things, because the degree of complexity may lie beyond our cognitive limits. And it's harder to place bets, because the past behavior of a complex system may not predict its future behavior. In a complex system the outlier is often more significant than the average.[4]

The distinction between complicated and complex systems and its implications are contentious. Some might argue that with enough data and enough computational power, *any* system could be modelled, so nothing is complex in the sense that it is not ultimately knowable in the way the previous passage suggests; others argue that complex systems are precisely such because they are impervious to scientific or intellectually modelling. This debate quickly leads to philosophical disputes about determinism and is the stuff of some compelling science fiction books and films.[5] If we were able to know the location, position and velocity of every atom at one point in time (T_0) could we accurately predict the state of the world or universe at some future point (T_1, T_2, and so on)? For the purposes of this chapter, I will assume that for all practical purposes – perhaps until such time as AI is advanced well beyond its current state, and possibly not even then – the distinction between complicated and complex remains important, and complex systems – while perhaps not ultimately incomprehensible – require us to approach the subject matter (in our case, complex global challenges) in a distinct, holistic way. The designation 'global' here serves as a provisional marker of problems or challenges that extend beyond national borders.

What about *crisis* or *crises*, especially *global* ones? We might think provisionally of a crisis as an uncommon situation that requires an out-of-the ordinary response by the community or the political authority or authorities in question. A destructive earthquake is a good example of a local crisis. It is, in most places, an

[4] Gökçe Sargut and Rita McGrath, 'Learning to Live with Complexity' (September 2011) *Harvard Business Review* (online), hbr.org/2011/09/learning-to-live-with-complexity.

[5] For a compelling dramatisation of these questions, see Alex Garland (ed), *Devs* (mini-series), UK/US production, released on 5 March 2020 (US) and 15 April 2020 (UK).

uncommon event that requires the community and the local political authority to set aside everyday activities and focus their energies on addressing the event and its consequences and seek, as much as possible, to restore normalcy. Of course, the response to a local crisis such as an earthquake has more dimensions that this simple formulation suggests. We would need to consider, for example, what the community might be able to do to *prepare* for an earthquake or, in its aftermath, to *rebuild* the community, physically, socially and psychologically, to be more resilient. For now, however, a devastating earthquake can serve as a local crisis, to help us distinguish it from a global one.

What international lawyers and international relations theorists consider an *international* crisis is not necessarily a *global* crisis as I use the term in this chapter. An international crisis might be an armed conflict between two or more countries and perhaps their proxies or even a disaster – such as a *tsunami* – that affects many adjacent countries. It can be devastating, to be sure, but is typically a one-off and geographically contained event (although, of course, regional conflicts can transform into global ones). A global crisis, as I define it, is closer to what recent scholarship calls *global catastrophic risk* – defined by Nick Bostrom and Milan Ćirković as 'a risk that might have the potential to inflict serious damage to human well-being on a global scale' – which would include events ranging 'from volcanic eruptions to pandemic infections, nuclear accidents to worldwide tyrannies, out-of-control scientific experiments to climatic changes, and cosmic hazards to economic collapse'.[6] More recent examples include risks posed by artificial intelligence[7] and ecological collapse.[8] These are events for which – due to the interconnected nature of the global system – 'catastrophic failure anywhere can mean catastrophic failure everywhere'.[9] Most of the situations described in this way involve a significant *existential* risk, although the threshold level of severity is open for debate.[10] Most of the examples in question involve extensive, worldwide loss of life, human and non-human, on a massive scale. Although some global catastrophic risks are not complex – eg, an asteroid strike – in many cases, the global crises that ensue from these risks are also *complex* and, as such, are multi-layered, contentious and not susceptible to a linear approach to problem-solving.

The problem with complex global challenges and crises is that neither is readily amenable to problem-solving within the legal and institutional structures of the modern state or the international institutions designed in the mid-twentieth century. States, for their part, are territorially bounded in ways that complex global challenges and crises are not. Even international institutions, which – in

[6] Nick Bostrom and Milan M Ćirković (eds), *Global Catastrophic Risks* (Oxford University Press, 2020) 1.

[7] Kreienkamp and Pegram (n 3) 781.

[8] Global Challenges Foundation, 'Global Catastrophic Risks 2022: A Year of Colliding Consequences' 57–63, globalchallenges.org/updates/a-year-of-colliding-consequences-the-global-catastrophic-risks-report-2022.

[9] ibid.

[10] Kreienkamp and Pegram (n 3) 781.

theory – are designed to address international, even global, problems, are often weighed down by inter-state conflict and geopolitical rivalries, making cooperation challenging. And while some international institutions are increasingly open to non-state, civil society participation, most are deeply state-centric, stymying efforts to cooperate on a global scale. It is perhaps unsurprising that, in the early aftermath of the COVID-19 pandemic, the Lancet Commission concluded in its 2022 report that the scale of devastation the pandemic unleashed could be attributed to 'a massive global failure at multiple levels' with the world's major powers having 'failed to collaborate to control the pandemic'.[11] What, then, are the structural problems at the state, international, and transnational levels that stand in the way of collaboration? And how, if at all, might these institutions be adapted to address complexity and crisis?

The international legal and institutional order that emerged after the Second World War was not designed to address global catastrophic risks. That order focused on state sovereignty, inter-state relationships and international agreements. That formulation assumed that international problems could be addressed by states coming together and signing international treaties, which would be implemented by international bodies designed for that purpose. And while this approach made sense for some coordination purposes – international development and finance (at least at that time), international aviation, postal services and even – eventually – arms control, it was always beholden to the geopolitics of the Cold War, and, in more recent times, to renewed geopolitical tensions and cleavages. As alluded to earlier, even institutions such as the World Health Organization (WHO) were unable to pre-empt the COVID-19 pandemic despite the many early warning signs.[12] While states could, theoretically, respond to an emerging epidemic by taking pre-emptive action on their own to contain it an early state and prevent contagion, not all risks can be addressed in this way. Some, such as climate change, require coordinated action by a variety of different actors on multiple scales. States can help to implement or enforce policies or 'orchestrate'[13] non-state actors (as we will see later in this chapter), but states on their own are increasingly unable to respond on their own to global complexity and crisis. Finally, while transnational regulation can be effective in some sectors and contexts (eg, sustainable forestry, factory safety, infrastructure project finance[14]), it remains relatively fragmented.[15] The challenge is to find ways of leveraging and extending these models to address

[11] Jeffrey D Sachs, et al, 'The Lancet Commission on Lessons for the Future from the COVID-19 Pandemic' (2022) 400 *The Lancet* (British edition) 1224.

[12] Victor V Ramraj (ed), *Covid-19 in Asia: Law and Policy Contexts* (Oxford, 2021).

[13] Thomas Hale, 'Transnational Actors and Transnational Governance in Global Environmental Politics' (2020) 23 *Annual Review of Political Science* 203.

[14] See Victor V Ramraj, 'Transnational Non-State Regulation and Domestic Administrative Law' in Susan Rose-Ackerman et al, *Comparative Administrative Law*, 2nd edn (Edward Elgar, 2017) 582–97; Victor V Ramraj and Thitinant Tenguamnuay, 'Privatization of Constitutional Law: Thailand' in David S Law (ed), *Constitutionalism in Context* (Cambridge University Press, 2022) 517–40.

[15] Michael W Dowdle, *Transnational Law: A Framework for Analysis* (Cambridge University Press, 2022).

climate change and other kinds of global catastrophic risk in a more effective and holistic way. The next section will consider how other disciplines have fashioned theories of complexity in an effort to capture the interconnected nature of the natural and socio-political world, and the importance of developing suitably nuanced and holistic responses.

II. Governance for Complexity and Crisis

Complexity, as noted earlier, refers – ambiguously at times – both to a kind of problem (eg, a complex, rather than complicated problem) and the possible responses to it. When it comes to global complexity and crises, the misalignment between these kinds of *problems* and the legacy international institutions available to us requires a more creative and holistic problem-solving *response*. Consonant with legal pluralism, another cluster of theories, arising from different disciplines, is helpful in this regard. These theories – of wicked problems,[16] systems thinking,[17] adaptive governance[18] and complexity theory itself[19] – push us to think about global problems in less linear, more holistic ways. For its part, complexity theory emerged in the physical sciences in the mid-twentieth century through the work of Nobel laureate Ilya Prigogine and others.[20] According to Prigogine, in contrast with classic science which sought simple models of complex systems, by 1987, a far-reaching 'reconceptualization of science'[21] was taking place which recognised that 'in a pluralistic world … we find deterministic as well as stochastic phenomena, reversible as well as irreversible'.[22] (For those unfamiliar with the term, a 'stochastic process or system', the Cambridge Dictionary tells us, 'is connected with random probability'.[23]) Extended to the social sciences, this way of thinking would encompass 'a wide range of chaotic, dissipative, adaptive, nonlinear and complex systems and phenomena' and 'a new and exciting interdisciplinary approach to science and society that challenges traditional academic divisions, frameworks and paradigms'.

While it is difficult to do justice to complexity theory or complexity-adjacent theories in a short chapter, a brief survey is revealing. For example, while 50 years of research on *wicked problems* has produced a voluminous body of scholarship,

[16] See Horst WJ Rittel and Melvin M Webber, 'Dilemmas in a general theory of planning' (1973) 4 *Policy Sciences* 155 and the vast body of literature over five decades that their work has inspired.

[17] Donella H Meadows and Diana Wright. *Thinking in Systems: A Primer* (Chelsea Green, 2008).

[18] Sirkku Juhola, 'Introduction to the Handbook on Adaptive Governance' in Sirkku Juhola (ed), *Handbook on Adaptive Governance* (Edward Elgar, 2023) 1–13. On complex adaptive systems, see also JB Ruhl and Daniel Martin Katz, 'Measuring, Monitoring, and Managing Legal Complexity' (2015) 101 *Iowa Law Review* 191.

[19] JB Ruhl, 'Law's Complexity: A Primer' (2008) 24 *Georgia State University Law Review* 885.

[20] Magnus Ramage and Karen Shipp, *Systems Thinkers* (Springer London, 2009).

[21] Ilya Prigogine, 'Exploring Complexity' (1987) 30 *European Journal of Operational Research* 97, 98.

[22] ibid.

[23] See dictionary.cambridge.org/dictionary/english/stochastic.

the general tenor and enduring influence of Horst Rittel and Melvin Webber's powerful idea can be discerned from this formulation almost four decades later:

> A wicked problem is a complex issue that defies complete definition, for which there can be no final solution, since any resolution generates further issues, and where solutions are not true or false or good or bad, but the best that can be done at the time.[24]

Systems thinkers also highlight the 'messy, more crowded, more interconnected, more interdependent' nature of our modern world,[25] stressing the need 'to look at it in terms of wholes and relationships rather than splitting it down into its parts and looking at each in isolation'.[26] The urge us to 'hone our abilities to understand parts, see interconnections, ask "what-if" questions about possible future behaviours, and be creative and courageous about system redesign'.[27] Another cluster of complexity-adjacent scholarship falls under the banner of *adaptive governance* (or relatedly, 'complex adaptive systems'[28]), which refers to 'a system of environmental governance with the potential to mediate the complexity and uncertainty inherent in' social-ecological systems and encompasses a 'range of interactions between actors, networks, organizations, and institutions emerging in pursuit of a desired state for social-ecological systems'.[29] The adaptive governance systems are characterised by their resilience in the face of rapidly changing conditions and their ability to 'connect individuals and organizations across multiple levels and scales'.[30] On this approach to governance, and in contrast with top-down managerial approaches, power is distributed to promote regulatory resistance in the face of systemic shocks,[31] policy experimentation is valued, and 'results are continuously monitored to further inform that policy'.[32] Adaptive governance is perhaps the closest of these theories to the concerns of public lawyers and is familiar to many scholars working in environmental law. But legal scholarship – particularly comparative law and comparative public law scholarship – has articulated other ways that law can engage with complex problems. The next part of this chapter shows how legal pluralism – especially as it has developed in Southeast

[24] Valerie A Brown, Peter M Deane, John A Harris and Jacqueline Y Russell, 'Towards a Just and Sustainable Future' in Valerie A Brown, John A Harris and Jacqueline Y Russell (eds), *Tackling Wicked Problems: Through the Transdisciplinary Imagination* (Earthscan, 2010) 4.

[25] Meadows and Wright (n 17) 6.

[26] Ramage and Shipp (n 20) 1.

[27] Meadows and Wright (n 17) 6-7.

[28] Law is increasingly understood in this way, particularly in the context of overlapping legal orders. For example, Steven Lierman, defines 'complex adaptive systems' as 'complex in that they are diverse and made up of multiple interconnected elements, and adaptive in that they have the capacity to learn from experience and adapt to the changing environment', citing 'the ecosystem, the biosphere, the brain and the immune system' as examples: 'Law as a Complex Adaptive System the Importance of Convergence in a Multi-Layered Legal Order' (2014) 21 *Maastricht Journal of European and Comparative Law* 611, 629.

[29] Chaffin et al (n 3) 6. See also the influential work of Niklas Luhmann, 'Law as a Social System' (1988–1989) 83 *Northwestern University Law Review* 136.

[30] Chaffin et al (n 3) 5.

[31] Ruhl and Katz (n 18) 209.

[32] Chaffin et al (n 3) 6.

Asia – points to an innovative approach to law, one that complements other theories of complexity and offers a way of harnessing law in response to global complexity and crisis.

III. The Promise of Legal Pluralism

Although the diversity of legal orders is not unique to Asia, the sheer diversity of legal, social and religious norms in the region[33] – and Southeast Asia in particular, as the epigraph to this chapter and the work by contributors to this volume demonstrate convincingly[34] – has made it a crucible for the study of and experiments in legal pluralism.[35] As a place of overlapping and competing legal orders and extraordinary political regime diversity, it is well positioned to help navigate global complexities and crises. Andrew Harding's account of the syncretic nature of law in Southeast Asia, from which the epigraph is drawn, depicts legal pluralism in a vivid way, as geological layers, overlayed on one another 'without actually replacing' the lower layers that remain visible – capturing both the history and contemporary legacy of the region's legal diversity.[36] Drawing on the pioneering work of MB Hooker[37] and Clifford Geertz,[38] Harding, along with his peers and protégés (many of whom are represented in this volume) have exposed to the world what once was known to only a small number of scholars outside Southeast Asia: in this region can be found almost every imaginable mixture of legal and political regime. As Harding's contemporary Werner Menski also put it, law 'beyond Europe' is not simply about state law, 'but about a plurality of voices and values' allowing 'negotiations of difference and diversity at many different levels, and at all times'.[39]

These pluralist insights are significant for three reasons. First, while some legal pluralist frameworks seek to promote legal diversity within the nation-state, most contemporary approaches to legal pluralism acknowledge that some

[33] See Lynette J Chua, David M Engel and Sida Liu, 'Legal Pluralism' in Lynette J Chua, David M Engel and Sida Liu, *The Asian Law and Society Reader* (Cambridge University Press, 2023) 74–113.

[34] Many scholars consider Southeast Asia the most religiously diverse part of the world: see Jaclyn L Neo, Arif A Jamal and Daniel PS Goh, 'Introduction: Regulating Religion in Asia' in Jaclyn L Neo, Arif A Jamal and Daniel PS Goh (eds), *Regulating Religion in Asia* (Cambridge University Press, 2019) 1–16.

[35] MB Hooker, 'Towards a Legal History of Southeast Asia' (1978) 51 *Journal of the Malaysian Branch of the Royal Asiatic Society* 110. See also Veronica L Taylor, with MB Hooker and Virginia Hooker, 'M.B. Hooker and Southeast Asian Law: Path-breaking Passions' in Gary F Bell (ed), *Pluralism, Transnationalism and Culture in Asian Law: A Book in Honour of M.B. Hooker* (ISEAS–Yusof Ishak Institute, 2017) 1–30; Brian Tamanaha, *Legal Pluralism Explained: History, Theory, Consequences* (Oxford University Press, 2021).

[36] See Harding (n 1) 205.

[37] Above n 19.

[38] Clifford Geertz, *Local Knowledge: Further Essays in Interpretive Anthropology* (Basic Books, 1983).

[39] Werner Menski, 'Beyond Europe' in Esin Örücü and David Nelken (eds), *Comparative Law: A Handbook* (Hart Publishing, 2007) 189–216, 195.

kinds of legal order (eg, customary, religious, Indigenous or transnational) can subsist independently of the state and do not depend on formal state recognition. Although it is widely acknowledged that states can *recognise* other legal orders as a kind of legal pluralism consistent with a statist understanding of law, it is also clear that legal traditions can exist and thrive even in the absence of state recognition: 'studies of legal pluralism "from the ground up" … give greater prominence to the multiple normative systems people actually experience, and they allow us to see more accurately how state law operates in complex, multilayered social environments'.[40]

Second, most legal pluralist accounts accept that legal orders can subsist and interact with other legal orders on different scales, from the local to the regional, and from the macro-regional to the global. Recent work has shown, for example, how local communities, including ethnic minorities operating within states, are able to provide a distinctive legal approach to the challenges of globalisation, including pressures arising from global capitalism.[41] Legal pluralism therefore offers a way of thinking about global problems in a manner that is holistic, multilayered, dynamic, entangled, and even contested and contradictory. For example, Keebet von Benda-Beckmann explains that legal pluralism opens the door to the possibility that a variety of legal instruments could be brought to bear on complex problems:

> Regulatory pluralism is premised on the idea that a mix of very diverse regulatory instruments, if carefully selected and sequenced, is more likely to facilitate successful outcomes than mere state regulation and legal procedures …. The idea is that the relevant stakeholders, such as government actors, citizens and civic institutions may together generate governance structures for complex issues.[42]

The notion that regulatory responses to complex issues could be addressed in a holistic regulatory way is consistent with ideas proposed in other fields, such as economic geography, which show how 'economic processes' in the global economy 'work at multiple scales *simultaneously*' – so trying to 'understand a set of processes at one scale alone will inevitably produce a very incomplete picture of what is happening'.[43]

The resonance of economic geography with law leads to a third point. Most legal pluralists recognise that law does not exist apart from society, and so legal

[40] See Chua et al (n 33) 102.

[41] See, for example, David Engel, 'Blood Curse and Belonging in Thailand: Law, Buddhism, and Legal Consciousness' (2016) 3 *Asian Journal of Law and Society* 71; John Gillespie and Hong Thi Quang Tran, 'Legal Pluralism and the Struggle for Customary Law in the Vietnamese Highlands' (2022) 70 *American Journal of Comparative Law* 1; Benjamin Lawrence, 'New constitutional rites: indigeneity, legal pluralism and the international finance corporation's performance standards in Cambodia' (2022) 54 *Legal Pluralism and Critical Social Analysis* 48.

[42] Keebet von Benda-Beckmann, 'Trajectories of Legal Entanglement: Examples from Indonesia, Nepal, and Thailand' (2022) 54 *Legal Pluralism and Critical Social Analysis* 13, 15.

[43] Neil M Coe, Philip F Kelly and Henry WC Yeung, 'Geography: How do we think spatially?' in Neil M Coe, Philip F Kelly and Henry WC Yeung, *Economic Geography*, 3rd edn (Wiley-Blackwell Publishing, 2020) 3, 30.

systems necessarily interact with other human and natural systems. Add to that observation the multifaceted nature of complex global problems and crises, and it readily becomes clear that not only to holistic *legal* responses to global challenges, but genuinely interdisciplinary – legal *and extra-legal* – responses are required. These insights together anticipate and sit comfortably alongside a cluster of theories – complexity theory and what I will call and explain later in more detail, collectively, complexity-adjacent scholarship – that can be brought to bear on complexity and crisis, helping us to redesign law and governance in a more appropriate way.

How does legal pluralism help us in responding to complexity and crisis? As in other disciplines, the response to complex problems is not to search for simple solutions; in this respect, legal pluralism's recognition of the complexity of the legal world provides a natural entry-point for lawyers to engage with complexity in other disciplines and helps fashion responses to complex global problems. Consider again that both complexity theory and complexity-adjacent theories use 'complexity' or cognate terms to refer both to the problem and possible solutions. While complex *problems* and complex *solutions* are often linked, it is possible that a problem that can be described in simple terms (the outbreak of lethal virus or an earthquake) requires increasingly complex solutions as its consequences multiply. COVID-19 was a classic example. The more the virus spread, the more devastating its public health consequences, but also the greater and more complex the political, economic and social costs. While the initial solution (local containment) might have been relatively simple, the wider the outbreak, the more complex and multifaceted the problems became, and the more complex the required solutions needed to be. Complexity theory and complexity-adjacent scholarship recognise that most complex *problems* cannot be understood in a linear way; they require a nuanced understanding of multiple, interconnected systems that interact with one another in ways that cannot be reduced to even very complicated or sophisticated models. In this respect, they reflect, and could easily draw on the need to shift away from state-centric approaches to, as long recognised by legal pluralists, the variety of socio-legal norms that shape individual and group conduct, as well as their overlapping and entangled[44] nature. While traditional legal analysis tries to shoe-horn legal problems into conceptual spaces – a domestic legal issue, a private law matter – to simplify legal analysis, many problems defy such straightforward characterisations. Indeed, some problems are so entangled with different legal traditions or systems that they give rise to competing legal claims within a multiplicity of legal orders.[45]

The COVID-19 pandemic and climate change stand out, respectively, as mostly negative and mostly positive examples of responses to complex global problems. The COVID-19 pandemic illustrated in stark terms how a threat to public health

[44] von Benda-Beckmann (n 42).

[45] ibid.

was linked to local and global politics, economics and financial stability, labour and immigration, equality in the workplace, food security, gender (including gender-based violence) and racism.[46] Over the course of the pandemic, many governments found themselves torn between competing priorities and trade-offs (public health measures and restrictions on individual liberty among them).[47] Their decisions could not reasonably be taken in isolation (although local politics often prevailed over other considerations) nor did they have exclusively local effects. Yet we have seen that the Lancet Commission bemoaned the 'massive global failure' of coordination 'at multiple levels'.[48] At the same time, a legal pluralist analysis of the response in Southeast Asia reveals a distinct role for non-state actors – eg, religious groups, Indigenous communities, villages in ethnic minority areas in Myanmar[49] – who tapped into global public health norms and sought to implement them locally. Unfortunately, these responses were largely unrecognised and uncoordinated in the face of the fast-moving threat, despite efforts on the part of the WHO to serve as a focal point.

The climate crisis too displays a similar set of challenges, with profound implications for ecological systems and sustainability, the global economy, local and global politics, livelihoods and economic inequality, and a range of other considerations – often pulling in different directions and defying simple solutions. But here, the experiences – from a law and governance perspective – differ from COVID-19. For one thing, environmental governance has a longer history of innovation by nonstate actors, predating the United Nations Framework Convention of Climate Change (UNFCCC) and the accords and agreements that have emerged under that umbrella. Since the 1960s and 1970s, a global environmental civil society movement has emerged 'composed of NGOs, local social groups, experts, and other nonstate actors that share values'.[50] Moreover, while transnational actors have been influential in several policy areas,[51] they have been particularly influential 'in building and strengthening intergovernmental treaties and organizations to protect the

[46] Ramraj (n 12).

[47] For an illustration of how these dynamics played out in Canada during the COVID-19 pandemic, see Victor V Ramraj, 'Coordination Failure, Pandemic Prevention, and Political Polarization in Global Perspective' (2023) 46 *Manitoba Law Journal* 179.

[48] Sachs et al (n 11) 1224.

[49] See Ramraj (n 12) (especially Benjamin Schonthal and Tilak Jayatilake, 'Religion amid the Pandemic: A Buddhist Case Study'; Azmil Tayeb and Heong Hong Por, 'Malaysia: Improvised Pandemic Policies and Democratic Regression'); and Myat Myat Mon, 'How One Myanmar Village is Fighting the COVID-19 Outbreak' *The Diplomat* (18 August 2021), thediplomat.com/2021/08/how-one-myanmar-village-is-fighting-the-covid-19-outbreak.

[50] Thomas Hale, 'Transnational Actors and Transnational Governance in Global Environmental Politics' (2020) 23 *Annual Review of Political Science* 203, 206.

[51] The shift in the early 2000s toward transnational private or non-state regulation involving civil society, industry, scientific, and sometimes governmental or intergovernmental organisations, in areas ranging from sustainable forestry to food safety, shows that a different model is possible: Colin Scott, Fabrizio Cafaggi and Linda Senden, 'The Conceptual and Constitutional Challenge of Transnational Private Regulation' (2011) 38 *Journal of Law and Society* 1. See also Michael W Dowdle, *Transnational Law: A Framework for Analysis* (Cambridge University Press, 2022).

environment' with environmental intergovernmental meetings 'increasingly open to transnational actor influence'.[52]

For their part, international agreements under the UNFCCC umbrella, such as the Paris Agreement, have themselves engaged multiple intergovernmental actors in their implementation, recognising the critical role nonstate actors such as business organisations and NGOs play 'in providing a supportive environment in which innovative initiatives can be encouraged and nurtured'[53] – allowing for a multiscale, multistakeholder response. While governments and international organisations continue to play an 'orchestrating' role in global environmental governance,[54] the overall governance landscape is increasingly complex. In recent years, the Conference of the Parties (COP) meetings under the UNFCCC offers another example of how stakeholders other than states – such as 'environmental groups, businesses, trade unions, NGOs, indigenous peoples, and scientific communities'[55] – can be involved in international climate policymaking alongside governments.

As in other areas involving complex global governance challenges, climate governance requires 'institutions and organizations … nested across levels of governance, structured with multiple centers of power, redundant in function, and connected across space and time through networks'.[56] These global challenges demand 'institutional diversity (a mixture of market, state, and community organizations) at the local, regional, and state levels, connected by formal and informal social networks',[57] a kind of institutional diversity that is familiar to scholars of legal pluralism. Despite these promising developments, the COP meetings – even with all their attendant problems (eg, the effectiveness of nonstate participation among Global South actors remains contentious) – are a rare exception of coordination that, unlike some forms of transnational private or nonstate regulation, remains dependent on state initiative.

These developments in climate law and governance would not surprise legal pluralists in Southeast Asia. By way of consolidation, let me offer, briefly, seven ways in which pluralist approaches to law resonate with complexity, complexity-adjacent theories, and complex problem-solving. First, legal pluralists see state and state-derived law as only one kind of law, allowing room for multiple legal responses. To paraphrase the late Patrick Glenn, state law is but one legal tradition among many.[58] Second, while legal pluralists acknowledge the importance of

[52] Hale (n 50) 206–07.

[53] Robert Falkner, 'The Paris Agreement and the new logic of international climate politics' (2016) 92 *International Affairs* 1107, 1125.

[54] Hale (n 50) 213.

[55] Mattias Hjerpe and Björn-Ola Linnér, 'Functions of COP Side-Events in Climate-Change Governance' (2010) 10 *Climate Policy* 167, 178. See also Shannon K Orr, 'Institutional Control and Climate Change Activism at COP 21 in Paris' (2016) 16 *Global Environmental Politics* 23.

[56] Chaffin et al (n 3) 7.

[57] ibid.

[58] H Patrick Glenn, 'The State as Legal Tradition' (2013) 2 *Cambridge Journal of International and Comparative Law* 704.

borders, territorial demarcations can sometimes be secondary, not primary, indicators of legal communities.[59] Third, actors in a pluralist context are not limited to state actors, and might include (for example) community elders, religious organisations, knowledge-holders, business leaders, and civil society organisations.[60] Fourth, legal pluralists recognise that in most legal contexts, a critical skill is knowing how to navigate between or among legal orders.[61] At the same time, legal pluralists are (as a fifth point) flexible rather than rigid in conceiving the relationship between state and non-state law.[62] In this respect, they would likely resist the suggestion that 'quantitative metrics and methods' are needed to measure and manage legal complexity.[63] On the contrary, the layering of legal systems and traditions, and the interplay among them, might be better conceived in less data-driven ways. Sixth, legal pluralists are accustomed to working with multiple layers of law and the vertical and horizontal entanglements of legal orders they inevitably produce.[64] Seventh and finally, legal pluralism at its best considers difference, disagreement, and even contradiction[65] – and thus, *unpredictability*[66] – to be natural conditions, but need not stand in the way of peaceful coexistence or effective governance. In Southeast Asia's encounters with Western law, 'that there will be many areas of non-convergence' such that 'Global doctrine must embrace all cultures and legal traditions, and take the best from them.'[67] That, at least, is the aspiration. Amid all the diversity, we might helpfully think of legal norms as dynamic, subject to adjustment and renegotiation in response to changing social,

[59] Roger Cotterrell, 'Transnational Communities and the Concept of Law?' (2008) 21 *Ratio Juris* 1.

[60] For a classic articulation of a capacious approach to legal actors, see Sally Falk Moore, 'Law and Social Change: The Semi-Autonomous Social Field as an Appropriate Subject of Study' (1973) 7 *Law & Society Review* 719; in a contemporary context, see Carrie Menkel-Meadow, 'Why and How to Study 'Transnational' Law' (2011) 1 *UC Irvine Law Review* 97, 120.

[61] Menkel-Meadow (n 60) 106–09.

[62] Harding (n 1); John Gillespie and Hong Thi Quang Tran, 'Legal Pluralism and the Struggle for Customary Law in the Vietnamese Highlands' (2022) 70 *American Journal of Comparative Law* 1, 36.

[63] Ruhl and Katz (n 18) 195. Contrary to Ruhl and Katz, the legal pluralist's claim of complexity is not that, say, the US Tax Code or 'statute or code' or a 'body of law' is too complex, but that the nature of law – in Southeast Asia and elsewhere – involves a dynamic interplay among multiple legal orders.

[64] Harding (n 1); von Benda-Beckmann (n 42).

[65] See Andrew Harding, 'Buddhism, Human Rights and Constitutional Reform in Thailand' (2007) 2 *Asian Journal of Comparative Law* 1: 'Living with contradiction is something with which the West, not just South East Asia which has much experience in this regard, needs to get used to in the postmodern, multi-culturalist world of international human rights' (21).

[66] On the idea of *emergence* and the unpredictability in the context of complex adaptive systems, see Ruhl and Katz (n 18) 229–31. I am grateful to Ngoc Son Bui for a helpful discussion on this point. While it is laudable *within* a legal system to aspire to consistency and predictability, once we acknowledge the reality of legal pluralism, the idea of inconsistency among legal *orders* seems inevitable. And while some degree of predictability is important for subjects of multiple legal orders, the presence of inconsistency and unpredictability – and divergence – suggests the normative complexity of problems that cannot always be settled by jurisprudential fiat. Sometimes the uncertainty is a product of the complexity of the problem, a feature to be acknowledged, rather than wished away.

[67] Andrew Harding, 'Global Doctrine and Local Knowledge: Law in South East Asia' (2002) 51 *The International and Comparative Law Quarterly* 35, 53.

political, cultural, economic and environmental conditions and the conflicts and disagreements, and moments of unpredictability, they inevitably produce.

These points certainly do not exhaust the many characteristics of legal pluralism that resonate with complexity theory; some might identify others features or characterise core elements in different ways. And to be sure, legal pluralism has its critics[68] (which a committed legal pluralist would welcome): it is a normative position that requires a rigorous intellectual defence. I will not undertake this defence here. But in mounting that defence, it would be helpful for legal pluralists to engage with complexity and complexity-adjacent theories. In so doing, they will find common cause in defending an approach to problem-solving that is more fluid and less linear; one that has much to contribute to a holistic response to global complexity and crisis.

IV. Conclusion

This chapter offers a snapshot of an approach to global problem-solving – inspired by the work of Andrew Harding and other public and comparative law scholars working on Southeast Asia – that takes seriously both the complexity of global challenges and crises and the inadequacy of state-centric approaches to law to respond to many of them. It demonstrates the complexity of global problems and the need for complex responses. It also shows how legal pluralism – especially the experience of legal pluralism in Southeast Asia, along with the extensive multidisciplinary scholarship on complexity – has grappled with complex global problems in different ways, recognising both the interconnectedness of problems, legal and extra-legal factors, and the importance of holistic, layered, multidisciplinary thinking. In a world beset by complexity and crisis, by global catastrophic risks, this chapter invites legal pluralists to engage with complexity. As they do, they would be well advised to have Andrew Harding's essays on the nomic din of Southeast Asia at their side.

[68] See, for example, Klaus Günther. 'Normative Legal Pluralism: A Critique' in Jorge Luis Fabra-Zamora (ed), *Jurisprudence in a Globalized World* (Edward Elgar Publishing, 2020) 84–99.

3

Why Comparative Public Law is no Longer a Neglected Discipline: A Tribute to Andrew Harding

JUSTIN O FROSINI*

I. That Fateful Meeting in Bari

I was first introduced to Andrew Harding (AH) by our mutual friend and colleague Peter Leyland at a conference on the British Constitution organised in a warm and pleasant Bari at the end of May 2003. I still have vivid memories of the delicious al fresco dinner in the old city centre with Andrew, Peter and Professor Nino Olivetti Rason, co-editor of an Italian book series called *Diritto pubblico contemporaneo. Gli ordinamenti costituzionali*,[1] which constituted one of the sources of inspiration[2] for Peter and Andrew's monumental book series, *Constitutional Systems of the World*.[3] Andrew was exactly as Peter had described him: empathic, knowledgeable and delightful to converse with. A few years later I spent the summer recess as a visiting professor at the University of Victoria's Law Faculty[4] co-teaching a Comparative Constitutional Law class with Andrew and another friend and colleague, Ben Berger. With some important guidance from

* Many thanks to Giovanni Di Carlo, Hanna Gesang and Allegra Wirmer at the Center for Constitutional Studies and Democratic Development for their invaluable research assistance in the preparation of this chapter, and to Peter Leyland for his insightful comments. Part of the research for this chapter was funded by the George Lawrence Abernethy Endowment.

[1] cris.unibo.it/handle/11585/31569.

[2] 'This project originates from an approach to contribute to a volume on the United Kingdom to an Italian series of books on World constitutions … As well as gratefully accepting the offer to write the Italian version … it immediately struck me and my friend and colleague Professor Andrew Harding that no such series was available for comparative constitutionalists to draw upon. This book is the first volume in a brand new series which seeks to fill what was perceived to us a serious gap in the literature': Peter Leyland: *The Constitution of the United Kingdom*, 1st edn (Hart Publishing, 2007) vii.

[3] www.bloomsbury.com/us/series/constitutional-systems-of-the-world.

[4] Here I must take the opportunity to thank the then Dean, Donna Greschner, for the exquisite hospitality on her part and all the faculty.

Andrew, I also finished my book on constitutional preambles.[5] I came back to Italy after that summer in British Columbia knowing much more about both comparative public law and the rules of cricket, in both of which Andrew is an expert.

II. The Contemporary Renaissance Scholar

Andrew's long academic career is 'comparative public law in action'. In nearly three decades he has worked across three continents. After eight years at SOAS, where he was also Head of Department (baptism by fire?), Andrew went on to become Professor of Asia-Pacific Legal Relations at the University of Victoria, British Colombia, Canada before becoming Professor of Law at the National University of Singapore in 2012. That Andrew has dedicated his life to research is testified by the fact that over the years he has directed three leading research centres (Centre for Asia-Pacific Initiatives, Centre for Asian Legal Studies and the Asian Law Institute) and is on the editorial board of several outstanding law journals such as the *Asian Journal of Comparative Law* and the *Chinese Journal of Comparative Law*. His research fellowships and visiting professorships have crossed four continents with appointments going from Harvard Law School to my home institution Bocconi University, where I had the honour of hosting Professor Harding in 2007 and 2011. Wherever he has gone, he has left his mark transmitting to hundreds of enthralled students his boundless knowledge of comparative public law and Asian law.

III. Harding's Impact on Comparative Public Law

A. The 1998 Public Lecture in the Golden Jubilee Series at SOAS

Andrew Harding has had a lasting impact on comparative public law and this emerges from a seminal work, published at the turn of the millennium, which has inspired the title of this chapter. First given as a public lecture in the Golden Jubilee Series at SOAS on 13 March 1998, AH's chapter in Ian Edge's *Comparative Law in Global Perspective*[6] is a powerful defence of the discipline of comparative public law.[7] Harding situates it between comparative law and public law, but also

[5] Justin O Frosini, *Constitutional Preambles. At a Crossroads between Politics and Law* (Maggioli, 2012).
[6] Andrew Harding, 'Comparative public law: A neglected discipline?' in Ian Edge (ed), *Comparative Law in Global Perspective* (Ardsley, 2000) 101–20.
[7] While assisting me with this chapter, CCSDD researcher Hanna Gesang wrote the following in an email exchange about Andrew's article: 'This was not just useful for my studies, it put into words why I want to study comparative public law better than I could have ever managed to, I found it genuinely moving.' Hanna Gesang, personal communication, 24 September 2024.

references politics and sociology. He addresses common criticisms, establishes a methodology, and, whilst doing so, makes a convincing case for the importance of comparative public law. Despite more than a quarter of a century passing since the speech was first given, it retains its timeliness. Indeed, it has in some ways increased in relevance since 1998.

Firstly, AH argues that studying law without studying comparative law is virtually impossible. In isolation, understanding is inherently limited. Within comparative law, Harding distinguishes 'theoretical' and 'applied' comparative law, where the first '[serves] purely intellectual ends',[8] yet is not without importance because it creates 'an indispensable foundation or framework for the second'.[9] However, the article focuses on application of comparative law in public law contexts. Applied comparative law is defined as

> a practical method by which we can decide inter-jurisdictional questions to do with legislation, legal transplantation and legal development or reform, with the possible higher aim of unification or standardisation of principles of justice in pursuit of humanistic, economic or environmental goals.[10]

Having defined his precise subject – applied comparative public law – Harding moves on to situate his subject between two other disciplines: public law and comparative law. Public law is defined as 'those parts of the law which deal exclusively with the state or with relations between the state and other legal persons'.[11] This definition is immediately problematised: as becomes obvious throughout the article, Harding does not believe in a precise distinction between public and private law, especially within the context of comparative law. This will be outlined in more detail in the section dedicated to methodology. Furthermore, the close connection between public law and the subcategory of political science sometimes referred to as 'comparative government' is noted. Comparative public law is 'the study of public law in a comparative vein',[12] that does not fit neatly into any box: 'it enjoys legitimacy as a branch of public law, and of comparative law, and indeed of comparative government too'.[13] This remark has not lost its relevance, as recognition of interdisciplinary scholars(hip) continues to divide.

According to Harding, the need for justification originates from the fact that scholars of comparative law and scholars of public law refuse to engage in dialogue – both with each other, and with those of comparative public law. In the following section of the chapter, Harding outlines a canon of comparative public law, or as he poetically asks, 'If there is such a thing as comparative public law, what are its

[8] Harding (n 6) 103.
[9] ibid.
[10] ibid.
[11] ibid, 104.
[12] ibid, 105.
[13] ibid.

antecedents, its classical propositions, its sacred or controversial texts? Who are its heroes and heroines?'[14]

Before he even gets to sketching the discipline's canon, Harding inserts a passionate paragraph on the raison d'être of the discipline. Constitutional lawyers, he argues, have made 'sizeable' contributions to deadly conflicts. 'Weimar was the Chernobyl of our subject',[15] and it is imperative that lessons from the past are taken into consideration in modern-day constitution-making. The passage is so impactfully written that it would certainly make a good introduction to any first lecture on comparative public law.

B. The History of Comparative Public Law

Moving on to outlining a canon, Harding traces the history of the discipline starting with Ancient Greek scholars, notably Aristotle's comparisons of Greek constitutions. He pinpoints the decline of the Roman Republic as the moment in which the study of constitutions was paused until the Enlightenment. Harding claims that 'the growth of elaborated forms of constitutional government elsewhere was stunted … principally by the continuous invasions of barbarous Aryan or Mongol warriors … who established vast military empires'. Portraying this as the cause of the 'interruption' does, in my opinion, deserve some scrutiny – the complex system of satrapies of the Achaemenid Empire comes to mind. He does point out that the 'long night' that lasted until Enlightenment nevertheless included philosophers who thought critically about statecraft and systems of governance and therefore approximated the purpose of comparative public law. After this, he briefly touches on enlightenment-era scholars – Tocqueville, Paine, Burke – and the role of comparative public law in constitution-making in the United States and beyond.

Harding then outlines the notable lack of a 'public' component in the development of comparative law. The focus on private law has led to a 'narrow definition of law', a 'conservative field of activity' in a 'highly Euro-centric' context.[16] Harding's nod to the impending importance of comparative public law in Europe, especially given the success of private legal integration, reads no less poignantly today. Meanwhile, political institutions have been left to political and social scientists, who Harding rightfully criticises for not taking legal perspectives into account. Comparative public lawyers thus find themselves 'in a pincer movement between the comparative lawyers and the social scientist'.[17]

[14] ibid.
[15] ibid.
[16] ibid, 108.
[17] ibid, 108–09.

C. Overcoming the Private Law Bias: Why Otto Kahn-Freund was Wrong

The 'private law bias' is explicitly addressed in the following section of his essay. Harding strongly criticises Otto Kahn-Freund, specifically the article 'The Uses and Misuses of Comparative Law'.[18] Harding dispels Kahn-Freund's notion that different national systems are too far apart to lead to meaningful comparison, citing a SOAS project which compared environmental justice mechanisms in cities across several continents. He comes to the conclusion that Kahn-Freund was literally and figuratively boxed in by the Berlin Wall and the cold war context. Of course, Harding's speech, given in 1998, is itself a child of its time. The optimism of the 'end of history' is evident in his paragraph about Thailand's 1997 Constitution – and how was he supposed to know that since then, Thailand has gone through what can only be described as continuous constitutional chaos?

D. Harding's Methodology of Comparison

The last section of the article proposes a methodology of comparison for the discipline.[19] Harding, pragmatically, suggests that this is the moment to put former disagreements aside and learn from comparative lawyers. Specifically, he applies the propositions of Zweigert and Kötz[20] to comparative public law by referencing his project on environmental justice, as well as Mauro Cappelletti's 'Florence project'.[21] Briefly put, the propositions are as follows:

(a) Functionality – the laws that are being compared must fulfil the same purpose, rather than being outwardly similar. In Harding's research project, that meant comparing even extra-legal mechanisms to laws and applying 'mid-range concepts'[22] to capture functionally similar processes. Of course, this also entails smoothly moving across the barrier between private and public law.
(b) Results and Value-Systems – Harding's project confirmed that the idea of 'legal systems [tending] to reach the same destinations by different routes' applied to public law just as much as to private law.
(c) Selection – Whilst Zweigert and Kötz recommend not to compare 'affiliated' systems as this does not yield interesting results, Harding maintains that this

[18] Otto Kahn-Freund, 'On the Uses and Misuses of Comparative Law' (1974) 37 *Modern Law Review* 1: important early contribution to the anti-formalist movement in comparative law.
[19] Andrew Harding and Peter Leyland, 'Comparative Law in Constitutional Contexts' in David Nelken and Esin Örücü (eds), *Comparative Law: A Handbook* (Hart Publishing, 2007).
[20] Hein Kötz and Konrad Zweigert, *An Introduction to Comparative Law*, 3rd edn (Oxford University Press, 1998).
[21] Mauro Cappelletti, *Access to Justice and the Welfare State* (European University Institute, 1981).
[22] Harding (n 6) 115.

is hardly an issue in public law. Indeed, his research project faced notable challenges when comparing the Chinese legal system to all other ones – so some closeness could prove helpful.

(d) Terminology – Harding suggests that in order to overcome terminological challenges when comparing fundamentally different systems, the comparativist should return to the aforementioned mid-range concepts, rather than trying to apply technical terms. The useful examples he gives is that rather than asking 'Do they have anything like the ombudsman?',[23] a public law comparativist may consider asking 'What mechanisms exist for citizens to make complaints against the administration?'

International norms, according to Harding, will only reinforce the usefulness of comparativist works in the public law sphere. Where there are international norms, there is a practical purpose behind comparison: that of fulfilling internationally set standards.

E. The Pursuit of Best Practices which Protect Democracy and Human Rights

In his conclusion, Harding mentions possible fields of exploration for comparative public law. He ends, powerfully, with a quote from Aristotle on the collection of constitutions. Applied comparative public law to AH has a clear purpose: that of establishing best practices, which protect democracy and human rights. By establishing this, he does not just successfully defend the discipline against its critics, but also endows it with a meaningful purpose.

Speaking in 1998 – just three years after the Dayton Agreement – Harding had the right to be optimistic about our discipline's power. More than a quarter century later, some of our optimism may have faded due to democratic backsliding and the decline in constitutional democracy around the world. Yet, AH's essay retains its relevance and may even serve as a reminder that studying comparative public law was significant then and has only become more important since.

IV. Andrew Harding Igniting Minds on the Debate Concerning Legal Transplanting

In the field of comparative law one of the most heated debates is of course related to whether one can transplant single rules, law or even an entire legal institution from one legal system to another. This topic is masterfully addressed by AH in a wonderful online seminar delivered to Jangran Lakecity University in 2020 as part

[23] ibid, 117.

of the International Igniting Minds Series.[24] During this seminar, AH discusses the topic of legal transplantation[25] by focusing on the scholarly dispute between Pierre Legrand[26] and Alan Watson.[27] He begins by defining legal transplantation as occurring when a donee system adopts a rule, an institution, a statute, or even has in place an entire legal system from another (donor) country.

Legal transplantation triggers a reflection about law and society. AH cites mirror theory (law as a mirror of a society and its values) and discusses how not only law is constructed by society, but also society is constructed by law. He highlights that laws can only function so far as individuals within society are willing to observe them, and this must be at the forefront of lawmakers' minds. Gaps between law and society may exist to varying degrees (he compares India, with a large gap, and Singapore, with a very small one). This link between law and society[28] may pose a problem to legal transplantation, though he argues that it is not impossible per se.

Harding goes on to compare the binary positions of Watson and Legrand, which he describes as two ends of the spectrum of perspectives on legal transplantation. Watson argues that legal transplantation is possible, and that it represents the main driver of legal development. He disregards the conditions of the donee system as a determining factor, and states that legal tradition and the 'adhesiveness of law' is secured by the donee system's legal profession. On the contrary, Legrand argues against the possibility of legal transplantation, in light of the determinative nature of societal and cultural understanding of rules, which cannot be transplanted in a foreign society.

AH then goes on to challenge both Watson and Legrand's arguments. For instance, he criticises Watson's argument that law may be abstracted from society, as consideration of the way a law functions in the donor society is important to evaluate its potential effectiveness in the donee society. However, he agrees that legal transplantation is the major method of legal change across time and space. With regard to Legrand, AH pushes back against the scholar's denial of the possibility of legal transplantation, which is self-evident,[29] as well as his argument that all rules – ie, their legal meanings – carry a specific cultural baggage which makes transplantation impossible. AH also discusses how Legrand's support for the mirror theory clashes with the reality of legal reform, as it undermines the idea that law may change society, rather than the other way around, 'although the

[24] Andrew Harding, www.youtube.com/watch?v=slJusFw-2es.

[25] See Andrew Harding, 'Comparative Law and Legal Transplants in South East Asia: Making Sense of the "Nomic Din"' in D Nelken and J Fest (eds), *Adapting Legal Cultures* (Hart Publishing, 2001).

[26] For a critique of formalism in comparative law: Pierre Legrand, 'The Impossibility of Legal Transplants' (1997) 4 *Maastricht Journal of European and Comparative Law* 111.

[27] Alan Watson, *Legal Transplants: An Approach to Comparative Literature*, 2nd edn (University of Georgia Press, 1993).

[28] Yong-Shik Lee and Andrew Harding, 'Law and Development: A Comparative Law Aspect' (2024) 17 *Law and Development Review* 393–415.

[29] Administrative law in Thailand is an excellent example. See eg Peter Leyland '"Droit Administratif" Thai Style: A Comparative Analysis of the Administrative Courts in Thailand' (2006) 8 *Australian Journal of Asian Law* 121.

term "transplantation" is not preferred due to its failure to capture the need for modification to fit the socioeconomic conditions on the ground'.[30] Nonetheless, AH does embrace the value of Legrand's invitation to tread carefully with transplantation. Finally, he criticises both scholars for failing to study whether their theories correspond to reality.

AH also addresses the debates on whether legal transplantation may be limited to private law or also applicable to public law (which he supports, though he recognises that private law transplantation is easier than public). He outlines how civilian lawyers reject the idea of public law transplantation on the basis of the differing political structures that exist across societies, while common lawyers are much less strict with the public vs private distinction.

Another feature that AH discusses is how to recognise successful transplantation, which depends on several factors and may be measured using different standards. He considers how some kinds of law seem to be more easily transplanted than others, arguing that this depends on the closeness of law to social values – family law is harder to transplant than company law, for example, though the process is by no means impossible.

AH proceeds to examine some examples from his experience in East Asia, including the adoption (and adaptation) of the concept of the trust from the common law system in the civil law systems of China and Thailand,[31] the adoption of the publication of leading cases in China from the common law system, and the transplantation of marriage registration and validity in societies where customary marriage was normal. He states that these examples show transplantation of legal ideas which are adapted to the receiving system, which is somewhat different from what was discussed by Watson and Legrand. He argues that care must be taken in the terminology used around legal transplantation, and that the absorption process of a new legal idea into a receiving system must be further studied to understand legal reform.

In concluding this section on legal transplantations, it is worth citing AH (and his co-author Yong-Shik Lee) once again:

> The debate in comparative law appears also to ignore the vast amount of legal transplantation that, increasingly, takes place (often with considerable modifications). It is a stretch of the imagination to consider that all such legal adoptions are unsuccessful, and billions of dollars wasted, even if law and development needs to be modest in its claims. The fact is that, in spite of the acknowledged need to engage with legal culture, or with 'real legal certainty' as it is sometimes called, as opposed to simply 'rule of law', legal problems do tend to repeat across jurisdictions, and the solutions available for solving such problems are in general rather few in number.[32]

[30] Lee and Harding (n 28) 409.

[31] Lee and Harding (n 28); Surutchada Reekie and Narun Popattanachai, 'Thai Trust Law: A Legal Import Rooted in Pragmatism' in Andrew Harding and Munin Pongsapan (eds), *Thai Legal History: From Traditional to Modern Law* (Cambridge University Press, 2021).

[32] Lee and Harding (n 28) 409.

This is clearly a polemical response to Pierre Legrand's total rejection of legal transplantation.

V. Comparative Public Law is no Longer a Neglected Discipline

In April 2011 I had the pleasure and privilege of hosting AH at Bocconi University to discuss together with Roberto Toniatti, a leading Italian scholar of comparative public law, whether ours was still a neglected discipline.[33] We all came to the conclusion that it no longer was. As Mark Tushnet has pointed out, interest in comparative public law and more specifically comparative law has 'historically come in waves, typically triggered by dramatic examples of constitution-making'.[34]

Mark Tushnet goes on to underline that:

> Current interest in comparative constitutional law is a legacy of the third wave in the late twentieth century. The field appears to have become 'self-sustaining', that is, not dependent upon triggering events. There is an International Association of Constitutional Law, with regular meetings drawing together scholars from around the world, as well as a leading journal, the *International Journal of Constitutional Law*, dedicated to comparative constitutional law.[35]

Moreover, 'the decade of the 2010s has already seen the publication of three major research handbooks on comparative constitutional law, each conceiving of the field in slightly different terms'.[36]

In 1999 a group of Italian public law comparatists led by Giuseppe Franco Ferrari founded a new journal entitled *Diritto pubblico comparato ed europeo* (*Comparative Public and European Law*) which celebrated its 25th Anniversary in Trento in November 2024. This is just one of many examples of how comparative public law has become an ever-growing discipline. Four years later, in 2003, Norman Dorsen from the New York University School of Law founded the above-mentioned *International Journal of Constitutional Law* (*ICON*) a quarterly law journal covering constitutional law, administrative law, international law and other branches of public law. From the Editorial Board of *ICON* emerged the idea of creating an International Society of Public Law:

> ICON has expanded its interests, its range of authors, its readers, its Editorial Board members, and above all, the issues it covers, to include not only articles in individual

[33] ius.unibocconi.eu/sites/default/files/files/media/attachments/abstract20110715095358.pdf.

[34] Mark Tushnet, *Advanced Introduction to Comparative Constitutional Law* (Edward Elgar, 2014) 1.

[35] ibid.

[36] ibid. The handbooks Tushnet refers to are Tom Ginsburg and Rosalind Dixon (eds), *Comparative Constitutional Law* (Edward Elgar, 2011); Michel Rosenfeld and Andras Sájo (eds), *The Oxford Handbook of Comparative Constitutional Law* (Oxford University Press, 2012); Mark Tushnet, Thomas Fleiner and Cheryl Saunders (eds), *Routledge Handbook of Constitutional Law* (Routledge, 2012).

> fields such as Administrative Law, Global Constitutional Law, Global Administrative Law and the like, but also – and increasingly so – scholarship that reflects both legal reality and academic perception; scholarship which, in dealing with the challenges of public life and governance, combines elements from all of the above fields with a good dose of political theory and social science.[37]

Every year there are several international conferences across the globe that deal with public law in a comparative perspective from Icon-S to the Global Summit on Constitutionalism.[38]

VI. The 'Villains' of Comparative Public Law

In the 2000 chapter illustrated above, AH posed the question of who the heroes and heroines of comparative public law were,[39] so with a little *divertissement* we shall now ask ourselves who are the '*villains*' of comparative public law.

A. Lost in Translation

As Vicki Jackson rightly underlines:

> [H]owever difficult it is to become *bilingual, bilegalism* is even harder to achieve. Not only is it necessary to understand foreign languages, or find reliable translations of foreign legal materials, but in order to understand one doctrine or institution of another legal system it is necessary to have at least some understanding of the broader canvas on which it exists.[40]

What does the word *doctrine* mean in English? Does it correspond to the Italian term *dottrina*? What does the word *jurisprudence* mean in English? Does it correspond to the Italian term *giurisprudenza*?

Other examples: in many respects the expressions 'form of state' and 'form of government' are notions that specifically derive from Italian public law. In fact, in the United States and in Britain these two terms are often treated as synonyms, with the term 'form of government' used more frequently than the expression 'form of state'. 'Government' in English has a far wider meaning than the word '*governo*' in Italian because, while the latter normally refers to the executive power (more precisely the Council of Ministers), the former often refers to the state has a whole – hence the use of the term 'branch of government' to define the legislative, executive and judicial powers. The legal linguist Gigliola Mariani Sacerdoti

[37] www.icon-society.org/history.

[38] law.utexas.edu/the-2025-global-summit.

[39] Harding (n 6) 105.

[40] Vicki C Jackson, 'Comparative Constitutional Law: Methodologies' in Michel Rosenfeld and Andras Sájo (eds), *The Oxford Handbook of Comparative Constitutional Law* (Oxford University Press, 2012) 70.

discovered this when she translated the Federalist Papers[41] because she had to translate the term 'government' in several different ways in Italian.

What in Italian are classified as '*forme di governo*' are often referred to as 'regime types' or 'systems of government' in English. We can find similar conceptual linguistic difficulties in other countries too. The French use the expression '*régime politique*' rather than '*forme du governement*', and although the Spanish do employ the expressions '*forma de estado*' and '*forma de gobierno*', they also use the term '*forma politica*', which in many respects is a combination of the two notions: in fact Article 1.3 of the Spanish Constitution states that '*La forma política del Estado español es la Monarquía parlamentaria*' ('The political form of the Spanish State is the Parliamentary Monarchy').[42]

Alongside the problem of 'lost in translation' there is also the problem of 'lost in *un*translation', ie when a word from one language is used in another. Again, Italy is an excellent example of this. An involution has hit Italian political communication, ie 'linguistic xenophilia', which often involves legal terminology. When Britain started its devolution process under the Blair Government in 1997, the supporters of greater decentralisation in Italy (in particular the then Lega Nord) started using the word 'devolution'.[43] But when this term, which derives from British public law, is used in Italy does it really have the same meaning that it has in the United Kingdom?[44]

Finally, the need for bilegalism may sometimes be required even among English-speaking countries. One example for all: the United States has 'judicial review' and so does the United Kingdom, but in the United States the term refers to 'judicial review of legislation' while in the United Kingdom it refers to 'judicial review of administrative action'. To avoid confusion, many comparative scholars now prefer the term 'constitutional review' when referring to judicial review of legislation.[45] Mark Tushnet also well illustrates this:

> Deeper issues of language and translation arise in the Benthamite tradition of functionalism and universal grammar. The 'natural' translation of some terms is misleading. The term 'judicial review' provides a good example even *without translation*. The US usage of the term refers to the judicial practice of determining whether a statute is consistent with the Constitution; in British usage it refers to judicial practice of determining whether administrative action is consistent with statutory authorization. The term used for the US practice is 'constitutional review', a phrase largely unknown in US constitutional discourse. (italics added)[46]

[41] Alexander Hamilton, John Jay and James Madison, *Il Federalista* (Gigliola Mariani Sacerdoti tr, Giappichelli, 2000).

[42] Justin O Frosini, 'Forms of State and Forms of Government' in Giuseppe Franco Ferrari (ed), *Introduction to Italian Public Law* (Giuffré, 2018) 33–34.

[43] David Wiley, 'Berlusconi creates history by naming devolution minister' *The Scotsman* (11 June 2001) 10.

[44] Justin O Frosini, 'Devolution' in Lucio Pegoraro, Silvia Bagni and Giorgia Pavani (eds), *Glossario di amministrazione locale comparata* (Giuffrè, 2002) 51–54.

[45] Justin O Frosini, 'Constitutional Justice' in Giuseppe Franco Ferrari (eds), *Introduction to Italian Public Law* (Giuffré, 2018).

[46] Tushnet (n 34) 6.

In a way, terms such as 'form of government' and 'constitutional review' are part of the specific language of comparative public law.

Finally, it is worth noting that these issues not only pertain to research in the field of comparative public law, but also to the teaching of comparative public law as Francesco Biagi justly underlines in an article published in *Diritto pubblico comparato ed europeo* which addresses the fascinating topic of teaching comparative law in English in Italy.[47]

B. Those who Stop at Textual Analysis

Another set of 'villains' of comparative public law are those researchers that consider textual analysis of constitutions as the *end* rather than the *means*. Textual analysis is an essential part of any comparative public law research, but it can't stop there. AH and Peter Leyland explain this very effectively in their book on the constitutional system of Thailand:

> The primary objective of this book has not been to offer a description of Thailand's current Constitution, but rather to consider the *broader issue of Thai constitutionalism* … The challenge of constitutionalism … is not simply to formulate rules at a constitutional level which embody principles of a particular conception of good governance, neither is it simply a matter of designing formal checks and balances; constitutionalism for us requires the *achievement of general conformity with such rules by all the main constitutional actors* (italics added).[48]

An example from Italy. If one wants to know what are the functions of the Italian Constitutional Court[49] a mere textual analysis of the Constitution would not provide you with the right answer. Article 134 therein tells us that:

> The Constitutional Court shall pass judgement on controversies on the constitutional legitimacy of laws and enactments having force of law issued by the State and Regions; conflicts arising from allocation of powers of the State and those powers allocated to State and Regions, and between Regions; charges brought against the President of the Republic and the Ministers, according to the provisions of the Constitution.

Taking the Constitution at face value, it would seem that the Constitutional Court only has three functions, but in actual fact it has four, because the procedure established by ordinary statute law for conducting a referendum as provided for by Article 75 of the Constitution assigns the *Corte costituzionale* a fourth function, ie that of declaring admissibility of abrogative referendums.

[47] Francesco Biagi, 'Insegnare diritto comparato in inglese. Sfide e prospettive' (2024) 26 *Diritto pubblico comparato ed europeo* 545.

[48] Andrew Harding and Peter Leyland, *The Constitutional System of Thailand* (Bloomsbury, 2011) 251.

[49] Justin O Frosini, 'Constitutional Court of Italy (La Corte Costituzionale della Repubblica Italiana)' in Rüdiger Wolfrum, Rainer Grote and Frauke Lachenmann (eds), *The Max Planck Encyclopedia of Comparative Constitutional Law* (Oxford University Press, 2017).

Other possible pitfalls for comparative public law scholars who limit their research to textual analysis are what we might define as 'self-definitions',[50] ie the cases where a constitution defines its respective legal system in a certain way, but where there is good deal of ambiguity as to the meaning of that term. In analysing 'self-definitions', one must not only be aware of the problems inherent in legal translations (see section A above), but also be very cautious because the self-definition may be misleading. A good example is the Constitution of Bulgaria, where Article 1 states that 'Bulgaria is a republic with a parliamentary form of government', but then Article 93(1) goes on to say that 'The President is elected directly by the voters for a period of five years by a procedure established by law.' The 'self-definition' contained in Article 1 does not correspond to how we might define the dispositional properties[51] of parliamentary forms of government, where the head of state is not directly elected.

This might appear to be a very theoretical line of reasoning, but it has been rendered very concrete in recent times through the clashes between the directly elected President Radev and the then Bulgarian prime minister Boyko Borisov, which led Radev (strengthened by his popular mandate) to frequently veto legislative proposals submitted by Borisov's GERB party to Bulgarian Parliament, issuing a total of 19 vetoes in the first two and a half years of his presidency: a decidedly interventionist stance for a president who ought to have a merely ceremonial role.[52]

C. Populists and Comparative Public Law: From 'Manipulative Borrowing' to 'Institutional Capturing'

Former Polish prime minister and co-founder of the right-wing populist Law and Justice Party, Jaroslaw Kaczynski, studied law at the Faculty of Law and Administration of the University of Warsaw, where in 1976 he obtained a Doctor of Law. The populist and illiberal prime minister of Hungary, Viktor Orbán, received a law degree from the University of Budapest in 1987. Kaïs Saïed, president of Tunisia, is a retired professor of constitutional law, and was secretary-general of the Tunisian Association of Constitutional Law between 1990 and 1995 then vice-president of the association from 1995. The populist prime minister of Slovakia, Robert Fico, graduated in law in 1986 from Comenius University Bratislava, and the violent populist Rodrigo Duterte, former president of the Philippines, obtained

[50] Lucio Pegoraro, 'Autoqualificazione ed eteroqualificazioni del federalismo: il linguaggio della Costituzione e delle proposte di riforma' in Serena Baldin, Lucio Pegoraro and Angelo Rinella (eds), *Tre lezioni sul federalismo* (Edizioni Università di Trieste, 1999) 19–30.

[51] Robert Elgie, 'The classification of democratic regime types: Conceptual ambiguity and contestable assumptions' (1998) 33 *European Journal of Political Research* 24.

[52] Anna Krasteva, *Citizens vs. Elites: Symbolic Battles Over the Uses of Political Crises in Bulgaria* (Österreichische Gesellschaft für Europapolitik, 2023).

a law degree from San Beda College of Law in 1972 and in the same year passed the bar exam.

Do I need to continue? These populist leaders are no fools and they know the law very well. They are the real villains of comparative public law because there can be no doubt that they study the laws and institutions of other countries with the aim of carrying out a very smart legal transplantation that serves their purposes. We all know that liberal democratic constitutions share some common features that safeguard pluralism and democratic resilience. Accordingly, constitutional entrenchment is justified because it guarantees that important decisions are taken with the participation of the minority. Using Viktor Orbán – the Villain of Villains? – and Hungary as a case study we discover that populist governments often pursue constitutional amendment to achieve goals that are exactly the opposite. What are these goals?

Under a populist government, the constitution acquires mythical traits that exalt the 'people' and tend to emphasise an emotional bond with the charismatic leader.[53] This *epos* of the constitution explains why populists entrench as many of their policies as possible.[54] An example can help clarify this point:

> Article 3 of the Ninth Amendment to the Hungarian Constitution which protects a child's right to identify with their gender at birth and to have an upbringing based on Hungary's constitutional identity and Christian culture. The government's explanatory notes state that Western ideology is changing in a way that necessitates guaranteeing the child's right to self-identity in line with their gender at birth in order to protect the child's physical and mental wellbeing. In the future, because of Article 3, a government sympathetic to the existence and claims of trans-gender people will have great difficulty developing affirmative policies unless they are able to win a majority in Parliament that allows them to amend the constitution.[55]

A second goal is to limit external interference, especially that of the EU, with executive decision-making. For example, in 2016, a judgment delivered by the Hungarian Constitutional Court upheld a law approved by the Orbán majority aimed at rejecting the EU proposal to reallocate refugees in various Member States.[56] The Court handed down this decision because it considered the law to be an epitome of Hungarian *national identity*. In other words, what second generation constitutional courts had termed, during the 1960s, the doctrine of counter-limits, has been reconfigured as an identity test[57] transforming the Constitution into a shield against external interference. Here we are in the presence of a much-studied

[53] Justin O Frosini and Sara Pennicino, 'The Impact of Populism on European Constitutional Systems: A Comparative Study' (2022) 3 *Percorsi costituzionali* 586.

[54] Nadia Urbinati, *Me the People* (Harvard University Press, 2019) 110–11; Frosini and Pennicino (n 53).

[55] Frosini and Pennicino (n 53).

[56] Judgment no 22/2016.

[57] Federico Fabbrini and Oreste Pollicino, 'Constitutional Identity in Italy: Institutional Disagreements at a Time of Political Change' in C Callies and G van der Schyff (eds), *Constitutional Identity in a Europe of Multilevel Constitutionalism* (Cambridge University Press, 2019).

topic in the realm of comparative public law, ie 'judicial cosmopolitanism',[58] but in this case it is being used for illiberal purposes.

A third goal is to reserve the power of adjudication to the Constitutional Court by means of constitutional entrenchment so as to limit the role of ordinary courts. In fact, a captured constitutional court will not only support populist governments' choices, but even offer a constitutional doctrine to justify them. This is part of a certain pattern of institutional control where Kelsenian-style constitutional courts become the enforcers of anti-pluralist populism; in other words, we have what Oreste Pollicino has define as 'manipulative borrowing' combined with 'bad judicial masters'.[59] This impact on European constitutional systems is extremely significant because a modern institution that was devised after World War II as a centrepiece for protection of democracy and fundamental rights is hollowed out and transformed from a guardian into an accomplice.[60]

VII. Andrew Harding the Botanist Emeritus

AH's copiously cited 2000 chapter begins with several quips about the SOAS Law Department, which Harding, upon his first encounter, perceived as a 'lofty place' where scholars are akin to:

> A collection of outrageously eccentric jurists that studied things one could barely imagine. They seemed to me rather like 19th Century botanists in safari jackets, peering through magnifying glasses at the extraordinary legal flora of Asia and Africa. The idea that I might one day myself enter this strange botanical garden and ascend the rain-tree of learning never entered my head.

As I hope this tribute has demonstrated, there is no doubt whatsoever that AH did enter that 'strange botanical garden' and 'did ascend the rain-tree of learning'. As Peter Leyland underlines in his chapter, 'Harding's studies on the nature of the so called Westminster Model and on the multi-layered character of constitutional systems, particularly from Southeast Asia' have been essential in understanding

[58] There is copious literature on this topic: Tania Groppi and Marie-Claire Ponthoreau (eds), *The Use of Foreign Precedents by Constitutional Judges* (Oxford University Press, 2013); Ran Hirschl, 'Judicial Review and the Politics of Comparative Citations: Theory, Evidence and Methodological Challenges, in Erin F Delaney and Rosalind Dixon (eds), *Comparative Judicial Review* (Edward Elgar Publishing, 2018); Giuseppe Franco Ferrari (ed), *Judicial Cosmopolitanism: The Use of Foreign Law in Contemporary Constitutional Systems* (Brill, 2019); Francesco Biagi, 'Foreign Law in Constitutional Interpretation' in Rüdiger Wolfrum, Rainer Grote and Frauke Lachenmann (eds), *The Max Planck Encyclopedia of Comparative Constitutional Law* (Oxford University Press, 2021).

[59] Oreste Pollicino. 'Populist Constitutional Grammar – Between Manipulative Borrowing and Bad (Judicial) Masters' in Martin Krieger, Adam Czarnota and Wojciech Sadurski (eds), *Anticonstitutional Populism* (Cambridge University Press, 2022) 434–61.

[60] Sara Pennicino, 'Has Liberal Constitutionalism yielded to populism or have the populists yielded to liberal constitutionalism? The case of Italy and the Five Star Movement' (2019) 2 *Percorsi costituzionali* 533; Frosini and Pennicino (n 53).

the development of constitutional systems that were inspired by the British model.[61] His research interests have spanned from country studies on the constitutional systems of Malaysia[62] and Thailand[63] to the forms, functions and practice of constitutional courts from across the globe.[64]

In a nutshell, AH really has spent his life 'peering through magnifying glasses at the extraordinary legal flora of Asia'. The convex lens that he has always used is the methodology of comparative public law thus making him both a leading scholar in our field and a Botanist Emeritus.

[61] Andrew Harding '"The Westminster Model" Constitution Overseas: Transplantation, Adaption and Development in Commonwealth States' (2004) 4 *Oxford University Commonwealth Law* 143.

[62] Andrew Harding, *The Constitution of Malaysia: A Contextual Analysis*, 2nd edn (Hart Publishing, 2022).

[63] Harding and Leyland (n 48).

[64] Andrew Harding, Peter Leyland and Tania Groppi, 'Constitutional courts: Forms, functions and practice in comparative perspective' in Andrew Harding and Peter Leyland (eds), *Constitutional courts: A comparative study* (Wildy, Simmonds & Hill Publishing, 2009).

PART II

Comparative Constitutional Law

4

Comparative Constitutional Law and Asia: Conspectus and Prospectus

KEVIN YL TAN*

I. Introduction: The Legacy of Comparison

The history of the development of comparative constitutional law as a field of study has been briefly documented elsewhere[1] and it is not my aim to revisit that narrative. What is clear from these various accounts is that comparative constitutional law has hitherto been dominated by scholars from Europe and North America, and that Asia – however defined – has not featured prominently in such studies. Writing in 2002, Andrew Harding found himself making an impassioned argument for comparativists to take Southeast Asia seriously and to assure public lawyers around the world that most states in Southeast Asia did indeed observe the rule of law and that trajectories of development were worthy of study.[2] This situation has changed quite dramatically in the following decade, so much so that Harding attributed the burgeoning comparative constitutional law scholarship to the rise of 'new Asian constitutionalism'.[3] This has led to the publication of a slew of books and articles on comparative constitutional law covering Asia. This chapter considers the development of the field of comparative constitutional law in

* I would like to thank my research assistant, Marcus Teo, for his initial research for this article. All errors are mine alone. An earlier version of this chapter was presented at the 'The State of Comparative Law in Asia' Conference held at the Faculty of Law, National University of Singapore on 27 September 2017.

[1] See Rosalind Dixon and Tom Ginsburg, 'Introduction' in Tom Ginsburg and Rosalind Dixon (eds), *Comparative Constitutional Law* (Edward Elgar, 2011) 1–15, 1–4; Michel Rosenfeld and András Sajó, 'Introduction' in Michel Rosenfeld and András Sajó (eds), *The Oxford Handbook of Comparative Constitutional Law* (Oxford University Press, 2012) 1–21, 2–9; Mark Tushnet, *Advanced Introduction to Comparative Constitutional Law* (Edward Elgar, 2014) 1–9; and Ran Hirschl, *Comparative Matters: The Renaissance of Comparative Constitutional Law* (Oxford University Press, 2014) 77–150.

[2] Andrew Harding, 'Comparative Public Law: Some Lessons from South East Asia' in Andrew Harding and Esin Örücü (eds), *Comparative Law in the 21st Century* (Kluwer, 2002) 249–66.

[3] Andrew Harding, 'Asian Law, Public Law, Comparative Law Stir-Fry: Theory and Method Considered' in Tania Groppi, Valeria Piergigli and Angelo Rinella (eds), *Asian Constitutionalism in Transition: A Comparative Perspective* (Giuffré, 2008) 19–45, 22–23.

Asia over the past six decades and offers some suggestions for future research and investigations.

II. The Pioneering Work of Harry E Groves

Few scholars know that the comparative study of constitutional law in Asia actually began in Asia. In 1962, at the University of Malaya in Singapore, an African-American professor of constitutional law compiled and published the first-ever comparative constitutional law casebook. It was a pioneering work on many fronts. His name was Harry Edward Groves, who arrived in Singapore in 1960 as Asia Foundation Professor of Constitutional Law and became Dean of the Faculty in 1963; and that groundbreaking book was his *Comparative Constitutional Law: Cases and Materials*.[4] Harry Edward Groves (1921–2013)[5] was born in Manitou Springs, Colorado and educated at the University of Colorado (*cum laude*), University of Chicago (JD) and Harvard Law School (where he obtained his LLM as Ford Foundation Fellow). An artillery officer in World War II, he was a member of the Judge Advocate General in the Korean War. He began his academic career as an Associate Professor at the North Carolina College Law School in 1949. Between 1951 and 1956, Groves served as a captain in the Judge Advocate General's corps and then practised law in Fayetteville, North Carolina. In 1956, he became Dean of the School of Law at Texas Southern University (now Thurgood Marshall School of Law). In 1962, he was appointed Asia Foundation Professor of Constitutional Law at the University of Singapore, and became Dean of the Faculty the next year. He left Singapore in 1964 to become President of the Central State University in Wilberforce, Ohio, a position he held until 1968 when he was appointed Professor at the School of Law, University of Cincinnati. From 1976 to 1981, he was Dean of the North Carolina Central University Law School before leaving to take up the position of Brandis Professor of Law at the University of North Carolina, Chapel Hill, where he later became Emeritus Professor.

Groves had been shortlisted for the appointment as the Asia Foundation Professor for one simple reason. While pursuing his LLM at Harvard Law School in 1958–1959 under a Ford Foundation Fellowship, he enrolled in Professor Arthur Sutherland's Comparative Constitutional Law class and wrote a paper on the new Federation of Malaya Constitution. Groves recalled:

> The course was lightly structured. Each student picked the constitution of some foreign country, researched and wrote on it and reported his progress to the class at the weekly

[4] Harry E Groves, *Comparative Constitutional Law: Cases and Materials* (Ocean Publications, 1963).

[5] For a brief account of Groves and his career, see John Charles Boger, 'Harry Edward Govers, Late Emeritus Henry Brandis Professor of Law: In Memoriam' (2013–2014) 92 *North Carolina Law Review* 1041.

> meetings. The professor and other students might address questions and comments to the one reporting. I chose the constitution of the then Federation of Malaya. The reasons for my choice were not very profound. I wanted to study a country emerging from one of the colonial empires and since I read no foreign language well, I felt constrained to limit my choice to one where the research materials would be in English. The Malayan constitution met that criterion, but, more interestingly, it had borrowed a number of its fundamental rights provisions from the civil rights and civil liberties provisions of the United States constitution; and having become effective only on August 31, 1957, when the country gained its independence from Great Britain, the constitution had not been much written about by September, 1958. When I began my research, knowing absolutely nothing about the country. Professor Sutherland advised me that he, also, knew nothing about Malaya or its constitution but encouraged me to plunge ahead.[6]

Groves' paper was subsequently published as 'Fundamental Liberties in the Constitution of the Federation of Malaya: A Comparative Study' in the *Fordham Law Review*,[7] and it was after reading this article that a colleague from the University of Pennsylvania encouraged Groves to apply for the Asia Foundation Professorship. Groves was appointed for two years during which he was expected to advise the University on legal education and in formulating the law curriculum, as well as 'assist in the training of an Asian successor' to himself.[8] In preparation for his new assignment, Groves spent several weeks gathering materials at the Harvard Law School library. He was anxious that the course he would teach would not simply be a cursory adaptation of an American constitutional law course:

> This phase of the project, i.e., the preparation of teaching materials, is, of course, of utmost importance to the success of the entire program. If I were simply preparing to teach a course in constitutional law in this country, I could select a textbook from at least a half dozen good ones available. Or if I were going abroad for a typical assignment, I would prepare a series of lectures. However, this assignment is of a more sustained nature, with the course designed in fact to become a permanent part of the curriculum of the University. There is simply no available collection of materials that could be put in the hands of the students … Casebooks for American courses in constitutional law would not be appropriate, since much of their material would be irrelevant and since, in any case, the purpose would not be to give them a course in American constitutional law but rather by the careful selection of relevant United States materials to show them a method for approaching their own constitution.[9]

[6] Harry E Groves, 'How Did You Get to Singapore?', unpublished manuscript, in Harry E Groves Papers #04975, Southern History Collection, The Wilson Library, University of North Carolina at Chapel Hill.

[7] Harry E Groves, 'Fundamental Liberties in the Constitution of the Federation of Malaya: A Comparative Study' (1959) 5 *Howard Law Journal* 190.

[8] Ryan to Harry E Groves, 20 April 1960, in the Harry E Groves Papers #04975, Southern History Collection, The Wilson Library, University of North Carolina at Chapel Hill.

[9] Groves to Bradley, 11 April 1960, Harry E Groves Papers #04975, Southern History Collection, The Wilson Library, University of North Carolina at Chapel Hill.

Groves chose the casebook format for his enterprise. While acknowledging that the casebook was a singularly American device developed by Christopher Columbus Langdell at Harvard, he nevertheless justified its more extensive use:

> Libraries seldom have more than one set of a particular series of reports, and the pressure on the library of an entire class if obliged to read specific cases for certain class discussions can be intolerable. Secondly, it is possible to shorten substantially many cases by appropriate editing, without lessening their value as teaching tools, thereby reducing the reading time of students of individual cases and making possible a wider coverage than would otherwise be feasible. Finally a casebook may make available cases not in the school's library. For these reasons and perhaps for others, the casebook method of teaching has spread, and continues to spread, beyond the borders of the United States.
>
> … The modern casebook is considerably more than a collection of cases. It is a guide to further reading, especially of articles in legal periodicals; and it frequently, as does this book, poses collateral and additional problems for analysis.[10]

Explaining his choice of the American casebook form, Groves said that it was useful to 'illustrate the methods by which courts in a number of jurisdictions whose source of fundamental law traces to the Anglo-American concepts have solved problems that arise under such constitutions'.[11] Groves' collection was arranged in five chapters over 628 pages: (1) Principles of Constitutional Interpretation; (2) Equal Protection of the Laws; (3) Emergency Powers; (4) Aliens and Citizens; and (5) Government Employment. Included in this collection were excerpted cases from Australia (two cases); Burma (six); Canada (six); the United Kingdom (three); India (23); Ireland (two); Malaya (three); Pakistan (seven); Singapore (one); and, of course, the United States (32). This was not only the first casebook to include material from the Asian states, albeit only from India, Pakistan, Burma, Malaya and Singapore, it was, until the appearance of *Constitutionalism in Asia: Cases and Materials*[12] in 2014, the one in which Asian material made up a substantial proportion of the book. In all, 40 out of the 85 cases excerpted by Groves emanated from the five jurisdictions in Asia.

III. Other Pioneering Efforts

Today, Harry Groves is a much-forgotten figure, and his pioneering work on comparative constitutional law neglected. Instead, most modern scholars trace the development of the field to the 1968 casebook of Professor Thomas M Franck (1931–2009) of New York University.[13] Franck's collection, *Comparative*

[10] Groves (n 4) vii.

[11] ibid, viii.

[12] Wen-Chen Chang, Li-ann Thio, Kevin YL Tan and Jiunn-rong Yeh, *Constitutionalism in Asia: Cases and Materials* (Hart, 2014).

[13] For example, Norman Dorsen, Michel Rosenfeld, András Sajó and Susanne Baer, authors of *Comparative Constitutionalism: Cases and Materials* (West, 2003) iii, wrote: 'Of course there have been

Constitutional Process: Cases and Materials – Fundamental Rights in the Common Law Nations,[14] contained a total of 175 excerpted cases, of which 31 were from three Asian states: India, Ceylon and Pakistan. This collection focused primarily on cases involving fundamental rights, rather than institutions and covers the following countries: Australia (five cases); Barbados (one); Buganda (one); Canada (three); Ceylon (13); India (17); Kenya (eight); Nigeria (four); Pakistan (one); South Africa (seven); Southern Rhodesia (six); Swaziland (one); Tanzania and Tanganyika (12); Uganda (seven); the United Kingdom (23); and the United States (66). In its 595 pages, Franck not only organises these cases, but also includes introductions and notes on the various decisions – so useful in contextualising the material – and his work could be said to be the precursor of the modern 'text, cases and materials' books that are now so popular with professors seeking to impart more than pure 'textbook knowledge' to their students, and where students still have to grapple with the original judgments, albeit in truncated form.

In 1963, the year Groves' book was published, a small volume of a dozen essays, entitled *Constitutionalism in Asia*,[15] was published in New Delhi under the editorship of Richard Neville Spann (1916–81), Chairman of the Department of Government and Public Administration at the University of Sydney. In August 1960, Spann had organised a symposium-themed 'Constitutionalism in Asia' seminar at the Australian National University in Canberra that brought together 38 scholars and jurists to 'consider how constitutional government was faring in some Asian countries which had achieved independence under Western-type constitutions since the war'.[16] The 12 papers that were presented –dealing with various aspects of constitutionalism in Burma, India, Indonesia and Pakistan – were edited and collated in this volume. Spann's volume was the very first collection of essays focusing on constitutions in Asia. It was, however, very much a look at constitutionalism in Asia through Western liberal lenses.

Writers of casebooks in the 1970s were less ambitious in scope and coverage than either Groves or Franck. Almost all of them were American scholars[17] who had only a passing interest in Asia. For example, Walter F Murphy and Joseph Tanehaus's 1977 work, *Comparative Constitutional Law: Cases and Commentaries*,[18] focuses on judicial policy-making through case law from six countries, only one

earlier casebooks in this field, going back at least to 1968, when Thomas Franck's notable *Comparative Constitutional Process* appeared.' Indeed, Michel Rosenfeld and András Sajó went so far as to call Franck's volume 'path-breaking'. See Michel Rosenfeld and András Sajó, 'Introduction' in Michel Rosenfeld and András Sajó (eds), *The Oxford Handbook of Comparative Constitutional Law* (Oxford University Press, 2012) 1–21, 8.

[14] Thomas M Franck, *Comparative Constitutional Process: Cases and Materials – Fundamental Rights in the Common Law Nations* (Sweet & Maxwell, 1968).

[15] RN Spann (ed), *Constitutionalism in Asia* (Asia Publishing House, 1963).

[16] ibid, vii.

[17] The exception was Mauro Cappelletti (1927–2004), an Italian scholar who also taught at Stanford University Law School.

[18] Walter F Murphy and Joseph Tanenhaus, *Comparative Constitutional Law: Cases and Commentaries* (St Martin's Press, 1977).

of which was Asian: Japan. Mauro Cappelletti and William Cohen concentrate on constitutional adjudication and procedures in Italy, the United Kingdom, the Soviet Union, the United States, Germany and the European Union in general in their casebook *Comparative Constitutional Law: Cases and Materials* (1979).[19] No Asian country is included in this study.

In the next half-century, few scholars attempted to study constitutions and constitutionalism in Asia as a whole. As a consequence, the literature consists of only a few edited collections of essays and one book. Two collections of essays were published under the hand of Professor Lawrence Ward Beer (1932–2014): *Constitutionalism in Asia: Asian Views of the American Influence* (1979);[20] and *Constitutional Systems in Late Twentieth Century Asia* (1992).[21] Beer (a Japanese law specialist), declared that his 1979 volume was 'inspired by the 1976 Bicentennial of the Declaration of Independence of the United States of America'. Comprising just nine chapters, the book features contributions from eight Asian countries: Bangladesh, China, India, Indonesia, Japan, Malaysia, the Philippines and Singapore. The authors were asked to consider the extent of American influence in the development of their respective constitutions. Another collection of this ilk is Joseph Barton Starr's *The United States Constitution: Its Birth, Growth and Influence in Asia*, published in 1988[22] and inspired by the bicentennial celebration of the American Constitution. Beer's 1992 volume is slightly less focused on the American experience in Asia and is thus a more valuable collection. This time, the scope was expanded to include contributions from 13 countries: China, Taiwan, Japan, North and South Korea, Vietnam, Brunei, India, Indonesia, Malaysia, the Philippines, Singapore and Thailand.

In 1984, the great Indian jurist Dr Durga Das Basu (1910–1997) issued the first volume of a projected series of books he entitled *Comparative Constitutional Law*,[23] a massive 528-page tome which was to have been the first in a planned series of treatises on constitutional law. It is unclear what the other projected volumes were intended to be, as there appears to have been no subsequent follow-up to this volume. In any event, Basu – known for his prodigious writings and commentaries on the Indian Constitution – ambitiously stated that this work was

[19] Mauro Cappelletti and William Cohen, *Comparative Constitutional Law: Cases and Materials* (Bobbs-Merrill, 1979). For a review of this volume and that of Murphy and Tanehaus, see Donald P Kommers, 'Comparative Constitutional Law: Casebooks for a Developing Discipline' (1981–1982) 57 *Notre Dame Law Review* 642.

[20] Lawrence Ward Beer, *Constitutionalism in Asia: Asian Views of the American Influence* (University of California Press, 1979). A second edition was published in 1988 as Lawrence Ward Beer, 'Constitutionalism in Asia: Asian Views of the American Influence', Occasional Papers & Reprints in Contemporary Asian Studies, No 6 – 1988–89) (School of Law, University of Maryland).

[21] Lawrence Ward Beer, *Constitutional Systems in Late Twentieth Century Asia* (University of Washington Press, 1992).

[22] Joseph Barton Starr, *The United States Constitution: Its Birth, Growth and Influence in Asia* (Hong Kong University Press, 1988); see also George Athan Billias, *American Constitutionalism Heard Around the World 1976–1989* (New York University Press, 2009).

[23] Durga Das Basu, *Comparative Constitutional Law* (Prentice-Hall, 1984).

unique in that it offered a 'legal interpretation of the various Constitutions and the universal propositions emerging therefrom' and

> deals critically, with burning topics which currently agitate the public mind, in different lands … and suggests solutions to the problems in the background of the special circumstances of each particular country and its national Constitution which call for variations, if any, in the application of the general principles arrived at on a comparative study.

Unfortunately, Das's vast learning and erudition are let down by a poorly organised text that jumps erratically from point to point, jurisdiction to jurisdiction in an incoherent stream-of-consciousness outburst that does little to advance the cause of comparative constitutional law.

In the 1980s and early 1990s, the comparative study of constitutional law seemed to have generally gone out of style and little literature was generated. Indeed, other than the volumes by Basu and Beer discussed above, there was little in the way of treatises, and there were certainly no casebooks. Things began to change in 1993 with a major initiative by the Centre for Comparative Constitutional Studies at the University of Melbourne to publish the *Asia-Pacific Constitutional Yearbook*. The Centre, which was established in 1988, was directed by the indefatigable Cheryl Saunders (born 1944), a major pioneer in advancing comparative constitutional legal studies in Asia.[24] In her introduction to the inaugural issue of the *Yearbook*, Saunders pointed out why countries in the region should become 'increasingly familiar with the structure and operation of government systems other than one's own' – 'While there will always be diversity in the way in which constitutions are established and allocate powers, most countries in the region aspire to a constitutional "rule of law" in some form', especially since constitutionalism 'has the advantage of concerning a certain level of legitimacy on government, … enhances confidence in the operation of governments which adhere to transparent rules and principles, and which make decisions in a predictable way'.[25] The *Yearbook* was thus launched to 'disseminate information about regional developments in constitutional law' in the hope that it will 'assist greater understanding of the constitutional issues facing regional countries'.[26]

The *Yearbook*, edited by Saunders and Graham Hassell, was structured quite simply, with a series of 'country reports' in the vein of the well-known *Asian Survey*,[27] and its first volume of the *Yearbook* contained country reports

[24] In 2022, Saunders – who was the first woman to be appointed professor at the University of Melbourne – was awarded the Tang Prize in recognition of 'her pioneering contributions to comparative constitutional law, and in particular her work on constitution-building in the Asia-Pacific region'. See www.tang-prize.org/en/owner_detail.php?id=1715&cat=13.

[25] [1993] *Asia-Pacific Constitutional Law Yearbook* v.

[26] ibid.

[27] *Asian Survey* is a bimonthly academic journal of contemporary Asian affairs (and its predecessor, the *Far Eastern Survey*) published by the Institute of East Asian Studies at the University of California, Berkeley. Each year, an issue is dedicated to country by country survey of key events and developments in each of the Asian states.

from 12 jurisdictions: Australia, China, Hong Kong, Macau, Indonesia, Nepal, New Zealand, Singapore, the Solomon Islands, Thailand, Tonga and Western Samoa. In subsequent years, reports from Bangladesh, Cambodia, Fiji, Guam, Japan, Kiribati, Pakistan, Papua New Guinea, the Philippines, South Korea, Sri Lanka, Taiwan, Vanuatu and Vietnam were also included, though not on a regular basis. One major shortcoming of the *Yearbook* was the inconsistency of its coverage. Invariably, in a large enterprise such of this, its editors had to rely on sympathetic and willing country rapporteurs to submit timely reports. This proved difficult to sustain in the long term and in 1997, after just five issues, the *Yearbook* ceased publication. Drawing from the rich resources of the *Yearbook* series, Saunders and Hassell later made a first attempt to explain constitutionalism on an Asia-wide scale in their brief but wide-ranging *Asia-Pacific Constitutional Systems*, which was published in 2002.[28] This volume focused primarily on the institutional arrangements of constitutional systems in the ASEAN states and a selection of the Pacific islands, including Papua New Guinea, the Solomon Islands, Vanuatu, Fiji and Tonga.[29]

It was only at the end of the 1990s that the first of two prominent casebooks was published, again by American scholars. This was *Comparative Constitutional Law* by Vicki C Jackson and Mark Tushnet.[30] The second, published four years later in 2003, was *Comparative Constitutionalism: Cases and Materials* by Norman Dorsen, Michel Rosenfeld, András Sajó and Susanne Baer.[31] Both these works were enormous tomes, weighing in at 1,500 and 1,400 pages respectively. They were written in the best tradition of the modern American casebook, with useful introductions, primary and secondary readings, and notes and questions to guide the reader along. Of the 15 countries discussed in the Jackson and Tushnet volume, only two Asian countries were featured: India and Japan. The book by Dorsen, Rosenfeld, Sajó and Baer is more consciously comparative and non-US- or West-centric in outlook. In their introduction, the authors make the point that 'As far as possible, the casebook presents issues generically' and avoids 'characterizations and classifications that present the US position as the norm and other positions as departures.'[32]

The reluctance to include Asian states in comparative constitutional law surveys may be attributed to two factors. First, many comparative constitutional law scholars view constitutionalism as embodying the best in liberal democratic ideals. As such, the kind of 'constitutionalism' practised by many states in Asia may not merit study or inclusion since they are non-liberal or fundamentally 'anti-constitutional'

[28] Graham Hassall and Cheryl Saunders, *Asia-Pacific Constitutional Systems* (Cambridge University Press, 2002).

[29] ibid, 2.

[30] Vicki C Jackson and Mark Tushnet, *Comparative Constitutional Law* (Foundation Press, 1999).

[31] Dorsen et al (n 13). A second edition of this book was published in 2010. Like the volume by Jackson and Tushnet, it grew considerably between editions and has a staggering 1,700 pages. The third edition of Jackson and Tushnet's casebook (2014) is over 1,800 pages in length.

[32] ibid, iv.

or 'non-constitutional'.[33] States that have no recognisable democratic institutions, independent courts and a robust constitutional culture, would not, in this paradigm, merit inclusion. The second reason is simply the fact that much of the material in Asia has hitherto not been available, much less in the English language.

IV. Revival of Interest in Comparative Constitutional Law … and Asia

The twenty-first century saw not only the revival of comparative constitutional law as a field of study,[34] but also the emergence of Asia as an increasingly important focus of that study. Writings in the field are methodologically diverse.[35] We have always had freestanding studies of the constitutions or facets of constitutional doctrines in the various states in Asia even if these are not, strictly speaking, comparative constitutional legal studies. Indeed, in one of his earlier articles, Ran Hirschl[36] argues that the term 'comparative constitutional law' is used loosely to refer to four different forms of 'comparative' enquiry or types of scholarship, one of which is 'freestanding single country studies', which are mistakenly referred to as 'comparative' only because they 'concern a country other than the author's own' and not because there is any kind of 'comparison' as such.[37] That said, the number of such studies available in the English language has, in recent years, ballooned.

Such studies will continue to be popular and their numbers will increase, and I do not propose to dwell further on such studies save to say Andrew Harding's and Peter Leyland's[38] effort in initiating the Hart series of books on the Constitution Systems of the World have added immensely to the literature. Beyond the usual encyclopedia-style compilations,[39] this series takes contextual analysis seriously and attempts to enable readers to understand 'the true context, purposes, interpretation, and incidents of a constitutional system' by offering historical, political and legal insights into the key events that shaped the constitutional landscapes of each country studied. At the time of writing, country studies of the following Asian

[33] See Harding (n 2).

[34] See Ran Hirschl, *Constitutional Matters* (Oxford University Press, 2014).

[35] On comparative constitutional law methodologies, see Vicki C Jackson, 'Comparative Constitutional Law: Methodologies' in Rosenfeld and Sajó (n 14) 54–74.

[36] Ran Hirschl, 'The Question of Case Selection in Comparative Constitutional Law' (2005) 53 *American Journal of Comparative Law* 125. Hirschl repeats this typology in his 'On the Blurred Methdological Matrix of Comparative Constitutional Law' in Sujit Choudhry (ed), *The Migration of Constitutional Ideas* (Cambridge University Press, 2006) 39–66.

[37] Hirschl (n 36) 126–27.

[38] In addition to Harding and Leyland, the series general editors now include Benjamin Berger, Rosalind Dixon and Heinz Klug.

[39] See for example, Kluwer's 'International Encyclopaedia for Constitutional Law' series edited by Andrew Alen and David Haljan; and Gerhard Robbers (ed), *Encyclopedia of World Constitutions* (Facts on File, 2007).

countries have been published: Central European Asian States,[40] China,[41] India,[42] Hong Kong SAR,[43] Indonesia,[44] Japan,[45] Malaysia,[46] Myanmar,[47] Pakistan,[48] Singapore,[49] South Korea,[50] Taiwan,[51] Thailand[52] and Vietnam.[53] At the time of writing, volumes on Bangladesh and the Philippines have also been planned. Hart's series on Constitutions of the World has been supplemented by its general 'Hart Studies in Comparative Public Law' and its Asia-centric series, 'Constitutionalism in Asia'.[54] Also underway at the time of writing is a new four-volume 'mini-series' by Hart entitled 'Asian Comparative Constitutional Law', which aims to 'provide an authoritative account of four major issues in comparative constitutional law across Asian jurisdictions'.[55]

Other than Hart, other established publishing houses like Cambridge University Press, Edward Elgar, Routledge and Brill have also contributed richly to the growing literature on constitutionalism in Asia through various book series they have instituted. Since 2012, Cambridge University Press's 'Comparative Constitutional Law and Policy' series[56] has spawned a large number of well-received volumes touching on Asia.[57] Although Edward Elgar does not have a dedicated series, it has

[40] Scott Newton, *The Constitutional Systems of the Independent Central Asian States: A Contextual Analysis* (Hart, 2017).

[41] Qianfan Zhang, *The Constitution of China: A Contextual Analysis* (Hart, 2012).

[42] Arun K Thiruvengadam, *The Constitution of India: A Contextual Analysis* (Hart, 2018).

[43] Albert HY Chen and Po Jen Yap, *The Constitutional System of the Hong Kong SAR* (Hart, 2024).

[44] Simon Butt and Tim Lindsey, *The Constitution of Indonesia: A Contextual Analysis* (Hart, 2012).

[45] Shigenori Matsui, *The Constitution of Japan: A Contextual Analysis* (Hart, 2011).

[46] Andrew J Harding, *The Constitution of Malaysia: A Contextual Analysis*, 2nd edn (Hart, 2022).

[47] Melissa Crouch, *The Constitution of Myanmar: A Contextual Analysis* (Hart, 2020).

[48] Sadaf Azia, *The Constitution of Pakistan: A Contextual Analysis* (Hart, 2017).

[49] Kevin YL Tan, *The Constitution of Singapore: A Contextual Analysis* (Hart, 2015).

[50] Chaihark Hahm, *The Constitution of South Korea: A Contextual Analysis* (Hart, 2025).

[51] Jiunn-rong Yeh, *The Constitution of Taiwan: A Contextual Analysis* (Hart, 2016).

[52] Andrew Harding and Peter Leyland, *The Constitution of Thailand: A Contextual Analysis* (Hart, 2011).

[53] Mark Sidel, *The Constitution of Vietnam: A Contextual Analysis* (Hart, 2009).

[54] The general editors of this series are Kevin YL Tan, Li-ann Thio and Jaclyn L Neo Volumes published in this series include: Chang, Thio, Tan and Yeh (n 12); Kevin YL Tan and Bui Ngoc Son (eds), *Constitutional Foundings in Southeast Asia* (2019); Jaclyn L Neo and Bui Ngoc Son (eds), *Pluralist Constitutions in Southeast Asia* (2019); Brian Christopher Jones (ed), *Democracy and Rule of Law in China's Shadow* (2022); Li-ann Thio and Jaclyn L Neo (eds), *Religious Offences in Common Law Asia: Colonial Legacies, Constitutional Rights and Contemporary Practice* (2022); Kevin YL Tan and Ridwanul Hoque, *Constitutional Foundings in South Asia* (2020); Eugénie Mérieau, *Constitutional Bricolage: Thailand's Sacred Monarchy vs The Rule of Law* (2023); Kevin YL Tan and Michael Ng (eds), *Constitutional Foundings in North Asia* (2022); and Wen-Chen Chang, Kelley Loper, Mara Malagodi and Ruth Rubio-Marin (eds), *Gender, Sexuality and Constitutionalism in Asia* (2024).

[55] See Ngoc Son Bui and Mara Malagodi (eds), *Asian Comparative Constitutional Law: Constitution*-Making (Hart, 2023) 1. Edited by Ngoc Son Bui and Mara Malagodi, this mini-series will comprise four volumes: 'Constitution-Making'; ''Constitutional Amendment'; 'Constitutional Structure'; and 'Constitutional Rights'.

[56] The general editors of this series are Tom Ginsburg, Zachary Elkins and Ran Hirschl.

[57] See for example, Shubhankar Dam, *Presidential Legislation in India* (2013), Susan H Williams (ed), *Social Difference and Constitutionalism in Pan-Asia* (2014); Albert HY Chen (ed), *Constitutionalism in Asia in the Early Twenty-First Century* (2014); Mark Tushnet and Madhav Khosla (eds), *Unstable Constitutionalism: Law and Politics in South Asia* (2015); Chaihark Hahm and Sung Ho Kim, *Making*

a long list of comparative law publications that straddle the field and which involve studies on Asia.[58] Brill – better known for its extensive catalogue of public international law publications – has two series: 'Asian Law' and 'Chinese and Comparative Law', under which several useful titles in the field have been published.[59] Recently, Routledge, well known for its interest in Asian subjects launched a new 'Asian Law' series, but with no particular focus on comparative law.[60] This new series – under the general editorship of Randall Peerenboom – absorbed the interesting triptych of works he initiated in the 2000s.[61]

Given the complexity and difficulties with comparing constitutions, constitutional ideas and constitutional systems across the Asian states, single-author

We the People: Democratic Constitutional Founding in Postwar Japan and South Korea (2015); Benjamin Schonthal, *Buddhism, Politics and the Limits of Law: The Pyrrhic Constitutionalism of Sri Lanka* (2016); Po Jen Yap (ed), *Courts and Democracies in Asia* (2017); Dian AH Shah, *Constitutions, Religion and Politics in Asia: Indonesia, Malaysia and Sri Lanka* (2018); Albert HY Chen and Andrew Harding (eds), *Constitutional Courts in Asia* (2018); Eric C Ip, *Hybrid Constitutionalism: The Politics of Constitutional Review in the Chinese Special Administrative Regions* (2019); Gerlad N Rosenberg, Sudhir Krishnaswamy and Shishar Bail (eds), *A Qualified Hope: The Indian Supreme Court and Progressive Social Change* (2019); Po Jen Yap and Chien-Chih Lin, *Constitutional Convergence in East Asia* (2021); Tom Ginsburg and Benjamin Shontal (eds), *Buddhism and Comparative Constitutional Law* (2022); and Qianfan Zhang, *Constitutional Reforms in China* (2024).

[58] See specifically, Baogang He, Brian Galligan and Takashi Inoguchi, *Federalism in* Asia (2007); Thomas WD Davis and Brian Galligan (eds), *Human Rights in Asia* (2011); Rosalind Dixon and Tom Ginsburg (eds), *Comparative Constitutional Law in Asia* (2014); John O Haley and Toshiko Takenaka (eds), *Legal Innovations in Asia* (2014); Philipp Dann and Arun K Thiruvengadam (eds), *Democratic Constitutionalism in India and the European Union* (2021); and more generally, Susan Rose-Ackerman, Peter L Lindesth and Black Emerson (eds), *Comparative Administrative Law*, 2nd edn (2017); Mark Tushnet (ed), *Comparative Constitutional Law*, 3 vols (2017); Tom Ginsburg, Pier Guiseppe Onsteri and Franceso Parisi (eds), *Classics in Comparative Law*, 4 vols (2014); Erin F Delaney and Rosalind Dixon (eds), *Comparative Judicial Review* (2018); Helena Alviar Garcia and Gunter Frankenberg (eds), *Authoritarian Constitutionalism: Comparative Analysis and Critique* (2019); Gary Jacohsohn and Miguel Schor (eds), *Comparative Constitutional Theory* (2019); David Landau and Hanna Lerner (eds), *Comparative Constitution Making* (2019); Susanna Mancini (ed), *Constitutions and Religion* (2020); Anthony F Lang Jr and Antje Weiner (eds) *Handbook of Global Constitutionalism*, 2nd edn (2023); Andrew J Harding, Jiaxiang Hu and Maartje de Visser (eds), *Legal Education in Asia* (2017).

[59] See, for example, Setsuo Miyazawa, Weidong Ji, Hiroshi Fukurai, Kay-Wah Chan and Matthias Vanhullebusch (eds), *East Asia's Renewed Respect for the Rule of Law in the 21st Century* (2015); Yu Gu, *Hong Kong's Legislature Under China's Sovereignty* (2015); Linzhu Wang, *Self-Determination and Minority Rights in* China (2018); Ragna Arli and Anne Sanders, *Courts in Evolving Societies: Sino-European Dialogue between Judges and* Academics (2020); and Bertus de Villiers, Saldi Isra and Pan Mohamad Faiz (eds), *Courts and Diversity: Twenty Years of the Constitutional Court of Indonesia* (2024).

[60] This new series absorbs Peerenboom's three earlier volumes: Randall Peerenboom (ed), *Asian Discourses of Rule of Law: Theories and Implementation of Rule of Law in Twelve Asian Countries, France and the US* (2004); Randall Peerenboom, Carole J Peterson and Albert HY Chen (eds), *Human Rights in Asia: A Comparative Legal Study of Twelve Asian Jurisdictions, France and the USA* (2006); and John Gillespie and Randall Peerenboom (eds), *Regulation in Asia: Pushing Back on Globalization* (2009). Another major collection published by Routledge is the Routledge Law in Asia series edited by Randall Peerenboom, Pip Nicholson and Michael Ng. To date, the following comparative constitutional law volumes have also been published: Tom Ginsburg and Albert HY Chen (eds), *Administrative Law and Governance in Asia* (2009); Andrew Harding and Penelope (Pip) Nicholson (eds), *New Courts in Asia* (2010); and Po Jen Yap (ed), *Judicial Review of Elections in Asia* (2016).

[61] ibid.

works covering aspects of constitutional systems in Asia are, understandably, rare. Among such ambitious monographs have been Tom Ginsburg's study of judicial review in the constitutional courts in Asia;[62] Po Jen Yap's study of constitutional dialogue among the common law jurisdictions in Asia,[63] Bui Ngoc Son's book on 'Confucian Constitutionalism' in East Asia,[64] and Dian Ahmad Shah's study of politics and religion.[65] Each study is an attempt to understand the work of institutions (Ginsburg), the nature of jurisprudential borrowings and adaptations (Yap) and philosophical underpinnings of states in Asia, with the caveat that each study is necessarily limited to three jurisdictions or so.[66] Finally, several academic journals have also published 'special issues' or 'special sections' on comparative constitutional law subjects.[67]

The bulk of the new literature in the field of comparative constitutional law in Asia have been in the form of edited volumes of essays covering different facets of the subject. Among general area studies, one of the earliest was a three-volume work entitled *Constitutionalism in Southeast Asia* by Clauspeter Hill and Jörg Menzel, published in 2008 by the Konrad Adenaur Stiftung (Foundation). The first volume contains the English versions of the 11 states in Southeast Asia (including East Timor), the second volume offered what the editors loosely called 'country reports',[68] while the third volume was a collection of papers on cross-cutting issues,

[62] Tom Ginsburg, *Judicial Review in New Democracies: Constitutional Courts in Asian Cases* (Cambridge University Press, 2003).

[63] Po Jen Yap, *Constitutional Dialogue in Common Law Asia* (Oxford University Press, 2015). The countries covered in Yap's work are: Hong Kong, Malaysia and Singapore.

[64] Bui Ngoc Son, *Confucian Constitutionalism in East Asia* (Routledge, 2016).

[65] Shah (n 57).

[66] Ginsburg study covers the constitutional courts of Taiwan, South Korea and Mongolia; Yap's compares jurisprudence in Hong Kong, Malaysia and Singapore; while Shah's study is limited to Indonesia, Malaysia and Sri Lanka. Bui's work deals specifically with the impact of Confucianism on ideas of constitutionalism in what he broadly terms 'East Asia' – China, Japan, Taiwan, Korea and Vietnam – although his work is more philosophically focused than regional.

[67] See for example, 'Las and Politics of Religion and Constitutional Practices in Asia' (2018) 13 *Asian Journal of Comparative Law* 207; 'Comparative Constitutional Amendment in Southeast Asia' (2019) 14 *Journal of Comparative Law* 46; 'Global Constitutionalism: Asia-Pacific Perspectives' (2021) 10 *Global Constitutionalism* 221; 'Constitutional Struggles in Asia' (2022) 50 *Federal Law Review* 131; and 'Law, Court, and Constitutions in Twentieth-Century South Asia' (2023) 41 *Law and History Review* 241–415.

[68] The country studies were: Tsun Hang Tey, 'Brunei: Entrenching an Absolute Monarchy'; Jörg Menzel, 'Cambodia: From Civil War to a Constitution to Constitutionalism?'; Christian Roschmann, 'East Timor (Timor Leste): Constitutional Framework for a Country in the Making'; Denny Indrayana, 'Indonesia: Search for a Democratic Constitution (1945–2008)'; Gerald Leather, 'Laos: A Constitution in Search of Constitutionalism'; CL Lim, 'The Constitution of Malaysia (1957–2007): Fifty Years, Fifty Amendments and Four Principal Developments'; Myint Zan, 'Myanmar (Burma): From Parliamentary System to Constitutionless and Constitutionalized One-Party and Military Rule'; Harry Roque, 'The Philippines: Quezon's Wish Granted'; Li-ann Thio, 'Constitution of the Republic of Singapore: The Indigenisation of a Westminster Import'; Chaowana Traimas and Jochen Hoerth, 'Thailand: Another New Constitution as a Way Out of the Vicious Cycle?'; and Clauspeter Hill, 'Vietnam: Constitutional Development in a Re-united Country'.

such as methodology,[69] emergency powers,[70] electoral systems,[71] federalism[72] and decentralisation,[73] constitutional rights[74] and constitutional reform.[75] As Hill and Menzel state, some of the country reports represented in this volume were 'the first ever systematic analysis of those respective constitutions'.[76] No other region-wide survey was attempted until the 2013 publication of *Comparative Constitutionalism in South Asia* edited by Sunil Khilnani, Vikram Raghavan and Arun Thiruvengadam.[77] This work was followed in quick succession by Albert Chen's *Constitutionalism in Asia in the Early Twentieth-First Century*[78] in 2014, which attempts a comprehensive snapshot survey of the state of constitutional law in 16 Asian states in the first decade of the twenty-first century;[79] and Mark Tushnet and Madhav Khosla's edited volume, *Unstable Constitutionalism: Law and Politics in South Asia* in 2015.[80]

Other edited volumes that have been published in the last decade cover broad and diverse subjects like constitution-making,[81] the judiciary,[82]

[69] See Menzel (n 68) vol 3, 9–31.

[70] See Victor V Ramraj, 'Constitutionalism and Emergency Powers', vol 3, 57–68.

[71] Tsun Hang Tey, 'Malaysia's Electoral System', vol 3, 69–97; and Tsun Hang Tey, 'Singapore's Electoral System', vol 3, 98–125.

[72] See Johan S Sabaruddin, 'A Background of Federalism in Malaysia', vol 3, 135–56.

[73] See Satya Arinanto, 'Decentralization and the Constitutional System of Government in Indonesia', vol 3, 157–80.

[74] See, for example, Katrin Merhof, 'Women's Rights in Southeast Asia's Constitutions and Their Implementation: The Start of a Long Process', vol 3, 181–215; and Harry L Roque Jr, 'The Binding Nature of International Human Rights and Humanitarian Laws in the Philippine Constitution', vol 3, 242–96.

[75] See Somphanh Chanthalyvong, 'The Lao PDR Constitution and Judicial Reform', vol 3, 297–310; and Tran Thanh Huong and Duong Anh Son, 'Economic Development and Constitutional Reform in Vietnam', vol 3, 311–20.

[76] Clauspeter Hill and Jörg Menzel (eds), 'Preface' in *Constitutionalism in Southeast Asia*, vol 1 (Konrad Adenaur Stiftung, 2008) 5.

[77] Sunil Khilnani, Vikram Rahavan and Arun K Thiruvengadam (eds), *Comparative Constitutionalism in South Asia* (Oxford University Press, 2013).

[78] Chen (n 57).

[79] The states covered in this volume are: India, Nepal, China, Japan, North Korea, South Korea, Taiwan, Hong Kong, Vietnam, Thailand, Cambodia, Myanmar, Indonesia, the Philippines, Malaysia and Singapore. Notable countries not covered in Chen's survey are Pakistan and Bangladesh.

[80] Tushnet and Khosla (n 57). South Asia has been the subject of much extensive study in recent years, see for example, Philipp Dann, Michael Riegner and Maxim Bonnemann (eds), *The Global South and Comparative Constitutional Law* (Oxford University Press, 2020); and Swati Jhaveri, Tarunabh Khaitan and Dinesha Samaratne (eds), *Constitutional Resilience in South Asia* (Hart, 2023).

[81] See Harshan Kumarasingham, *Constitution-making in Asia: Decolonisation and State-Building in the Aftermath of the British Empire* (Routledge, 2016); Tan and Son (n 54); Tan and Hoque (n 54); Kevin YL Tan and Michael Ng (eds), *Constitutional Foundings in Northeast Asia* (Hart, 2022); and Son Bui and Malagodi (n 55).

[82] See Harding and Nicholson (n 60); Jiunn-rong Yeh and Wen-chen Chang (eds), *Asian Courts in Context* (Cambridge University Press, 2015); and Yap (n 57).

judicial decision-making,[83] constitutional review,[84] constitutional amendment,[85] emergency powers,[86] elections,[87] public interest litigation,[88] politics and the constitution,[89] social differences and constitutional practice,[90] law and religion,[91] legal transplants and adaptations,[92] authoritarian legalism[93] and models of constitutional practice.[94]

V. Comparative Constitutional Law in Asia: What Next?

A. The 'Why' before the 'What' and 'How'

The growth of scholarship in comparative constitutional law in Asia has been remarkable. The establishment of key institutions and centres encouraging comparative legal studies in Asia has no doubt contributed immensely to this growth. Centres for the study and research into 'Asian law' or law in Asia have existed for many years, but mostly in non-Asian universities. Quite possibly the oldest is the Asian Law Centre at the University of Washington, which was established in 1962. Closer to Asia is the University of Melbourne's Asian Law Centre which was set up in 1985, and its Centre for Comparative Constitutional Studies, established in 1988. However, starting in the 2000s, Asian universities began establishing their own centres to promote Asian legal scholarship. In 2002, Nagoya University launched its Centre for Asian Legal Exchange while the National University of Singapore (NUS) established the Asia Law Institute (ASLI) in 2003 – comprising law school members from Asia – to foster Asian legal scholarship and facilitate greater interaction among legal scholars in Asia. It also worked positively to galvanise and generate scholarship in all fields, including comparative constitutional

[83] See Yap (n 63); and Yvonne Tew, *Constitutional Statecraft in Asian Courts* (Oxford University Press, 2020).

[84] See Ginsburg (n 62).

[85] See, Rehan Abeyratne and Ngoc Son Bui (eds), *The Law and Politics of Unconstitutional Constitutional Amendments in Asia* (Routledge, 2021).

[86] Victor V Ramraj and Arun K Thiruvengadam (eds), *Emergency Powers in Asia: Exploring the Limits of Legality* (Cambridge University Press, 2010).

[87] Yap (n 60).

[88] Po Jen Yap and Holning Lau (eds), *Public Interest Litigation in Asia* (Routledge, 2011).

[89] Björn Dressel (ed), *The Judicialization of Politics in Asia* (Routledge, 2012); and Marco Bünte and Björn Dressel (eds), *Politics and Constitutions in Southeast Asia* (Routledge, 2016).

[90] Williams (n 57).

[91] See, for example, Shah (n 57); Jaclyn L Neo, Arif A Jamal and Daniel PS Goh (eds), *Regulating Religion in Asia: Norms, Modes and Challenges* (Cambridge University Press, 2019); and Thio and Neo (n 54).

[92] Neo and Son (n 54).

[93] Hualing Fu and Weitseng Chen, *Authoritarian Legality in Asia* (Cambridge University Press, 2019).

[94] Michael W Dowdle and Michael A Wilkinson (eds), *Constitutionalism Beyond Liberalism* (Cambridge University Press, 2017).

law. In 2012, the NUS set up the Centre for Asian Legal Studies among which one of its key strengths is comparative constitutional law. These developments augur well for the field of comparative constitutional law, as more and younger scholars turn their attention to the field. Notwithstanding the burgeoning interest in the field, many law schools in Asia do not offer courses on the law of other Asian states as part of their curriculum.[95]

But what next? Given the flurry of activity in the field and the copious literature currently being generated, what should scholars in the field focus on? What do we really need? To answer these questions, we first need to ask ourselves, as scholars in the field, why we do what we do. Why are we so interested in comparing constitutions in Asia? Put another way: Why *should* we be interested in comparing constitutions in Asia? We could, of course, respond in the same way the crack mountaineer George Mallory did when asked why he wanted to climb Mount Everest: 'Because it's there.' The 'field' is certainly there, even if it was not 30 years ago,[96] but such a response could hardly sustain a lifetime of dedication and work in what is ultimately a difficult though rewarding field of research. We must seriously examine the a priori 'why' question before answering the *how* and *what* questions that flow therefrom.

Unfortunately, it would be a gargantuan task to poll scholars in the field to ascertain *why* they do what they do. In any case, I am not sure such a poll would yield any consistent or coherent set of responses. But if we look at the nature of comparative constitutional scholarship, it may be possible to discern *why* scholars do what they do. Ran Hirschl identifies four types of comparative inquiry. The 'first and most basic' is the 'free-standing, single-country studies that are mistakenly characterized as comparative mainly because they concern a country other than the author's own'.[97] The second type of scholarship – mainly by judges in search of 'the *right* or *just* solution for a given constitutional challenge' – is 'geared toward self-reflection or betterment through analogy, distinction, and contrast'.[98] Scholars of this ilk typically refer 'to constitutional jurisprudence and practices of other presumably similarly situated polities' to gain a better understanding of their 'own set of constitutional values and structures and enrich, and ultimately advance, a more cosmopolitan or universalist view' of their constitutional discourse. The third type of comparative scholarship is universalist in outlook, 'emphasising the broad similarity of constitutional challenges and functions across relatively open,

[95] See Maartje de Visser and Andrew Harding, 'Mainstreaming Foreign Law in the Asian Law School Curriculum' (2019) 14 *Asian Journal of Comparative Law* S149–S172.

[96] See, for example, Harding's plea for more research on comparative public law in 2000: Andrew Harding, 'Comparative Public Law: A Neglected Discipline' in Ian Edge (ed), *Comparative Law in Global Perspective: Essays in Celebration of the 50th Anniversary of the Founding of the SOAS Law Department* (Transnational Publishers Inc, 2000) 101–20.

[97] Hirschl (n 36) 125. He repeats this typology in his 'On the Blurred Methodological Matrix of Comparative Constitutional Law' in Choudhry (n 36) 41–46.

[98] Hirschl (n 36) 127. See also, Cheryl Saunders, 'The Use and Misuse of Comparative Constitutional Law' (2006) 13 *Indiana Journal of Global Legal Studies* 37.

rule-of-law polities'. Hirschl explains that scholars of the third variety often study 'various manifestations of and solutions to roughly analogous constitutional challenges' in order to sharpen their analysis. He refers to this type of scholarship as 'concept formation through multiple description'.[99] The fourth and final type of comparative constitutional law scholarship attempts to build theory 'causal inference', where hypotheses concerning causal links are postulated and falsified.[100]

Assuming that Hirschl has indeed covered the entire gamut of comparative constitutional scholarship with his typology – and I think he has – then scholars study comparative constitutional law for the following reasons. First, to better understand what is going on in a particular jurisdiction; second, to develop a 'better' and more responsive jurisprudence; third, to better understand constitutional concepts and phenomena in the abstract; and fourth, to build better theories about law. None of these objectives are quite independent of each other; nor do scholars eschew one type of scholarship for another. To a greater or lesser extent, we jump between these various objectives when writing about a subject, depending on what piques our intellectual curiosity at the time. So, while I may work extensively on the constitutional law and development of one country, I could just as well be interested in how the theory of basic structure might operate across jurisdictions like mine. In that sense, we need more of *all* of these types of writings – expository single-jurisdictional works, normatively driven and conceptually driven comparisons.

B. How Do or Should we Compare?

Our scholarly objectives define the form of our writings. As such, I think we are all comparativists to a greater or lesser extent, depending on where our research takes us. In her survey of the literature, Vicki Jackson identifies five methodological categories of comparative constitutional law scholarship: (a) classificatory; (b) historical; (c) normative; (d) functional; and (e) contextual.[101] Jackson quickly adds that these categories overlap and that within each category, 'different techniques may be used' depending on the nature of the scholarly inquiry.[102]

One of the big methodological debates in the field of comparative constitutional law concerns the fissure that has divided scholars adopting universalist or normative methodologies on the one end and scholars with a more contextualist bent on the other. Universalists take as their starting point a transnational or supranational principle, concept or model and then assess how the constitutional laws of particular jurisdictions fare against them.[103] Universal norms may take

[99] ibid, 129.
[100] ibid, 132.
[101] Jackson (n 35) 55.
[102] ibid.
[103] ibid, 60–62.

the form of 'theories of the good society' or answers to other jurisprudential or philosophical questions, or perhaps 'the nature of constitutionalism itself'.[104] This form of universalism appears in the work of scholars like Beer,[105] Chen,[106] Yap,[107] Peerenboom[108] and Patapan.[109] The universalist approach to comparative constitutional law has been criticised by several leading scholars like Tushnet,[110] Hirschl[111] and Choudhry.[112]

At the other end of the spectrum are scholars who adopt a contextualist approach. Contextualists[113] argue that that we need to take constitutional systems on their own terms and that we need to try to understand their workings within their particular contexts. As Tushnet pointed out, such an approach has a heavy historical or anthropological bent and the peculiarities of a nation's constitutional history feature heavily in the development of its constitutional law.[114] There are, according to Tushnet, two forms of contextualism: *simple contextualism*, which 'insists that constitutional ideas can only be understood in the full institutional and doctrinal context within which they are placed; and *expressivism*, 'which takes constitutional ideas to be expressions of a particular nation's self-understanding'.[115] In the abstract, contextualist studies see constitutional law as path-dependent, and strive to show how a nation's legal culture, institutions and arrangements, doctrinal history and other factors led ineluctably to the system observed.[116] Critics of contextualism argue that the kind of particularism engendered by this

[104] ibid, 60–61.
[105] Beer (n 21) 24 and 33–34.
[106] Albert HY Chen, 'Conclusion: Comparative Reflections on Human Rights in Asia' in Peerenboom, Petersen and Chen (n 60) 487–516, 488–89.
[107] Yap (n 63) 22–27.
[108] Randall Peerenboom, 'Varieties of Rule of Law: An Introduction and Provisional Conclusion' in Peerenboom (n 60) 3–5.
[109] Haig Patapan, 'Leadership, Law, and Legitimacy: Reflections on the Changing Nature of Judicial Politics in Asia' in Dressel (n 89) 223–27.
[110] Mark Tushnet, 'Comparative Constitutional Law' in Mathias Reimann and Reinhard Zimmermann (eds), *The Oxford Handbook of Comparative Law* (Oxford University Press, 2006) 1230–32; Mark Tushnet, 'Some Reflections on Method in Comparative Constitutional Law' in Sujit Choudhry (ed), *Constitutional Design for Divided Societies: Integration or Accommodation* (Oxford University Press, 2008) 67–83; and Mark Tushnet, 'The Possibilities of Comparative Constitutional Law' (1999) 108 *Yale Law Journal* 1225, 1239.
[111] Hirschl (n 34) 205.
[112] Sujit Choudhry, 'Introduction' in Choudhry (n 110) 8–9.
[113] Proponents of contextualism would include scholars like Mark Tushnet, Andrew Harding, Peter Leyland, Gunter Frankenberg, Ralf Michaels and Kevin Tan.
[114] Tushnet (2008) (n 110) 76–79.
[115] ibid, 68. Works that might be labelled 'expressivist' include three works from Peerenboom's *Rule of Law* (n 94): Thio Li-ann, 'Rule of Law within a Non-Liberal "Communitarian" Democracy: The Singapore Experience' (183–224); Raul C Pangalangan, 'The Philippine "People Power" Constitution, Rule of Law, and the Limits of Liberal Constitutionalism' (371–84); and Hahm Chaihark, 'Human rights in Korea: Rhetoric and Implementation' (385–416). See also Surya Deva, 'Public Interest Litigation in India: A Quest to Achieve the Impossible?' in Yap and Lau (n 88) 57–79; and Andreas Ufen, 'Undermining Religious Minority Rights in Indonesia and Malaysia: Fragile Coalitions, Wavering Executive Chiefs, and Rogue Groups as Proxies' in Bünte and Dressel (n 89) 186–206.
[116] Tushnet (n 114) 81.

methodology might cause scholars to overplay the salience of 'culture' as a key and immutable variable[117] and to 'lose sight of the complexity of global constitutional archetypes – and the importance … of locating regional constitutional patterns within their full global context'.[118]

Another popular approach to comparative constitutional law studies is 'functionalist' in nature. Scholars in this mould assume that 'political institutions perform certain tasks common to all (well-functioning) systems of government', and that 'only by examining different political systems can [we] identify the functions common to all and the institutions [we] think serve those functions'.[119] Functionalist scholars try to find commonalities across constitutional systems by focusing on specific institutions (eg courts) or doctrines (eg separation of powers), rather than on specific norms or principles. For example, much of the work of the prolific Tom Ginsburg may well be categorised as functionalist.[120] Yet other scholars have adopted a hybridised approach in hope of establishing some kind of middle-ground. Classification and categorisation in the form of ideal types have long been a helpful tool in the social sciences and some scholars have adopted this strategic approach.[121]

This is all very confusing. Is there an ideal approach we should adopt in our studies of constitutions in Asia? I venture not. Approaches are useful as guides to help us establish methods and agenda, but they do not in themselves reveal truths. I would suggest that in the work of comparing constitutions in Asia – or anywhere else for that matter – we might first concern ourselves with the questions

[117] Ginsburg (n 62) 14–15; and Tushnet (2006) (n 110) 1300.

[118] Dixon and Ginsburg (n 58) 16.

[119] Tushnet (1999) (n 110) 1238.

[120] In his *Judicial Review in New Democracies: Constitutional Courts in Asian Cases* (n 62), he develops an 'insurance' theory of judicial review to explain through functional analysis, why 'explicit constitutional power of and access to judicial review will be greater where political forces are diffused than where a single dominant party exists at the time of constitutional design'; why judicial review expands with democracy; and why parties in competitive democracies thereafter acquiesce in or even support the exercise of judicial review (at 25, 71–72 and 78–79). Ginsburg and Moustafa have also analysed the courts' power-consolidating functions in authoritarian regimes, the circumstances in which such regimes are likely to turn to the courts for help, why a regime's reliance on courts necessarily leads to challenges to its policies, and how regimes may constrain courts to limit them only to the function of consolidating that regime's power (see Tamir Moustafa and Tom Ginsburg (eds), *Rule by Law: The Politics of Courts in Authoritarian Regimes* (Cambridge University Press, 2008) 4–13. In his work on constitutions in authoritarian regimes, Ginsburg and Simpser assess problems of governance that might be solved with the adoption of a constitution, and consider how constitutions still limit power in authoritarian societies, and why, despite their possible limiting effects, such regimes continue to draft constitutions. See Tom Ginsburg and Alberto Simpser (eds), *Constitutions in Authoritarian Regimes* (Cambridge University Press, 2014) 3–5 and 10–14.

[121] See for example Peerenboom (n 60) xvi; Albert HY Chen, 'Constitutions, Constitutional Practice and Constitutionalism in East Asia' in Christoph Antons (ed), *Routledge Handbook of Asian Law* (Routledge, 2017) 75–93; Jiunn-rong Yeh and Wen-chen Chang, 'The Emergence of East Asian Constitutionalism: Features in Comparison' (2011) 59 *American Journal of Comparative Law* 805; Dressel (n 89) 6–7; Yap (n 57) 4–5 and 17; and Thio Li-ann, 'Varieties of Constitutionalism in Asia' (2021) 16 *Asian Journal of Comparative Law* 285–310. See also Andrew Harding and Ngoc Son Bui, 'Recent Work in Asian Constitutional Studies: A Review Essay' (2016) 11 *Asian Journal of Comparative Law* 163.

that need answering.[122] 'Asia' is a vast region, immensely diverse in its political ideology, culture, economic development, colonial history, legal transplants and autochthonous constitutional experiments. A study of Asian constitutional practice in terms of principles, institution-building and operation within the political process and rights adjudication, yields rich insights and perspectives into how we understand the role of law and government in issues like legitimacy, accountability and the construction of national identity. We should attempt to get a picture of what is *actually going on*, rather than normatively suggesting what should be done or determining if an act or device qualifies as 'constitutional'.[123]

In a nutshell, we want to take Asia on its own terms and consider how constitutions and constitutional laws are used in a variety of ways to respond to problems in each society. Allow me to end by repeating my proposal for a methodology that treats the study of comparative constitutional law as the interplay between the challenges and corresponding challenges arising in the various Asian states:

> How then might we contextualize the study of constitutionalism in Southeast Asia without becoming too specific and descriptive? Might not these developments be seen in a more universal light? In this respect, I have been particularly drawn to historian Arnold J. Toynbee's thesis of 'challenge and response'. In his monumental *A Study of History*, Toynbee looked at civilizations in terms of challenge-and-response and argued that civilizations arose in response to some set of challenges of great difficulty if 'creative minorities' devised solutions and reoriented their societies. When civilizations respond to challenges, they grow, and when they stop responding creatively to these challenges, the societies decline. In the same way, I see the development of constitutionalism in each Southeast Asian country as an attempt by its people to respond to the challenges of a modem, post-colonial environment.[124]

Such an approach to studying constitutionalism enables us to understand how each society deals with the challenges it is confronted with and the nature of these challenges. Oftentimes, the challenges are not mere political challenges from within, but also legal challenges from abroad. Any internal discourse on what is good, and right is necessarily informed by what is being said about the same subject somewhere else in the world.

[122] See Andrew Harding and Peter Leyland, 'Comparative Law in Constitutional Contexts' in Esin Örücü and David Nelken (eds), *Comparative Law: A Handbook* (Hart, 2007) 313–38, 331.

[123] See Mark Tushnet, 'Some Skepticism About Normative Constitutional Advice' (2008) 49 *William & Mary Law Review* 1473; and Eugenie Merieau, 'Area Studies and the Decolonisation of Comparative Law: Insights from Alternative Southeast Asian Constitutional Modernities' (2020) 51 *International Quarterly for Asian Studies* 153.

[124] Kevin YL Tan, Jiunn-Rong Yeh, Chao-Ju Chen and Li-Ju Lee, 'History and Culture: Complexities in Studying Southeast Asian Constitutionalism' (2010) 5 *National Taiwan University Law* Review 197, 205–06.

5

The Westminster Model Constitution Home and Abroad: Texts and Contexts?

PETER LEYLAND*

I. Introduction

This chapter is meant as a tribute to the work and achievements of Andrew Harding, a close friend and colleague. Our intense and fruitful collaboration over many years has ranged from co-writing a book on Thailand's constitutional system,[1] launching and developing the 'Constitutional Systems of the World' series as founding editors,[2] co-authoring journal articles[3] and co-authoring book chapters.[4]

Andrew Harding (AH) is an exceptional scholar and, as such (to borrow Ferdinand Mount's compliment to Sir Ivor Jennings), is no exception to the rule that constitutional writers who wish to hold our attention must charm as well as instruct and it is, above all, the incessant evolution of practice which he exposes so brilliantly.[5] This observation is particularly apposite here because although AH is acutely aware of theoretical debates in the field of comparative public law, his hugely diverse output has studiously avoided theoretical abstraction. Rather, the concern is to adopt a suitable methodology on a pragmatic basis in order to permit rigorous analysis of aspects of public law in a national, historical and often comparative context.[6] His output covers a vast range of issues and is remarkable

* Many thanks to Justin Frosini and Andrew Harding for their assistance in the preparation of this chapter.

[1] Andrew Harding and Peter Leyland *The Constitutional System of Thailand* (Hart Publishing, 2011).

[2] www.bloomsbury.com/uk/series/constitutional-systems-of-the-world.

[3] Andrew Harding and Peter Leyland 'The Constitutional Courts of Thailand and Indonesia: Two Case Studies from South East Asia' (2008) III *Journal of Comparative Law* 118; Andrew Harding and Peter Leyland, 'Constitutional Design in Thailand: the Management of Electoral Process in an Emergent Democracy' (2010) 4 *The Journal of Parliamentary and Political Law* 299.

[4] Andrew Harding and Peter Leyland, 'Comparative Law in Constitutional Contexts' in D Nelken and E Örücü (eds), *Comparative Law: A Handbook* (Hart Publishing, 2007).

[5] Ferdinand Mount, *The British Constitution Now* (Mandarin Books, 1993) 65.

[6] See eg Andrew Harding, *The Constitutional System of Malaysia*, 2nd edn (Hart Publishing, 2022) 34. 'The problem is, that of interpreting conventions which developed in Britain as unwritten customs

for the depth of knowledge revealed across the entire field of comparative public law.

As a follow up to Justin Frosini's authoritative critical review which forms the basis of chapter 3 AH's studies on the nature of the so-called Westminster Model (WM) and on the multilayered character of constitutional systems, particularly from Southeast Asia, prompts further discussion on how to approach contextual work from the standpoint of comparative constitutionalism. This chapter is presented as a comparative case study which seeks to revisit these ideas from a different critical standpoint and investigates whether they can be applied together to provide a distinct form of critical analysis.

II. What is the Westminster Model?

Turning first to AH's work on the Westminster Model Constitution Overseas (WMCO).[7] There has to be a common embarkation point for a comparatist anxious to engage directly with many diverse constitutional systems.[8] It is remarkable that there are 54 nations, mostly ex-Commonwealth, that live under constitutional arrangements corresponding to elements of Westminster-style governance or heavily influenced by it.[9] At the same time it is axiomatic that constitutions share a range of characteristics in many different ways (Westminster, Paris, Washington) although the resemblance may be for diverse reasons. The classification of constitutions can be, in part, approached by isolating certain characteristics. The problem is that surface resemblance can prove misleading as a guide to how any constitution in question actually functions.

In fact, classification of a WM is no simple task and reaching a clear definition is somewhat illusory.[10] For example:

(1) It could be attached to the current UK constitutional system, including all its recent innovations such as devolution for Scotland, Wales and Northern Ireland, the incorporation of the European Convention on Human Rights under the Human Rights Act (HRA), the introduction of a Supreme Court and the effect of constitutional measures relating to UK withdrawal from the EU.

dependent on precedent and political practice but which now find themselves as written law in Malaysia.'

[7] Andrew Harding, '"The Westminster Model" Constitution Overseas: Transplantation, Adaption and Development in Commonwealth States' (2004) 143 *Oxford University Commonwealth Law Journal* 143.

[8] There are different ways of categorising constitutions: written/unwritten; flexible/rigid; unitary/federal; separated/fused power; republican/monarchical.

[9] Harding (n 7).

[10] See eg Ian Ward, *The English Constitution: Myth or Reality* (Hart Publishing, 2004).

(2) The style or type of constitution deriving from the UK Constitution which in certain crucial respects resembles the UK Constitution not as it is today, but as it was, or at least appeared to be, particularly during the second half of the twentieth century when many commonwealth constitutions were drafted. The Westminster-type Constitution of this vintage prior to devolution was unitary, there was no charter of rights and no clear separation of powers was recognised.[11]

(3) A distinct account of the Westminster as opposed to Whitehall model used by constitutional commentators explains how power is actually exercised in the domestic Constitution. It draws a contrast between a Westminster model where power is exercised by a sovereign Parliament – emphasising the role of the Westminster Parliament as sovereign lawmaker – with a Whitehall view of the Constitution – which is regarded as driven not by the Westminster Parliament but by a dominant executive in Whitehall.[12]

(4) In his study of the export model AH isolates salient characteristics of mainly the second version.[13] For him a combination of such characteristics typify the hybrid constitutions, often constitutions of Commonwealth nations, based on Westminster, and this comes to represent the WMCO. He provides an insightful study which draws upon an intimate knowledge of a wide range of constitutions. But, as already mentioned, the idea of any Westminster model is itself illusory. This is because it is framed around the Westminster system, one that is reliant on an unwritten constitution, heavily dependent upon constantly evolving conventions,[14] as well as other changes made from time to time by a sovereign parliament through legislative intervention. In consequence, it is not rigid in any sense.[15] Each account may be fundamentally different, because there is no common starting points except perhaps rather broad characteristics (many of which also apply to other constitutions).

To continue with the motoring metaphor adopted by AH, the so-called Export Model (WMCO) conveys information about the engineering characteristics, the type of body, the size of the engine, the type of braking system together with the relevant catalogue of optional extras, but these elements alone do not explain the performance of the vehicle, nor its handling characteristics. Neither does a listing of this kind distinguish between the core elements and incidental characteristics. It

[11] Many Commonwealth constitutions were drafted at this time with the involvement of Sir Ivor Jennings, Stanley De Smith, Kenneth Diplock and others. See Mara Maragoldi, 'Ivor Jenning's Constitutional Legacy beyond the Occidental Oriental Divide' (2015) 42 *Journal of Law and Society* 1012, 1013.

[12] Anthony Birch, *The British System of Government*, 10th edn (Routledge, 1998) 22 ff.

[13] In summary under the headings: 1. Written or unwritten. 2. Parliamentary sovereignty or constitutional supremacy. 3. Unitary or federal state. 4. Head of state versus head of government and related issues; 5. Elections parties and the alternation of power; 6. Judiciary.

[14] Geoffrey Marshall, *Constitutional Conventions: The Rules and Forms of Political Accountability* (Oxford University Press, 1987).

[15] See Alison L Young, *Unchecked Power* (Bristol University Press, 2024).

helps us to be aware in a comparative sense of approximately the kind of constitution, but we also need to inquire into how the constitution operates. How is power exercised as part of a democratic constitution based on an elected parliament and a cabinet system of government? Thus far the conception of the WMCO is necessarily descriptive in the sense that characteristics are assessed in the specific context of a range of constitutional systems.

III. A Multilayered Dimension?

Given that there is a very strong historical element surrounding the discussion a broad sweep, from colonisation to Empire to Commonwealth, it occurred to me that perhaps this approach to classifying constitutions might be wedded to another idea developed by Andrew Harding, namely the concept of multilayered constitutionalism. In seeking to provide a contextual understanding of constitutions AH has developed and applied incisively the related idea of multilayered constitutionalism. The most credible way of understanding legal culture in any nation is to observe an accretion of successive layerings, rather than to view the process in terms of new beginnings. Most, if not all, nations have legal systems beyond the constitution and law, itself reflecting multiple experiences in various combinations of ancient civilisation, colonisation and modern constitutionalism. In respect to Southeast Asia he observes that:

> The extent of legal 'reception' … is truly staggering. … It is appropriate to think of law in South East Asia geologically, as a series of layers each of which overlays the previous layers without actually replacing them, so that in places, due to tectonic shifts, the lower layers are still visible, although not perfectly distinguishable from each other.[16]

In each case these layering have been distinctive … the system which emerges is dynamic and it may draw upon customs and traditions, but it displays its own characteristics to varying degrees. AH proceeded to demonstrate how these layers were formed and how they inter-relate to each other.[17]

IV. The Spirit of the Westminster Model

A discussion of the wider historical context seeks to expose a latent cultural dimension associated with the Westminster system itself and Westminster model

[16] See Andrew Harding, 'Comparative Law and Legal Transplants in South East Asia: Making Sense of the "Nomic Din"' in David Nelken and Jan Fest (eds), *Adapting Legal Cultures* (Hart Publishing, 2001). Nomic = to do with law, Din = loud and variegated noise.

[17] ibid 205 ff. 'The original or bottom layer of South East Asian law is that referred to as "aboriginal" or "native" custom, still extant and recognised by the official legal system.'

constitutions that lie beyond any discussion of formal constitutional provisions and related laws – a series of signifiers that might be understood to be the discernible spirit of such constitutions.

The unwritten Westminster constitutional system is, and has always been, susceptible to radical change. Its flexibility stands out as a significant feature, but perhaps the crucial point is that the contemporary system at any moment is only ever coherent as a form of multilayered constitution which always retains certain traditional elements woven into its fabric;[18] one that represents certain qualities at its very core, but these are not necessarily replicated as a strictly rule-based system. It would seem reasonable to suppose that at least some of those qualities or characteristics have been integrated as part of the export version. In fact, at any moment this multilayered constitution is fully intelligible only if interpreted as the accumulated result of the past and the various layerings which have accrued since.

In one sense any Westminster model might be understood through the recognition of foundational moments,[19] often associated with conflict, particularly in the seventeenth century, but not with any single event.[20] For the UK version of Westminster constitutionalism[21] the idea of restoring or retaining traditional values through the issuing of charters and codes that dealt with matters fundamental to the functioning of society reverts back to pre-conquest times, hundreds of years prior to Magna Carta.[22] Magna Carta was itself reissued on many occasions to reassert certain constitutional norms. Other episodes might include the formation of elements of common law[23] and the recognition of privileges of Parliament, particularly freedom of speech.[24] Above all, the Bill of Rights of 1689 was a response endorsed by Parliament to what was perceived as arbitrary government under James II. This piece of legislation set the seal on a form of government by consent. Many conventions and the confirmation of the privileges of Parliament

[18] Nicholas Bamforth and Peter Leyland, *Public Law in a Multi-Layered Constitution* (Hart Publishing, 2003). See introduction.

[19] See eg Raoul Van Caenegem, *An Historical Introduction to Western Constitutional Law* (Cambridge, Cambridge University Press, 1995) 74 ff.

[20] Ivor Jennings, *The Law and the Constitution*, 5th edn (University of London Press, 1959) 8 ff.

[21] Parliament as a representative body was meeting in the 13th century and the two chambers met separately from the 14th century. See John Goodall, 'The Medieval Palace of Westminster' in Christine Riding and Jacqueline Riding (eds), *The Houses of Parliament: History, Art, Architecture* (Merrell, 2000) 55.

[22] Andrew Blick, *Beyond Magna Carta: A Constitution for the United Kingdom* (Hart Publishing, 2015) 36, 82.

[23] 'In a series of famous cases, including Dr Bonham's Case and the Case of Proclamations, Coke CJ thwarted James's attempts to use his prerogative as a means of subverting the authority of the ordinary courts. … Myth countered myth; that of divine right countered by that of the common law.' See Ward (n 10) 183. See also Adam Tomkins and Paul Scott, *Entick v Carrington: 250 Years of the Rule of Law* (Hart Publishing, 2015); Mark Elliott and Kirsty Hughes (eds), *Common Law Constitutional Rights* (Hart Publishing, 2020).

[24] See Alistair Horne, Gavin Drewry and Dawn Oliver (eds), *Parliament and the Law* (Hart Publishing, 2013).

(Article 9) originate from it, and it is perhaps the closest the UK has come to having a single foundational constitutional document.[25]

V. Dignified versus Efficient Elements

These elements exist and can be observed as a series of distinct signifiers, but they are also etched into the system arguably carrying with them (whether as myth or reality) the notion of accountable institutions and a democratic culture. (This does not mean that such rules will not be subverted or ignored, but the system itself serves as a constant reminder of this aspect.)

Walter Bagehot recognised the combination of the old and the traditional with the capacity to adopt and integrate the new on a pragmatic basis to provide 'checks and balances'.[26] Bagehot's account in Queen Victoria's reign (1867) identifies a special kind of dichotomy – what he termed the 'dignified' and the 'efficient' elements of the Constitution. Of course, for him this involves a deliberate justification of the hereditary principle associated at an institutional level with the monarchy and the House of Lords.

Nevertheless, the dignified version, though indefensible now, still survives (conspicuously with the monarchy and House of Lords) and provides a form of constitutional continuity. It reflects the ancient, complex and ceremonial; those features Bagehot claimed were capable of exciting and preserving the reverence of the population and generating its motive power. Not withstanding political turmoil, wars, pandemics, etc, the monarch as Head of State remains constant as a powerful symbol of the nation's unity and strength. For Bagehot this reverence, to the extent that it exists, is partly because the institution is shrouded in mystery. (In 2021, while prime minister Boris Johnson was throwing parties in No 10 Downing Street during the COVID-19 pandemic, Queen Elizabeth II was solemnly obeying the rules at Prince Philip's funeral at Windsor.)[27]

By way of contrast, the efficient version recognises the modern, simple and functional aspects. Rather, this verges towards the way Jennings saw the Constitution as facilitating the efficient working of the democratic system.[28] This involves an understanding of the deployment of power – the part which works and which actually rules. The Prime Minister and the Cabinet rule according to the 'efficient' view, but the monarch remains head of the 'dignified' version. It appears that the WM (both domestic and export versions) arguably engenders a grasp of both dignified and efficient elements, but does so in radically different combinations and concentrations. In some versions of the WM, of course the

[25] Neil McCormick, *Questioning Sovereignty* (Oxford University Press, 1999). McCormick would perhaps take issue on this point given Scotland's role in the formation of the United Kingdom; see ch 4.

[26] Walter Bagehot, *The English Constitution* (Fontana, 1963) 60 ff.

[27] 'Prince Philip's funeral in pictures' *The Guardian* (17 April 2021).

[28] Mara Marigoldi, 'Ivor Jennings: The Law and the Constitution' in Patrick O'Brien and Ben Young (eds), *Leading Works in Public Law* (Routledge, 2024).

monarch is retained as head of state but with an even less active role than in the UK. In other versions the role has been replaced by an elected head of state with more powers.[29] At another level, it is interesting that despite any political tensions frequent royal visits to the Commonwealth nations during the reign of Queen Elizabeth II (1952–2022) underpinned the association with Westminster, which includes the preservation of accompanying traditions. The respective manifestations of the dignified version in terms of ceremony and ritual extended beyond the formal provisions of the Constitution itself.

VI. Deconstructing the Westminster Iconography

An entirely different type of layering encountered by any participant in or observer of British constitutional culture is the formal but imposing architectural iconography of Westminster itself. In response to the destruction by fire in 1834 of the St Stephen Parliament House at Westminster, a competition was held for its replacement. The Whigs/liberals proposed a building in a neo-classical style while the Conservatives, whose will prevailed, favoured a design in the Gothic or Elizabethan style.[30] The outcome is relevant as a neo-classical building with semi-circular chambers might have influenced the development of procedural rules, which have been based on the traditional oblong shape with two opposing rows of benches. Not only was Gothic back in fashion but there was also a need to blend in with surviving medieval buildings – Westminster Hall, the Cloisters and Chapter House of St Stephen's, and the Undercroft Chapel – to form part of a complex. The main structure along the River Thames displays a harmonious symmetry, but in Gothic form has frequently been celebrated as the mother of democratic parliaments (whether or not the reputation is fully deserved). In its ambition and detailing the imposing new building resembles a medieval cathedral with its pointed arches, ribbed vaulting and flying buttresses (echoing a national British style displaying traditional craftsmanship).[31]

Within the palace, artists painted frescoes depicting victorious battles, often against France, already a republic, and showing philanthropic values such as courtesy, religion and hospitality.[32] The building is equally remarkable for the cohesion of Pugin's design aesthetic which radiates the spirit of traditional medieval craftsmanship often at the expense of the needs of everyday functionality (lack

[29] See Harding (n 7).

[30] Robert Furneaux Jones, *Victorian Architecture* (Penguin, 1966) 75, 84 ff.

[31] The design attracted prominent criticism as well as praise. Ruskin referred to the reconstructed Houses of Parliament as the most effeminate and effectless heap of stone ever raised by man. See John Ruskin, *The Seven Lamps of Architecture* (George Allen, 1907). In William Morris's utopian vision of socialism, Parliament has become a dung house piled high with manure. See William Morris, *News from Nowhere* (Penguin, 2004).

[32] See eg William Vaughan, '"God Help the Minister who Meddles in Art": History Painting in the New Palace of Westminster' in Riding and Riding (n 21).

of offices).[33] Pugin believed that every feature of the building must be necessary for convenience, construction or propriety, and that all ornamentation should be integral to the essential construction of the building. The result is an edifice which projects its unique symbolic design philosophy not only in its lavish decoration and furnishings, but extending to the carpets, furniture and even the crockery in the dining rooms. In establishing the layout, Barry, principally responsible for the architectural structure, placed the location of the Sovereign's throne, the Lords Chamber and the Commons Chamber in a straight line, thus linking the three elements of Parliament in continuous form. One end contains the Commons Chamber with its relatively modest dimensions and humble simplicity, and the other, the striking grandeur of the House of Lords.[34]

We turn next to consider how the constitutional business of the House of Commons is acted out in the Palace of Westminster and in related parliaments. English is in many instances the shared vernacular as a common language of engagement, with nothing lost in translation, and the Parliament comes with many of the same accompanying rules.[35] Surveying the layout of other mainly Commonwealth (WM) parliaments it becomes plain that this is the widely imitated cockpit of democracy[36] and comprises a series of green tiered benches contrasting starkly with the lavishly adorned House of Lords at the opposite end of the building. In its essence the simplicity of the Commons Chamber with two sides facing each other contributes to an adversarial style of any Westminster-based parliamentary system. This is also related to the electoral system which tends to favour a mainly two-party system because one party often emerges with an overall majority. The lower house is presided over by a Speaker, dragged to the chair, who enforces familiar procedural rules forming the standing orders of the House derived from Erskine May, and the proceedings are reported according to the style adopted in Hansard.[37] Parliamentary privilege allows MPs to expose improper conduct in the House without fear of any legal repercussions. Indeed, from a comparative

[33] Nicholas Pevsner, *An Outline of European Architecture*, 7th edn (Pelican, 1974) 382.

[34] See David Cannadine, 'The Palace of Westminster as Palace of Varieties' in Riding and Riding (n 21). See also www.parliament.uk/about/living-heritage/building/palace/architecture.

[35] See Arun Thiruvengadam, *The Constitution of India: A Contextual Analysis* (Hart Publishing, 2017). The initial catastrophe of Indian independence was followed by the promulgation of a distinctive constitution. It differs from a Westminster model, but it retains a parliamentary system with elements related to it. For example, the subsequent reorganisation of parliamentary committees in India shadowing government departments to provide enhanced accountability mirrors the Westminster reforms creating departmental select committees introduced in 1979.

[36] See eg David Natzler, David Bagnall, Jean-Phillipe Bochu and Peter Fowler, 'Controversy at the Antipodes (and Elsewhere): The International Cousins of the Treatise' in Paul Evans (ed), *Essays on the History of Parliamentary Procedure in Honour of Thomas Erskine May* (Hart Publishing, 2017). It is stressed that links between Commonwealth parliaments (New Zealand, Canada, Australia) had always been and remains strong, with May's treatise quickly accepted as an authoritative work of reference, 143.

[37] See eg William McKay, 'A Sycophant of Real Ability: the Career of Thomas Erskine May' and S Patrick, 'A History of Standing Orders' in Evans (n 36).

perspective a Westminster genealogy is often striking notwithstanding the passage of time and the diversity of the Constitution in other respects. For example, AH observes in his seminal study of the Malaysian Constitution that there are features typical of Westminster-style parliaments partly mirroring the rules and practices of the Dewan Rekyat (Malaysia's Lower House).[38] Such aspects would include the derivation of standing orders of the House ruled upon by the Speaker, committees within Parliament and the more recent adoption of Public Accounts Committee presided over by a senior member of the opposition.[39]

In another respect the relatively intimate Westminster-style architectural layout of opposing benches establishes an intimate theatrical tone[40] to the proceedings.[41] Benches are divided into government on one side, and opposition parties on the other (the UK has *never* had a strictly two party system). Crucially, the official opposition plays a very important part in Parliament. It is represented on all committees and always has the right to reply in debates. Also, the opposition choses the subject of debate for the supply days following the budget. Mount reminds us of the value of established institutions notwithstanding their shortcomings:

> The fact that checks and balances may be partial, informal or self imposed does not entail that they are trivial or ineffective. The Lower House may have the ultimate power to impose its will under modern constitutions, but that does not mean that whatever restraint or delay may be given to the Upper House cannot act as a powerful inhibitor.[42]

In attempting any comprehensive evaluation there would of course be countless variables, but in a general sense a nation such as Kenya might serve as another interesting example to consider briefly, since under its 2010 Constitution it has a well-established democratic parliamentary system.[43] Unlike the UK Westminster system, it now has an elected president as head of state, elected National Assembly and prime minister, and regionally elected Senate.[44] The National Assembly, however, is still modelled on the House of Commons, with a similar layout featuring a tension between government and opposition, and once again it follows many of the same procedures. Essentially, it is a nation with a system of elected representative democracy adopting many traditions traceable to Westminster.

[38] Andrew Harding, *The Constitution of Malaysia: A Contextual Analysis*, 2nd edn (Hart Publishing, 2022) 89 ff.

[39] Mohamad Yusof, Roosme Hamzah and Shad Faruqi, *Law, Principles and Practice in the Dewan Rakyat of Malaysia* (Thomson Reuters, 2020).

[40] See Riding and Riding (n 21).

[41] Giovanni Rizzoni, *Parliamentarism and Encyclopaedism: Parliamentary Democracy in an age of fragmentation* (Hart Publishing, 2024) 44 ff.

[42] Mount (n 5) 83.

[43] Elizabeth O'Loughlin, 'Kenya's Constitution in a global context' (2017) 15 *ICON* 839.

[44] www.parliament.go.ke.

VII. Cabinet Government and Executive Layerings

A multilayered approach to unscrambling the WM from the standpoint of the executive branch exposes overlapping and evolving institutional features. In turn, these elements reveal historical episodes from the era of empire to the present that have shaped each system in a distinct fashion. Under the classic UK model the Prime Minister and ministers of the Crown exercising a general control over their departments have relied on a permanent civil service that provides both continuity and stability.[45] As Professor King explains:

> More important than either the House of Lords or the monarch … was the civil service. Although the constitutional role of the senior civil service was defined only informally, it was defined with remarkable clarity. On the one hand, senior civil servants were indeed servants, Crown servants – that is servants of the government of the day. When ministers knew what they wanted to do civil servants were there to do it and the minister in question could be a member of either party. The British civil service was strictly neutral in party political terms, and senior officials … almost invariably loyal to the government of the day. Civil servants were permanent officials and their permanency was a function of their loyalty.[46]

While the combination of measures to distribute powers between head of state, the Prime Minister and ministers differ considerably under the many codified versions related to the WM,[47] a permanent civil service stands out as a characteristic which has been widely shared.[48]

Interestingly, the embryonic Indian Civil Service (ICS) was the first Westminster-related system to incorporate principles characteristic of a modern bureaucracy,[49] including hierarchical structure, increased centralisation and the adoption of competitive examinations for recruitment.[50] These mid-nineteenth-century innovations in India signalled a gradual shift towards an elite service, anticipating some of the key recommendations of the Northcote Trevelyan report of 1854 which eventually resulted in the full professionalisation of British Civil Service.[51] In a colonial setting a relatively small, uniform civil service was fashioned to perform the task of establishing British control over a vast nation with only limited military resources.

Certainly, from an Indian perspective the ICS in its original form had manifest deficiencies. The service was dominated top-down by a class of overpaid officials of British stock and limited competence, and until well into the twentieth century the

[45] For an outline of the traditional 20th-century civil service, see Jennings (n 20) 200 ff.

[46] Anthony King, *The British Constitution* (Oxford University Press, 2007) 43.

[47] Harding (n 7) 153ff.

[48] See eg, Derek O'Brien, *The Constitutional Systems of the Commonwealth Caribbean: A Contextual Analysis* (Hart Publishing, 2014) 126.

[49] Zafar Mohyuddin and Muhammad Yasir Ali, 'The Development of Indian Civil Service in British India: An Analysis' (2021) VII *Journal of Historical Studies* 80, 83.

[50] See the Charter Act 1853, which streamlined administrative process in India.

[51] See eg Peter Hennessey, *Whitehall* (Pimlico, 2001), esp ch 1.

recruitment system discriminated strongly against Indians, however well qualified they turned out to be. Given that the ICS had been a hostile colonial administration not directly accountable in constitutional terms, and frequently perceived as being indifferent to the well-being of the greater population of India, it might appear surprising in retrospect that the bureaucratic structure has remained intact post-independence.[52] Among its many formidable challenges, the Indian Constitution, and the system of governance it heralded post-independence, had to contend with a radical transition from 600 princely states to a newly created federation. This called for a strong and efficient centralised and local administration.[53] The framers of the Indian Constitution appear to have retained a modified Westminster form of executive and legislature from the outset as the ICS was and continued to be (renamed as the Indian Administrative Service) the existing 'efficient' (in the Bagehot sense) mechanism available for the delivery of policy and to establish the rule of law under a new constitution.

Since the 1980s the institutional profile of the civil service in the UK and other nations with WM constitutions has been fundamentally transformed in response to ideological challenges to big government[54] related to the application of Public Choice theory.[55] In practical terms such ideas have been applied in a range of different ways under the general guise of what has been termed new public management (NPM).[56] In essence, the Whitehall Revolution in the UK that followed involved the incorporation of business models, including the agencification of the Civil Service[57] with the emergence of chief executives responsible for policy delivery, an increasing reliance on the contracting out of services provided by government and customer-orientated citizen participation with the introduction of citizen charters.[58] These were changes that were not easily reconciled with political neutrality, anonymity and security of tenure viewed as signature characteristics of a permanent service, but also regarded as fundamental to the traditional view of cabinet government and ministerial responsibility, where ministers are seen to be directly answerable to Parliament for the entire administration, including civil servants responsible for implementing policy.[59]

Turning once again to India, the advent of economic liberalisation in India in the early 1990s was an important 'constitutional moment' for the nation that fundamentally altered the structure and operation of the state in respect to

[52] Shasi Tharoor, *Inglorious Empire: What the British Did to India* (Penguin Books, 2017) 55 ff.
[53] Thiruvengadam (n 35) 30 ff, 73 ff.
[54] Harding (n 38) 44 ff.
[55] See eg David Osborne and Ted Gaebler, *Reinventing Government* (Addison Welsley, 1992).
[56] Carol Harlow and Richard Rawlings, *Law and Administration*, 2nd edn (Butterworths, 1997) 132.
[57] Departments broken down into agencies dedicated to an aspect of policy delivery headed by a chief executive run according to a business model, eg Passport Agency under Home Office.
[58] Jonathan Tonge, *The New Civil Service* (Baseline Books, 1999) 1, 35 ff.
[59] Diana Woodhouse, 'Ministerial Responsibility' in Vernon Bogdanor (ed), *The British Constitution in the Twentieth Century* (Oxford University Press, 2003) 316 ff.

regulation, governance and policy making.[60] Certain aspects of NPM[61] have since been superimposed on an Indian system of cabinet government with a view to reducing corruption and inefficiency, but without disrupting the formal hierarchy of the IAS.[62] The recognition of citizen participation as part of this trend assumes that an administration cannot be successful if it is not living up to democratic values. Citizens can expect to be treated fairly in asserting their (public law) rights and will have recourse to a remedy if their expectations as customers are not met. To take one such example, the NPM concept of the Citizen's Charter[63] has been adapted to streamline the process of administration across many Indian states, and, at the same time, to radically improve citizen rights of access to public services. Under this initiative hundreds of charters have been introduced across India under Public Services legislation to standardise performance.[64] The legislation provides that in dealing with routine tasks, such as approving or rejecting applications for a public service, failure by officials to meet a pre-set deadline can lead to an automatic right to appeal followed by a mandatory order to act and a fine. It has been argued that this initiative not only provides greater empowerment of citizens over lower officials in many Indian states, but is also a legal means through which top officials and politicians can seek to regain some control over the lower tiers of the Indian bureaucracy.[65]

In sum, this discussion of the civil service as part of the executive branch provides further evidence of the diversity and illusiveness of so many aspects of WM constitutions. On the one hand, the UK and India have a bottom layer of shared foundational elements comprising a permanent hierarchical civil service, widely recognised as a pivotal characteristic of cabinet government; and, on the other, as part of the respective constitutional dynamics there have been widely divergent approaches to development and reform, particularly in the field of NPM.

VIII. Conclusion

For the purposes of this analysis the multilayered character of constitutions has been conceived in a structural quasi-semiotic fashion.[66] We have identified certain

[60] Thiruvengadam (2017) 229.

[61] Including contracting out services by the local administration and public–private partnerships to deliver infrastructure and transport. See Abhinav Sharma, 'New Public Management in India: Reinventing Administration' (2017) 54 *Indian Journal of Public Administration* 91.

[62] The prime minister and cabinet as members of the elected government are accountable directly to Parliament while the secretary to the Government of India, who is the senior permanent official of the Indian Administrative Service (IAC), acts as the most senior ministerial advisor.

[63] Gavin Drewry, 'Whatever Happened to the Citizen's Charter' [2002] *Public Law* 9.

[64] Nick Robinson, 'Right to Public Service Acts in India: The Experience from Bihar and Madhya Pradesh' Accountable Government: Policy Research Series, AI Policy Briefs, November 2012 (Introduction).

[65] ibid (Lessons).

[66] Roland Barthes, 'Introduction to the Structural Analysis of Narratives' in Susan Sontag (ed), *Barthes: Selected Writings* (Fontana, 1982) 251 ff.

signifiers discernible at different levels well beyond any formal legal/constitutional text itself. This approach involves the search for elements that persuade us that there might really be residual values as well as features (even if illusive) related to the constantly evolving democratic culture of the Westminster system which reach beyond any formally recognised and listed characteristics in the law or the constitution of any single nation.[67] Finally, there is the problematic question of overall evaluation. For AH in his WMCO article the measure of success or failure is assessed generally, for example, in terms of providing overall constitutional stability, good governance or a residue of characteristics resulting from Westminster, or the ability to embrace new constitutional technologies.[68] On the other hand, an obvious shortcoming with some Westminster-related constitutions identified by AH arises at a political level and relates to the difficulty in functioning effectively without an established party system to achieve the alternation of power. This fundamental drawback

> has [in some instances] facilitated the emergence of a dominant-party system, where one party or a coalition of parties has enjoyed power over a long period of time, and has used its in-built majority to fashion the constitution so as to give it more power, controlling even the amendment process.[69]

In terms of measuring basic democratic credentials, the relative merit of any constitution depends upon the degree of accountability to the people. Ultimately, this largely boils down to a political question – does it (the constitution as it applies) deliver the capacity to change the complexion of the government under whatever system of universal suffrage is deployed? Then, this accountability may also be linked to the degree of parliamentary and judicial oversight of the executive, etc. The second requirement, which may of course be related to the first, concerns the extent to which any system establishes constitutionalism under the rule of law[70] and guarantees the protection of citizen rights, particularly minority rights.[71] Any answer to this second question depends upon the recognition of such rights at a constitutional level and the capacity of the courts under the rule of law to ensure that such rights are upheld and protected.[72]

[67] Obviously, the multilayered dimension acknowledges other, and at times, competing latent values operating beyond the constitutional or legal text.

[68] Harding (n 7) 165.

[69] ibid, 160.

[70] Harding and Leyland (n 1) 27 ff.

[71] What Lord Bingham explains as his thick view. See Thomas Bingham, *The Rule of Law* (Penguin, 2010); and John Laws, *The Constitutional Balance* (Hart Publishing, 2021) 14 ff.

[72] Mount (n 5) 88.

6

Wrestling with Eastminster: Monarchy in Malaysia

TOM GINSBURG

A recent play imagines the Prime Minister of the Kingdom of Great Britain and Northern Ireland presenting King Charles III with a bill restricting the freedom of the press.[1] It has long been a convention that the king's assent to parliamentary legislation is *pro forma*; the last refusal to grant it was in 1707, and, since then, the king has not been a material part of the legislative process. Nonetheless, in the play, Charles refuses to assent to legislation passed by Parliament. He seeks to negotiate with Parliament, creating a constitutional crisis in which the Prime Minister threatens to remove the requirement of royal assent to statutes, but Charles first disbands Parliament. The future of the monarchy is at stake. Parliament puts up a tremendous fight. The play ends with Charles's abdication, leaving the reins in the hands of his son, Prince William, and the monarchy survives in the face of rising republican sentiment.

This narrative illustrates a dynamic that often plays out in constitutional monarchies. Whatever formal powers are assigned to the monarch in a constitutional text, they are surrounded by conventions and understandings that both expand and contract them. The Westminster system is one in which the conventions developed in the idiosyncratic process that created the British Constitution, which was essentially a set of repeated interactions among elites who all attended the same schools. Westminster rules as written do not always conform to the real powers of government actors, who operate under the euphemism of the 'King in Parliament', a formulation that is as transparent as that of trans-substantiation.

In other constitutional systems, the written text understates the actual powers of the monarchy. Thailand's monarchy has been constrained by a constitutional text since 1932, but during the long reign of King Rama IX, it fused old Buddhist ideas with new political idioms to move to the very centre of Thai society.[2] Seen as a divine character, Rama IX clearly could exercise far more power than one might have thought by simply reading the constitutional text.

[1] Mike Bartlett, *King Charles III* (2014).
[2] Eugénie Mérieau, *Constitutional Bricolage* (Brill, 2022).

By both accident of birth and scholarly interest, Andrew Harding has spent his life living in countries that are monarchies. He has also contributed profoundly to our understanding of how that institution works in Southeast Asia, informed by his understanding of Westminster conventions. This short chapter revisits some of Harding's work on constitutional monarchy, alone and with co-authors, from a distinct theoretical perspective. I draw on ideas of constitutional political economy to examine the persistence and utility of constitutional monarchy in a world of republics. I focus on recent developments in Malaysia to illustrate general themes that have resonance beyond its borders.

The chapter is organised as follows. First, I define terms, and provide a framework for thinking about the relative power of monarchy vis-à-vis civilian powerholders. Next, I examine recent developments in Malaysia, as recounted by Harding along with Kumarasingham.[3] The final section considers general implications of the analysis.

A note on my use of gender. I refer to kings generically to denote male and female monarchs, in part because many of the monarchies I will discuss are patriarchal in character. No offence is meant by this designation, as the logic of constitutional monarchy applies to the holders of office regardless of gender.[4]

I. The Emergence and Endurance of Constitutional Monarchy

Monarchy is an ancient form of political organisation that can bring together groups larger than those connected by kinship, enabling cooperation across greater geographic and demographic scope.[5] The monarch provides a focal point for members of society, and has the ability to integrate them into a new fictive community, which in turn can facilitate new interactions and reduce conflict. A single authority can reduce intergroup conflict, as new and integrative forms of identity can emerge among common subjects, and the king can provide justice as one of the services to the population.[6] As Gerring et al point out, monarchy becomes more attractive as the size of the polity increases, as the value of a single individual as a coordination point becomes more important as the society expands.[7]

Monarchies come in various forms. Constitutional monarchy is a subtype in which: 1) the head of state is a monarch, either appointed or hereditary; (2) the powers of the monarch are laid out in a constitution or set of constitutional texts;

[3] Andrew Harding and Harshan Kumarasingham, 'The Malay Monarchies in Constitutional and Social Conception' (2022) 9 *Asian Journal of Law and Society* 399.

[4] See also Maartje De Visser and Andrew Harding, 'Monarchical Constitutional Guardianship and Legal Métissage in Asia.' (2022) 9 *Asian Journal of Law and Society* 345, 347 fn 5.

[5] John Gerring et al, 'Why Monarchy? The Rise and Demise of a Regime Type.'(2021) 54 *Comparative Political Studies* 585.

[6] Deborah Boucayannis, *Kings as Judges: Power, Justice and the Origins of Parliaments* (Cambridge University Press, 2022).

[7] Gerring (n 5).

and (3) the head of government is not the monarch and is responsible to electoral institutions. This remains a fairly popular form of government. Some 17 per cent of all countries and the vast majority of monarchies fall into this category, including some of the world's richest and most successful countries.

It should be noted that a small number of countries (eight at the time of writing) remain absolute monarchies, including Brunei. With the exception of Swaziland, these countries are all oil-rich Muslim-majority countries, in which monarchies were secured and entrenched by the British.

Many think of political history as a kind of teleological progression from absolute monarchy to constitutional monarchy, and thence to republic. In an absolute monarchy, the king has all power, whereas in constitutional monarchy, he has virtually none. De Visser and Harding are surely correct that the shift is not linear, and that the distinction between these two types is not a sharp one.[8] They also note that formal and informal powers can vary within each type. We might situate particular monarchies on a spectrum from more to less power, on both formal and informal dimensions.

In high monarchy, a king is the fictive owner of land and in some cases has a role in a state church. Certainly, he always seeks to be allied with religious elites. Examples here include the King of England, who is the head of the Anglican church; the Scandinavian monarchs, who head their national churches; the Japanese Emperor, who is the living descendent of the Sun Goddess, and plays a central role in Shinto ritual; the Kings of Thailand, portrayed as *dhammaraja*; and the longstanding bargain between the House of Saud and the Wahhabi *ulema* to legitimate the rule of the family. A connection with religion can be mutually beneficial for king and keepers of the faith. The former earns some legitimacy in exchange for patronage and support. Sometimes this close link allows for the deployment of religious elites to resolve intrafamily disputes.

A monarch faces a two-sided bargaining problem. First, there is the internal problem within the ruling family about who gets to serve as the ruler. Royal lines claim descent from a common ancestor, but they often involve many branches. The Tudors and Stuarts, the House of Hanover and the current British monarchs from the House of Windsor are all related, having a common ancestor in the ninth-century monarch Alfred the Great. But common descent has never prevented vicious internal fighting among branches of royalty. Thus a king must secure his own position within the family. The potential for contestation requires an internal bargain so as to remain the focal point for the extended clan.

But the king also has to bargain with elites and society outside the family to ensure a stream of rents for distribution within the governing group. The long history of the English monarchy can be summarised as a series of deals with elites, and over time the relative power of the monarchs has declined.

[8] De Visser and Harding (n 4) 347.

Two-sided bargaining has the interesting feature that constraint at one level can enhance leverage at the other. One might imagine that the higher the level of power vis-à-vis society, the more valuable is the throne for potential insiders. Thus, exceptionally powerful monarchs might become vulnerable internally because the stakes of sitting on the throne are very high. Conversely, monarchs with limited external power might be more secure internally. Constitutional monarchs, though they lack as much external power as enjoyed by absolute monarchs, might have more stable tenure on the throne because they reduce the incentive to fight over the job.

What determines the relative power of the monarchy vis-à-vis non-royal elites? It is standard in political science to consider this problem in terms of a bargaining process between king and society. European feudalism required kings to make deals with prominent members of society. As time went on, there was pressure to write these deals down into compacts and charters. In England, *Magna Carta* symbolised the power of the barons to extract concessions from the King in exchange for supporting his rule, and similar documents were created in other places. The classic model of king-and-council was a mechanism for making elite bargains, under quasi-constitutional rules in which each had power.

These arrangements could be relatively stable for a time but, like all such bargains, are subject to exogenous and endogenous shocks. When an invader shows up, or the economy changes, or populations shift, the parties to a constitutional bargain can change their positions and demand more, or less, from each other. A large literature devoted to crisis bargaining discusses these arrangements, and the long history of European monarchy describes these shifts over time. Most prominently, North and Weingast have this model in mind in their history of the United Kingdom, in which a long series of bargains erodes monarchic power over taxation.[9] This, they argue, led to liberalisation and the emergence of stable property rights that underpinned British industrial development. A major part of this process was the development of sources of wealth that were not based on land. Non-monarchic elites gain power to the extent that their wealth depends on trade and industry, which are not in the direct or figurative control of the king. In contrast, where a king controls geographically concentrated resources like oil or gas, he need not bargain with elites at all – something identified in the literature on the resource curse.[10]

To illustrate these dynamics, let us take a stylised example consisting of the king, elites, and the people, who each have some ability to influence the bargain among the other two. Imagine a king negotiating with a set of elites who believe they can demand a greater share of power than they enjoy under the status quo.

[9] Douglass North and Barry Weingast, 'Constitutions and Commitment: The Evolution of Institutions Governing Public Choice in Seventeenth-Century England.' (1989) 49 *The Journal of Economic History* 803.

[10] Benjamin Smith and David Waldner, *Rethinking the Resource Curse* (Cambridge University Press, 2020).

When challenged in such a situation, the monarch has roughly three choices: he can repress the opposition, potentially triggering conflict; he can concede and give up some power; or he could throw the issue to a third party, for example to a court or to an election in which some parties are aligned with the monarchy and others with challengers. This last strategy introduces a random element into the negotiations.

One might think the easy answer for the king when challenged is to keep all power by repressing. But repression has costs. It creates a risk of over-empowering the military, which might itself become a challenger. Many modern monarchies have been deposed by militaries: Afghanistan (1973), Cambodia (1970), Iraq (1958) and Libya (1969) come to mind. Conflict also risks a loss of legitimacy for the throne. Concession, in contrast, keeps the peace but leads to a reduction in the monarch's relative share of power. Concession also creates more stability for private property rights, which reinforces the power of challengers during the next round of crisis. Concessions are something of a one-way ratchet; they are hard to recover once granted.

The most interesting possibility is for a king to ask the people for their view. If the election goes the way of the king, the monarch survives with power intact. If the election empowers civilian parties, however, the king loses an increment of power. This in turn can trigger more repression. Something like this happened in Kuwait in May 2024, when the Emir disbanded parliament after an election and appointed a new Crown Prince.

A Southeast Asian example is found in the ignoble end of the Nguyen Dynasty, which had ruled Vietnam since 1802. With French colonial conquest, the Nguyen ruler Bảo Đại became the emperor of Annam, and then the constitutional monarch of unified Vietnam when the Japanese ousted the French in March 1945. He served as a monarch for a few months before abdicating at Ho Chi Minh's request in August 1945. From 1949 to 1955 he returned to serve as head of state of the French State of Vietnam, but was then ousted by a referendum organised by Ngô Đình Diệm. One can view this sequence as a series of attempts by the Emperor to retain some power, but civilian elites were unwilling to accommodate him.

The inverse dynamic occurred in Brunei. As the British prepared the territory for independence with a 1959 Constitution, the Sultan was given significant power and did not even have a duty to consult with civilian elites. After an indirectly elected legislature was introduced in 1962, the political party that won challenged the British for power. This rebellion was shut down quickly by British forces from Singapore, leaving the Sultan as the unchallenged power holder. He subsequently banned the political party and abolished the constitutional provision for elections. This case easily fits the resource curse model of an absolute monarch defending a jointly controlled oil field with the British colonialists. The monarchy survived precisely because of its weakness during the key period of challenge by civilians, leaving it unchecked in the next stage, and it remains the only absolute monarchy outside the Middle East that is based on oil.

Once a monarch's power is negotiated away, politics occurs among different elite factions without much attention to the king's preferences. We then need an account as to why civilian elites retain a monarch without power. What resources does a monarch bring to the bargaining table in circumstances in which material power has declined severely, as occurred for most monarchies over the last two centuries? Two ideas in particular stand out, which I call *stakes reduction* and *insurance*. By stakes reduction, I mean the idea that a monarch can reassure certain members of society that their core interests are protected. In a series of papers, Weingast along with co-authors argues that democratic constitutions endure when they successfully reduce the stakes of politics.[11] When people's core interests, be they religion, language or property, are threatened, it triggers what Weingast calls the rationality of fear: the very fear that core interests are threatened can lead people to take pre-emptive actions that cause political disruption and might undermine the social order. Groups whose core interests might be reassured through the presence of a monarchy include ethnic minorities, who can signal loyalty to the nation even if they are not seen as being an essential part of it. It might also include conservatives, since monarchies tend to be associated with conservative politics. Conservatives favour property rights and religion. A long history of political thought considers the threat posed to power holders by 'excessive' democracy, with constitutions as a device to codify a social arrangement between the wealthy few and the populous poor. Property owners can feel protected and empowered when monarchy is preserved. In particular, ideological radicals who oppose property are also very likely to be opposed to the existence of a monarchy. An attack on the king as an institution might serve as a tripwire warning that property rights more broadly are threatened.

Another service we may see monarchs provide is what I and co-authors call *crisis insurance*. Even without any power, monarchs can play a special role in providing focal points during times of true crisis. This means that as a last resort, a constitutional monarch can serve to prevent the surrendering of democracy or the unravelling of political order. A central example in Asia occurred in 1992, when King Rama IX of Thailand called military leader General Suchinda Kraprayoon and protest leader Chamlong Srimuang together in the midst of major upheavals. In front of the television cameras, he excoriated both men, leading to a de-escalation of conflict and the setting in motion of a process that led to the restoration of democracy. This was a form of crisis insurance, in which the King reset the bargain after a breakdown between two rival factions.

Crisis insurance fits the idea that the monarch is a 'guardian of the constitution' of last resort.[12] Such a role makes several assumptions about the monarch. First, the

[11] Sonia Mittal and Barry R Weingast, 'Self-Enforcing Constitutions: With an Application to Democratic Stability In America's First Century' (2013) 29 *Journal of Law, Economics, and Organization* 278.

[12] Harshan Kumarasingham (ed), *Vice-Regalism: The Crown as Head of State in Political Crises in the Postwar Commonwealth* (Palgrave MacMillan, 2020); Anne Twomey, *The Veiled Sceptre: Reserve Powers*

role assumes that the individual has invested energy into knowing what the constitution actually entails; second, that she can act as a disinterested observer, that is, unbiased between sides to a conflict; and third, that she can identify a moment of crisis and the appropriate action to be taken. Perhaps because these can be strong assumptions, kings are not always able to play this role. It is risky, as it draws on an accumulated stock of reputational capital that might be hard to rebuild once it is squandered. An effective monarch will have a reputation for being able to discover potential solutions to crises that the parties themselves may not be able to identify. This is a kind of epistemic power, and not everyone has it.

Furthermore, the powers to be utilised in providing crisis insurance may be formal or informal in nature. Formal constitutions often give the monarch a role in opening or dismissing parliament, identifying formateurs of government, approving laws and exercising powers like pardon. Informal powers may depend on the particular charismatic authority of the ruler, or perhaps from the emergence of conventions through repeated practice over time.

Integrating a diverse polity, along with reducing the stakes of politics and providing occasional crisis insurance, are services to society. Elites, even bitterly divided ones, might prefer to keep a powerless monarch around as a symbol, so as to stabilise politics and prevent conflict from escalating. Hence monarchy can survive even without power.

II. Malaysia's Constitutional Monarchy

This section applies some of these ideas to Malaysia. The focus is not on the internal struggle over who will hold the throne, but on the second part of the two-level game, namely the relative amount of power enjoyed by kings and civilian elites.

Malaysia is one of the most unusual monarchic systems in the world today, in that it is a collective, elective monarchy. Malaysia is a federal state formed by the British out of a set of territories that were historically distinct and had their own traditional rulers, now typically called sultans.[13] Malay ideas of monarchy draw on Islamic and local traditions, tracing descent from the Sultanate of Malacca, and remain in effect in the nine peninsular Malay states, each of which has a hereditary ruler.

After independence, these monarchies were preserved by the British in part to provide symbolic primacy for the Malays, who had their numbers diluted through mass immigration from China and India during colonial rule.[14] This meant they were given only a few reserve powers and were, from independence

of Heads of State in Westminster Systems (Cambridge University Press, 2018); De Visser and Harding (n 4) 349–55.

[13] Harding and Kumarasingham (n 3) 400.

[14] G Braighlinn, *Ideological Innovation under Monarchy: Aspects of Legitimation Activity in Contemporary Brunei* (VU University Press, 1992) 4.

in 1957, always 'constitutional monarchs' in our sense. The nine individual rulers get together every five years to elect a new national monarch from among their number, called the *Yang di-Pertuan Agong*. The convention is rotation among the different state rulers. As Harding and Kumarasingham describe, this office, as well as the state level monarchies, inherited the roles accorded to the Governor General in the Westminster colonies, and were expected to govern in accord with conventions.

In practice, however, the state rulers did not always follow Westminster conventions.[15] Like King Charles in the play mentioned at the outset of this chapter, they sometimes refused to sign bills and engaged in conflicts with the chief ministers. This is an example of what Kumarasingham called an 'Eastminster' system. For example, when the Sultan of Johor was about to assume the position as the Yang di-Pertuan Agong in 1983, he threatened to stop signing bills and to exercise more direct power at the federal level, critiquing politicians. Prime Minister Mahathir proposed a bill that would have transferred the power to declare an emergency to the prime minister alone, and to provide for automatic assent to bills, so as to prevent pocket vetoes by the leaders. This led to a constitutional standoff, the result of which was a compromise settlement, with the rulers retaining the right to oversee emergency declarations, but giving up some of their veto power.[16] The Constitution provided background rules for the negotiation of a bargain over power between rulers and government.

A subsequent round of negotiations over the constitutional powers of the rulers was occasioned by a crisis around ruler immunity. The Sultan of Johor and his sons had engaged in a number of criminal acts, including assaults and financial improprieties. When negotiations and persuasion proved ineffective, the Government passed a constitutional amendment that removed ruler immunity, and established a special court to hear cases against the rulers.[17] The rulers, however, unanimously decided not to consent to the bill, which led to a further round of negotiation and compromise.[18] A Special Court was eventually set up and, according to Harding and Kumarasingham, has addressed two cases in its 30 years of operation.[19]

A crisis at the state level occurred in Perak in 2008.[20] The ruler had appointed a chief minister who had the ability to command the majority of votes in Parliament, but some members switched allegiance, depriving the governing coalition of sufficient votes to remain in office. The appropriate constitutional remedy according to the state Constitution was dissolution of Parliament, but the monarch appointed a new chief minister without putting the prior Government to a vote of no confidence.

[15] Andrew Harding, 'The Rulers and the Centrality of Conventions in Malaysia's "Eastminster" Constitution' in Harshan Kumarasingham (ed), *Viceregalism* (Palgrave Macmillan, 2021).

[16] ibid.

[17] HP Lee, 'Malaysian Royalty and the Special Court' in Andrew Harding and Pip Nicholson (eds), *New Courts in Asia* (Routledge, 2010).

[18] The rulers had special authority in this realm because the statute concerned ruler power.

[19] Harding and Kumarasingham (n 3) 407.

[20] ibid, 411.

This led to legal disputes that clarified the matter, providing an example of a confrontation in which monarchic power expanded.

In short, the history of Malaysia's monarchy since independence has been one in which rulers exercised powers beyond what might be expected in the British tradition, but consistent with the constitutional text. Over time, however, the civilian government has confronted the rulers on multiple occasions, leading to a gradual reduction of powers. In each case, the result of the conflict has been one in which the monarchs wield some resources, and have neither completely surrendered nor pushed too hard.

How have the services provided by monarchs evolved over time? Harding and Kumarasingham contend that the crises over powers have had some effect on the conception of the monarchical role. As they put it, the crisis generated an

> understanding on the part of the Rulers that their public behaviour must be vastly improved, if not beyond all reproach. Moreover, they need to be seen to perform an important public function, namely that of upholding constitutional values and protecting society from what have come to be seen as the worst excesses of politicians.[21]

One transformation has been toward a greater role in integrating the polity. The retention of traditional rulers was originally designed, not so much to integrate Malaysia's diverse population, but rather to symbolise the dominance of the majority Malay group, and to alleviate its sense of demographic and cultural threat. At the same time, the Constitution of Malaysia allows the monarch some role in the protection of minorities. Article 153 of the Constitution, while allowing quotas to benefit the majority Malays and other native populations, provides that the monarch can intervene in the quotas to protect the 'legitimate interests of other communities'.[22]

In recent years, the role of the monarchs are shifting toward what Harding calls the 'Nazrinian' monarchy.[23] Under this conception, the monarchs are shifting their role from serving as a symbols of the ontological priority of the Malays, toward a more general one of serving all the communities of Malaysia. Harding and Kumarasingham point to the example of a monarch intervening in a dispute about a business refusing to serve non-Muslims.[24] While it is not clear to me whether this vision has been completely adopted throughout the nine states, it clearly represents a broader conception of the role played by the traditional rulers.

Occasionally Malay's monarchs provide a form of crisis insurance. One recent, if dubious, instance occurred in May 2020, in the midst of a pitched political battle between supporters of former Prime Minister Mahathir Mohamad and his erstwhile allies in the United Malays National Organization (UMNO). After a set of

[21] ibid, 407.

[22] Constitution of Malaysia (1957), Art 153.

[23] Andrew Harding, '"Nazrinian" Monarchy in Malaysia: The Resilience and Revival of a Traditional Institution' in Andrew Harding, and Dian A Shah (eds), *Law and Society in Malaysia* (Routledge, 2017) 72–95.

[24] Harding and Kumarasingham (n 3).

demonstrations, UMNO Prime Minister Najib Razak was ousted in a massive corruption scandal in 2018. Mahathir came back, leading a fractious coalition.

But in 2020, one of his allies, Muhyiddin Yassin, defected and joined forces with the UMNO Old Guard. Malaysia's King at the time exercised his discretion to appoint Mr Muyyiddin as Prime Minister.[25] Muhyiddin then immediately cancelled the parliamentary session, allegedly because of coronavirus risk. At a May session, the Yang di Pertuan Agong did not allow an investiture vote or motion of no confidence. We thus had a situation in which a monarch, ostensibly to resolve a political crisis, may have set democratic governance back.

Perhaps because of the particular partisan status of the monarchs in Malaysia's complex ethnic politics, however, this did not cause widespread demand for a change in the system, or a move toward republicanism. And some months later in October, the King exercised or even abused his discretion to reject a declaration of emergency that would have left Parliament suspended indefinitely.[26] Whatever the formal legality of these acts, Harding and Kumarasingham assert that the public was generally happy with the role of the Yang di-Pertuan Agong. A sense of political chaos, combined with the pandemic and economic challenges, may have contributed to this state of affairs. It thus seems to be an example in which the King throws the issue to the voters in some sense, and ends up coming out on top.

Malaysia's idiosyncratic monarchy plays an unusual role in national integration, in reducing the stakes of politics for the Malay majority, and in providing an active form of crisis insurance. It clearly enjoys some power, but in response to recent threats from political elites to reduce that level of power, has had to transform its role. In shifting to the 'Nazrinian' conception, Malaysia's rulers are extending the set of services they offer to society to a broader base, helping to ensure the survival of the institution into a new era.

III. Conclusion

Readers can be forgiven for thinking the foregoing is but a reframing in different language of ideas already present in Harding's work on monarchy. To that I plead guilty, as I have learned much from Harding's prodigious output over the years. My language is one of bargaining, while Harding writes in a law-and-society vein. We have agreement that one cannot understand institutions, including monarchy, without some attention to the broader social context and how it changes across time.

What are the implications of Malaysia's idiosyncratic monarchy for the broader understanding of the phenomenon? In some ways, we are watching in

[25] Richard Paddock, 'Democracy Fades in Malaysia as Old Guard is Restored Without a Vote' *New York Times*, 24 May 2020, A19.

[26] Dian H Shah, *Constitutions, Religion and Politics in Asia* (Cambridge University Press, 2022).

real time dynamics that played out over centuries of British history. Constitutional monarchy results from a process of giving up power over time, but this is not a unidirectional process. Kings will sometimes deploy their formal powers when they were not expected, and this can serve to resolve crises or exacerbate them.

At the same time, ideas of monarchy change over time. The shift toward a more responsive, inclusive role, as embodied in the Nazrinian conception of kingship, seems well designed to allow the monarchies to endure for the foreseeable future. To do so, the rulers will have to stay in their lane, intervening to resolve crises only when asked. A shift back toward more absolute forms of ruling, such as is found in neighboring Brunei, is totally out of the question for Malaysia. And that is a good thing.

7

Negotiating Religious Federalism in Malaysia

DIAN AH SHAH*

I. Introduction

Among Professor Andrew Harding's vast contribution to Asian legal studies, his scholarship on (and intellectual commitment to) pluralism stands out. Whether it is pluralism in the legal and political sense, or in the cultural and socio-economic sense, Harding's work consistently engages with this theme in various ways, and in doing so, he shows us that pluralism is indeed a lived reality in Asia. One especially notable facet of his contribution in this regard is examining the ways in which states could recognise, protect and manage pluralism through constitutional governance, and in particular through the devolution of powers. In what is also characteristic to his contextual, empirically grounded legal scholarship, Harding has made a foundational contribution to our appreciation of the gap between the theory and practice of devolution, particularly in the Asian context. For example, in his study of East Malaysia, Harding has developed a rich account on both the promises and pitfalls of federalism in protecting the rights and interests of indigenous peoples.[1] This chapter engages with these various dimensions of the interaction between pluralism and federalism, by focusing on a relatively understudied issue: religious federalism in Malaysia.

Analysis of constitutional law and religion in Malaysia has largely focused on the implications of the recognition of Islam as the religion of the Federation; the jurisdictional contestations between the civil and *Syariah* branches; and, by

* Parts of this chapter are adopted and adapted from my article, 'Navigating Navigating State-Religion Relations through Religious Federalism' (forthcoming, 41(1) *Journal of Law and Religion* 2026).

[1] See, eg, Andrew Harding, 'Asymmetric Federalism and Protection of Indigenous Peoples: The Case of Sabah and Sarawak in Malaysian Federalism' 50 Shades of Federalism (25 January 2021), 50shadesoffederalism.com/case-studies/asymmetric-federalism-and-protection-of-indigenous-peoples-the-case-of-sabah-and-sarawak-in-malaysian-federalism; and Andrew Harding, 'A Measure of Autonomy: Federalism as Protection for Malaysia's Indigenous Peoples' (2018) 46 *Federal Law Review* 557.

extension, the tussles between fundamental rights and *Syariah* law. However, what has thus far received scant scholarly attention is the religious federalism framework that undergirds the entire relationship between Islam, the state and its institutions. What I mean by religious federalism here is the devolution of power to sub-national governments on religious policy- and lawmaking. Indeed, in Malaysia's context – as we shall see in the next section – religious federalism manifests in the constitutional arrangement that places selected matters implicating Islam under the purview of state governments. The precise boundaries of this arrangement (and by extension, the centre-state division of power on Islamic matters) was tested in two relatively recent cases: *Iki Putra Mubarrak* in 2021 and *Nik Elin Nik Rashid* in 2023.

By way of background, Mr Mubarrak was charged by the Selangor state *Syariah* prosecutor for attempting to commit acts of sodomy (or what is legally defined as sexual intercourse against the order of nature with another male). The *Syariah* Criminal Offences Enactment of Selangor criminalises 'sexual offences against the order of nature' by imposing penalties including a fine, imprisonment or caning, and it is enforced to regulate same-sex sexual intercourse among persons professing the Islamic faith. However, the problem – Mr Mubarrak claimed – was that the same offence was already regulated by Section 377A of the Penal Code, and therefore, under the terms of the centre-state division of powers in the Federal Constitution, the Selangor provision was null and void. This is because the Selangor state legislature lacked competence to legislate on a matter that is exclusively under the 'Federal list' of legislative authority.[2] In 2021, the Federal Court of Malaysia ruled that the provision in the Selangor *Syariah* Criminal Offences Enactment was unconstitutional. In its reasoning, the Federal Court grounded its decision in the core principles and mechanics underpinning Malaysia's scheme of federalism. While reiterating that state legislatures are constitutionally empowered to enact laws in specific matters relating to Islam, the Court nonetheless held that they do not have the authority to legislate on matters included in the Constitution's Federal List.

This case – and indeed this chapter – brings to light broader questions about the theory and practice of formal constitutional arrangements devolving power to sub-national governments on religious matters. The theoretical appeal of devolution, particularly in multiethnic and multireligious states, is clear. For one, it represents a commitment to upholding diversity and the right to self-determination and autonomy, which in turn creates a foundation for peace-building. In countries where ethnic and/or religious divisions overlap with deeply rooted historical grievances and territorial claims, the prospect of autonomy and self-governance may help facilitate peace negotiations and allay demands for secession. In addition, when it comes to governance, the decentralisation of government power

[2] List I of the Ninth Schedule, Federal Constitution of Malaysia (1957). The list explicitly includes criminal law and procedure, and these areas of law are governed by the Penal Code and the Criminal Procedure Code.

allows some degree of counterbalance against the concentration of authority in the central government. This is said to be conducive for democracy and government accountability, not only by 'bringing government closer to the people',[3] but also by enhancing checks and balances at the local level. In the realm of religious policy-making, devolution of powers may even encourage plurality of religious thought and ideas that reflect local nuances and development.

Yet, as Harding recognises in the specific context of federal arrangements, the trajectory, operation and outcomes of devolution of power may well be more dynamic and complex than conventional theory suggests.[4] Indeed, as we shall see in Malaysia's case, devolution of powers is accompanied by centrifugal tendencies that may, under certain conditions, generate polarisation and conflict. To complicate matters further, depending on the broader political and constitutional complex, there is a risk that repressive laws may emerge (and be sustained), as well as unchecked exercises of authority at the sub-national level. In exploring the operation of religious federalism in Malaysia, this chapter illustrates precisely how these tensions play out. It posits three principal dynamics that have materialised in Malaysia's context: the *perversion* of religious federalism to enhance control over religious affairs; the *promise* of religious federalism in managing religious plurality; and the *abuse* of autonomy under religious federalism arrangements.

In these respects, the Malaysian experience serves as a potent illustration of the dynamic, contextual and complex nature of federal arrangements in devolving power. More broadly, it encourages us to rethink the normative imperatives and implications of federalism, particularly in the context of Asia's divided societies. It highlights the importance of institutional design, but at the same time it also draws our attention to the institutional (legal and political) conditions that must be present for countries to reap the benefits of federalism and devolution of power. In other words, legal and constitutional arrangements may spell out rights, entitlements and spheres of authority in matters implicating religion, but these are ultimately defined and controlled by the shifting (and competing) political fundamentals of the state. This may be exacerbated by the presence of legal loopholes in the scheme of devolution, which may weaken the benefits and operation of federalised solution as a means of managing religious divisions and plurality. The lessons here are instructive for other countries in the region grappling with the demands for autonomy, inclusivity and rights in the realms of religion. In Indonesia, for instance, debates on decentralisation and its implications on religious policy-making remains salient today, more than two decades after the fall of Soeharto's authoritarian government in 1998. In the Philippines, the extent of autonomy and devolution of powers in Muslim-majority Mindanao continues

[3] Andrew Harding and Rawin Leelapatana, 'Possibilities for Decentralisation in Thailand: A View from Chiang Mai' (2021) 1 *Thai Legal Studies* 76, 80.

[4] Andrew Harding, 'Devolution of Powers in Sarawak: A Dynamic Process of Redesigning Territorial Governance in a Federal System' (2017) 12 *Asian Journal of Comparative Law* 257, 257.

to be a contested issue, despite the constitutional dispensation creating specific autonomous regions.[5]

The rest of the chapter will be organised as follows. Section II explores the concept of religious federalism and the constitutional schemes on religion in Malaysia, including the question of how federal-state relations on religion are organised. It explains how the constitutions distribute, regulate and control powers relating to religion, and address issues such as the extent of state discretion to legislate on religion and whether federal or national laws or governments can restrict state policy. Section III offers insights into the *perversion* of religious federalism in Malaysia by showing how it is invoked to maintain central government control on Islamic matters. Section IV then demonstrates the *promise* of religious federalism in managing religious (Islamic) plurality and the boundaries and content of *Syariah* laws in the country. In section V, I explore both the potential and pitfalls of autonomy in religious matters, highlighting the *abuse* of religious federalism and its implications on rights protection. Finally, to conclude this Chapter in section VI, I offer some reflections on the factors shaping the operation of religious federalism in Malaysia, demonstrating how it unfolds within particular institutional, legal and political imperatives and contexts.

II. Religious Federalism in Malaysia

The Federation of Malaya, as it was first conceived in 1948 and retained at independence in 1957, comprised 11 states. In this 'original' arrangement, state powers are mainly restricted to Islamic law and Malay customs, local government, land, agriculture, forestry and natural resources. With regard to Islam, this meant that in the nine individual states with a hereditary Malay monarch (the Sultan), there is a degree of autonomy in legislating, regulating and administering Islamic law.[6] Indeed, even as the Federal Constitution recognises Islam as the 'religion of the Federation', the constitution-making settlement in 1957 provided that Sultan remains the Head of Islam in his state, and the rights, privileges, prerogatives and powers he enjoys are 'unaffected and unimpaired' by such constitutional dispensation on Islam.[7]

The Federation later expanded in 1963 as Singapore, Sabah and Sarawak joined to create the Federation of Malaysia, but the nature of these arrangements changed[8] – what has emerged is an asymmetric federal arrangement with the Sabah and Sarawak enjoying more powers than other partners in the Federation in a range

[5] Amanda Cats-Baril, 'Self Determination', International IDEA Constitution Brief (September 2018) 6, www.idea.int/sites/default/files/publications/self-determination-constitution-brief.pdf.

[6] For the remaining four states and the three federal territories of Putrajaya, Labuan and Kuala Lumpur, such matters fall under the purview of the *Yang di-Pertuan Agong* (the federal monarch).

[7] Article 3(1)–(2) of the Federal Constitution of Malaysia.

[8] Singapore left the Federation in August 1965.

of issues including immigration, the legal system and legal profession, and fiscal matters. The question of religion is also implicated in the special arrangements vis-à-vis the two states – when the 1963 Malaysia Agreement (MA63) was negotiated and signed, it made clear that the constitutional status of Islam at the federal level was not applicable to Sabah and Sarawak. This is justified due to the cultural, demographic and historical circumstances of these two states – they are ethnically, linguistically, culturally and religiously heterogenous and in fact, more so than any other state in West Malaysia. If the Malay-Muslims are the majority in West Malaysia, no single ethnic group comprises the majority in any of these two states. In Sarawak, the Iban is the biggest ethnic group, comprising 30 per cent of the population, and they are largely Christians. In fact, in the 2010 census Christianity is the largest religion in Sarawak, while in Sabah, Islam remains the biggest religion (approximately 60 per cent of the population).[9] Yet, there is a great degree of inter-religious marriage amongst the Sabahans, which contributes to the ethnic, religious and cultural diversity in the state. That said, it is worth noting that an amendment to the Sabah state Constitution in 1973 made Islam the state religion – an episode that demonstrates concretely just how precarious commitments and agreements about religion may be as political fundamentals evolve in Malaysia. Therefore, as I shall illustrate in more detail throughout this chapter, the practice of religious autonomy may in reality also be limited, and this must be considered alongside several contextual factors.

First, historically, although a federal structure of government was a 'necessary condition' for independence,[10] the personalities involved in negotiating and making the Constitution at independence did not envision federalism as an arrangement to accommodate ethnic or religious difference nor to meaningfully pull power away from the centre. As Harding notes, federalism in Malaysia was adopted to further a 'cultural' purpose, that is to maintain and support the continuance of state constitutional monarchies[11] whose authority over Islam and Malay customs have been long-held, even during the British colonial occupation. Sultans, as the *Khalifahs* (God's Regent on Earth), maintained a spiritual role – they were the heads of religion for their Malay subjects. They were also the centre of gravity for every aspect of Malay life. Thus the content of 'Islamic law' invariably depended on the Sultan's inclinations and the influence of *adat* at state level.[12] In the state of Negeri Sembilan, for example, the passing of property under inheritance laws is shaped by the matrilineal *adat perpatih*, as opposed to the patrilineal traditions of Islamic law.[13] That said, in the bigger scheme of things the orientation of federalism (including religious federalism) was, and has been, very much centre-heavy.

[9] Department of Statistics Malaysia (DOSM), 'Demographic Statistics, Fourth Quarter 2025', www.dosm.gov.my/portal-main/release-content/demographic-statistics-fourth-quarter-2024.

[10] Andrew Harding, *The Constitution of Malaysia: A Contextual Analysis* (Hart, 2012) 133.

[11] ibid, 134.

[12] ibid, 227.

[13] MB Hooker, 'The Challenge of Malay Adat Law in the Realm of Comparative Law' (1973) 22 *International and Comparative Law Quarterly* 492.

This 'mentality' or orientation surrounding federalism is reflected in the constitutional arrangements on religious federalism. In general, Malaysia's federalism is focused on a strong central government with limited legislative and executive power for the states. For instance, Article 75 of the Federal Constitution provides that federal law *shall* prevail where there are any inconsistencies between federal and state laws. The Federal List (List I, Ninth Schedule) is extensive, covering matters such as external affairs, defence, citizenship, finance and the civil and criminal justice systems. Furthermore, Article 76(1)(b) of the Constitution states that the Federal Parliament *may* legislate on any matter within the State List (List II, Ninth Schedule) to promote legal uniformity in two or more states, although such legislation would only take effect when it is adopted by the state legislature. With regard to religion (Islam), the Ninth Schedule (List II, Paragraph I) of the Federal Constitution delineates the parameters of states' legislative powers vis-à-vis Islam. These matters mainly revolve around personal and family law issues for 'persons professing the religion of Islam', but the Constitution also empowers state legislatures to create and spell out punishments for 'offences against the precepts of Islam'. This category, as we shall see later, has emerged as a contentious point in Malaysia's constitutional politics, owing to the presence of state *Syariah* criminal laws that arguably cover matters that are in the Federal List. That said, the broader takeaway point here is that state powers over Islamic matters are clear, but they are also regulated – they must not trespass into the realms of federal authority and they may be subject to federal legal harmonisation initiatives.

The third factor implicates specific federal limits on the powers of *Syariah* Courts to enforce *Syariah* laws. In a way, this also reinforces the point made earlier about the limits on devolved power on Islam under Malaysia's religious federalism scheme. A 1988 constitutional amendment (Article 121(1A)) carved out an exclusive sphere of authority for *Syariah* courts in certain Islamic matters provided in List II of the Ninth Schedule. The objective of this amendment was to ensure that decisions of the *Syariah* courts within its exclusive jurisdictional sphere are final and they cannot be altered by the civil (secular) courts. Then, in 1993, a three-tier system of *Syariah* courts was established in each state, comprising the *Syariah* subordinate courts, the *Syariah* high courts and the *Syariah* court of appeals. However, the 1965 *Syariah* Courts (Criminal Jurisdiction) Act prescribes limits on punishment – *Syariah* courts are thus only authorised to impose a maximum of three years' imprisonment, a fine not exceeding RM5,000, and/or six strokes of the cane. Since the courts are creatures of statute and possess limited jurisdiction, they could be regarded as inferior courts (compared to the High Courts), but their pronouncements on matters properly within their jurisdiction would be regarded as final.

To promulgate, administer and enforce Islamic laws and policies, as well as advise the Heads of Islam in the state, each state has its own religious council, religious department and a system of *Syariah* courts. However, at the federal level, there is the Department of Islamic Development (JAKIM), which is set up under and overseen by the Prime Minister's Department. Despite the existence of state-level religious departments, JAKIM has played a crucial and extensive role in carrying out the Federal Government's policies and agenda on Islam across state lines. This is despite assurances during the constitution-making process that the recognition of Islam as the 'religion of the Federation' will not encroach upon the powers of the Sultans regarding Islamic affairs in their respective states and that if any federal-level religious department was set up, it would merely serve a coordination function across state lines.[14] This suggests the Federal Government would play a minimal role at state-level and the states would continue to enjoy whatever measure of autonomy they have on Islamic affairs.

The combination of historical, structural and political conditions has produced an asymmetric federal system that is riddled with complexity. This complexity, when combined with evolving political imperatives, has defined the centre-state tensions in managing Islamic laws and affairs. As the following sections illustrate, these tensions also bear significant implications for the protection of fundamental rights in the country.

III. The Perversion of Religious Federalism?

As explained above, from the outset Malaysia's federalism bore strong centralisation tendencies, notwithstanding the constitutional arrangements carving out some measure of autonomy for states in Islamic matters. The Constitution enables and supports the prevalence of federal power through Article 75, and to a lesser extent, Article 76. I also alluded to the role of JAKIM, a department formally set up under the Prime Minister's Department in 1997, but its roots are traceable to what was called the National Council for Islamic Affairs in 1968. The Council purportedly served a 'coordination role' and as the 'highest forum' to 'discuss and advise' the Council of Malay Rulers on Islamic affairs in the country.[15] Strictly speaking in these respects, the autonomy accorded to states to chart and implement their policies on Islamic affairs seems very much intact. However, what I will show in this section is that there has also been some pattern of incremental perversion of the religious federalism arrangement in Malaysia, which in effect dilutes state-level authority on Islam. The crucial background to this was the rapidly changing political imperatives implicating Islam in the late 1970s, in which the *Barisan Nasional* (BN) Government felt that it had to respond to the demands of Islamic revivalism in the society and the growing influence of a rival Islamic political party, PAS.

[14] Dian AH Shah, *Constitutions, Religion and Politics in Asia: Malaysia, Indonesia and Sri Lanka* (Cambridge University Press, 2017), p. 45.

[15] See Jabatan Kemajuan Islam Malaysia (JAKIM), 'JAKIM Constitutional', www.islam.gov.my/en/corporate-info/jakim-constitutional.

Central control over the Islamic discourse through legal and institutional reforms was one strategy to achieve these aims. Instead of upholding state autonomy over Islamic affairs, the Government employed federal-level institutions to control the Islamic discourse that it feared would be utilised to drive anti-government rhetoric. In the sphere of legal reforms, for instance, the Government passed an amendment to the Penal Code in 1983 to criminalise actions such as alleging another person has ceased to profess his/her religion, undermining the actions of a religious official, and claiming that the actions of such official are inconsistent with the doctrines of the religion.[16] Another provision – Section 298A(5) – prohibits a person who is not an appointed religious official (ie, not appointed by the state) from performing any functions 'of a religious character'. This effectively gave the Federal Government significant control over religious activities and the kinds of persons authorised to carry out those activities. Of course, these provisions are neutral in these that they do not explicitly address Islam. However, they were enacted with the rise in religiously motivated, anti-government propaganda in mind. For instance, an influential PAS leader at the time had issued a 'mandate' declaring that Muslims who supported and worked with UMNO (the dominant, Malay-Muslim party in the BN coalition) were *kafirs* (unbelievers).[17] In addition, the Government was also anxious about the spread of Islamic doctrines or practices that fell outside the official denomination endorsed by the state, ie, Sunni Islam. From the perspective of the state, anything other than its brand of Sunni Islam translates into Muslim deviancy, and the lack of uniformity in Islamic doctrines and praxis and conformity to the state's brand of Islam, risks religious conflict and disharmony within the Muslim community. In some cases, these were also deemed a threat to national security.

The provisions of the Penal Code and their position within Malaysia's religious federalism scheme were tested before the courts in the late 1980s, when four individuals were charged under Section 298A for engaging in an 'act which is likely to prejudice unity among persons professing the Islamic religion'. They had acted as a *Bilal* (a person who performs the call to prayer), an *Imam* (a person who leads congregational prayer, and a *Khatib* (a person who delivers Friday prayer sermons) during Friday prayers in the state of Terengganu without prior government authorisation.[18] These individuals then challenged the constitutionality of Section 298A, arguing that the provision in pith and substance dealt with Islam, which ought to be regulated by state as opposed to federal legislature. In a majority three to two decision, the Supreme Court upheld the petitioners' claim, stating that the acts covered by Section 298A 'had nothing to do with public order' (a federal matter) but rather they concerned religious matters (a state matter).[19]

[16] Section 298A(2), Penal Code.

[17] Norshahril Saat and Afra Alatas, 'Islamisation in Malaysia Beyond UMNO and PAS', ISEAS Perspective (26 September 2022) 4.

[18] *Mamat bin Daud v Government of Malaysia* [1988] 1 MLJ 119 (Kuala Lumpur, Supreme Court).

[19] ibid, at 125.

Central control was further buttressed by strengthening the position and functions of JAKIM beyond its original coordination and advisory roles mentioned above. In the early years of Prime Minister Mahathir's first administration (1981–2003), the size of the religious bureaucracy expanded considerably – its staff increased from 100 in 1982 to 608 in 1987.[20] Though suspicious of the political role of the *ulama* and political Islam, Mahathir coopted trained Islamic scholars and religious figures and they became state-sponsored to power his agenda of building a modern and progressive Islamic community. JAKIM's role in 'centralising' and 'standardising' Islam and Islamic laws nationwide became crucial for that agenda.[21] For example, it vets Friday sermons to be distributed to state religious departments (and subsequently to local mosques in the districts); it standardises *fatawa* (religious edicts) issued by state-level *fatwa* committees;[22] and it monitors the spread of Islamic doctrines that the Government deemed 'deviant' (ie, they do not conform to the Government's view and interpretation of Islam) and facilitates rehabilitation for followers of deviant groups.

To illustrate JAKIM's power and influence, consider its role in the development and dissemination of *fatawa*. JAKIM oversees the National Fatwa Committee (NFC) – a federal-level body comprising state-level *mufti* and professionals (such as academics) appointed by the Council of Malay Rulers. The NFC issues a *fatwa* either through deliberation in response to a query by the Council of Malay Rulers, or through a national discussion (*Muzakarah Fatwa Kebangsaan*) conducted at least six times a year.[23] Once a *fatwa* is issued and presented to the Council of Malay Rulers for assent, it is then sent to state religious councils. Depending on how the NFC issues the *fatwa*, state councils are either: (1) bound to accept the *fatwa* as is and recommend its adoption or otherwise to the state-level ruler; or (2) allowed to make amendments and choose whether to adopt the NFC-issued *fatwa*.[24] Although theoretically each state may ignore federal-level authority, the participation of state *muftis* in deliberations at the NFC means that in practice, there is little deviation from what has been decided at federal level. In addition, federal authorities view the lack of uniformity and diverging views as irritants. Thus, while state *fatwa* committees may issue contradictory *fatawa*, JAKIM works to standardise them. Other federal efforts at streamlining Islamic thought and practice include the organisation of dialogues between *muftis* and overseeing the development of Islamic education in national religious schools. These efforts, in turn, shape policy-making on Islamic affairs at state level.

[20] Joseph Chinyong Liow, *Piety and Politics: Islamism in Contemporary Malaysia* (Oxford University Press, 2009) 49.

[21] See Maznah Mohamad, 'The Ascendance of Bureaucratic Islam and the Secularization of the Sharia in Malaysia' (2010) 83 *Pacific Affairs* 505.

[22] Norshahril Saat, *The State, Ulama and Islam in Malaysia and Indonesia* (Amsterdam University Press, 2018) 84.

[23] ibid 78.

[24] ibid.

Although one might make a (rather weak) case that these are merely 'coordination' initiatives that are in no way overbearing, the reality is that JAKIM's role vis-à-vis the states has become salient, particularly insofar as state religious councils and officials have become more reliant on, and tempted by, ample funds from the Federal Government. It is no longer a mere coordinator or advisor; it is, for all intents and purposes, the chief policymaker on matters relating to Islam at federal level, and its policies determines – to a significant extent – how Islam is practised, implemented and developed throughout the country. Another instructive example in this regard is the prohibition on the use of the word 'Allah' as a reference to God in Malay-language bibles. The policy adopted by the Federal Government is implemented uniformly nationwide, and JAKIM was instrumental in supporting and justifying such prohibition. At the height of a legal challenge at the Court of Appeal, for instance, a Friday sermon reiterated the position that 'Allah' was a term exclusive for Muslims and that those who sought to use the term were out to confuse Muslims and lure them away from Islam. The Court of Appeal eventually ruled unanimously that the prohibition was not unconstitutional and did not infringe the right of non-Muslims to practice their religion.

IV. The Promise of Devolved Power?

I have demonstrated thus far how Malaysia's religious federalism operates in ways that may lead to the concentration of power over Islamic affairs in the hands of the central government. There is yet another mechanism through which religious federalism is navigated, which is more discursive in nature and pays *some* regard to state authority over Islamic affairs. This involves a continuous *process* of political and bureaucratic interaction between federal and state authorities to manage Islamic plurality and define the boundaries (and content) of Islamic laws at sub-national levels. It bears emphasis here that even though the overall *outcomes* of that interactive process may lie closer to the legal centralism end of the centralism–pluralism spectrum, the discourse allows the negotiation of some deviation from federal preferences and mitigates potential problems that full devolution might generate (which will be explored further in section V).

The most illustrative example of this horizontal approach in navigating religious federalism could be seen from the Federal Government's series of reforms of Islamic laws and institutions in the 1980s. These initiatives entailed more than just changing the content of Islamic law to institute modern and progressive Islamic thought in the country;[25] it also meant standardising substantive laws across state lines and, to some extent, expanding the corpus of Islamic laws governing Muslims. It is worth noting here that the BN Federal Government – as part of the

[25] Donald L Horowitz, 'The Qur'an and the Common Law: Islamic Law Reform and the Theory of Legal Change' (1994) 42 *American Journal of Comparative Law* 233, 253.

so-called 'Islamisation' project – was never interested in creating a theocratic state or in pursuing the full range of Islamic laws, including *hudud* crimes and punishment (such as amputation and stoning for certain types of crimes). These were instead championed by PAS – which took control of the state of Kelantan following the 1990 elections – as part of its political rhetoric that it was more committed to upholding Islamic principles than the BN-led Government. Indeed, the PAS Government quickly passed the Kelantan *Syariah* Criminal Code II 1993 within three years of its electoral victory, but the Code was never enforced due to the limits imposed by federal law on the sentencing power of *Syariah* courts.[26] That said, politically, the Federal Government could not ignore or dismiss the groundswell of Islamic revivalism and the demands that accompanied it. The strategy, therefore, turned on anchoring 'Islamisation' initiatives within the pursuit of modern, moderate and progressive Islam for national development.

At this juncture, it would be apt to recall that under List II of the Ninth Schedule to the Federal Constitution, certain Islamic matters are well under the jurisdiction of the states. Thus, the principal challenge for the federal government was to engineer and achieve uniform laws in these areas, especially 'with separate sultanates and different political configurations' in the states resisting reforms.[27] To meet this challenge, the Federal Government formed a *Syariah* Technical Committee – comprising Islamic law as well as common law scholars and lawyers – tasked to discuss, formulate and promote draft statutes to be adopted by states nationwide. The Committee then 'toured' the states in the Federation to discuss with, and convince, state legal advisors, executive committees and representatives of the Sultans to enact the Federal model laws.[28] What becomes obvious here is that while there remained a strong imperative from the centre to reform and standardise Islamic laws, this was pursued through a fairly organised and inclusive process of communication, negotiation and persuasion with the states.

The efforts of the Technical Committee bore more fruit in some areas than others. For example, Islamic laws of procedure and evidence are virtually uniform across all states, and the reforms produced provisions that very heavily influenced by common law rules of procedure and evidence.[29] As Horowitz notes, the statutes in these areas are characterised by 'hybridisation'– Islamic rules and features were certainly present, but by and large they are comparable to federal (secular) statutes.[30] By contrast, the most controversial tensions took place in the field of Islamic family law, where the Technical Committee produced a model family law statute dubbed the 'Federal model'.[31] This was resisted by Kelantan, where the state Government set up another committee which produced a competing draft.

[26] Malik Imtiaz Sarwar and Surendra Ananth, 'Confronting the Constitutionality of Hudud' (2016) 4 *Malayan Law Journal* xii, xiii.

[27] Horowitz (n 25) 269.

[28] ibid, 253.

[29] ibid, 272.

[30] ibid, 270–72.

[31] ibid, 268.

The major differences between these two models pertain to the issues of consent to marriage, divorce and polygamy.[32] For example, with regard to polygamy, the original Kelantan statute merely stipulates that a man is not allowed to enter into a polygamous marriage unless he obtains a 'written permission' from the Qadhi Court (that is, the *Syariah* Court) and if he enters into such marriage without such permission, he is subject to a fine of up to RM300 or a jail term of up to a month.[33] The original Federal model, by contrast, prescribed stricter and detailed conditions for the permission application and circumstances in which the Court may grant permission, including an assessment of whether the marriage was 'just and necessary', and whether the applicant was able to accord equal treatment to all wives.[34]

Efforts at uniformity and standardisation were thus not fully successful in the 1980s, because while most states that opted for the Federal model, several others adopted the Kelantan model. However, the discourse continued over the next two decades or so, resulting in changes to both models. Subsequent amendments to the Federal model introduced provisions that are less than favourable towards women.[35] There is, for instance, a pattern of liberalisation in divorce and polygamy rules (such as allowing divorces to be pronounced by the husband outside the courts and allowing the registration of polygamous marriages without court permission upon payment of a small fine).[36] In addition, notwithstanding the earlier lack of state-to-state uniformity due to the adoption of the Federal model in some states and the Kelantan model in others, subsequent changes have produced largely uniform Islamic family law across state lines today. Even the latest Kelantan Islamic Family Law Enactment, enacted in 2002, reflects the current amended Federal model (the Federal Territory Islamic Family Law Enactment 1984).

Two implications are immediately discernible from this case study, both of which are in turn relevant in thinking about the relationship between federalism, pluralism and religion. First, the continuous discourse between federal and state religious authorities – notwithstanding federal efforts to standardise and control the content of Islamic laws across state lines – may temper the emergence and effects of discriminatory and repressive laws, which political actors on the extreme flanks might pursue under the guise of 'autonomy'. The original Kelantan statute on family law (1983) was eventually replaced in 2002, and its provisions on polygamy, for instance, now include the kinds of conditions that are prescribed in the Federal model.

[32] ibid, 273.

[33] Section 19, Islamic Family Enactment 1983 (Kelantan).

[34] Section 23(4), Islamic Family Law Act 1984 (Federal Territories).

[35] See Mohamad Hashim Kamali, 'Islamic Law in Malaysia: Issues and Developments' (1981) 4 *Yearbook of Islamic and Middle Eastern Law* 153, 154, 161–65; Maznah Mohamad, 'Making Majority, undoing family: law, religion and the Islamisation of the state in Malaysia' (2010) 39 *Economy and Society* 360, 375.

[36] Musawah and Sisters in Islam, *Joint Report on Muslim Family Law and Muslim Women's Rights in Malaysia* (February 2018) 6, www.musawah.org/wp-content/uploads/2019/02/Malaysia-SIS-Musawah-Joint-Thematic-Report-2018-CEDAW69.pdf.

Second, this method of navigating religious federalism may blunt impulses (be they at federal or state levels) to concentrate authority, but this may well hinge on how the process and outcomes unfold and the issues at stake. Consider the efforts by PAS to implement *hudud* punishments since their electoral victory in Kelantan in 1990. When the PAS-led state legislative assembly unanimously passed the Kelantan *Syariah* Criminal Code II 1993, which prescribed *hudud* punishments for offences such as theft, robbery and sexual intercourse outside wedlock, it was the first and the only state to do so at that time. To be sure, this contravenes the constitutional scheme of religious federalism in Malaysia and the Kelantan Government had clearly encroached into the realms of federal power in regulating criminal law. It was only in February 2024, following a constitutional challenge, that the Federal Court struck down several provisions of the Enactment for violating the federal–state division of powers.[37] But the fact that the Kelantan Code remained on the books for so long, despite it being unenforceable due to the federal limits on *Syariah* courts' powers, brings to light the political dilemma: the Federal Government could not be seen as vociferously opposing the expansion of Islamic law, even if it regarded provisions of the Code to be 'inappropriate for the modern world'.[38] In this instance, therefore, federal–state discourse was defunct – the issue of *hudud* was such a high-stakes political game that no side was willing to compromise on.

V. The Abuse of Religious Federalism

The Kelantan Code example in the preceding section is a good segue into the discussion of how religious federalism may be abused in ways that magnify social polarisation and constitutional rights violations. Here, we are presented with a paradox: on the one hand, devolution of powers facilitates self-determination, enhances political accountability of state governments to their electorates, and allows a plurality of religious thought and ideas to be practised, particularly those that may be deemed 'minority views' within the national discourse on Islam. On the other hand, as scholars have noted elsewhere, federal solutions may reduce attachment to the national state, identity and agenda,[39] foster enduring identity-based cleavages (in Malaysia's case, intra-Islam cleavages that could potentially spur broader social and political conflict), and lead to corruption and authoritarian (religious) governance at state level (which is plausible in the Malaysian context

[37] This is the case of Nik Elin Nik Rashid. The challenge against the constitutionality of Kelantan's *Syariah* Criminal Enactment was similar to the challenge in Iki Putra (above), but this time it implicated at least 16 provisions relating to a range of offences.

[38] Horowitz (n 25) 264.

[39] Tom Ginsburg, 'Constitutional Design Options for Territorial Cleavages in the Middle East' in Asli U Bali and Omar M Dajani (eds), *Federalism and Decentralization in the Contemporary Middle East and North Africa* (Cambridge University Press, 2023) 67, 72.

given weak institutionalisation of checks and balances and tolerance of religious dissent). These implications could well be intended, unintended, or even both.

The issue of child marriage provides an instructive example of the abuse and adverse consequences of religious federalism. In July 2018, the Gua Musang *Syariah* Court (in Kelantan) fined a 41-year old man RM1,800 (approximately USD400) for marrying a minor without prior permission from the *Syariah* court and for entering into a polygamous marriage without consent from his existing spouse.[40] Later in September, reports emerged about a 15-year-old girl who married a 44-yearold man as his second wife, having obtained approval from another *Syariah* court in Kelantan. These cases, plus a few others that emerged throughout 2018, led to calls from the civil society for the Government to raise the minimum age of marriage to 18 years old for Muslim girls.

Most states provide that the legal minimum age of marriage of 18 years for boys and 16 years for girls. As of January 2024, only two states – Selangor and Kedah – have raised the minimum age to 18 years for girls. That said, in all states (and federal territories), marriage below the age of 18 is still permissible with state *Syariah* court approval. Statistics from the Malaysian Department of *Syariah* Judiciary revealed that there were 10,240 child marriage applications from 2005 to 2015.[41] In a study by UNICEF Malaysia in 2018 reported that *Syariah* court judges typically took three main considerations into account before allowing an application for child marriage: sexual and reproductive health issues (for instance, if the applicant was pregnant and had had pre-marital sexual intercourse); the child's maturity and preparedness for marital life; and family matters (including possible pressures that the applicant faced from his or her family).[42]

Following the public controversy generated by the cases in Kelantan in 2018, the Federal Government attempted to work with state governments to raise the minimum age for marriage. But in November 2019 the then-Deputy Prime Minister revealed that while some states had agreed to amend their laws to set the minimum age of marriage at 18 years old, seven states – including Kelantan – refused to make such amendments. The divergence between state and federal views on this matter is further illustrated by the fact that the Fatwa Committee of the National Council of Islamic Religious Affairs (a federal body) had published a *fatwa* in 2014 declaring that child marriage was neither obligatory, nor a healthy practice, and that the current legal exceptions allowing child marriage should not be encouraged. Yet, this view is not necessarily shared by *muftis* (Islamic legal jurists recognised by the Government) at state-level, some of whom believe that increasing the minimum age for marriage poses more negative risks.[43] Here, the

[40] Rohaniza Idris, 'Investigation on child marriage in Gua Musang still ongoing, says DPM' *New Straits Times* (17 July 2018), www.nst.com.my/news/nation/2018/07/391802/investigation-child-marriage-gua-musang-still-ongoing-says-dpm.

[41] ibid, 19.

[42] ibid, 57. This study drew on data from the *Syariah* courts of seven states in Malaysia.

[43] ibid, 27.

full force of state-level authority over Islamic affairs is apparent – state refusal to increase the minimum age of marriage for girls is arguably within their jurisdiction, and any legal reform pushed by the federal authorities would have to secure the buy-in of state religious authorities. However, the insistence of 'autonomy' here becomes a real impediment to instituting progressive reforms that better-protect constitutional rights of citizens.

The disagreements between state and federal religious authorities are also obvious in other areas of *Syariah* law. I have previously alluded to the sharp divergence in Islamic criminal law between the Kelantan and Terengganu on the one hand, and the remaining states as well as the Federal Territories (under the authority of the Federal Government). As in the issue of child marriage, the regulation of apostasy remains a significant point of contention. After the *Lina Joy* case in 2009 – where a woman (born Muslim) in the Federal Territories converted to Christianity and failed to obtain official state recognition of her conversion without a 'certificate of conversion' from the *Syariah* courts – the Federal Government mooted the idea of a federal law to regulate Muslim apostasy nationwide. Part of the controversy generated by the *Lina Joy* case stemmed from the absence of a clear set of legal procedures in the Federal Territories for apostasy. Such laws exist in some, but not all states, and where they do exist, the procedures for apostasy vary across state lines.

The Federal Government's proposal to standardise apostasy laws never reached the parliament for debate. The 'official' version of events was that the Government needed more time to deliberate on the contents of the bill and that it wanted to avoid any hasty decisions on a politically sensitive issue. It was not only sensitive as far as religious relations were concerned, but also on the issue of centre–state relations. Unlike other areas of Islamic law such as family law, apostasy opens debates on fundamental issues concerning punishments for 'offences against the precepts of Islam', and given the prerogatives of the Sultans in Islamic matters within their own states, asserting federal authority over 'Islamic crimes' may not sit well with the states. In addition, it left the Federal Government with the choice between upholding its progressive, moderate image by introducing 'permissive' laws on apostasy (that eschews capital punishment or a jail sentence) or articulating more punitive approaches, along the lines adopted by the PAS-led Government in Kelantan. The latter would have been politically difficult, given potential objections from non-Muslim parties in the government coalition, but the Federal Government also did not wish to be perceived as 'soft' on what is deemed as a serious crime in the Islamic tradition.

VI. Conclusion: The Institutional and Political Imperatives of Religious Federalism in Malaysia

In discussing the various modalities in navigating religious federalism in Malaysia, one issue has stood out thus far: operationalising centre–state relationships on religion and Islamic laws is a political issue in as much as it is a legal one. This accentuates both the opportunities and limitations of devolution of powers in matters implicating religion – in this case, Islam as the majority religion. Where states have strongly asserted their authority over Islamic affairs, it has proven difficult to institute legal reforms to enforce constitutional rights protections and temper divisive religious political mobilisation within the society. While technically pluralism within and between religions is to be celebrated, divergences in opinion, thought and praxis within the Malay-Muslim majority has been a potent source of conflict that foments animosities and sometimes even violence. The Federal Government's centralisation impulses and efforts – where successful – have yielded significant advances in protecting the rights of women, for example. However, some of the cases above also suggest that these patterns may not always be persistent. To understand these complexities, I suggest that a closer look at the institutional and political factors is warranted.

First, the centre-heavy orientation of Malaysia federalism both in terms of institutional arrangement and practice have undoubtedly shaped the forces and counter-forces surrounding religious federalism. The constitutional dispensation on federal–state powers clearly prioritises laws passed by the Federal Parliament where there are inconsistencies between federal and state laws (Article 75). In relation to this, even the residual power of state legislatures to make laws beyond what is explicitly stated in the List II of the Ninth Schedule is limited, in that such laws cannot address matters that fall within the federal legislative authority (Article 77). The constitution drafters had also explicitly envisaged Parliament as the sole lawmaking authority in matters enumerated in the Federal List, and, while in general states retain exclusive power to legislate in matters that fall under their exclusive jurisdiction, in certain circumstances spelled out in Article 76, the Federal Parliament possesses overriding powers. This scheme has been authoritatively upheld by the Federal Court in the *Iki Putra Mubarrak* case, with the Court emphasising that

> the terms of our [Federal Constitution] and the history of its founding make it abundantly clear that the primary legislative powers of the Federation shall lie ultimately with Parliament save and except for specific matters over which the States shall have legislative powers.[44]

The Court also determined that the constitutionality of state laws would be assessed as against the subject matter included in the Federal List, not against any existing federal law.[45] The upshot, in this case, is that a provision of the Selangor *Syariah* Criminal Offences Enactment 1995 that criminalised same-sex sexual intercourse was deemed unconstitutional, as it addressed a matter that is clearly under the jurisdiction of the Federal Parliament (ie, regulation of criminal law).[46]

[44] *Iki Putra Mubarrak v Kerajaan Negeri Selangor and Others* [2021] 1 LNS 47, para 68.
[45] Paras 51–52.
[46] The same offence is regulated by Section 377A of the Penal Code.

Second, a complicating factor that still looms over any legal disputes implicating Islam concerns the issue of how and where Islamic laws and actions of Islamic bodies sit within the broader constitutional and administrative law framework, where rights such as freedom of expression, freedom of religion and equality are afforded to all citizens. At one extreme end of the spectrum, there seems to be a belief – in constitutional culture and practice – that anything that raises Islamic law questions is exceptional, in that it rests outside of the reach of the civil courts and the constitutional rights guarantees. Thus, where such issues arise, the *Syariah* courts will adjudicate the matter as purely an 'Islamic law' question, and their decisions are deemed final and authoritative. The root of this complexity is mainly structural – it concerns Article 121(1A) of the Federal Constitution, which institutes an autonomous sphere of authority and legal development for *Syariah* courts. Following this amendment, the civil (secular) courts are said to be precluded from reviewing *Syariah* court decisions in certain matters that are *exclusively* within the *Syariah* jurisdiction. This view has shaped the trajectory of Malaysia's constitutional culture and judges' understanding about their roles vis-à-vis cases on religion for decades. Thus, there has been a tendency amongst judges to avoid authoritative decisions on issues implicating Islam, even where they raise important constitutional law questions. And once a case is adjudicated before the *Syariah* courts, there is virtually no way to overturn the decision at the civil courts. That said, the intention behind this scheme was straightforward and relatively innocuous. It was thought that questions involving *Syariah* law (in the limited areas where the law applies) required the expertise of those trained in Islamic jurisprudence. In addition, as a matter of legal certainty, the provision was intended to resolve conflicting decisions between civil and *Syariah* courts in cases implicating Islamic law. However, as experience has shown time and again, a legal problem may raise both Islamic law and constitutional law questions, and the answers to both may well diverge.

It was only in 2018 that the Federal Court decided that civil courts are empowered to review the Islamic authorities' decision-making processes.[47] It also held that Article 121(1A) does not strip the authority of the civil courts to interpret the Constitution, 'even where the determination of Islamic law is required for such interpretation'.[48] This effectively meant that religious authorities (and the courts) could no longer shield themselves behind Article 121(1A) to avoid the supervisory jurisdiction of the civil courts. The case in question involved conversion – more specifically, it was about the unilateral conversion of children to Islam (overseen and secured by a state religious authority) without the knowledge or consent of their non-Muslim mother. The Court held that the way the religious authority secured the conversion of the children had exceeded the scope of his administrative powers. It bears emphasis, therefore, that Article 121(1A) does not oust

[47] *Indira Gandhi a/p Mutho v Pengarah Jabatan Agama Islam Perak* [2018] 1 MLJ 545 (Federal Court).

[48] ibid, 584–86.

the civil court's supervisory powers over the *Syariah* courts, nor does it elevate the *Syariah* courts to a status parallel to that of the civil courts. The former are creatures of state legislation with limited jurisdiction as defined in the Federal Constitution's Ninth Schedule, List II, paragraph I.

Finally, as readers may realise at this juncture, the preceding points, individually and in combination, cannot fully account for the practice and operationalisation of religious federalism in Malaysia. If indeed centralisation impulses are so strong to the point that state authority is circumvented or disregarded completely, why do federal authorities retreat or exercise restraint in some cases? What I have attempted to suggest implicitly as I unpacked the modalities and case illustrations is that the Federal Government's broader political agenda and position does matter to some extent. The issue of Islamic criminal punishments has had an enduring political significance, and it arguably is growing in significance as the Malay-Muslim society in general becomes more conservative in the past two decades. This has been the 'signature' political pledge of the Islamic party, PAS, as it attempts to prove to the Malay-Muslim voter that it is the only party that would champion 'true' Islamic causes and principles. In the 1990s, the Federal Government maintained its resilience in resisting state-level pressures to implement *hudud* punishments for various criminal offences.[49] It could afford to do so given its super-majority strength in Parliament,[50] and its political dominance, particularly among the Malay-Muslim majority, meant that it possessed a great degree of legitimacy in managing demands on Islam.

However, more than two decades later, when the *hudud* debate resurfaced after the PAS Government passed a new *Syariah* Criminal Code in Kelantan (2014), the Federal Government changed its tone – it expressed greater openness to accommodate the implementation of the Code. This sparked proposals to table a Private Member's Bill to amend the 1965 *Syariah* Courts (Criminal Jurisdiction) Act to 'upgrade' the *Syariah* Court's powers to allow it to enforce *hudud*. Indeed, the tabling of the Bill took place in 2016 and it was listed on the Parliament agenda, but it was never debated. Be that as it may, it has become almost customary for these debates around Islamic criminal law to revolve around the *political* question of which parties or coalitions display more commitment to Islamic interests and development (even if those 'interests' and 'development' are selectively and narrowly construed). The legal and institutional reform efforts by the Mahathir

[49] Except Kelantan and Terengganu, *Syariah* criminal enactments are almost identical (except for minor differences in the wording and organisation of the provisions) to the *Syariah* Criminal Offences (Federal Territories) Act 1997. The two states have retained *hudud* punishments on the books, but they have yet to be able to implement those punishments due to limitations on the *Syariah* courts' sentencing powers, as explained above. These enactments are applicable only to Muslims (this is typically stated in section 1 of the enactments), and they are organised into several parts covering, among other issues, offences relating to 'aqidah (creed), offences relating to the sanctity of Islam and its institutions, and offences relating to decency'. See, eg, *Syariah* Criminal Offences (Selangor) Enactment 1995 (Enactment No 9 of 1995), s 7; and *Syariah* Criminal Offences (Federal Territories) Act 1997, s 4. Both provisions deal with the offence of propagating 'false doctrine'.

[50] Implementing *hudud* would require a constitutional amendment.

administration from the 1980s were also, for the most part, a response to PAS and a way of assuring the Malay-Muslim electorate that the Government, too, was serious about championing Islam, albeit in a modern and progressive direction. This also served to placate concerns among non-Muslims about 'Islamisation' in the country.

What has often become secondary in these debates is the constitutional arrangements and dispensation – how and when they structure exercises of power in relation to Islam. The implications, as we have seen above, are significant. Religious federalism is set to become contested issue in the years to come. In a climate where politics is becoming more fragmented, where the constitutional culture is lagging behind, and where institutional weakness is prevalent, the elasticity and integrity of this arrangement will continue to be challenged and tested in ways that shape not only federal–state division of powers, but also state–religion relations, religious diversity and constitutional rights guarantees. More broadly, Malaysia's experience with religious federalism raises critical questions about the nature and characteristics of particular institutional arrangements on religion, and how they operate and evolve over time.

8

Gender Constitutionalism and Reproductive Politics – Lessons from Asia

MARA MALAGODI*

It is a great honour to write this short chapter in celebration of Professor Andrew Harding's extraordinary career and scholarship. I met Andrew in 2010, and over the past 14 years he has become a mentor, a collaborator and most of all a friend. This chapter on gender constitutionalism and reproductive politics with a comparative focus on Asia aims to showcase some of the lessons that I have learnt from Andrew over the years, to channel the spirit that informs his scholarly engagement, and ultimately to record my deepest admiration for him and his many contributions to the field of comparative constitutional law and Asian constitutionalism. This chapter begins with a brief biographical anecdote to explain how Andrew's scholarship on Asian constitutionalism has influenced my career trajectory. Then, it explores two elements of his longstanding intellectual engagement with Asian constitutional systems that have shaped my work. These two elements are as follows.

First, Andrew has always been vocal about the fact that Asia is integral to the advancement of comparative constitutional law as a global field of intellectual inquiry.[1] His scholarly engagement has also consistently highlighted that many innovative constitutional developments have been taking place across Asian jurisdictions, but they often go unacknowledged due to the Eurocentric bias of the discipline, except for the few 'usual suspects' such as India and Japan. Crucially Asia offers important constitutional lessons for the rest of the world, and the world should take notice. In 2006, Andrew reflected on the scope of comparative constitutional law from a deeply contextual perspective and from the vantage point of a scholar embedded in Asia:

> I do not wish to be seen as saying that constitutionalism in Asia must of necessity follow the general contours of Western constitutional history, although sometimes there are

* Thanks to Professor Peter Leyland for his very insightful and helpful comments on an earlier draft.

[1] Andrew Harding and Ngoc Son Bui, 'Recent Work in Asian Constitutional Studies: A Review Essay' (2016) 11 *Asian Journal of Comparative Law* 163.

> striking parallels between the two. Rather I would see new Asian constitutionalism as part of a global convergence towards a more just legal order.[2]

This approach was both empowering and liberating for me as a young scholar and continues to be the guiding light of my work.

Precisely for this reason, this chapter focuses on gender constitutionalism and reproductive politics. For instance, Nepal – a 'non-standard' jurisdiction in the corpus of comparative constitutional law – offers important lessons for the world with respect to the constitutional treatment of sexual and reproductive health rights (SRHR), punching well above its weight.[3] However, these lessons have regrettably not informed global discussions, strategies and campaigns about abortion, pregnancy care, sexual health and education, etc. More broadly, the comparative study of the constitutional treatment of abortion across a significant number of Asian jurisdictions provides us with a terrific comparative framework to understand the challenges and opportunity of gender constitutionalism in matters of reproductive autonomy. This is particularly important in the current climate in which questions of comparative constitutional law surrounding reproductive rights have been dominated and shaped almost entirely by American developments post-*Dobbs*.[4] The US anti-abortion movement has undoubtedly been a catalyst for global regressive reproductive politics worldwide with a pushback on abortion rights in many jurisdictions. However, there have been many progressive constitutional moves around the world to protect reproductive rights that provide crucial strategies to enhance reproductive rights.

Conversely, questions of reproductive politics cannot be disentangled from the constitutional treatment of gender and sexuality. Asian jurisdictions provide an enormous variety of culturally consonant approaches to gender fluidity and sexuality. These jurisdictions have also developed different strategies to navigate the complex terrain of colonial legacies, religious traditions and liberal reforms that merit meticulous comparative analysis. There is now a growing body of scholarship emerging from across the world demonstrating that Asian jurisdictions and other historically marginalised constitutional experiences teach important lessons for global developments. This body of scholarship is not just shifting the focus of the academic field of comparative constitutional law, but it is also informing the work of activists, civil society organisation, intergovernmental agencies, government bodies and judicial decisions. I believe Andrew's

[2] Andrew Harding, 'New Asian Constitutionalism: Myth or Reality?' (2006) 14 *International Islamic University of Malaysia Law Journal* 153.

[3] Mara Malagodi, 'Challenges and Opportunities of Gender Equality Litigation in Nepal' (2018) 16 *International Journal of Constitutional Law* 527; Mara Malagodi, 'Intersectional Inequalities and Reproductive Rights: An India-Nepal Comparison' (2020) 3 University of Oxford Human Rights Hub Journal 195.

[4] *Dobbs v Jackson Women's Health Organization*, 597 US 215 (2022).

pioneering approach to the study of Asian constitutionalism was instrumental in spearheading and supporting these recent developments rooted into cosmopolitan constitutional values geared at securing fairer and more inclusive legal frameworks.

Second, Andrew's contribution has not been solely of a scholarly nature. His work as an *impresario* of comparative constitutional law should not be overlooked as it has been crucial in shifting the jurisdictional focus of the discipline and placing the study of Asian constitutional systems at the centre of the field. In this respect, Andrew made an enormous contribution to the creation and fostering of scholarly networks in the domain of Asian constitutionalism. This sub-field has seen an exponential growth and much more close-knit forms of collaborations through joint publication initiatives in journals,[5] edited volumes[6] and book series,[7] scholarly conferences and networks such as the *Asian Constitutional Law Forum*,[8] and the support and nurturing of emerging academic talent through doctoral scholarships and postdoctoral fellowships alongside the inclusion of junior scholars into collaborative initiatives with leading scholars in the field. The list of the contributors to this collection is a testimony to Andrew's creation of a truly global network of scholars committed to the contextual study of Asian constitutional systems. So, this chapter is for you, dear Andrew, to express my gratitude for the unfailing support and constant inspiration that you have provided over the years – always with your charming wit and good humour.

[5] For instance, *Asian Journal of Comparative Law* (Cambridge University Press), *Asian Journal of Law and Society* (Cambridge University Press), *Asia-Pacific Journal on Human Rights and the Law* (Brill), *Asian Journal of Law and Policy* (MMU Press), etc.

[6] For instance, Tom Ginsburg and Albert HY Chen (eds), *Administrative Law and Governance in Asia: Comparative Perspectives* (Routledge, 2009); Albert HY Chen and Tom Ginsburg (eds), *Public Law in East Asia* (Ashgate, 2013); Wen-Chen Chang, Li-ann Thio, Kevin YL Tan and Jiunn-rong Yeh (eds), *Constitutionalism in Asia: Cases and Materials* (Hart, 2014); Tom Ginsburg and Rosalind Dixon (eds), Comparative Constitutional Law in Asia (Elgar, 2014); Albert HY Chen and Andrew Harding (eds), *Constitutional Courts in Asia: A Comparative Perspective* (Cambridge University Press, 2018); Po-Jen Yap (ed), *Constitutional Remedies in Asia* (Routledge, 2019); Rehan Abeyratne and Ngoc Bui Son (eds), *The Law and Politics of Unconstitutional Constitutional Amendments in Asia* (Routledge, 2022); Po-Jen Yap and Rehan Abeyratne (eds), Routledge Handbook of Asian Parliaments (Routledge, 2023); Ngoc Bui Son and Mara Malagodi (eds), *Asia Comparative Constitutional Law Vol 1: Constitution Making* (Hart, 2023); Ngoc Bui Son and Mara Malagodi (eds), *Asia Comparative Constitutional Law Vol 2: Amendments* (Hart, 2024); David Law, Holning Lau and Alex Schwarz (eds), *The Oxford Handbook of Constitutional Law in Asia* (Oxford University Press, forthcoming 2025); Ngoc Bui Son, Mara Malagodi and Christopher Roberts (eds), *Asia Comparative Constitutional Law Vol. 3: Structure* (Hart, forthcoming 2025; some chapters available at academic.oup.com/edited-volume/55080).

[7] See for instance, the new book series, 'Oxford Studies in Asian Laws' (Oxford University Press) created in 2024, www.law.ox.ac.uk/content/news/announcement-oxford-studies-asian-laws.

[8] See the 10th Biannual Forum of the ACLF to be held at the University of Hong Kong: ccpl.law.hku.hk/call-for-papers-10th-asian-constitutional-law-forum-december-2024-hong-kong.

I. Asia in Comparative Constitutional Law: A UK Perspective

I first met Andrew in 2010 at the Hart Workshop held at the Institute of Advanced Legal Studies (IALS) of the University of London, a few months after defending my doctoral thesis at the School of Oriental and African Studies (SOAS) on Nepal's constitutional developments. I was particularly excited to meet Andrew. Of course, his reputation preceded him: he had been the Head of the Law School at SOAS until 1999, he had created with Professor Peter Leyland the extraordinary series, 'Constitutional Systems of the World', for Hart Publishing that brought contextual approaches to the study of constitutional law at the centre of the discipline,[9] he had co-authored the book on Thailand in that very global series,[10] and he had already published an eclectic and groundbreaking body of work in the area of Asian comparative constitutional law.[11]

When I met Andrew, he was Professor of Asia-Pacific Legal Relations at the University of Victoria in Canada. He was not just the kind of constitutional scholar I deeply admired and aspired to become; he was also a beacon of hope. His career path represented both a range of exciting intellectual possibilities, but also a unique professional way of being. Andrew was able to build an extraordinary career at the time in which British public law academia was neither particularly comparative nor Asia-focused. It is also that specific context that makes Andrew's intellectual and professional achievements even more extraordinary. In fact, following the process of decolonisation in the 1950s and 1960s, the public law curriculum in most British law schools started to focus almost exclusively on the UK, with some modest comparisons with Global North jurisdictions. In fact, the discipline had radically moved away from what Ivor Jennings or Stanley De Smith were writing and teaching only a few decades before. For instance, a perusal of Jennings' syllabus for his Constitutional Law class in 1938–39 at the London School of Economics and Political Science (LSE) demonstrates that 'constitutional law of the Overseas Commonwealth and Empire' used to be seen as integral to the British

[9] 'Accessible, contextual introductions to the constitutional systems of the world'. See: www.bloomsbury.com/uk/series/constitutional-systems-of-the-world.

[10] Andrew Harding and Peter Leyland, *The Constitutional System of Thailand: A Contextual Approach* (Hart, 2011).

[11] For instance: Andrew Harding, 'The 1988 constitutional crisis in Malaysia' (1990) 39 *International & Comparative Law Quarterly* 57. Andrew Harding, 'Global doctrine and local knowledge: Law in Southeast Asia' (2002) 51 *International & Comparative Law Quarterly* 35. Andrew Harding, 'The "Westminster Model" constitution overseas: Transplantation, adaptation and development in Commonwealth states' (2004) 4 *Oxford University Commonwealth Law Journal* 143. Andrew Harding, 'Buddhism, human rights and constitutional reform in Thailand' (2007) 2 *Asian Journal of Comparative Law* 1. Andrew Harding and Peter Leyland, 'The constitutional courts of Thailand and Indonesia: Two case-studies from Southeast Asia' (2008) 3 *Journal of Comparative Law* 118.

Constitution and to the curriculum of UK law schools.[12] The end of Empire made British constitutional law a more inward-looking affair.

In terms of legal research, the contextual study of the legal systems of Asia and Africa in the UK became progressively relegated to the domain of law and anthropology with much emphasis on legal pluralism, personal laws, customs, cultural norms and religious law.[13] While these developments were crucial in developing law-in-context approaches to the study of law, they did not focus on constitutional law. In fact, the study of the constitutions of Asia and Africa was often linked to a focus on positivist law. As a result, very little emphasis was placed on the constitutional aspect of state governance and the comparative lessons that the contextual study of constitutional law beyond Europe, North America and selected Commonwealth jurisdictions could impart. This position developed notwithstanding the fact that constitutional law in postcolonial jurisdictions like India and Kenya amongst many others was both a thriving intellectual pursuit and a crucial domain of political engagement. Andrew's work was instrumental in bridging this gap between law-in-context approaches to constitutional law and the comparative study of constitutional law across Asia.

Andrew's professional advice singlehandedly changed the trajectory of my career. When I spoke to Andrew at IALS 15 years ago, I sought his views on how to pursue my interests in both constitutional law and Asia in the context of UK public law academia. With the pragmatism of a lawyer, Andrew said that it was crucial to bring British constitutional law and history in conversation with South Asian constitutional developments to enhance both. Over the years, I have felt profoundly vindicated by Andrew's approach to the study of Asian constitutional law and his goal of building a truly global field of comparative constitutional law, in which there were valuable lessons to be learnt from Asian jurisdictions as well, and not just the other way around. This was the crucial epistemic change that was needed in an otherwise still rather Eurocentric discipline. And not because we thought 'everyone should be interested in Asia' – as a senior colleague once insinuated – but because a discipline built on a skewed and exclusionary selection of jurisdictions as case studies is an intellectual endeavour that simply does not reflect reality and is methodologically weak.

Andrew's scholarship has been instrumental in challenging the Eurocentrism of the field of comparative constitutional law, in making Asia an integral part of the discipline and in shifting the epistemology of comparative constitutional law. This shift has been key to undermining conceptualisations of the rule of law and constitutional democracy as new forms of the 'white man's burden' with clear colonial roots. Andrew's impressive publication and teaching records have spearheaded these changes, but also his incredible ability to build scholarly networks with a

[12] Ivor Jennings' Private Papers at the Institute of Commonwealth Studies (ICS) at the University of London. ICS 125/D/3.

[13] See for instance the monumental body of work by Professors Simon Roberts and William Twining, but their scholarship was tangential at best to public law scholarship in the UK.

research focus on Asia, nurture a new generation of scholars across the globe, and provide publication outlets and professional opportunities for constitutional law academics working in Asia *and* on Asia. We all owe Andrew a great debt and our gratitude for his vision, and for pioneering these initiatives and networks.

II. Gender Constitutionalism: Lessons from Asia

The choice of gender constitutionalism as a topic to celebrate Andrew Harding and his work might seem an odd one as he has not engaged directly with this area of law. Nonetheless this chapter aims to show how far-reaching Andrew's contribution is to the field of comparative constitutional law through these examples. My recent work on gender constitutionalism in Asia follows in the footsteps of Andrew's approach to Asian constitutionalism much more than it would appear at first glance. For instance, the volume *Gender, Sexuality and Constitutionalism in Asia* built on pre-existing networks of scholars of Asian constitutional law that Andrew was instrumental in creating, adopted the deeply contextual approach that Andrew's scholarship has promoted, and capitalised on the momentum that the push to mainstream Asian constitutionalism had finally gained, in no small part thanks to Andrew's work.[14] Moreover, since the early 2000s, the area of gender constitutionalism has grown significantly as the equal citizenship status of women and sexual and gender diverse people (SGDP) has been increasingly fought for on the constitutional battlefield, at least in jurisdictions that broadly operate within the parameters of constitutional democracy. However, no systematic comparative constitutional analysis of Asian jurisdictions with respect to sex, gender and sexuality had been carried out until we started our collaborative project in 2019.

In our volume we aimed to assess the ability of constitutionalism to affirm and sustain the equal citizenship of women and SGDP. More specifically, we wanted to develop a comparative constitutional framework to assess to what extent constitutional law and litigation have been successful avenues to advance the equality claims of women and SGDP. Thus, we selected 12 Asian jurisdictions in which the constitutional domain has been crucial to gender equality claims. In short, the aim was to map the opportunity structures internal and external to the Constitution for the advancement of gender equality. This endeavour required a deeply contextual analysis of the constitutional domain in each of the Asian case studies included in the volume, upon which we developed from a bottom-up perspective a qualitative comparative framework. By way of example, one of the aspects that we investigated in our comparative analysis was the relationship between gender architecture and constitutional change (taken to encompass both the making of a new constitution and constitutional amendments). We garnered two main comparative insights.

[14] Wen-Chen Chang, Kelley Loper, Mara Malagodi and Ruth Rubio-Marín (eds), *Gender, Sexuality and Constitutionalism in Asia* (Hart, 2024).

First, the moment of constitution-making determined only to a certain extent the recognition of gender equality. Constitutional texts drafted in more recent times feature more explicit and extensive forms of constitutional guarantees in matters of gender equality in line with global cosmopolitan developments. In fact, more recent constitutions, such as the 2015 Constitution of Nepal, feature extensive sections on justiciable fundamental rights protecting and empowering women and SGDP, alongside far-reaching affirmative action measures, Directive Principles of State Policy and 'pink quotas' reflecting what is considered global best practice and in line with international advice. Older constitutions, instead, did not feature at the time of promulgation extensive references to gender or sex, even as prohibited grounds of discrimination or even any at all, for instance Indonesia, Malaysia and Singapore.[15] Instead, a number of constitutions since 1997, such as Taiwan, Japan, South Korea and Hong Kong, recognise sex and/or gender as prohibited grounds of discrimination. Others, such as India, Pakistan, Sri Lanka, and the Philippines, went a little further and included limited forms of affirmative action measures for women, alongside non-discrimination clauses.

The temporal dimension is however just indicative and does not determine by itself specific instances of gender-based discrimination at the time of constitution-making. A much more contextual analysis of the individual case studies is required. For instance, gender-based discrimination in terms of the inability of women to pass on their citizenship featured both in the 1965 Constitution of Singapore and in the 2015 Constitution of Nepal at the time of promulgation. In 1965 this type of framing was not uncommon; instead in the case of Nepal it points to specific political concerns about the demographics of certain groups, especially those living in the areas adjacent to the open border with India. In fact, Singapore amended the Constitution's citizenship clause in 2004 to ensure gender equality in line with international standards,[16] while Nepali lawmakers have shown no intention to do so notwithstanding repeated calls by international bodies and domestic activists to make the new Constitution compliant with international law.[17]

Second, constitution-making processes that feature the inclusion of women and SGDP representatives amongst the ranks of their constitution-makers (or that have at least embraced the gender equality demands of civil society actors) tend to produce more gender-inclusive constitutional texts. However, in line with most of the literature on constitution-building, we concluded that the degree of

[15] Andrew's book on Malaysia in the Hart series 'Constitutional Systems of the World' explores in depth the question of discrimination and engages with the conflicting approaches to these issues in the context of Islamisation; for instance, the ratification of The Convention on the Elimination of all Forms of Discrimination Against Women (CEDAW) despite countervailing trends. Andrew Harding. *The Constitution of Malaysia: A Contextual Approach* (Hart, 2022).

[16] Daryl WJ Yang and Jaclyn Neo, 'Gender Equality in Singapore: Wither the Constitution?' in Wen-Chen Chang, Kelley Loper, Mara Malagodi and Ruth Rubio Marín (eds), *Gender, Sexuality, and Constitutionalism in Asia* (Hart, 2024) 173–200.

[17] Mario Gomez, 'Women, Gender and the Constitution in Sri Lanka' in Chang, Loper, Malagodi and Rubio Marín (n 16) 281–310.

inclusion and participation of diverse voices in the constitution-making process did not necessarily guarantee a more inclusive outcome even in terms of gender equality. Nepal was again a case in point. Even with 33 per cent of women in both Constituent Assembly the citizenship chapter discriminated against women with respect to passing on their citizenship.[18] Conversely, the presence of Sunil Babu Pant – Asia's first openly gay MP – in Nepal's first Constituent Assembly was instrumental in having the rights of sexual and gender minorities recognised in the text of the 2015 Constitution in a groundbreaking development. In fact, our comparative analysis of the 12 case studies in the volume did not offer straightforward answers as much depended on contextual factors specific to each of the case studies. A participatory and inclusive constitution-making process fosters the legitimacy of the constitutional transition, but it is not in itself sufficient because it ultimately depends on whether those diverse voices are reflected in the outcome of the constitution-building process.

In terms of constitutional lessons that the study of gender constitutionalism in Asia offers, it is argued that the advancement of LGBTQI+ rights goes hand-in-hand with the progressive treatment of sexual and reproductive health rights (SRHR), and that they are both integral to the advancement of gender constitutionalism. This kind of claim cannot be made without deploying a contextual approach. Let us start with a striking set of developments surrounding transgender rights. South Asian jurisdictions have recently pioneered innovative postcolonial constitutional solutions to move beyond the gender binary in constitutional adjudication, legislative and policy reforms, and even constitution-making. The recent constitutional recognition of gender nonconforming identities that have existed in South Asia for centuries has been inextricably intertwined with the historical legal treatment of gender and sexuality since colonial times. Over the past 15 years successful constitutional litigation on the legal recognition of non-binary gender identities in Nepal (*Sunil Babu Pant*, 2007, 2017),[19] Pakistan (*Dr Khaki*, 2009–12),[20] and India (*NALSA*, 2014)[21] had a cascading effect leading to the translation of removal of harm as non-discrimination into positive entitlements for gender nonconforming individuals through new legislative and policy developments across these jurisdictions Significantly, nonbinary gender recognition culminated in the inclusion of LGBTQI+ individuals into the text of Nepal's new 2015 Constitution, the only one in Asia – and one of the few in the world – to recognise explicitly the rights of sexual and gender minorities. A similar attempt to recognise explicitly LGBTQI+ rights has been made in Sri Lanka during the 2016 constitutional reform process, but it remains to be seen whether the final document will do so.[22]

[18] ibid.

[19] *Sunil Babu Pant v Government of Nepal* NKP 2065 Vol 50 N.4 485.

[20] *Dr Muhammad Aslam Khaki v SSP (Operations) Rawalpindi* PLD 2013 SC 188.

[21] *NALSA v Government of India* AIR 2014 SC 1863.

[22] Mario Gomez, 'Women, Gender and the Constitution in Sri Lanka' in Chang, Loper, Malagodi and Rubio Marín (n 16) 339–65.

On the one hand, local cultural notions of non-binary gender identities (eg, Sanskrit-era 'third nature' and Mughal-era '*khawaja sira*') have been deployed as effective advocacy tools by activists to advance LGBTQI+ constitutional rights in an otherwise socially conservative milieu. Judges across South Asia have looked favourably at these links to local history and culture put forward by activists, and adopted the nomenclature of 'third gender', '*khawaja sira*' and 'third nature' to justify their decision and partly shield themselves from accusations of being 'Westernised' by relying exclusively on international legal standards and foreign precedents, while distancing themselves from the colonial treatment of gender, for instance the criminalisation of gender-non conforming communities under the Criminal Tribes Act 1871 applied mainly in the northern regions of British India. On the other hand, South Asian forms of gender constitutionalism suffer from similar pitfalls that can be explained comparatively through their comparable constitutional structures, and shared legal and cultural history linking gender and sexuality. These include emphasis on heteronormative and patriarchal local cultural and religious notions (eg, Sanskrit-era '*kliba*' to denote any form of deviation from culturally constructed notions of masculinity) and the enduring legacy of colonial legal interventions (eg, 'sodomy laws' and the criminalisation of 'eunuchs').

As a result, the focus on non-binary gender identity as an autochthonous socio-cultural identity marker has been instrumentally deployed by the post-colonial states to sideline questions of sexual orientation. This is particularly problematic since so-called 'sodomy laws' remain in force in Pakistan, Bangladesh and Sri Lanka, while India only decriminalised in 2018 via constitutional litigation in the landmark *Navtej Johar* case,[23] and Bhutan in 2020 via legislative intervention.[24] In 2023, Pakistan's Federal Shariat Court ruled in *Hammad Hussain* that the Pakistan Transgender Persons (Protection of Rights) Act 2018's provision on self-declaration of legal gender was un-Islamic and invalidated it, citing the fact that individuals might fall foul of the enduring colonial-era 'sodomy laws' that continue to criminalise same-sex intimacy in the country. Similarly, the use of 'third gender' in Nepal to classify the entire LGBTQI+ spectrum has erased the identities of binary-identifying transgender and gender non-conforming individuals, alongside those identities based on sexual orientation. In the 2022 case of *Adheep Pokhrel*, Nepal's Supreme Court stated in *obiter* that the terms 'third/other gender' should be superseded, and that gender self-identification should be mandated in accordance with the 2015 Constitution.[25]

These case studies encapsulate groundbreaking legal development that help think beyond the gender binary in the constitutional sphere and provide important comparative constitutional lessons for debates and reforms in other jurisdictions

[23] *Navtej Johar v Union of India* AIR 2018 SC 4321.

[24] On 10 December 2020 the Parliament of Bhutan voted to repeal ss 213–214 of the Penal Code on 'unnatural sex'.

[25] *Adheep Pokhrel v Government of Nepal* Writ N 079-WO-0198 (decided 19 December 2022).

grappling with the same legal questions. In 2023, the expert report in support of Rukshana Kapali's case in the Supreme Court of Nepal, eventually published as an article in the *University of Pennsylvania Journal of International Law*, sought to harness contextual approaches to comparative constitutional law to support forms of legal activism seeking constitutional inclusion.[26] Ms Kapali, a binary transgender woman, sought to identify as female on her identity documents, not as 'third gender' or 'other'. Ms Kapali legally challenged government authorities that had rejected her repeated requests. The Supreme Court ruled in favour of petitioner Rukshana Kapali on 6 November 2023 but handed down its full judgment only in August 2024, paving the way for the advancement of trans rights in Nepal. The socio-political implications of the legal categorisations on the basis of sex, gender and sexuality are far-reaching as they shape a crucial modality of belonging to the polity. Conversely, the constitutional treatment of forms of non-reproductive sexuality and the stigma traditionally associated with them illuminates the remit and extent of sexual and reproductive health rights.

III. Rethinking Reproductive Politics from an Asian Perspective

Reproductive politics has been historically associated with women's struggles to secure bodily self-determination on an individual level, but it is also about reproduction of the body politic on both a symbolic and biopolitical level.[27] The notion of reproductive politics has shifted over time and questions of gender identity and sexual orientation are critical to understanding these debates and developments. In this respect, the constitutional sphere has become a crucial battlefield for competing visions about the scope and limits of reproductive choices and policies. In fact, the notion of sexual and reproductive health rights includes the constitutional and legal frameworks surrounding the issues of abortion, contraception, sexual health, maternal health, surrogacy, sterilisation, sex education and education supporting informed reproductive decisions. The nature of these rights, their extent and degree of implementation have always been politically contested terrain.

In Asia, like in the rest of the world, deeply patriarchal social mores have shaped the dominant legal structures regulating reproduction and patrolling sexuality. These legal frameworks have been designed to exercise control people's bodies, ossify patriarchal hierarchies and reinforce both the gender binary and heteronormativity. Broadly speaking, sexual activity has been condoned only if for reproductive purposes and within heterosexual marriage. Asian jurisdictions

[26] Holning Lau and Mara Malagodi, 'Legal Gender Recognition in Nepal and Comparative Context' (2024) 45 *University of Pennsylvania Journal of International Law* 269.

[27] Nira Yuval-Davis and Floya Anthias, 'Introduction' in Nira Yuval-Davis and Floya Anthias (eds), *Woman-Nation-State* (Palgrave Macmillan, 1989) 1, 7.

broadly operating within the parameters of constitutional democracy offer crucial comparative insights into the constitutional dimension of reproductive politics. They feature different approaches depending on whether the political or judicial branches dominate the debate, and factors internal and external to the constitutional system provide crucial explanatory value.

At the one end of the spectrum, we find more recent constitutions that include a vast array of justiciable fundamental rights. For instance, the 2015 Constitution of Nepal includes specifically, under the rights of women, a right to safe motherhood and reproductive health, while the non-justiciable Chapter of Directive Principles, Policies, and Responsibilities of the State under the provision on social inclusion reiterate the importance of securing reproductive services and facilities. The clear constitutional underpinning of these rights since the promulgation of the 2007 interim Constitution has enhanced the centrality of Nepal's Supreme Court, which has handed down groundbreaking decisions in this area. In Nepal abortion was partially legalised only in 2002; until then it featured one of the most repressive legal regimes in the world. In 2010, the Supreme Court issued a landmark judgment in the case of *Lakshmi*, in which abortion rights were deemed to be at the core of sexual and reproductive rights and integral to the right against discrimination and the right to equality.[28] It held that abortion equates to the right to self-determination for women and as such it holds a special place within reproductive rights. It clearly stated that a woman is the master of her own body and must have the final word in deciding whether to have sexual relations, when to give birth to a child, and how to use her body.

The Court also held *in obiter* that the criminalisation of abortion disproportionally impacts women, and that abortion should be entirely decriminalised. More specifically, it ruled that it was inappropriate to criminalise abortion, since under Nepali law the foetus is not classified as human life. Thus, the foetus cannot be granted more importance than the protection of the physical and mental health of the mother. The Court concluded that a forced pregnancy and a forced continuation of pregnancy constitute violence against women. Nepal's Parliament, however, did not follow the Court's recommendations to decriminalise abortion entirely. Abortion outside the scope of Section 15 of the Safe Motherhood and Reproductive Health Rights Act 2018 remains a criminal offence under Section 188 of Nepal's new Penal Code in Chapter 13, Offences against the Protection of Pregnancy. Significantly, any termination beyond the 28-week gestational limit regardless of reason – even if the pregnant person's life is at risk – attracts criminal sanctions. Thus, constitutional litigation demanding the complete decriminalisation of abortion both for pregnant women and service providers has been pending in the Constitutional Bench of the Supreme Court since 2021; this petition which I have helped draft has relied extensively on the *Lakshmi* decision, comparative

[28] *Lakshmi v Office of the Prime Minister* 2067, 52(9) NKP 1551 (2010).

legal analysis and international human rights standards.[29] In this respect, Nepal has been urged to decriminalise abortion both by the CEDAW Committee in 2018 and during the Universal Periodic Review in 2021.[30] Efforts are under way also to lobby the legislature to decriminalise on its own initiative rather than in response to judicial intervention.

At the opposite end of the spectrum, Singapore's Constitution does not protect gender at the constitutional level, but the People's Action Party delivered on its electoral promise to foster gender equality by enacting the Women's Charter as early as 1961. Thus, most reforms towards gender equality have been executive driven. Unsurprisingly, Singapore features one of the most permissive abortion laws in the world. Adopted in 1969, this legislation was motivated more by economic pragmatism demanding women's participation into the workforce rather than constitutional concerns about individual bodily autonomy and dignity.[31] On an intermediate position of the spectrum, jurisdictions where there is a significant influence of religion on state authorities and political legitimacy have suffered setbacks in the advancement of SRHR. In South Korea, it was only in the wake of the 2018 #MeToo movement that a broad coalition succeeded in persuading the Constitutional Court to decriminalise abortion in a bold jurisprudential move, notwithstanding the longstanding opposition of religious forces.[32] In the Philippines, due to the prominent role of the Catholic Church, the life of the foetus was granted explicit constitutional protection, and the penal law retains to this day a complete ban on abortion, with the judiciary and the political branches so far unwilling to intervene.[33] Colonial legacies and religious influences are also a crucial hurdle to the accessibility of abortion service, such as in Hong Kong, where many women have been travelling to Mainland China to obtain pregnancy terminations.

Asian case studies teach us an important lesson with respect to SRHR. It is in the jurisdictions in which the political branches have spearheaded reforms in matters of SRHR that the place of these rights is the most secure and their implementation most effective. Nepal is a case in point with its state-of-the-art constitutional jurisprudence on SRHR that should be included in any comparative constitutional law analysis on the subject. However, the legislative articulation of these rights is

[29] Bandana Upreti and Samana Kafle v. Government of Nepal (Writ No 077 of year 2077). Petition filed on 7 March 2021.

[30] Centre for Reproductive Rights and FWLD, 2021. *Decriminalisation of Abortion in Nepal: Imperative to Uphold Women's Rights*. Available at: https://reproductiverights.org/wp-content/uploads/2021/06/Decriminalization-of-Abortion-in-Nepal_02June021_-Final-Version-1.pdf.

[31] Yang and Neo (n 16).

[32] Constitutional Court of Korea, 2017 Hun-Ba 127 (11 April 2019). See: Yoon Jin Shin, 2024. 'Gender Equality, Individual Empowerment, and Constitutional Rights Review: South Korea's Dynamic Development' in W. Chang, K. Loper, M. Malagodi, and R. Rubio Marín (eds) *Gender, Sexuality, and Constitutionalism in Asia* (Hart), 117–144.

[33] *Imbong v Ochoa*, GR No 204819, 732 Phil 1 (8 April 2014). See: Bryan Dennis G Tiojanco, 'Gender, Sexuality, and Constitutionalism in the Philippines' in Chang, Loper, Malagodi and Rubio Marín (n 16) 201–30.

partly in contradiction with the Supreme Court's jurisprudence, and the implementation of SRHR is often very limited due to both lack of resources and political will. At a time in which reproductive rights are under attack around the globe, Asian jurisdictions impart crucial lessons to rejuvenate reproductive politics and devise constitutional strategies for the advancement of SRHR and gender constitutionalism more in general. These important lessons about the centrality of Asian constitutional experiences to global debates would not have been possible without the renewed interest in Asian constitutional law that Andrew's scholarship was able to ignite.

IV. Conclusions

Andrew Harding's work opened the way to the mainstreaming of Asian constitutional law into comparative constitutional law. Andrew's strategy has been multipronged: first-class scholarly publications on Asian comparative constitutional law, policy and public engagement; the revision of law school curricula; the creation of scholarly networks; professional associations and publication outlets; alongside his ability to mentor new generations of academics in the field. All of this has taken place over an extraordinary career spanning decades that took Andrew across the globe. This process of mainstreaming Asian constitutional law is by no means complete, but it is under way, and now appears to be both momentous and irreversible. Andrew's visionary and truly global approach to the field of comparative constitutional law has made a crucial contribution to the advancement the discipline from which we are all benefitting. It is with gratitude and admiration that I dedicate these reflections to Andrew.

9

Moving Forward in a Backward Democracy: Reflections on the Thai Constitutional Court's *Lèse-Majesté* Campaign Decision

RAWIN LEELAPATANA

I. Introduction

On 31 January 2024, the Thai Constitutional Court (CC) found itself once again embroiled in a political dispute between the dominant royalist-conservative faction and its pro-democracy counterpart. The conflict at issue involved the daring campaign launched by the left-wing, pro-democracy Move Forward Party (MF) to democratically reform Thailand's *lèse-majesté* law in S-112 of the Criminal Code prior and during the run-up to the general election in May 2023. The CC eventually affirmed the necessity of S-112 and thereby the dominance of the royalist establishment. My main focus in this chapter is not the legitimacy of S-112 per se, but rather the theoretical implications of the CC's approach and precedent for liberal constitutionalism. In this chapter, I ask: *How and to what extent does the* lèse-majesté *campaign decision affect the development of liberal constitutionalism in Thailand?*

This chapter proceeds by examining the context in which the calls for S-112 reform took place (section II) before delving into the details of the MF's proposal (section III). After elaborating the CC's 2024 decision (section IV), section V analyses its effects on the three dimensions of liberal constitutionalism – legal, political and social. The chapter argues normatively that Thai constitutionalism should be liberal. The January decision constitutes an example of how the CC's ruling conflicts with Thailand's pursuit of liberal constitutionalism and the younger generation's aspirations for democratisation. This chapter is connected to Professor Andrew Harding's writing on Thai constitutionalism and the CC.

It shares his concerns about the CC's partisan decisions in highly political cases and their effects on the country's polarised politics, as well as his desire for democratisation in Thailand.[1]

II. An Ultra-Royalist Right-Wing Turn in Post-2014 Thailand

Starting in 2006, the contemporary tussle for political dominance between the dominant royalist–military alliance and its pro-democracy counterpart has plunged Thailand into a series of mass protests, street violence and acts of vandalism. While the latter advocates political liberalisation and demilitarisation, the former embraces the form of royalist democracy formally known as 'the Democratic Regime with the King as Head of State' (DRKH), which seeks to bring parliamentary politics under the tutelage of the royalist-conservative elites.[2] For the royalist-conservative elites and the military, the King embodies the unity of the Thai nation, and thereby occupies the fulcrum of its security.[3]

Repelled by the sturdier anti-establishment movements and the approaching end of the revered King Bhumibol's 70-year reign (1946–2016), the royalist-backed junta – the National Council for Peace and Order (NCPO) – eventually carried out the most recent coup in May 2014 to reinforce royal hegemony under the DRKH.[4] The 2014 coup has significantly escalated the climate of 'hyper-royalism', the term coined by Thongchai Winichakul to describe 'the divinization of royals, their pervasive visual and discursive presence in the "space and time" of everyday life, and strict limits on what can be said about the monarchy.'[5] The rampant use of S-112 by the military is integral in actualising this project.[6] The provision makes it illegal for any individual 'to defame, disparage, or insult the King, the Queen, the Crown Prince, and the Regent', with anyone knowing its violation allowed to file complaints with the police. Conviction carries prison terms of three to 15 years. The NCPO-leader-turned-prime-minister Prayuth Cha-ocha showed no qualms

[1] Andrew Harding and Peter Leyland, 'The Constitutional Courts of Thailand and Indonesia: Two Case Studies from South East Asia' (2008) 3 *Journal of Comparative Law* 118.

[2] Thongchai Winichakul, 'Toppling Democracy' (2008) 38 *Journal of Contemporary Asia* 11, 20–21.

[3] Kevin Hewison and Kengkij Kitirianglarp, 'Thai-Style Democracy' in Søren Ivarsson and Lotte Isager (eds), *Saying the Unsayable: Monarchy and Democracy in Thailand* (Nordic Institute of Asian Studies, 2010) 187–88.

[4] Prajak Kongkirati and Veerayooth Kanchoochat, 'The Prayuth Regime: Embedded Military and Hierarchical Capitalism in Thailand' (2018) 6 *Trans-Regional and -National Studies of Southeast Asia* 279, 281.

[5] Serhat Unaldi, *Working towards the Monarchy: the Politics of Space in Downtown Bangkok* (University of Hawaii Press, 2016) 41; Thongchai Winichakul, *Thailand's Hyper-royalism: Its Past Success and Present Predicament* (ISEAS – Yusof Ishak Institute, 2016) 2–10.

[6] Kanokrat Lertchoosakul, 'The Paradox of the Thai Middle Class in Democratisation' (2021) 9 *TRaNS-Regional and -National Studies of Southeast Asia* 65, 75; Tyrell Haberkorn, 'A Hyper-Royalist Parapolitics in Thailand' (2016) 172 *Bijdragen tot de Taal-, Land- en Volkenkunde* 225, 227–28.

about boldly resorting to this provision to eliminate purported threats to the monarchy.[7]

Despite the reinstatement of some semblance of electoral politics and the parliamentary assembly under the junta-initiated 2017 Constitution, post-2020 youth-led protests for monarchy reform instigated pervasive *lèse-majesté* charges. Between November 2020 and February 2024, more than 260 individuals were accused of royal defamation, 20 of whom were aged below 18.[8] Sedition charges were sometimes brought again S-112 offenders.[9] Moreover, the courts have expanded the scope of S-112 to cover defamatory or offensive behaviours directed at 'the monarchy as an institution' and other actions such as sharing an article containing content critical of King Vajiralongkorn (2016–present), mocking his utterance, and spraying anti-S-112 messages on his portraits.[10] Worried by the situation, the MF chose to campaign for reforming S-112.

III. The MF's Proposed Reform of the *Lèse-Majesté* Law

The MF was a left-wing political party, with Pita Limjaroenrat serving as its first leader. The party sought to carry on progressive policies initiated by its dissolved predecessor, the Future Forward Party (FF), including decentralisation, demilitarisation, the creation of a welfare state, same-sex marriage, the abolition of compulsory military conscription and, most daringly, the reform of S-112.

In 2021, led by Pita, 44 MPs of the MF initiated the *lèse-majesté* law amendment Bill. Fundamentally, the Bill sought to abolish S-112, which is listed as 'an offence related to the security of the kingdom' under Title 1 of the Criminal Code, with the *lèse-majesté* offence transferred to the new Title 1/2, 'Offences related to the dignity of the King, the Queen, the Heir-apparent, and the dignity of the Regent'. Were the Bill to become law, royal insult would no longer be classified as a public offence but as a compoundable one, with a maximum penalty being a year in jail or a fine of THB300,000. Additionally, the Bureau of Royal Household (BRH) would be the only body permitted to bring *lèse-majesté* complaints, with 'honest and fair criticisms' of the monarchy exempted from legal consequences

[7] 'Lese-majeste explained: How Thailand forbids insult of its royalty' BBC (6 October 2017), www.bbc.com/news/world-asia-29628191.

[8] 'สถิติผู้ถูกดำเนินคดีมาตรา 112 "หมิ่นประมาทกษัตริย์" ปี 2563–67' ['Statistics on individuals prosecuted under S-112 "Defaming the King" in 2020-24'] TLHR (16 February 2024), tlhr2014.com/archives/23983.

[9] 'Thailand: Sedition, lèse-majesté charges against protesters proliferate' Article 19 (25 November 2021), www.article19.org/resources/thailand-sedition-lese-majeste-charges-against-protesters-proliferate.

[10] 'มาตรา 112 แก้ไข ≠ ยกเลิก ≠ ล้มล้าง' ['S-112 amended ≠ Abolition ≠ Overthrow'] Thairath (24 May 2023), plus.thairath.co.th/topic/politics&society/103221; 'Decoding Thailand's lese majeste law' *The Isaan Record* (7 February 2021), theisaanrecord.co/2021/02/07/decoding-thailands-lese-majeste-law; 'Thai activist gets prison for sharing king's profile on Facebook' BBC (15 August 2017), www.bbc.com/news/world-asia-40938914.

('the exemption clause').[11] The Bill no doubt stirred outrage among the pro-establishment parties and the NCPO-appointed Senate, and was undoubtedly blocked from being presented before Parliament.

In the run-up to the general election in May 2023, the MF listed the reform of S-112 as one of its campaigns. Having garnered more than 14 million votes, to a surprise of many, the party clinched the highest number of seats in Parliament (151 of 500).[12] Despite their initial frustration, however, the 2017 Constitution gives the royalist-conservative faction considerable leeway to veto the election outcome. In contrast to other parliamentary systems, the NCPO-picked Senate of 250 members were allowed to join with MPs to elect the prime minister.[13] Having explicitly expressed their disdained towards the MF's call for amending S-112, conservative MPs and most of the senators either voted against or abstained from voting for Pita, making him unable to secure enough votes to take over as prime minister.[14] Outside Parliament, a series of lawfare was launched against Pita and the MF, including the *lèse-majesté* campaign case.

IV. The *Lèse-Majesté* Campaign Case

The *lèse-majesté* campaign lawsuit was initiated by Theerayuth Suwankesorn, a lawyer representing Suwit Thongprasert, an ultra-royalist former monk. The case was processed through the procedures set out in the 'militant democracy clause' (MDC) in S-49 of the 2007 Constitution.[15] S-49 allows anyone with knowledge of attempts to use constitutionally guaranteed rights and liberties to overthrow the DRKH to request the Attorney-General to examine the matter.

As the Attorney-General failed to take action within 15 days, the 2017 Constitution allows the claimant, Theerayuth, to present his claim straight to the CC. In general, his main accusation made before the CC was that by initiating the lèse-majesté Bill and advocating for S-112 reform in the run-up to the election, Pita and the MF violated S-49. To gain full comprehension of the 2024 decision, it is useful to first examine the patterns of how the MDC has been construed as well as the CC's stance in Thailand's intractable political conflict.

[11] For details of the MF's Bill (available at drive.google.com/file/d/1mfL3j0-AbLxVAL8Z0lod8jTn8wh_DaQV/view?fbclid=IwY2xjawJgt9hleHRuA2FlbQIxMAABHso88rlilb46Tt--QD1rDkUVXBj_W6g-hYjlSoVhrSum8tqtlzmj56CrtDig_aem_WE3xTUXnHpFSr2qg6SKmgg) see Napon Jatusripitak, 'Thailand's Lèse-majesté Law: A Subtle Referendum in the Upcoming Elections?' Fulcrum (21 April 2023), fulcrum.sg/thailands-lese-majeste-law-a-subtle-referendum-in-the-upcoming-elections.

[12] 'Thailand's tectonic political shift' Eastasiaforum (11 November 2023), eastasiaforum.org/2023/11/11/thailands-tectonic-political-shift.

[13] The 2017 Constitution, s 272.

[14] 'Article 112 makes Pita fail to get enough votes to become PM' Khaosodenglish (13 July 2023), www.khaosodenglish.com/news/2023/07/13/article-112-makes-pita-fail-to-get-enough-votes-to-become-pm.

[15] See Karl Loewenstein, 'Militant Democracy and Fundamental Rights, II' (1937) 31 *The American Political Science Review* 638, 644.

Initially incorporated in the 1997 Constitution, widely heralded as Thailand's most democratic constitution, the MDC was originally designed to prevent the recurrence of another military coup.[16] Nonetheless, over the course of the two decades of intermittent political turmoil, the provision has been turned into a convenient means for the royalists to veto majoritarian politics. This is partially galvanised by higher costs and risks for protecting royal hegemony through a military coup raised by studier liberal demands fostered by the 1997 Constitution.[17] In parallel with this, a closer relationship between the judiciary and the royalist-conservative faction has also been fostered, with many pro-establishment supporters appointed as CC judges.[18]

The CC has construed 'acts of overthrowing the DRKH' to encompass a broad range of actions that their proponents claimed to be essential for political liberalisation. Examples of these actions include an attempt to dissolve the junta-appointed Senate[19] and calls for monarchy reform.[20] On the contrary, between 2013 and 2014, the Court ruled that the pro-monarchy protests constituted a proper exercise of the right to freedom of political expression guaranteed by the then 2007 Constitution. This series of CC orders, however, disregarded the protesters' anti-democracy actions of disrupting the general election process and assaulting people who attempted to exercise their right to vote.[21]

As we can see, the above decisions and orders turned the MDC into a mechanism for consolidating the dominance of the monarchy against intermittent calls for democratisation and demilitarisation. In a broader picture, the CC's decisions during the political conflict tend to be more hostile to political parties than the military. Between 2008 and 2024, it dissolved three major political parties stigmatised by the royalist-conservative faction as threats to the throne, including the FF.[22] However, it upheld the legitimacy of the 2014 coup and even helped streamline Prayuth's ultra-royalist rule.[23] The *lèse-majesté* campaign decision was a more recent instance that lawfare was waged against a purported anti-establishment political party, with a rigid standard of proof adopted and most of the MF's defences disregarded.

[16] 'สภาป้องกันรัฐประหาร' ['Assembly for Pre-empting Future Coups'] Thairath (10 May 2017), www.thairath.co.th/newspaper/columns/935717.

[17] Michael K Connors, 'Article of Faith: The Failure of Royal Liberalism in Thailand' (2008) 38 *Journal of Contemporary Asia* 143, 143–44.

[18] Björn Dressel and Khemthong Tonsakulrungruang, 'Coloured Judgements? The Work of the Thai Constitutional Court, 1998–2016' (2019) 49 *Journal of Contemporary Asia* 1, 11.

[19] CC Decision No 15-18/2556 (2013).

[20] CC Decision No 19/2564 (2021).

[21] eg, CC Orders No 45/2557 (2014), 50/2557 (2014). Rawin Leelapatana and Suprawee Asanasak, 'Constitutional Struggles and Polarised Identities in Thailand: The Constitutional Court and the Gravitational Pull of Thai-Ness upon Liberal Constitutionalism' (2022) 50 *Federal Law Review* 156, 165.

[22] CC Decision No 3/2562 (2019); CC Decision No 5/2563 (2020).

[23] eg, Decision No 5/2551 (2008); CC Decision No 29/2563 (2020); CC Decision No 30/2563 (2020).

The CC began by upholding the reasoning from its earlier decision[24] that S-112 is integral for protecting the King's sacred and inviolable status and thereby the DRKH as 'the honour of the King is constitutive of the nation's dignity'.[25] In general, it did not completely close off possibilities for amending this provision, but required that this be carried out through 'an appropriate legislative process'.[26] Though the nine judges did not elaborate on what constitutes the appropriate process as such, they unanimously concluded that the MF's S-112 Bill failed to meet this requirement.

Having asserted that the King and the Thai nation have coexisted and are inseparable, the nine judges highlighted the importance of the monarchy as the cornerstone of national security and unity. They ultimately regarded the MF's proposal to remove royal defamation from Title 1 of the Criminal Code as a downplaying of the significance of the *lèse-majesté* offence, as well as an endeavour 'to detach the monarchy from the Thai nation, which posed an imminent threat to national security'.[27]

Additionally, the CC ruled against the MF's proposal for the exemption clause. The nine judges asserted that this demand would effectively enable parties to S-112 proceedings to use materials that 'allude to or accuse the monarchy' to prove whether the factual circumstance in dispute falls within the clause as such or not, a consequence blatantly contradicting Section 6 of the 2017 Constitution which guarantees the King's sacred and inviolable status.[28]

Moreover, the CC stated that making royal defamation a compoundable offence would 'lower the protection status of the monarchy', which 'would be offensive to the feelings of the Thai people who love and respect the monarchy'.[29] In the meantime, the Court claimed that if the BRH were designated as the only qualified plaintiff in S-112 proceedings, the monarchy 'would be [ultimately] enmeshed in a conflict with the people'. Again, this would undermine the King's sacred and inviolable status under Section 6 of the 2017 Constitution.[30]

Apart from examining the substance of the S-112 Bill, a number of incidents prompted the CC to conclude that the MF itself held an antagonistic view towards S-112. These include the facts that some of its MPs had actively participated in anti-establishment protests which eventually led to calls for monarchy reform between 2020 and 2021, with many others using their position as MPs to bail out S-112 offenders. Pita's vote-canvassing speech and action, expressing his personal support for the repeal of S-112, was also referred to by the CC.[31] In addition to these, the Court maintained that the MF's 'intention to reduce protection of the

[24] CC Decision CC No 28-29/2555 (2012).
[25] CC Decision No 3/2567 (2024) 25.
[26] ibid, 33.
[27] ibid, 26.
[28] ibid, 26–27.
[29] ibid, 27.
[30] ibid.
[31] ibid, 29–31.

monarchy' was further shown by the fact that it was the only political party that persisted in the agenda of amending S-112 notwithstanding Parliament having previously rejected it.[32] Campaigning for this in the run-up to the election even signified the party's intention to turn the sacred monarchy into a mere means for garnering public support.[33]

Ultimately, the CC ruled that Pita and the MF had acted in violation of S-49, and ordered them to stop campaigning for S-112 abolition through whatever means.[34]

V. Analysis of the *Lèse-Majesté* Campaign Decision

Before analysing how the *lèse-majesté* campaign decision impacts Thailand's trajectories of liberal constitutionalism, I must first provide an overview regarding the core ideas of this concept. Nowadays, it can hardly be disputed that liberal constitutionalism has become a global discourse that appeals to of all stripes of governments, not just democratic ones.[35] This idea accordingly sets a benchmark for 'a desirable state of affairs'.[36]

In general, liberal constitutionalism assumes individuals to be rational and self-governing rightsholders, with authoritarianism castigated for hindering their ability to 'pursue their own version of the good life'.[37] It instead insists on 'freedom *from* state interference' – individual liberties are '*in principle unlimited*', with state power to transgress into this realm placed under *legal restraints*.[38] From this underlying assumption, its three dimensions can be deduced – legal, political and social.[39] It should be noted that the political and social dimensions share a common trait: both recognise the legislature as the representative of the people. However, they differ in that the political dimension is more institutionalised, while social counterpart involves the mobilisation of activists. Below, I analyse how the 2024 decision affect each dimension.

[32] ibid, 27–28.
[33] ibid, 28.
[34] ibid, 32–33.
[35] Paul Blokker and Chris Thornhill, 'Sociological Constitutionalism: An Introduction' in Paul Blokker and Chris Thornhill (eds), *Sociological Constitutionalism* (Cambridge University Press, 2017) 1.
[36] Thio Li-ann, 'Varieties of Constitutionalism in Asia' (2021) 16 *Asian Journal of Comparative Law* 285, 285.
[37] Andrew Hambler, *Religious Expression in the Workplace and the Contested Role of Law* (Routledge, 2015) 62.
[38] Rune Slagstad, 'Liberal constitutionalism and its critics: Carl Schmitt and Max Weber' in Jon Elster and Rune Slagstad (eds), *Constitutionalism and Democracy* (Cambridge University Press, 1988) 104–05.
[39] Leelapatana and Asanasak (n 21) 161–63; Victor V Ramraj, 'Constitutional Tipping Points: Sustainable Constitutionalism in Theory and Practice' (2010) 1 *Transnational Legal Theory* 191, 193–99.

A. The Legal Dimension

Central to the legal dimension of liberal constitutionalism ('the legal dimension') is 'the normative priority of legality's value'.[40] This means that *ex ante* legal authorisation is a prerequisite for the exercise of legal authority by all state organs, with the independent and impartial judicial review process institutionalised to ensure that state power is wielded within its remit.[41] As a result, state officials can claim to 'act qua state' only on the basis of law.[42] In the absence of this, individuals will fall prey to the 'norm-less will' of the state.[43] The impacts of the *lèse-majesté* campaign decision on the legal dimension involve two issues. The first concerns the composition of the panel that delivered this decision, while the second pertains to the correct application of law.

To explicate the first issue, we need to first look at the composition of the 2017 CC. The 2017 CC is composed of nine judges of whom are five career judges (three Supreme Court judges and two Administrative Court judges), two are selected from academia (one each from among prominent law professors and political science professors), and the remaining two must be either a former Attorney-General or deputy Attorney-General, or a former Director General.[44] The nine judges sitting in the 2024 decision were all selected by the NCPO-established bodies. Shortly after its seizure of power, the NCPO promulgated the Interim Constitution of 2014, which established the National Legislative Assembly (NLA), comprising 200 members chosen by the junta, to carry out both legislative functions and grant approval for the selection of judges to the CC.[45] The 2017 Constitution allows these NLA-selected judges to continue in office.[46] Meanwhile, names of judges who joined the panel after 2017 were endorsed by the NCPO-picked Senate of 250 members.[47] Ostensibly, these processes run against the legal dimension's underlying principles of judicial impartiality and independence. The name of the CC President himself, Nakarin Mektrirat, heightened this concern. Before being appointed the CC judge, Nakarin, a former political science professor at Thammasat University, had written a book that glorifies

[40] Lars Vinx, *Hans Kelsen's Pure Theory of Law: Legality and Legitimacy* (Oxford University Press, 2007) 31.

[41] MJ Peterson, 'Legislatures' in Anthony F Lang and Antje Wiener (eds), *Handbook on Global Constitutionalism*, 2nd edn (Edward Elgar, 2023) 424–25.

[42] David Dyzenhaus, 'The Compulsion of Legality' in Victor V Ramraj (ed), *Emergencies and the Limits of Legality* (Cambridge University Press, 2008) 36.

[43] William E Scheuerman, 'Carl Schmitt's Critique of Liberal Constitutionalism' (1996) 58 *Review of Politics* 299, 314–15.

[44] Thailand's Constitution of 2017, s 200.

[45] ibid, s 263; Thailand's 2014 Interim Constitution, s 6.

[46] Thailand's Constitution of 2017, s 273.

[47] ibid, ss 204, 269.

the monarchy, and appointed by the NCPO to serve as the drafter of the 2017 Constitution.[48]

Secondly, it is also problematic, both practically and theoretically, for the CC to treat the S-112 amendment Bill proposal as falling within the purview of S-49, which only provides room for investigation over whether an individual exercised his/her constitutionally guaranteed rights and liberties in such a way that subverts the DRKH. Apparently, S-49 is enshrined in Chapter III of the 2017 Constitution, 'Rights and Liberties of the Thai People'. Taking a literal interpretation of this provision, the term 'the *rights and liberties* to overthrow [the DRKH]' in its first paragraph can only be referred to those articulated in Chapter III, which does not include a submission of draft legislation, a process that is stipulated in Chapter VII – 'Parliament'. Meanwhile, from the theoretical perspective, the submission of draft legislation is integral to the legislative function, which is a manifestation of public authority rather than an exercise of individual rights.[49] Based on the above analysis, by straying into the realm of parliamentary affairs, the CC in the *lèse-majesté* campaign case went beyond its legal jurisdiction, in effect, reflecting 'A bad faith approach to interpreting and implementing [legal] obligations.'[50]

More importantly, in the 2024 decision, the defence of the monarchy *qua* the fulcrum of national security was used as a justification for expanding the reach of S-49 beyond its literal scope. This effectively leads to 'the logic of the state of exception' (SoE) – the idea that a commitment to legality can be legitimately suspended in the interest of national security – being more deeply '[imprinted] upon the concepts of legal authority and accountability' in Thailand.[51]

B. The Political Dimension

The political dimension of liberal constitutionalism, meanwhile, emphasises 'the importance of Parliament-based mechanisms in fostering core values of a liberal-democratic constitution.'[52] By providing a forum for competing interests to voice, debate and eventually reconcile their divergent viewpoints, such mechanisms are crucial not just for averting an enactment of legislation that facilitates an

[48] นครินทร์ เมฆไตรรัตน์ [Nakarin Mektrirat], พระผู้ทรงปกเกล้าฯ ประชาธิปไตย: *60* ปี สิริราชสมบัติกับการเมืองการปกครองไทย [*The Protection of Thai Democracy: 60 Years on the Throne and Thai Political Administration*] (Thammasat University, 2007).

[49] Bogdan Lancu, *Legislative Delegation: The Erosion of Normative Limits in Modern Constitutionalism* (Springer, 2012) 8; Piyabutr Saengkanokkul's comment: www.youtube.com/watch?v=Lm7w7fY0WMQ.

[50] Daniel Ghezelbash, 'Hyper-Legalism and Obfuscation: How States Evade Their International Obligations towards Refugees' (2020) 68 *The American Journal of Comparative Law* 479, 485.

[51] Carl Schmitt, *Political Theology: Four Chapters on the Concept of Sovereignty, translated by George Schwab* (University of Chicago Press, 2005) 6–7, 26; Leelapatana and Asanasak (n 21) 171.

[52] Leelapatana and Asanasak (n 21) 162.

authoritarian rule by '[prioritising] one interest at the expense of [the] other', but also for monitoring the exercise of state power.[53]

Following the precedent set by the *lèse-majesté* campaign decision, royalists may resort to S-49 to thwart the passage of any future draft law they regard as inimical to the monarchy's hegemonic status. Such precedent endows the future CC with full legitimacy to apply the MDC to usurp Parliament's authority to oversee the enactment of legislation especially through parliamentary debates.[54] It even turns the CC judges into the ultimate arbiter who decides what constitutes 'a proper legislative process'. Moreover, the 2024 decision carries with it overtones of 'elitist condemnation' that the parliamentary system is nothing but a nest of 'self-interested, factional, and unpatriotic politicians'.[55] This justifies the royalist defence of retaining 'veto power on majoritarian politics'.[56]

Overall, by giving the CC more authority to venture into the legislature's preserved domain and confirming its superior legitimacy, the *lèse-majesté* campaign decision undermines the importance of Parliament-based mechanisms in promoting political pluralism and checks and balances on the exercise of state authority. In the process, it effectively hinders the political dimension from becoming institutionalised 'as the primary ground of political authority'.[57]

C. The Social Dimension

Finally, the social dimension of liberal constitutionalism ('the social dimension') calls for 'the protection of individual rights' against arbitrary government intervention and the application of law, with 'the people' seen as instrumental in bolstering the Government's *social legitimacy*.[58] This dimension thereby encourages the people to play an active role in providing checks on the exercise of state power. To accomplish this, a variety of techniques can be used, 'such as influencing agenda setting, fostering political mobilization, gaining bargaining leverage, raising awareness of issues, and creating new alliances'.[59]

Contrary to the notion of 'active citizenry' that underpins the social dimension, the conservative rationale that most Thais are benighted people who tend

[53] Ramraj (n 39) 196–97; Hans Kelsen, *General Theory of Law and State* (Anders Wedberg (tr), Harvard Univrsity Press, 1945) 13.

[54] *cf* Piyabutr's comment above.

[55] Rawin Leelapatana, 'Thailand's Competing Notions of Constituent Power: The Making of the 2017 Constitution in the Binary-Star Scenario' in Son Ngoc Bui and Mara Malagodi (eds), *Asian Comparative Constitutional Law, Vol 1: Constitution-Making* (Hart Publishing, 2023) 330.

[56] Eugénie Mérieau, 'Thailand's Deep State, Royal Power and the Constitutional Court (1997–2015)' 46 *Journal of Contemporary Asia* 445, 451.

[57] Leelapatana (n 55) 331.

[58] ibid, 162–63; Li-ann (n 36) 288–89; Peterson (n 41) 424.

[59] Devyani Prabhat, *Unleashing the Force of Law: Legal Mobilization, National Security, and Basic Freedoms* (Palgrave, 2016) 2.

to be easily deceived by unpatriotic politicians is evidently reflected in the *lèse-majesté* campaign decision. This partially justified the CC's strict standard of proof imposed upon the MF.[60] Plus, by ruling that the MF's push for public discussion over the S-112 amendment and its enforcement would bring about public scepticism of the monarchy which possibly results in the overthrow of the DRKH, the CC's precedent sets a limitation for the social dimension and more fully accepts the idea of 'a two-tier space for civil society activism'.[61] It confirms that the Thai people are allowed to exercise their right to freedom of expression to discuss and criticise to the extent that it does not subvert the monarchy. With regard to monarchy-related topics such as the status of S-112, their role is nonetheless restricted to 'protecting' and 'acclaiming' royal hegemony.[62] As a result, the ruling aligns more favourably with the mobilisation of S-112 supporters within the real-world political arena, while simultaneously exhibiting an inclination to subject reformists – regardless of their aim to ensure accountability in the use of this provision for the sake of the monarchy's long-term stability – to royalist vigilantism.[63] The ruling ultimately ingrains the conservative rationale that 'the politics of inclusion and exclusion based on groups and individuals' identity', rather than the idea of universal human dignity, determines the protection of political rights in the Thai constitutional system.[64]

VI. Conclusion

The precedent set by the *lèse-majesté* campaign decision does not bode well for Thailand's quest for 'genuine' democracy and liberal constitutionalism. More importantly, such democratic subversion not only intensifies the phenomenon of hyper-royalism, but also fosters the growth of the other two Hs: hyper-legalism and hyper-moralism. Apparently, the approach to the interpretation of S-49 adopted by the CC 'proliferates … zones of exception' cloaked with a veneer of legality.[65] Apart from that, the 2024 ruling effectively infuses the Thai constitutional topography

[60] CC Decision No 3/2567 (2024) 28; David Streckfuss, *Truth on Trial in Thailand* (Routledge, 2011) 28.

[61] Rawin Leelapatana and Chompunoot Tangthavorn, 'The Constitutional Court and civic activism in polarised Thailand since 2014: turning back time?' in Amy Barrow and Sara Fuller (eds), *Activism and Authoritarian Governance in Asia* (Routledge, 2023) 109.

[62] Rawin Leelapatana and Abdurrachman Satrio Pratomo, 'The Relationship Between a Kelsenian Constitutional Court and an Entrenched National Ideology: Lessons from Thailand and Indonesia' (2020) 14 *ICL Journal* 497, 508.

[63] Rawin Leelapatana, 'The Gravitational Pull between Liberalism and Authoritarianism in Thailand's Color-Coded Politics: Civil Society in a Binary-Star-System' in Anthony J Spires and Akihiro Ogawa (eds), *Authoritarianism and Civil Society in Asia* (Routledge, 2023) 54.

[64] Leelapatana and Asanasak (n 21) 172.

[65] James Martel, 'The Law of Rules: Hyperlegalism, Emergency and the Violence of Procedure' (2021) 17 *Law, Culture and the Humanities* 53, 56–57.

with 'a fanatical obsession with clean politics and a disdain for politicians'.[66] As it turns out, the decision heightens the tension between the royalist-conservative faction and the younger generation, making political reconciliation between both sides more flickering, if not absolutely impossible, than ever before.

[66] Khemthong Tonsakulrungruang, 'Thailand's Obsession with Clean Politics Dismantles its Democracy' Verfassungsblog (2 March 2020), verfassungsblog.de/thailands-obsession-with-clean-politics-dismantles-its-democracy.

10

Independence Captured: Thailand's Independent Accountability Agencies and Democratic Backsliding

KHEMTHONG TONSAKULRUNGRUANG

I. The Overlooked Accomplice

For the past two decades, Thai politics has been characterised by the rise of a judiciary that frequently intervenes in electoral politics through its aggressive and arbitrary judicial review. In a phenomenon known as judicial activism, the Constitutional Court abruptly changes Thailand's political landscape when it dissolves major political parties, bans hundreds of politicians from politics, removes prime ministers and declares key policies unconstitutional.[1] Such judicial manoeuvring challenges the notion of separation of power and causes serious tension within the constitutional system. It also draws much attention to the judiciary, specifically to the Constitutional Court. Scholars write extensively about the role of the Constitutional Court in contributing to Thailand's political turmoil.[2] These studies shed light on how the crisis is developed and maintained through expansive judicial review. However, a focus on the Constitutional Court can easily lead onlookers of Thai constitutional law to miss the lesser known accomplice of watchdog agencies, or independent accountability agencies (IAA).

The Constitutional Court cannot act alone. It needs other bodies (the IAA) to investigate complaints and refer cases to the Court. In 1997, Thailand introduced a group of constitutionally entrenched, autonomous agencies specialised in

[1] Bjoern Dressel and Khemthong Tonsakulrungruang, 'Colored Judgements? The Work of the Thai Constitutional Court, 1998–2016' (2019) 49 *Journal of Contemporary Asia* 1, 4–6; Khemthong Tonsakulrungruang, 'Entrenching the Minority: The Constitutional Court in Thailand's Political Conflict' (2017) 26 *Washington International Law Journal* 247, 254–67.

[2] See Eugenie Meriaeu, 'Democratic Breakdown Through Lawfare by Constitutional Courts: The Case of Post-"Democratic Transition" Thailand' (2022) 95 *Pacific Affairs* 475; Yap Po Jen, 'The Constitutional Court of Thailand and Partisan Judges' in Yap Po Jen, *Courts and Democracies in Asia* (Cambridge University Press, 2017).

enforcing accountability upon the political branches. Almost 30 years have passed since the concept of IAA was first introduced. It is one of few surviving legacies of the 1997 Constitution. It is expanded every time Thailand drafts a new constitution. However, once hailed as a success, they now play a critical role in triggering a constitutional crisis. For example, the Election Commission (EC) and National Anti-Corruption Commission (NACC) obstructed political process and set the stage for *coup d'état* twice, in 2006 and 2014.[3] Public trust in IAA quickly eroded. But despite the critical role they play, little is discussed about evaluating IAA's performance and analysing the mistake in designing them. IAA deserves much more attention.

This chapter focuses on what has been missing from the current studies of IAA. It does not look at a specific body, but the overall concept of IAA. It does not address the technical issues, for example, of how to empower or strengthen IAA; to make them more effective or efficient. Instead, it asks a series of fundamental questions. What exactly is IAA? What does it mean to be independent? Most importantly, what has gone wrong? This chapter argues that an independent watchdog is a commendable idea implemented amidst an illiberal environment, leading to its independence being captured.

Section II explores the concept of IAA, tracing its beginning that defies the conventional separation of power in non-Western democracies, and Thailand's adoption. Section III then looks at Thailand's transplantation of the idea into its 1997 Constitution. It asks how IAA is placed within the Thai constitutional system. Section IV concerns the work of IAA in democratic backsliding scenario, with emphasis on the EC and NACC. Section V identifies mistakes in designing the agencies and discusses challenges in correcting these issues.

II. The Origin of IAA: The Fourth Branch of Power

Constitutional democracy can only thrive if all players respect the text and norms laid down by the Charter itself. Every player keeps its assigned role and tries not to usurp others'. Separation of power prevents a ruler from becoming a tyrant. The legislative, executive and judiciary are meant to check one another.

But this conventional separation of power is seemingly no longer adequate to foster a vibrant democracy.[4] That arrangement of a parliament, a cabinet and a court does not always work out. Often, the executive controls the majority in the house, therefore the two branches are captured by the same political faction that the house is not willing to scrutinise the cabinet. Instead, they collude to dominate

[3] Khemthong Tonsakulrungruang, 'Thailand: an abuse of judicial review' in Po Jen Yap (ed), *Judicial Review of Elections in Asia* (Routledge, 2016); Khemthong Tonsakulrungruang, 'Thailand's Forgotten Key' New Mandala (10 June 2014), www.newmandala.org/thailands-forgotten-key.

[4] Mark Tushnet, *The New Fourth Branch of Power* (Cambridge University Press, 2021) 11–14. See also, Bruce Ackerman, 'The New Separation of Powers' (2000) 113 *Harvard Law Review* 633.

the political landscape. A strongman founds a party under which every MP stays loyal to him, not to the Constitution.[5] The court, meanwhile, is too passive or too incompetent to review the rogue government. This problem is particularly acute in a new democracy where unwritten norms that could have served as internal, unofficial restrains are yet to develop and mature. As a result, constitution-drafters in the Global South look for a practical solution. They experiment with a new group of constitutional bodies that is not part of the three conventional branches. This fourth branch of power is a recent innovation.

Why would a jurisdiction need an extra branch of power? The first reason is the need for expertise. The idea of the fourth branch is a hybrid between administrative and constitutional law. As the modern administrative state has to deal with increasingly complicated issues, there grows the need for an impartial expert decision on those matters.[6] Naturally, that leads to the creation of a new type of agency, an independent regulatory agency that can deliver expertise isolated from political interference. These regulatory agencies still belong to the administrative branch under the cabinet's control, but they stay at arm's length.[7] The executive appoints them, but their decision-making is shielded from the executive's direction. Their tenure guarantees that they can only be removed for a specific cause, not at the will of a politician. Independent agency is hoped to revitalise the decaying administration which is captured by business interest and politicians' short-sightedness.[8] It provides the government with informed decisions. Most of them are concerned with scientific research, nuclear power, financial markets, commerce, the environment, workplace safety, highway traffic, and so on, while a few are tasked with certain functions, either in auditing the government's spending or managing an election.[9]

The second function is integrity. Democracy relies on the trust of the people that politicians are still representing them and not sold to the highest bidder.[10] If people are convinced that politics is all about enriching themselves and cronies, trust erodes and democracy is doomed. The integrity branch that operates outside normal political structure could provide much needed checks upon the politicians and bureaucrats.[11]

[5] See Kim Lane Scheppele, 'The Party's Over' in Mark Graber, Sanford Levinson and Mark Tushnet (eds), *Constitutional Democracy in Crisis?* (Oxford University Press, 2018); Mouli Banerjee '"Here", There, and Everywhere: Locating the Political Party in Democratic Transitions and Backslides' in Tom Daly and Dinesha Samararatne (eds), *Democratic Consolidation and Constitutional Endurance in Asia and Africa* (Oxford University Press, 2024) 88–90.

[6] Frank Vibert, *The Rise of the Unelected* (Cambridge University Press, 2007) 42–54.

[7] Martin Shapiro, 'A Comparison of US and European Independent Agencies' in Susan Rose-Ackerman and Peter L Lindseth (eds), *Comparative Administrative Law* (Edward Elgar, 2010) 294295.

[8] Vibert (n 6) 2.

[9] ibid, 19–30.

[10] Ackerman (n 4) 694.

[11] ibid,.

The concern of integrity is sure in the mind of Sun Yat Sen, the founder of modern China. Writing for the emerging republic, Sun Yat Sen tried to combine the western concept of separation of power with the oriental tradition. He identified the flaw of the conventional tripartite separation of legislative, executive and judiciary. Although the check function rests within the executive, under the President's command, that function could never work.[12] Instead, Sun proposes having an independent check body, drawing the idea from the ancient Chinese administration that had an independent officer to travel and investigate wrongdoing outside the Emperor's control.[13] Sun's idea resulted in Taiwan's Five-Power Constitution where two additional powers, the Control Yuan and the Examination Yuan, are introduced.[14] The Control Yuan of Taiwan is directly elected from the people and operates away from political oversight.[15] It investigates a wide range of misconduct, from disciplinary infraction to serious crime.[16] Despite its broad jurisdiction, its power is only recommendatory: the administration decides whether to pursue legal or disciplinary action per the Control Yuan's recommendation.[17]

But the fourth branch goes beyond busting an abuse of power. The new branch is installed to act as a guarantor of constitutional norms too.[18] A constitution contains fundamental values that it holds dear, for example, the rule of law, accountability, transparency and human rights. Politicians may attempt to encroach upon these norms which place limits upon their exercise of power. An independent body helps safeguard those norms through both expressive and material capacities.[19] It could send a signal to every player in that field that such norm is to be upheld, and it could enforce such norm as well.

Generally, the fourth branch of power includes anti-corruption, election management, human rights, budgetary auditing, and truth and reconciliatory bodies. It may also refer to the ombudsman, general comptroller or public prosecutor. Each body fulfils the three purposes – expertise, integrity and constitutional norms – but with different priorities. An election commission would require an expertise in managing a vote and axing a cheating candidate, preventing a prospective corrupt politician from entering into politics. A human rights commission is concerned less about corruption since it enshrines the principle of human and civil rights. The same goes for a truth and reconciliation, or a multi-cultural, body, whose power is mostly declaratory but not punitive. An auditor, meanwhile, is an expert in investigating fiscal irregularities.

[12] Herbert Ma, 'Chinese Control Yuan: An Independent Supervisory Organ of the State' (1963) 1963 *Washington University Law Quarterly* 402.

[13] ibid, 403–04.

[14] Jiunn-Rong Yeh, *The Constitutional of Taiwan: A Contextual Analysis* (Bloomsbury, 2016) 52–54.

[15] Constitution of the Republic of China, Art 91.

[16] ibid, Arts 97–98; 2019 Annual Report of the Control Yuan (2020) 2–3.

[17] Yeh (n 14) 123–25.

[18] See Tarunabh Khaitan, 'Guarantor Institutions' (2021) 16 *Asian Journal of Comparative Law* 540, 545–50.

[19] ibid, 553–58.

When does a country need the fourth branch of power? There is no hard and fast rule. The fourth branch is entirely optional, unlike the conventional three powers which have become a canon of modern democracy. The fourth branch is more common in new democracies. A more fragile regime, especially after a major trauma, is very vulnerable to political capture. Trust in conventional political institutions is low. Thus, a new organism outside the old structure could gain more trust to safeguard the system.[20] One of the best examples is South Africa. After Apartheid ended, the new Constitution introduced agencies to oversee election, corruption and reconciliation.[21] Together, they are known as Chapter 9 agencies. They are appointed by the House, but are not part of the House or the Presidential branch. They report their work to the House, but are not subject to the House's control.[22] Latin American and Asian countries have also introduced them.[23] Some fourth branch institutions are grouped together under a specific title, as in the South African Constitution, but many are scattered throughout a constitution.[24]

A constitutionally independent body specialised in integrity and accountability is only part of a larger phenomenon: the rise of the judiciary or the judicialisation of politics. When conventional political mechanisms fail to adequately restrain politicians, people turn to rely on the court to replace or supplement these mechanisms. Political parties and parliamentary processes are increasingly inadequate in restraining politicians so the Supreme Court or the Constitutional Court take that role.[25] They turn political dispute into a legal case and settle it not by vote or political convention, but law. The fourth branch takes what were formerly administrative jobs and assists the court by investigating and referring cases to the bench.

III. Introduction of the Thai IAA

In 1992, Thais rose up against the Government of General Suchinda Kraprayoon, the military leader of the 1991 coup, in the incident known as the Black May.[26] Suchinda agreed to resign after at least 44 were killed and many more were injured

[20] John Ackerman, 'Understanding Independent Accountability Agencies' in Rose-Ackerman and Linsedseth (n 7) 271–72.

[21] The Constitution of the Republic of South Africa 1996, ch 9.

[22] ibid, Art 181(2); Christina Murray, 'The Human rights Commission et al: What is the Role of South Africa's Chapter 9 Institutions?' (2006) 9 *Potchefstroomse Elektroniese Regsblad* 127.

[23] Ackerman (n 20) 272.

[24] ibid, 272–73.

[25] See Aharon Barak, *The Judge in a Democracy* (Princeton University Press, 2006) 27–35; Luis Roberto Barroso, 'Countermajoritarian, Representative, and Enlightened: The Roles of Constitutional Courts in Democracies' (2019) 67 *The American Journal of Comparative Law* 109.

[26] Chris Baker and Pasuk Phongpaichit, *A History of Thailand*, 4th edn (Cambridge University Press, 2022) 277–78.

or reported missing by the military's use of deadly force. Suchinda's resignation was considered to mark the end of the four decades of military intervention in Thai politics. The jubilant people then demanded political reform and a new constitution which could permanently prevent another coup and consolidate Thailand's fragile democracy.[27] On a larger scale, Thailand was joining the wave of liberalisation in East Asia where the emerging middle class toppled the military dictators, similar to Taiwan and Korea.[28]

Why did Thai constitutions repeatedly fail? Corruption was identified as the major cause of the vicious cycle where the Government became so corrupt that it lost public trust, triggering a coup to cleanse politics; the junta drafted a new Constitution and allowed an election that reinstated these politicians before another corruption scandal hit the administration; hence, another coup.[29] Constitution-drafters must think beyond the question of designing an efficient political process, eg an electoral system and a legislative procedure. They must figure out how to introduce a thicker version of democracy beyond a majoritarian rule to include more substantive norms, such as transparency and good governance. Moreover, they have to consider how to safeguard the new system. It is obvious that politicians – short-sighted, selfish and corrupt – were inadequate to shoulder such tasks.

A series of studies on a prospective reform was conducted in 1995 and would later become the basis of the 1997 Constitution design. Researchers, many of whom would later be appointed drafters, understood that the existing legal mechanism could no longer address the problem because they were placed in the administrative branch, under the cabinet's oversight. Thus, they proposed creating a cohort of autonomous bodies to provide checks on politicians. The research series suggested that the new Thai politics would require independent regulatory bodies of experts to improve the Government's efficiency as well as a number of independent bodies dealing with accountability, namely the constitutional court, the anti-corruption commission and the electoral management body.[30] Taiwan's Control Yuan was used as a case study,[31] but the final design of Thailand's independent accountability agencies bore little resemblance to Taiwan's.

The 1997 Constitution introduced a number of constitutionally entrenched, politically independent bodies: the Constitutional Court; the Administrative Court; the EC; the National Anti-Corruption Commission (NACC); the Ombudsman; the

[27] ibid, 279; Prawase Wasi, 'An Overview of Political Reform' in Duncan McCargo (ed), *Reforming Thai Politics* (NIAS Press, 2002) 21–22.

[28] See Jiunn-Rong Yeh and Wen-Chen Chang, 'The Emeregence of East Asian Constitutionalism: Features in Comparison' (2011) 59 *American Journal of Comparative Law* 805.

[29] Andrew Harding and Peter Leyland, *The Constitutional System of Thailand: A Contextual Analysis* (Hart Publishing, 2011) 18–21.

[30] See chs 5, 7 and 11– 15 of Thanapol Ewsakul (ed), การปฏิรูปการเมืองไทย: ฐานคิดและข้อเสนอว่าด้วยการออกแบบรัฐธรรมนูญฉบับประชาชน ปี 2540 [*Thailand's Political Reform: Original Concepts and Proposal for Designing the People's Constitution 1997*] (Thailand Research Fund, 2017).

[31] Borwornsak Uwanno, 'ระบบการตรวจสอบทุจริตของผู้ดำรงตำแหน่งระดับสูง' ['Designing Counter-Corruption Measures for High-Ranking Office Holders'] in Thanapol (n 30) 591–94.

National Human Rights Commission (NHRC); and the National Economic and Social Advisory Council. These either elevated existing administrative agencies or were created anew.

Initially, these agencies were scattered throughout the 1997 Constitution under different chapters, leading to confusion, but eventually agreement was reached that constitutionally independent organisations included the NACC, the EC, the Audit Commission, the NHRC and the Ombudsman. These bodies all shared some common traits.[32] First, they were established not by parliamentary statute, but by the Constitution itself. Second, their main mission was restoring the accountability of politicians and high-ranking bureaucrats. Third, they were nominated by a committee, comprised of limited numbers of representatives from political parties, the judiciary and civic society, before an approval by the senate. Fourth, they enjoyed operational, budgetary and personal autonomy. Fifth, their tenure was very secure; their office outlasted the Lower House's four-year term and they could not be dismissed unless specified by the law. Lastly, they were still subject to a certain level of accountability – mostly criminal liability in case of serious crime – or impeachment,[33] but they were largely free from judicial review. Thus, IAA was a non-partisan body that belonged to none of the three conventional branches of power. It was subject to little or no political oversight at all, and it occurred mostly at the vetting stage, not in its operation. Its mandate came directly from the Constitution, not the Government.

IAA is the only enduring legacy of the 1997 Constitution. Other ideals, such as direct public participation, decentralisation, and strong and stable government, are already gone. Two coups and two constitutions later, IAA remains stronger than ever. It evolves, though. The 2007 Constitution tried to clarify the concept of IAA by defining the EC, Ombudsman, NACC and Audit Commission as constitutionally independent organisations while defining the Attorney General, NHRC and Economic and Social Advisory Council as 'other constitutional organizations'.[34] No drafter could precisely define the latter. The 2017 Constitution classified the EC, the NACC, the Audit Commission, the Ombudsman and the NHRC under the heading 'Independent Organization', which is the closest to the idea of IAA.[35]

The biggest change is how IAA is recruited. Under the 1997 Constitution, half of the Commission were former Supreme Court judges nominated by the Supreme Court of Justice.[36] The other half was nominated by an ad hoc nomination committee comprised of the President of the Supreme Court of Justice, the President of the Supreme Administrative Court, presidents of public universities on behalf

[32] Distat Hotrakitya, 'องค์กรของรัฐที่เป็นอิสระในระบบกฎหมายไทย' ['Independent Governmental Agencies in Thai Legal System'] in Narongdech Srukosit (ed), แทนดอกไม้ไหว้ครู รวมบทความทางวิชาการด้านกฎหมายเนื่องในโอกาสวันคล้ายวันเกิดปีที่ 60 ของศาสตราจารย์ ดร. วิษณุ เครืองาม [*A Memo to Commenmorate Professor Wissanu Kreu-ngam's 60th Birthday*] (S Chareon Press, 2011) 43–49.

[33] ibid, Art 134.

[34] The Constitution of Thailand BE 2550 (2007), ch 11.

[35] ibid, ch 12.

[36] For example, see the Constitution of Thailand BE 2540 (1997), Art 138 (2).

of the civil society, and MPs.[37] Candidates would later be confirmed by the non-partisan Senate, which, in 1997, was elected directly.[38] But the combination of an ad hoc nomination committee was changed under the 2007 Constitution, which removed university presidents and reduced the number of MPs from four to two, to be replaced by one representative each from the Supreme Court of Justice and the Supreme Administrative Court.[39] Therefore, the judiciary played a more critical role. Finally, the 2017 Constitution sets up an ad hoc committee comprising of the President of the Supreme Court of Justice, the Speaker of the House of Representatives, the Head of the Opposition, the President of the Supreme Administrative Court, and representatives of all other independent bodies.[40] The process is therefore becoming more exclusive and homogenous. Moreover, since 2007, an indirect change to IAA is senatorial confirmation. The Senate has moved form being half-appointed, half-elected in 2007 to being fully appointed, by the military junta, from 2017 to 2024.[41] The change in the Second House severed the remaining ties of IAA with the people.

In reality, these provisions were not always observed. The 2006 junta directly appointed the NACC without parliamentary consent.[42] The National Assembly Council, which under the control of Prayuth Chan-ocha, the head of the Council of Peace and Order that staged a coup in 2014, appointed the majority or all of the Constitutional Court, the NACC, the EC, and the Auditor General, even after the 2017 Constitution had come into effect.[43]

IV. IAA and Democratic Backsliding

The first few years of the 1997 Constitution were promising. An election was considered free and fair. The EC handed candidates 'red' and 'yellow' cards for possible frauds.[44] The NACC investigated many politicians for failure to truthfully declare their assets and irregular wealth. One case involved a public health minister who was sentenced to 15 years' imprisonment and had more than THB200 million confiscated.[45] Another case concerned a deputy prime minister who was banned from politics for five years because he did not fully disclose his

[37] ibid, Art 138 (1).
[38] ibid, Art 121.
[39] For example, see 2007 Constitution, Art 231.
[40] 2017 Constitution, Art 217.
[41] ibid, Art 107.
[42] The Decree of the Council of Democratic Reform No 19 BE 2549 (2006).
[43] '8 ปี คสช. สภาแต่งตั้งเลือกสรรคนไปเป็น "องค์กรตรวจสอบ"' ['Over 8 years, the NCPO appointed members of the Watchdog Agencies'] iLaw (2 June 2022), www.ilaw.or.th/articles/5228.
[44] Harding and Leyland (n 29) 63.
[45] 'Thai ex-minister found guilty of corruption' Australian Broadcasting Corporation (28 October 2003), www.abc.net.au/news/2003-10-28/thai-ex-minister-found-guilty-of-corruption/1500788.

properties.[46] The Ombudsman and the NHRC actively investigated human rights violations and other cases against the state. In one famous case, the Ombudsman referred to the Constitutional Court section 12 of the Personal Name Act BE 2505 (1962) which mandated that a married woman shall adopt her husband's last name. The Constitutional Court agreed with the Ombudsman that section 12 was contrary to the equality clause in the 1997 Constitution, and therefore invalid.[47] The decision was hailed as a major breakthrough for gender equality in Thailand and the Ombudsman was praised for such advanced reading of the law. Overall, IAA was able to bring integrity into the constitutional system and earned much respect from the public.

In 2001, Thaksin Shinawatra ascended to power. A tycoon-cum-politician, Thaksin was fast-thinking and innovative, qualities that made him very popular. He launched several policies that addressed the grassroot majority who had long been neglected.[48] But Thaksin was also ruthless. His administration was tainted by terrible human rights record. Thaksin gave police *carte blanche* during the war on drugs to extra-judicially cull drug dealers, resulting in thousands of deaths of probably innocent victims.[49] He let the security forces commit grave atrocities in the Deep South in retaliation to the Muslim-Malay insurgency there.[50] Furthermore, he was accused of blatant corruption.[51] However, using his immense wealth and connection, Thaksin was able to co-opt a few senators whom he could lobby to pick an IAA candidate who was sympathetic to his party.[52] As a result, the functioning of the IAA began to fail. The NACC would not investigate a case against Thaksin, and other political parties complained that the EC allowed vote-buying to take place in the 2005 election.[53] The NHRC found itself powerless to hold Thaksin accountable for the human rights violations mentioned above.[54] Public trust further slid when members of the NACC were sentenced to imprisonment for unlawfully granting themselves financial rewards.[55] IAA's inability to stop Thaksin was partly the reason the anti-Thaksin protest grew, triggering a house dissolution, subsequent political deadlock, and ultimately the 2006 coup.

The year 2006 marked a watershed for Thailand's democratisation effort. The anti-Thaksin mob grew into a sizeable anti-democratic movement that eventually triggered the coup. The 1997 Constitution was abolished. Thai society was split

[46] Const Ct Decision 31/2543 (2000); Harding and Leyland (n 29) 180.

[47] Const Ct Decision 21/2546 (2003).

[48] Kewin Hewison, 'Thaksin Shinawatra and the Reshaping of Thai Politics' (2010) 16 *Contemporary Politics* 119, 122; Kasian Tejapira, 'Toppling Thaksin' (2006) 39 *New Left Review* 5, 14–15.

[49] Human Rights Watch, 'Not Enough Graves: The War on Drugs, HIV/AIDS, and Violations of Human Rights' (2004) 6–26.

[50] Kasian (2006) 29–31.

[51] See Hewison (n 48) 119; Aim Sinpeng, 'Corruption, Morality, and the Politics of Reform in Thailand' (2014) 6 *Asian Politics and Policies* 523, 530.

[52] Hewison (n 48) 123.

[53] Harding and Leyland (n 29) 64–65.

[54] Human Rights Watch (n 49) 20–21

[55] Sup Ct Criminal Division for Political Office Holders Decision Or Mor 1/2548 (2005).

into those who were for and against the coup, the beginning of the Red–Yellow contestation.[56] The 2006 junta ordered IAA, except the Auditor-General, the NACC and the EC, to cease operations. However, the 2006 junta set up another body, the Asset Scrutiny Committee, to deal with Thaksin's cases, barring the NACC from handling such issues.[57]

The second period was from 2006 to 2014. IAA assumed a more prominent role in interrupting parliamentary politics. One major change under the 2007 Constitution was that the Senate was half-elected and half-nominated. Effectively, the Senate became a bastion of anti-majoritarian conservatives who in turn filled IAA with the like-minded individuals.

As democracy declined, laws on politicians and political parties became increasingly hostile to the people's representatives. Even the smallest infraction lead to disproportionately severe punishment. Under the 2007 Constitution, a political party would be dissolved if a single member was found violating an election law.[58] The result was an onslaught of major political parties, including Thaksin's new party, the People's Power Party.[59] The only exception was the Democrat Party, whose case the EC failed to meet the deadline to indict.[60] The procedural mistake was perceived to be deliberate to spare the Democrat Party, which represented the anti-Thaksin faction.

Thaksin proved to be resilient. Although he had to flee into self-exile and had his assets confiscated, he won the 2007 election through a proxy and remained highly popular. But his proxy government faced strong resistance from the Yellowshirts, who employed lawsuits as a political weapon. This is not to say that all accusations were fabricated or unfounded. In many instances the case was credible, but the public doubted the neutrality of the investigator and judges. The Constitutional Court found that the Government failed to observe a treaty-making procedure as prescribed in the Constitution when signing a joint communique with Cambodia, prompting the NACC to investigate the Prime Minister and the Foreign Minister for serious misconduct.[61] But the NACC refused to investigate the President of the Supreme Administrative Court for intervening in the subsequent case concerning the same joint communique.[62] The NACC indicted Thaksin for legalising

[56] Barren J Terwiel, *Thailand's Political History: From the 13th Century to Recent Times* (River Books, 2005) 292–93.

[57] The Decree of the Council of Democratic Reform No 3 BE 2549 (2006).

[58] 2007 Constitution, Art 237.

[59] See Khemthong (2016) (n 3) 180–82.

[60] ibid, 182.

[61] 'Supreme Court acquits Noppadon' *Bangkok Post* (5 September 2015), www.bangkokpost.com/thailand/politics/681568/supreme-court-acquits-noppadon.

[62] Prasong Lertrattanawisut, การเปลี่ยนองค์คณะศาลปกครองสูงสุดคดีปราสาทพระวิหาร [Bench Switching in Supreme Administrative Court in Preah Vihear Case] (Individual Study, The Rule of Law and Democracy Diploma Program, the Constitutional Court Office, 2015).

underground lotteries[63] and ordering a bank to give the Myanmar Government a loan.[64] It investigated the Government for using deadly force to crackdown the anti-Thaksin protest in October 2008.[65] But the NACC refrained from probing into the army for a deadly crackdown of pro-Thaksin protesters in April–May 2010 under the Democrat's command.[66] The NHRC was also criticised for being sympathetic to the royalist Government while blaming the victims.[67]

The final showdown of this second period was a series of four incidents. First, the NACC investigated Yingluck Shinawatra, Thaksin's youngest daughter and the Prime Minister from 2011 to 2014, for her rice pledging scheme. Economists were divided over the idea of heavy-handed government subsidy, but the NACC labelled the policy as corrupt, therefore significantly undermining Yingluck's credibility.[68] Then, when Yingluck dissolved the House, the EC refused to cooperate with the Government to organise a smooth and fair election. The EC allowed protesters to disrupt the voting process, leaving many voting booths empty.[69] Later, the Ombudsman challenged the constitutionality of the general election despite that fact that the matter did not fall within the jurisdiction of the Ombudsman and the Constitutional Court.[70] Shortly after the Constitutional Court ruled that the 2014 election was invalid, it removed Yingluck as interim prime minister for wrongfully promoting a civil servant.[71] The NACC followed suit by opening an investigation into her case. A combination of these efforts led to another deadlock, and eventually a coup.

Leading up to the 2014 coup was the anti-Yingluck protest that lasted six months, occupying the heart of Bangkok's business district. Protesters were armed and unruly, beating up innocent bystanders.[72] Protest leaders employed vulgar, violent, obscene and derogatory speech to incite hatred and bodily harm to Yingluck and her family.[73] Clearly, these actions violated the principle of human

[63] 'Thaksin gets two years for abuse of power in lottery case' *Bangkok Post* (7 June 2019), www.bangkokpost.com/thailand/general/1690568/thaksin-gets-two-years-for-abuse-of-power-in-lottery-case.

[64] 'Thaksin gets three years in Exim Bank case' *Bangkok Post* (23 April 2019), www.bangkokpost.com/thailand/politics/1665840/thaksin-gets-three-years-in-exim-bank-case.

[65] 'Somchai doubts NACC's motive in reviving crackdown lawsuit' *Bangkok Post* (1 February 2015), www.bangkokpost.com/thailand/politics/473602/somchai-doubts-nacc-motive-in-reviving-crackdown-lawsuit.

[66] 'Red-shirt leader pressures NACC over 2010 crackdown' *Bangkok Post* (12 January 2018), www.bangkokpost.com/thailand/politics/1394686/red-shirt-leader-pressures-nacc-over-2010-crackdown.

[67] Puangthong Pawakapan, 'ใบอนุญาตให้ลอยนวลพ้นผิด: องค์กรอิสระในกรณีการสลายการชุมนุมปี 2553' ['License for Impunity: Independent Agencies in 2010 Protest Crackdown'] (2016) 14 *Same Sky Journal*.

[68] 'Rice scheme damaging, corrupt political tactic, says NACC' *Bangkok Post* (22 January 2015), www.bangkokpost.com/thailand/general/459155/rice-scheme-damaging-corrupt-political-tactic-says-nacc.

[69] See Prajak Kongkirati, 'Thailand's Failed 2014 Election: The Anti-Election Movement, Violence, and Democratic Breakdown' (2016) 46 *Journal of Contemporary Asia* 467; Duncan McCargo, 'Thailand in 2014: The Trouble with Magic Swords' (2015) *Southeast Asian Affairs* 337, 341.

[70] Const Ct Decision 5/2557 (2014).

[71] Const Ct Decision 9/2557 (2014).

[72] Prajak (n 69) 479–80.

[73] ibid, 475.

rights, but the NHRC did not act upon them. The sense of anarchy intensified and justified the military intervention. Unlike the 2006 coup, the National Council for Peace and Order (NCPO) ordered the IAA to continue their operation, suggesting better trust in these agencies.

From 2014, the anti-majoritarian conservatives fought not only with Thaksin, but also an emerging liberal force. The NCPO rounded up hundreds of people whom it suspected to be dissidents.[74] Arbitrary detention came with torture. But the NHRC never condemned the NCPO's operation, which instilled fear and suppressed dissent.

Investigation of Thaksin's and Yingluck's abuse of power continued after the coup. The NACC added an extra charge against a cabinet member, forcing Yingluck to flee abroad in 2016. That enthusiasm contrasted with the NACC's reluctance to scrutinise the NCPO. Again, the NACC refused to act upon a corruption scandal involving the army or the junta's keyperson, for example, the case of luxurious watches owned by General Prawitr Wongsuwan.[75]

During the 2016 Constitutional Referendum campaign, the EC ruthlessly punished anyone who dared to voice disapproval of the draft under the law prohibiting false information.[76] The NCPO successfully passed the 2017 Constitution and ordered a general election which was finally held in 2019. In general, the 2019 election was poorly organised.[77] In addition, the election was clearly rigged in favour of the junta-backed party. It allowed the junta to campaign ahead of others and put the emerging contestant, the Future Forward Party, at a disadvantage.[78] The new party, whose main agenda was to implement a major reform of the country's main institutions of the monarchy and the military, surely became the new enemy of the conservatives. The EC filed for the dissolution of the Thaksin-affiliated Thai Raksa Chart[79] and later, the Future Forward Party.[80] The EC also petitioned the Constitutional Court to disqualify the party leader, Thanathorn Jungrungruangkij.[81] As a result, scepticism over the EC remained high during the 2023 election.[82] Supporters of the opposition, the Move Forward Party, felt that the EC specifically targeted their party after flimsy accusations.[83]

[74] Amnesty International, 'Thailand: Attitude Adjustment 100 days under martial law' (2014).

[75] 'NACC clears Prawit of luxury watch assets scandal' *Bangkok Post* (27 December 2018), www.bangkokpost.com/thailand/politics/1601718/nacc-clears-prawit-of-luxury-watch-assets-scandal.

[76] Asian Network for Free Elections (ANFREL), 'Thailand Constitutional Referendum 2016: A brief assessment report' (2016) 11–13.

[77] Khemthong Tonsakulrungruang, 'Thailand' in Richard Albert et al, (eds) *2019 Global Review of Constitutional Law* (I.Connect-Clough Center, 2020) 345.

[78] See Jacob I Ricks, 'Thailand's 2019 Vote: The General's Election' (2019) 92 *Pacific Affairs* 443.

[79] Const Ct Decision 3/2562 (2019).

[80] Const Ct Decision 5/2563 (2020); see Khemthong Tonsakulrungruang, 'Thailand' in Richard Albert et al (eds), *2020 Global Review of Constitutional Law* (I.Connect-Clough Center, 2021) 307–08.

[81] Const Ct Decision 14/2562 (2019); see Khemthong (n 80) 348.

[82] ANFREL, '2023 Thai General Election: Democracy at Crossroad' (2023) 39.

[83] 'Pita survives media shareholding case' *Bangkok Post* (24 January 2024), www.bangkokpost.com/thailand/politics/2729909/pita-survives-media-shareholding-case.

IAA seemingly fails to achieve the three missions. They prove themselves incapable of managing a free and fair election, leading a counter-corruption effort, and protecting human rights and liberties. They cannot restore integrity to the political system. The more they function, the worse Thai politics becomes. Lastly, it is unclear what norm they seek to uphold. IAA are criticised for failing to meet the rule of law, transparency and human rights standards, yet performed well in engineering a crisis and guarding the authoritarian governments in 2006 and 2014–2023. But IAA conveniently evade addressing these issues by claiming themselves independent agencies.

V. Independence in Thailand's Illiberal Context

Disappointingly, independent agencies neither revitalise nor consolidate Thailand's fragile democracy. The more IAA exercise power, the faster democracy seems to decline. Thailand has lately been ranked either 'not free' or at best 'partially free' on a democracy index.[84] Corruption and human rights index scores have worsened.[85] The story of IAA fits into Thailand's much larger crisis of accountability deficit where certain public institutions, especially the watchmen, act arbitrarily and go unpunished. What went wrong with the constitutional design of Thailand's IAA?

In their study of election management bodies, Desatova and Alexander suggest that an independent election commission under an illiberal context would not be able to deliver a free and fair election.[86] In other words, sometimes an independent agency contributes negatively to democracy. The study serves as a reminder that independence or autonomy is not panacea.

Drafters of the 1997 Constitution faced a very difficult dilemma.[87] Many of them were western-educated and middle class with a liberal agenda. On one hand, these scholars and intelligentsias disdained military intervention as an undemocratic and anachronical act. They understood that corruption was bad and yearned for values such as human rights, transparency and the rule of law – hence the need to eradicate corruption so as to stop the vicious cycle of coup and election. Drafters were convinced that military intervention was no longer a sound solution to Thailand's chronic problem of democratisation. On the other hand, they shared with the middle class a deep distrust in elected politicians, whom they considered a bunch

[84] 'Thailand falls 8 places in Democracy Index' *Bangkok Post* (17 February 2024), www.bangkokpost.com/thailand/general/2743780/thailand-falls-8-places-in-democracy-index.

[85] See www.transparency.org/en/countries/thailand.

[86] See Petra Desatova and Saowanee Alexander, 'Election Commissions and Non-Democratic Outcomes: Thailand's Contentious 2019 Election' (2021) 43 *Politics* 505.

[87] Michel K Connors, 'Article of Faith: The Failure of Royal Liberalism in Thailand' (2008) 38 *Journal of Contemporary Asia* 143, 144–47.

of local mobsters; selfish, corrupt or short-sighted.[88] To be fair, their doubt was justified and would later be confirmed with the rise of Thaksin's clique. But without an election and politicians, Thailand could never be democratised. The result was the 1997 Constitution, which promoted parliamentary politics but placed the responsibility of enforcing accountability in the hands of the middle class.[89]

Harding and Leyland identify a cause of failure of Thai constitutionalism as a result of the hierarchical nature of the society.[90] Thai society resembles a pyramid where the King sits at the top and others are placed down the rank depending on power, wealth or birth status.[91] The design of the 1997 Constitution somehow aligns with such thinking. The arrangement reflects different focuses on democracy: on an electoral process or democratic values. An election was naturally for the majority but electoral politics was overseen by only a few. Here, the separation of power was not horizontal but vertical. Non-elected elites made sure that politicians could not deviate from the planned path. The entire design rested on an assumption that both the majority and the upper-class elites shared the same understanding of democracy. Unfortunately, the Thai middle class never considered democracy as the only game in play.[92] When they were disappointed by Thaksin Shinawatra in 2005–2006, they saw election and liberalism as two competing notions of democracy. They then abandoned the 1997 project to join the anti-majoritarian mob that invited the 2006 coup and judicial interventions. They would exploit the flaw of the IAA design in an attempt to get rid of Thaksin, at the price of democracy.

Why is IAA easily captured? IAA cannot be cowed by a military junta. It takes something more than that to convince IAA to cooperate. Harding and Leyland point out that Thai politics is conducted without political ideology.[93] That remark is true as electoral politics is more a politics of personality. However, the upper socio-political strata is strongly driven by certain ideology. As Harding and Leyland observe, the monarchy is the most important institution, its own branch of power beyond others' reach, royalist nationalism binding the military, the judiciary, the bureaucracy and watchdog agencies.[94] Thaksin was accused of sidestepping King Bhumibol and began to act like a president.[95] So, Thaksin was not just corrupt, like other ordinary politicians, but was also too dangerous, too ambitious and too

[88] ibid, 146.

[89] ibid, 147. See also Michael K Connors, 'Framing the Peoples' Constitution' in McCargo (n 27) 37–39.

[90] Harding and Leyland (n 29) 253.

[91] ibid.

[92] See Thorn Pitidol and Chanon Techasunthornwat, 'The Rise of Thai Upper Middle Class and its Turn against Democracy' in Micheael J Montesano et al (eds), *After the Coup: The National Council for Peace and Order Era and the Future of* Thailand (ISEAS-Yusof Ishak Institute, 2019); Chris Baker, 'The 2014 Thai Coup and Some Roots of Authoritarianism' (2016) 46 *Journal of Contemporary Asia* 388, 400–01.

[93] Harding and Leyland (n 29) 252.

[94] ibid, 29–33.

[95] Hewison (n 48) 128–29.

arrogant.[96] When the royalists perceived the popular Thaksin, and later, majoritarian democracy, as a threat to the palace, the entire mechanism turned against politicians and the electorate.

Harding and Leyland warn that, to give constitutionalism a chance and prevent further coups or other non-democratic interventions, public institutions must function as designed, within clearly demarcated roles.[97] That warning applies to elected as well as non-elected institutions. However, there has been little discussion about IAA. There is no real mechanism to hold IAA accountable. They are largely exempted from judicial review. They do not fall under the Administrative Court's jurisdiction and the Constitutional Court can only review certain issues, but not those directly mandated by the Constitution itself.[98] IAA can only be persecuted for serious crime, which was almost impossible.[99] The only two cases of ECT and NACC personnel being jailed (2005–2007) were widely considered to be a political ploy to punish pro-Thaksin members.

Any attempt to address IAA's accountability is labelled an encroachment upon independence. But independence does not automatically translate into impartiality, expertise or integrity. These ideas are often erroneously conflated. Unrestrained independence presents no less a problem to democracy than abusive politicians. IAA is also inclined to claim that they are 'above' politics. It is true that no party is capable of influencing the operation of IAA. But Thai political contestation is not confined to a partisan level where parties compete in an election. Political contestation in Thailand is at a more fundamental level: should the country adopt democracy or reject the idea of majoritarianism?[100] At their extreme is the total demolition of majoritarian politics and election, subjugating ignorant majorities under a handful of noble rulers.[101] When the Constitution prohibits partisan participation in IAA's selection, the law then leaves IAA in the hands of anti-democratic elites, who emphasised the 'apolitical' to evade accountability of their own.

IAA presents a classic dilemma of who watches the watchmen. To their credit, the view of the 1997 Constitution-drafters on Thai politicians was not too far from the truth – but it was incomplete. The drafters did not realise that, if left unchecked, these elites could harm democratisation as much as corrupt politicians did. As with the judiciary, the most difficult part is how to instil a sense of accountability into IAA without compromising their independence.

[96] ibid, 129.
[97] Harding and Leyland (n 29) 253.
[98] Const Ct Decision 14/2566 (2023).
[99] 2017 Constitution, Art 218 (3).
[100] Thongchai Winichakul, 'Toppling Democracy' (2008) 38 *Journal of Contemporary Asia* 11; Kewin Hewison, 'Thailand: Contestation over Elections, Sovereignty, and Representation' (2015) 51 *Representation* 51, Kasian Tejapira, 'Disguised Republic and Virtual Absolutism: Two Inherent Conflicting Tendencies in the Thai Constitutional Monarchy' (2023) 12 *Southeast Asian Studies* 105.
[101] Khemthong (n 1) 265–67; Khemthong Tonsakulrungruang, 'Coup and Decay: How Thai-style Democracy Abuses Constitutionalism' in Daly and Samararatne (n 5).

PART III

Legal Transplants, Law and Development

11

Echoes of Veracity: Localising the War on Fake News in Malaysia, Singapore and Thailand

LASSE SCHULDT

In his seminal article, 'Global Doctrine and Local Knowledge', Andrew Harding noted that 'the depressingly small number of scholars in the field of law in South East Asia have in truth trodden a somewhat lonely path'.[1] Andrew drew attention to the deplorable fact that mainstream (read: Global North) comparative law scholarship had largely ignored Southeast Asian legal experiences while, in fact, 'the region presents an ideal laboratory in which … global doctrine and local knowledge are and always have been, partners locked in a dizzying embrace'.[2]

More than 20 years later, comparative legal scholarship from Southeast Asia has grown remarkably in volume and global influence. Andrew's very own contributions played a key part in this fortunate development, and his continued and dedicated support of younger scholars in the region has at least been equally important. I am also personally grateful for his valuable advice and our close cooperation over the last decade.

In his article, Andrew acknowledged that 'legal systems converge because global economics and international politics are determinative, and the fronds of these are growing like the undergrowth of a tropical rainforest'.[3] But he strongly argued for more awareness of the defining role of Southeast Asian *local* knowledge in the process of norm diffusion and legal transplantation. It is in this spirit that this chapter aims to harness the concept of norm localisation for comparative legal studies.

[1] Andrew Harding, 'Global Doctrine and Local Knowledge: Law in South East Asia' (2002) 51 *International and Comparative Law Quarterly* 35, 47.

[2] ibid, 47.

[3] ibid, 51.

I. Norm Diffusion and Localisation

Southeast Asia's rainforests have suffered continuous cutbacks since Andrew's article was published. But new fronds of transnational norms have nonetheless taken root. A particularly influential diffusion process is the subject of this chapter: the war on fake news. The term 'fake news' was popularised by US President Donald Trump during his first term, mainly to discredit what he considered unwelcome reporting about himself and his political team. The phrase took the world by storm, either in English or in local languages. Its meaning consolidated, adding 'fake news' to many people's vocabulary.

At the same time, governments around the globe began identifying what they considered the problems of social media. They adopted the catchy 'fake news' label as a signifier for all sorts of false, forged or misleading information that could potentially cause harm to a variety of broadly defined interests. The global anti-fake news paradigm emerged. Governments of all colours joined hands to highlight the threats, moving to tackle them with a variety of regulatory measures. The European Union developed policies that led to the adoption of the Digital Services Act, and ASEAN issued its 2018 Joint Declaration to Minimise the Harmful Effects of Fake News. The global judicialisation of truth consists of the preparation and enactment of laws against online falsehoods, their practical application and corresponding litigation.

In academia, some authors believed they found the anti-fake news silver bullet that would not only work everywhere, but also comply with international human rights standards: criminal sanctions. While responses should of course be proportionate and 'tailored', penal punishment was found to be the universally best solution, apparently outperforming correction and removal mechanisms.[4] However, the authors showed limited interest in the 'tension between the irresistible surge of globalisation and the undeniable facts of society as it actually exists in the various localities'.[5] Apart from manifest difficulties to circumscribe the types of misinformation that merited governmental responses, the attempt to argue for anti-fake news measures without regard to local realities neglected the contingencies that Andrew had in mind. Consequently, the authors found that anti-disinformation efforts in Hun Sen's Cambodia, in Najib Razak's Malaysia, and in the Socialist Republic of Vietnam were 'promising' examples. A closer look may be required.

I therefore aim to discuss how the global anti-fake news paradigm diffused into three Southeast Asian legal systems. I examine the processes in Malaysia, Singapore and Thailand through the prism of norm localisation. As a theory of norm diffusion, localisation proves a particularly useful concept to connect the

[4] Rebecca K Helm and Hitoshi Nasu, 'Regulatory Responses to 'Fake News' and Freedom of Expression: Normative and Empirical Evaluation' (2021) 21 *Human Rights Law Review* 302.

[5] Harding (n 1) 35.

international with the local, but also the legal with the political. It considers the insertion of foreign and international norms as a process driven by local actors' agendas and strategies, and it focuses on acts of political framing and discourse. I attempt to show that comparative legal studies may benefit from interdisciplinary links to localisation scholarship.

Norm diffusion is concerned with the travelling of normative standards and ideas from international to domestic levels or between the latter. The diffusion concept has been shaped by constructivist international relations scholarship.[6] While it can rightfully be treated as an umbrella that also covers legal transplants, *norm* diffusion includes the spread of discourses and paradigms that are not necessarily consolidated in legal terms. The 'war on terror' and the 'green transition', but also 'Asian values', are examples of such broadly conceived (pre-legal) norms. *Diffusion* appears to be more open-ended than transplantation and evokes a process that occurs naturally and without human intervention. But the influential localisation approach to norm diffusion, quite conversely, emphasises the decisive role of local actors.

Localisation was introduced by Amitav Acharya. Studying the transnational spread of 'Cooperative Security' and 'Flexible Engagement' norms in ASEAN, he highlighted the agency and strategies of local stakeholders in the process.[7] He defined localisation as 'the active construction (through discourse, framing, grafting, and cultural selection) of foreign ideas by local actors, [which] may result in the former developing significant congruence with local beliefs and practices'.[8] In subsequent publications, he added that this process may not necessarily be linear due to local contingencies.[9] Localisation partly resembles Stefan Vogenauer's idea of localised legal transfers[10] as both concepts highlight adaptations to the specificities of receiving jurisdictions. However, Acharya's localisation differs in two key aspects: firstly, it focuses more on the diffusion of policy paradigms rather than the transfer of legal concepts and institutions; and, secondly, localisation appears to put a stronger emphasis on studying local actors' discourse and framing in the process.

[6] Margaret E Keck and Kathryn Sikkink, *Activists beyond Borders: Advocacy Networks in International Politics* (Cornell University Press, 1998); Martha Finnemore and Kathryn Sikkink, 'International Norm Dynamics and Political Change' (1998) 52 *International Organization* 887; Thomas Risse and Kathryn Sikkink, 'The Socialization of International Human Rights Norms into Domestic Practices: Introduction' in Thomas Risse, Stephen C Ropp and Kathryn Sikkink (eds), *The Power of Human Rights: International Norms and Domestic Change* (Cambridge University Press, 1999) 1.

[7] Amitav Acharya, 'How Ideas Spread: Whose Norms Matter? Norm Localization and Institutional Change in Asian Regionalism' (2004) 58 *International Organization* 239.

[8] ibid, 245.

[9] Amitav Acharya, 'Norm Subsidiarity and Regional Orders: Sovereignty, Regionalism, and Rule-Making in the Third World' (2011) 55 *International Studies Quarterly* 95.

[10] Stefan Vogenauer, 'Interpretation of Contracts and Control of Unfair Terms in Asia: A Comparison' in Mindy Chen-Wishart and Stefan Vogenauer (eds), *Studies in the Contract Laws of Asia Vol. III: Contents of Contracts and Unfair Terms* (Oxford University Press, 2020) 477, 554.

Localisation scholarship subsequently branched out into a variety of sub-concepts that include vernacularisation, mimetic adoption, norm translation, friction, interest convergence and layered localisation.[11] Relevant studies have analysed the spreading of regional and cooperative security norms, the prohibition of small arms, norms related to post-conflict peace-building, international criminal justice, and international human rights such as child rights or the freedom from torture and enforced disappearance. These works all share the focus on local actors' interests in their domestic arenas, the deployment of language and discourse, acts of contestation, and the strategic exploitation of opportunities in international relations. The Southeast Asian war on fake news is a similar norm diffusion process. But what is gained by adding yet another approach to the comparative law discipline?

Localisation emerged as a constructivist concept. As such, it assumes that social problems and their solutions are never pregiven. They are, in Foucauldian terms, constructed through language and power. The localisation concept draws attention to the process and the actors that turn global social issues into local social *problems*. It takes into full account that human agents select only some issues while neglecting others. Discourse is what gives importance to the limited range of matters. The localisation concept thus requires a relativist distance to law. It follows, for instance, that the 'success' of norm diffusion can be judged only in relation to the goals that acting persons pursued, rather than from any objectivised perspective. When localisation studies explain diffusion processes, examine the role of key actors, and compare rules and their enforcement to prior discourse and framing, they avoid making any absolute statements about success. From such constructivist perspective, norms are 'successfully' integrated mainly where the expectations of influential actors are served.

The localisation concept may help legal comparatists move away from objective notions of success – a move that Andrew also suggested.[12] My localisation case studies from Malaysia, Singapore and Thailand illustrate how a renewed focus on process and actors can be put into practice.

[11] Peggy Levitt and Sally Merry, 'Vernacularization on the Ground: Local Uses of Global Women's Rights in Peru, China, India and the United States' (2009) 9 *Global Networks* 441; Hiro Katsumata, 'Mimetic Adoption and Norm Diffusion: "Western" Security Cooperation in Southeast Asia?' (2011) 37 *Review of International Studies* 557; Lisbeth Zimmermann, 'Same Same or Different? Norm Diffusion Between Resistance, Compliance, and Localization in Post-conflict States' (2016) 17 *International Studies Perspectives* 98; Annika Björkdahl et al, 'Introduction: Peacebuilding through the Lens of Friction' in Annika Björkdahl et al (eds), *Peacebuilding and Friction: Global and Local Encounters in Post-conflict Societies* (Routledge, 2016) 1; Salvador Santino Fulo Regilme Jr, *Aid Imperium: United States Foreign Policy and Human Rights in Post-Cold War Southeast Asia* (University of Michigan Press, 2021); Lasse Schuldt, 'Layered Localization of International Human Rights Law: Signaling and Contestation in the Context of Thailand' (2024) 23 *Journal of Human Rights* 404.

[12] Andrew Harding, 'The Legal Transplants Debate: Getting Beyond the Impasse?' in Vito Breda (ed), *Legal Transplants in East Asia and Oceania* (Cambridge University, Press 2019) 13.

II. From Global to Local: The War on Fake News in Southeast Asia

The COVID-19 pandemic made the dangers of fake news a frequently repeated commonplace. But the ostensible 'infodemic' was, in fact, just an accelerator of a development that had begun roughly four years before. Since the 2016 presidential election campaign in the United States, policymakers, journalists and scholars devoted increasing attention to the impact of 'alternative facts' on Western societies. Studies found that intentionally false reporting may in some cases shape traditional media discourses, affect trust in institutions and polarise people.[13] From a psychological perspective, it became a truism that people's memories register falsehoods better than subsequent corrections. Studies on the benefits of fact-checking, however, returned much more differentiated results.[14] Some authors nonetheless considered the very concept of truth more contested than ever,[15] also because of politicians and state representatives who weaponised the fake news label against political opponents or unfavourable reports.[16]

In Southeast Asia, the worst possible effects of fake news occurred when Myanmar state agencies and the military allegedly distributed false rumours that incited large-scale violence against Rohingya people in Rakhine state. The Rohingyas' ensuing mass exodus to Bangladesh peaked in the years 2016–17. In the Philippines, the presidential office under Rodrigo Duterte was reportedly engaged in active disinformation operations that targeted critical voices and political opponents. It appeared that Southeast Asian governments were, ironically, *themselves* sources of fake news. But state policymakers framed the disinformation threat unabashedly as a matter of national security that necessitated decisive responses. Over the course of a few years, legislators created a variety of mechanisms to tidy up the Internet, including the 'silver bullet' criminal sanctions. The region quickly became a laboratory for anti-fake news laws. Official discourse tied the local steps to the global trend, frequently referring to Western democratic role models that were ostensibly treading a similar path. But the patterns of localisation were largely

[13] Chris J Vargo, Lei Guo and Michelle A Amazeen, 'The Agenda-Setting Power of Fake News: A Big Data Analysis of the Online Media Landscape from 2014 to 2016' (2018) 20 *New Media & Society* 2028; Jana Laura Egelhofer et al, 'From Novelty to Normalization? How Journalists Use the Term "Fake News" in Their Reporting' (2020) 21 *Journalism Studies* 1323.

[14] Dustin Carnahan and R Kelly Garrett, 'Processing Style and Responsiveness to Corrective Information' (2020) 32 *International Journal of Public Opinion Research* 530; Brendan Nyhan et al, 'Taking Fact-Checks Literally but Not Seriously? The Effects of Journalistic Fact-Checking on Factual Beliefs and Candidate Favorability' (2020) 42 *Political Behavior* 939.

[15] Silvio Waisbord, 'Truth is What Happens to News' (2018) 19 *Journalism Studies* 1866.

[16] Ahmed Al-Rawi, 'Gatekeeping Fake News Discourses on Mainstream Media Versus Social Media' (2019) 37 *Social Science Computer Review* 687; Sander van der Linden, Costas Panagopoulos and Jon Roozenbeek, 'You Are Fake News: Political Bias in Perceptions of Fake News' (2020) 42 *Media, Culture & Society* 460.

driven by domestic actors' political considerations and, in fact, strongly differed from their Western counterparts.

In Malaysia, Prime Minister Najib Razak was embattled in the 1MDB corruption scandal and faced the fourteenth general election on 9 May 2018 that would result in the crushing defeat of his Barisan Nasional coalition. In Singapore, consecutive surveys confirmed that the ruling People's Action Party (PAP) was losing popularity. It had to expect significant losses in the upcoming 2020 General Election. And in Thailand, the military Government that had taken power in the 2014 coup was just cautiously allowing political activities. In the run-up to the first post-coup election in March 2019, the new liberal Future Forward Party was rapidly gaining ground in nationwide polls. Powerholders were under pressure in all three countries. The stage was set for the localisation of the anti-fake news paradigm.

This study proceeds in four steps: from a brief overview of the legal-political settings it moves to examine the discursive framing of the fake news threat, the scope and content of newly enacted laws and, finally, to the patterns of law enforcement. This incremental approach largely follows Lisbeth Zimmermann's distinction between discourse, law and implementation,[17] but adds attention to individual localities. While the legal-political settings and fake news discourses of Malaysia, Singapore and Thailand exhibit several similarities, it will become apparent that relevant laws and their enforcement differed substantially.

A. Legal-Political Settings

Malaysia and Singapore can be very broadly described as non-substantive democracies. The United Malays National Organisation (UMNO) and the PAP, respectively, have dominated politics and controlled legislative agendas for decades. Malaysia's 'regularised authoritarianism' has manifested itself not only in internal security laws but also in the limited legal weight of fundamental rights and, consequently, the marginal role of courts in these matters.[18] The Government of neighbouring Singapore has successfully perpetuated its discourse of state survival and the nation's vulnerability. The PAP's calibrated coercion[19] is 'enveloped within administrative and regulatory mechanisms'[20] while state-licensed

[17] Zimmermann (n 11).

[18] HP Lee, *Constitutional Conflicts in Contemporary Malaysia*, 2nd edn (Oxford University Press, 2017) 166–81; Ariel Heryanto and Sumit K Mandal, 'Challenges to Authoritarianism in Indonesia and Malaysia' in Ariel Heryanto and Sumit K Mandal (eds), *Challenging Authoritarianism in Southeast Asia: Comparing Indonesia and Malaysia* (Routledge Cavendish, 2003) 1, 6.

[19] Cherian George, 'Consolidating Authoritarian Rule: Calibrated Coercion in Singapore' (2007) 20 *The Pacific Review* 127.

[20] Jothie Rajah, *Authoritarian Rule of Law: Legislation, Discourse and Legitimacy in Singapore* (Cambridge University Press, 2012) 20.

media largely refrains from criticising governmental action.[21] In Thailand, the military, the judiciary, the bureaucracy and the monarchy are considered the traditional powerholders that provide only limited space for electoral democracy.[22] A cycle of coups, the most recent ones occurring in 2006 and 2014, highlights the extraconstitutional roles of key domestic players.[23]

Written constitutions nonetheless include explicit provisions to protect freedom of expression,[24] the right most affected by measures against fake news. In all three jurisdictions, freedom of expression can lawfully be restricted for various purposes, including the protection of national security and public order. What amounts to public disorder, however, is largely left for lawmakers to define. The Supreme Court of Malaysia, as it was called at the time, ruled in a 1994 decision that a provision of the Printing Presses and Publications Act that prohibited to maliciously publish false information was a lawful restriction of freedom of expression: Parliament enjoyed discretion in choosing the legal measures to protect public order.[25] In Singapore, the High Court affirmed in a 2005 landmark case that Parliament had an 'extremely wide discretionary power' to determine the proper balance between freedom of expression and public interests, while the judiciary should adopt 'a generous, not a pedantic interpretation'. The 'manifest intent and purport of both the Constitution and domestic legislation, not … abstract notions of permissible conduct', shall be binding for the courts.[26] Turning to Thailand, it can be observed that public interests are defined with a strong security focus, allocating key definitional powers to the executive branch while leaving limited space for rights-based judicial control.[27] In a 2012 decision, the Constitutional Court confirmed the constitutionality of a law criminalising the spread of false information through computer systems (to which we will return below). It decided that the provision served national security and public order, which was sufficient to uphold it. Questions of proportionality remained unaddressed.[28]

Over time, these constitutional settings permitted the creation of various restrictive laws that include libel and defamation, internal security and social harmony legislation, but also anti-falsehood rules – long before the war on fake

[21] Diane K Mauzy and RS Milne, *Singapore Politics Under the People's Action Party* (Routledge, 2002).

[22] Duncan McCargo, 'Network Monarchy and Legitimacy Crisis in Thailand' (2005) 18 *The Pacific Review* 499; Henning Glaser, 'Constitutional Conflict and Restatement: The Challenge and Transformation of the Hegemonic Basic Consent in Thailand' in Henning Glaser (ed), *Norms, Interests, and Values: Conflict and Consent in the Constitutional Basic Order* (Nomos, 2015) 291.

[23] Andrew Harding and Peter Leyland, *The Constitutional System of Thailand: A Contextual Analysis* (Hart Publishing, 2011) 29–33.

[24] Art 10, Federal Constitution of Malaysia; Art 14, Constitution of the Republic of Singapore; Art 34, Constitution of the Kingdom of Thailand BE 2560 (2017).

[25] Supreme Court of Malaysia, *Public Prosecutor v Pung Chen Choon* (1994) 1 MLJ 566 SC.

[26] High Court of Singapore, *Chee Siok Chin v Minister for Home Affairs* (2005) 1 SLR 582 [135] SGHC.

[27] Harding and Leyland (n 23) 189–215.

[28] Constitutional Court of Thailand, Order No 46/2555 (2012).

news began. In Malaysia, provisions in the Penal Code (Section 505(b)), the Printing Press and Publications Act 1984 (Section 8A(1)), and the Communications and Multimedia Act 1998 (Section 233(1)(a)) criminalise the publication of falsehoods under different conditions. In Singapore, earlier grounds to punish people for false reporting can be found in the Penal Code (Section 505(b)), the Internal Security Act 1960 (Section 26, 39), the Sedition Act 1948/64 (Sections 3–4), the Telecommunications Act 1999 (Section 45(b)), and in the Protection from Harassment Act 2014 (Sections 3, 4 and 15). And in Thailand, provisions in the Criminal Code (Section 384), the Consumer Protection Act 1979 (Section 22(2) No 1), and the Computer Crime Act 2007 (Section 14) prohibit spreading falsehoods in various ways.

The global anti-fake news discourse thus arrived in three Southeast Asian jurisdictions that share several characteristics: the semi-authoritarian systems subscribe to thin notions of the rule law; constitutional review by courts is largely limited to non-substantive matters, leaving lawmakers wide discretion; and existing legal frameworks already permit significant restrictions of individual freedoms, including with respect to the distribution of allegedly false information. With these commonalities, however, the settings differ quite substantially from 'Western' jurisdictions where freedom of expression is protected more robustly. When governments localised the war on fake news, they nonetheless borrowed legitimacy from the 'West', as we shall see in the following paragraphs.

B. Discursive Framing of the Fake News Threat

While the regulatory problem of fake news was being recognised around the world, local discourses with distinct characteristics emerged: governments in Southeast Asia described the new threat in especially forceful terms reminiscent of the 'war on terror'. State representatives referred to allegedly similar legislative steps in other places, mainly in liberal democracies. In addition, governments communicated a constant fake news threat via state-administered fact-checking services.

In 2017, Malaysia's Prime Minister, Najib Razak, already under pressure in the 1MDB corruption case, described fake news as the new plague while social media was the 'Wild West'. He thus called on traditional media to 'fight to the last this tide of fake and false news'.[29] When the Anti-Fake News Bill was in the making, a cabinet member tried to quell worries about restrictions of freedom of expression, alleging instead that 'some countries such as Germany, Singapore, France, the Czech Republic and the European Union have also taken and are taking the same

[29] 'Free Speech Thriving in Malaysia but Fake News a Plague: PM Najib' Channel News Asia (19 April 2017), www.channelnewsasia.com/news/asia/free-speech-thriving-in-malaysia-but-fake-news-a-plague-pm-najib-8741726.

measures to curb the dissemination of fake news'.[30] The Anti-Fake News Act 2018 (AFNA) nonetheless differed substantially from anything enacted in Europe, as we will see below. But a state minister confirmed that 'Germany and the Czech Republic have done it, and the French government intends to do it'.[31]

After Barisan Nasional's historic defeat in the 2018 general election, AFNA was soon repealed by the incoming Pakatan Harapan coalition. Only a few days before the vote in the lower house, however, the new Prime Minister, Mahatir Mohamad, said, 'the anti-fake news law is good',[32] and governmental discourse did not subside with the Act's revocation. In 2019, a Sabah minister stated that the 'the question of fake news, hate speech is taking over humankind and somehow we must be able to fight this battle'.[33] However, when the COVID-19 pandemic swept the world, the Federal Government under Prime Minister Muhyiddin Yassin temporarily reintroduced AFNA in the form of the Emergency (Essential Powers) (No 2) Ordinance 2021. An UMNO-linked think tank was quick to reassure that 'Germany, Singapore, and Russia, for example, introduced such laws within the past three years which, like Malaysia, have attracted sharp criticism regarding potential restriction on free speech.'[34]

In the case of Singapore, the Government prepared the public for what was coming with the creation of the parliamentary Select Committee on Deliberate Online Falsehoods in early 2018. A preparatory Green Paper asserted that 'countries around the world and technology companies have begun taking steps to address online falsehoods. In Germany, the Network Enforcement Act was enacted last year'.[35] Prime Minister Lee Hsien Loong said, 'Singapore is not the only one which has taken legislation on this issue. The French have done so, the Germans have done so. … So, Singapore had to do this.'[36] He highlighted Singapore's specific vulnerability as a multi-ethnic English-speaking country with high Internet

[30] 'Azalina: Anti Fake News Law Protects, Not Stifle Freedom of Speech' *New Straits Times* (4 April 2018), www.nst.com.my/news/government-public-policy/2018/04/352726/azalina-anti-fake-news-law-protects-not-stifle-freedom.

[31] 'Sabah Minister Backs Proposed Law Against Fake News' *Free Malaysia Today* (26 February 2018), www.freemalaysiatoday.com/category/nation/2018/02/26/sabah-minister-backs-proposed-law-against-fake-news.

[32] 'Tackle Fake News without Hindering the Truth, Says Dr M' *Free Malaysia Today* (4 October 2019), www.freemalaysiatoday.com/category/nation/2019/10/04/tackle-fake-news-without-hindering-the-truth-says-dr-m.

[33] 'Kit Siang Says Govt Can Effectively Fight Fake News, Hate Speech' *Malay Mail* (27 November 2019), www.malaymail.com/news/malaysia/2019/11/27/kit-siang-says-govt-can-effectively-fight-fake-news-hate-speech/1813651.

[34] Jia Vern Tham and Khairil Ahmad, 'Malaysia's Fake News Ordinance: Rigid Rules For A Nuanced Problem' The Centre (26 March 2021), www.centre.my/post/malaysias-fake-news-ordinance-rigid-rules-for-a-nuanced-problem.

[35] Ministry of Communications and Information and Ministry of Law of Singapore, Deliberate Online Falsehoods: Challenges and Implications: A Green Paper (Misc 10 of 2018) paras 61–62, www.mlaw.gov.sg/files/news/press-releases/2018/01/Annexe%20A%20-%20Green%20Paper%20on%20Deliberate%20Online%20Falsehoods.pdf.

[36] 'Singapore PM Defends Proposed Law Combating Fake Online News' AP (9 April 2019), apnews.com/general-news-29b66dfffec345f2b78ed8d357797977.

penetration,[37] where hate speech and fake news were 'spreading like wildfire'.[38] A minister in the Defence Department mentioned terrorism and fake news as global security threats and continued that 'this is not conventional warfare, but a battle within all our societies'.[39]

While the committee's report came to the expected conclusion that 'deliberate online falsehoods are a real and serious problem for the world, and Singapore',[40] the public hearings allowed the Government to lay out its anti-fake news policy on a prominent stage. Critical voices were the exception. Some organisations and experts declined invitations to give opinions.[41] Others claimed their statements were misrepresented in the final report.[42] The most memorable episode was certainly the six-hour-long 'interrogation' of a well-known historian by Law and Home Affairs Minister, K Shanmugam. It became evident that the hearings were a legitimising act: 'performing legitimacy through select committees'.[43] Parliament passed the Protection from Online Falsehoods and Manipulation Act 2019 (POFMA) in May 2019. I will discuss its content below.

In Thailand, the public framing of the fake news threat was clearly tied to domestic political turmoil and the challenge from the Future Forward Party. A statement of the Army's Commander-in-Chief reflected the ruling elite's worries after Future Forward won almost 20 per cent of the vote in the 2019 parliamentary election:

> The threat now is fake news. … It's like cyber warfare. And when it combines with the [bombing] incident that happened last week, it's like hybrid warfare. … Now it is not just an open enemy like the old time. … So, we have to reorganise and improve our knowledge, and reorganise our units and many things to maintain peace and national security. … Some political parties, just born a couple of years ago … had the platform of their propaganda directed to [people] when they were 16 and 17. … They try to educate them with fake news.[44]

[37] Prime Minister's Office Singapore, 'PM Lee Hsien Loong at the CNA 20th Anniversary Gala Dinner' (29 March 2019), www.pmo.gov.sg/Newsroom/CNA-20th-Anniversary-Gala-Dinner.

[38] Prime Minister's Office Singapore, 'PM Lee Hsien Loong at the 29th Inter-Pacific Bar Association Annual Meeting and Conference' (25 April 2019), www.pmo.gov.sg/Newsroom/PM-Lee-Hsien-Loong-at-the-29th-Inter-Pacific-Bar-Association-Annual-Meeting-and-Conferenc.

[39] 'Special Address by Second Minister for Defence Ong Ye Kung at the Dinner Reception for the 6th International Institute of Strategic Studies Fullerton Forum: The Shangri-La Dialogue Sherpa Meeting' (29 January 2018), www.nas.gov.sg/archivesonline/data/pdfdoc/MINDEF_20180129001_2.pdf.

[40] Parliament of Singapore, *Report of the Select Committee on Deliberate Online Falsehoods – Causes, Consequences and Countermeasures* (2018), www.parliament.gov.sg/sconlinefalsehoods.

[41] 'Human Rights Watch Declines Singapore's Invite to 'Fake News 'Hearing' Reuters (30 March 2018), www.reuters.com/article/us-singapore-politics-fake-news/human-rights-watch-declines-singapores-invite-to-fake-news-hearing-idUSKBN1H60XQ.

[42] Reporters Without Borders, 'RSF Explains Why Singapore's Anti-Fake News Bill is Terrible' RSF (8 April 2018), rsf.org/en/news/rsf-explains-why-singapores-anti-fake-news-bill-terrible.

[43] Rajah (n 20) 139–44; Howard Lee and Terence Lee, 'From Contempt of Court to Fake News: Public Legitimization and Governance in Mediated Singapore' (2019) 173 *Media International Australia* 81.

[44] 'Apirat: Fake News Feeds "Hybrid War"' *Bangkok Post* (9 August 2019), www.bangkokpost.com/thailand/general/1727615/apirat-fake-news-feeds-hybrid-war.

A minister for digital affairs confirmed that fake news is a 'critical threat' that is 'embedded within every aspect of our society'.[45] In late 2019, the Thai Government launched the Anti-Fake News Center as a platform to inform the public about falsehoods circulating in social and traditional media. Similar websites (Sebenarnya.my and Factually) are operated by the Malaysian and Singaporean Governments. In prior research, I found that these platforms mainly function as constant reminders of the fake news threat, while questions regarding the criteria to select specific news items remain unanswered.[46] From a liberal perspective, state-operated fact-checking appears problematic due to the possible lack of independence.

Overall, governmental discourses localising the anti-fake news paradigm in Malaysia, Singapore and Thailand were characteristically bellicose, borrowing legitimacy from abroad, while positioning the state as the ultimate security provider.

C. Scope and Content of Anti-Fake News Laws

The legal-political settings and localisation discourses showed several similarities across the three countries. The resulting laws, however, differ in many respects. Malaysia's law focused on criminal sanctions and content removal, defining 'fake news' in the broadest possible way. In Singapore, Parliament created a much more comprehensive piece of legislation that addresses various types of falsehoods with a wide range of possible interventions. Thailand's criminal law addresses certain types of potentially problematic information, but raises significant questions regarding clarity and constitutionality.

Malaysia's AFNA was a short law of 14 sections. It introduced 'fake news' (*berita tidak benar*) as an actual legal term that included 'any news, information, data and reports, which is or are wholly or partly false, whether in the form of features, visuals or audio recordings or in any other form capable of suggesting words or ideas' (Section 2). 'Any person who, by any means, maliciously creates, offers, publishes, prints, distributes, circulates or disseminates any fake news or publication containing fake news' committed a crime punishable with imprisonment of up to six years and/or a fine (Section 4(1)). The Act did not require proof that fake news could, at least abstractly, impact any interests. Heavy on the subjective side, the sweeping offence just required malicious action. Direct and indirect financial assistance to the offence and a duty for everyone to remove impugned content carried the same criminal sanctions as the principal offence.

[45] 'Thailand to Set Up Center to Combat "Fake News"' Khaosod English (22 August 2019), www.khaosodenglish.com/news/crimecourtscalamity/2019/08/22/thailand-to-set-up-center-to-combat-fake-news.

[46] Lasse Schuldt, 'Official Truths in a War on Fake News: Governmental Fact-Checking in Malaysia, Singapore, and Thailand' (2021) 40 *Journal of Current Southeast Asian Affairs* 340.

AFNA went out of effect in late 2019. Its 2021 reincarnation as a COVID-19 emergency ordinance inserted 'intent to cause, or [acting by any means] which is likely to cause fear or alarm to the public' instead of malice. The punishment for the principal offence was reduced to not exceeding three years, while financial assistance still carried the same six years maximum. The emergency ordinance was revoked in late 2021. In sum, Malaysia's legislative approach to fight fake news was characterised by a focus on broadly phrased offences that carried significant criminal penalties. AFNA was apparently the legal weapon of a prime minister to silence roaring corruption rumours. Rushed through Parliament just weeks before the doomed 14th general election, the Act was meant to serve political purposes rather than the public.

The Government of Singapore opted for a much more comprehensive approach that comprised the 62 sections-long POFMA as well as accompanying Regulations and Supreme Court Rules. POFMA offers ministers a wide range of responses to what they perceive as harmful communications of 'false statements of fact'.[47] The powers include orders to post official messages (Correction Directions), to take steps to ensure that a statement is no longer communicated (Stop Communication Directions), to mandate Internet intermediaries or media to distribute ministerial corrections (Targeted or General Correction Directions), and to cut off access to impugned statements (Disabling Directions). Persons who fail to comply with any of these orders face criminal liability, while the communication of harmful falsehoods is itself also a crime (Section 7). The Government can also mark websites that have been the subject of at least three Directions as Declared Online Locations. Such websites are, among other consequences, banned from receiving any financial support, for example through advertisements.

In addition, POFMA substantially differs from AFNA as it ostensibly focuses on certain types of harmful falsehoods. The Act addresses false and misleading statements that are 'likely' to impact one of several enumerated public interests such as national security, public health, safety, tranquillity and finances, undisturbed international relations, orderly presidential or parliamentary elections or referenda, peaceful relations between different societal groups, and trust in government institutions. Proof of actual effects on any of these interests is not required: an abstract threat is sufficient.[48] And while addressees of Correction Directions may request the High Court to rule on the question of truth, claimants are barred from challenging the existence of an abstract threat (Section 17(5)). Thus, the Government of Singapore created a detailed legal framework that allows calibrated coercion, offering itself full discretion to identify relevant threats. How it was put into operation is discussed below.

[47] POFMA defines a false statement of fact in Section 2(2): 'a statement is false if it is false or misleading, whether wholly or in part, and whether on its own or in the context in which it appears'.

[48] Lasse Schuldt, 'Abstract Panic: On Fake News, Fear and Freedom in Southeast Asia' Verfassungsblog (14 April 2020), dx.doi.org/10.17176/20200415-032701-0.

Thailand's Act on Computer-Related Offences ('Computer Crime Act') was enacted in 2007, before the fake news paradigm began to spread. While large parts of the Act focus on offences related to the integrity of computers and computer data, the law also criminalises the communication of false information via computer systems (Section 14(1) Nos 1 and 2). Initial drafts were, in fact, meant to address only 'forged' computer data, analogous to forged paper documents.[49] But as the drafting progressed, 'false' information was included, and in a 2017 revision of the Act, legislators extended the scope to 'distorted' information. When global awareness of the fake news problem was rising, the 2017 amendment thus expanded the scope of the law. The relevant provision was also changed to penalise the communication of false information not only where detrimental effects on national security or a public panic were 'likely' to occur, but also where public safety, national economic security, or public infrastructure serving national interest might be affected (Section 14(1) No 2). In addition, spreading false, forged or distorted information would also be punishable if it was likely to cause damage to 'the public' quite generally (Section 14(1) No 1).

The Thai law on criminal online falsehoods thus contains partly overlapping provisions that are broadly phrased. In addition to interpretational pitfalls, parts of the law are arguably unconstitutional because of disproportionately high criminal penalties.[50] The sweeping character of the law is not surprising when considering that both the Act's initial version of 2007 as well as its 2017 revision were enacted at a time when lawmaking was in the hands of unelected legislative assemblies following the 2006 and 2014 military coups. The COVID-19 pandemic triggered additional emergency regulations that targeted related falsehoods. They have since been repealed.

The war on fake news thus resulted in differing legislative responses. Malaysia's short-lived experiments contrast with Singapore's and Thailand's permanent laws. Both the Malaysian and the Thai approaches relied heavily on criminal sanctions while Singapore opted for a more comprehensive toolbox of measures. The three jurisdictions are nonetheless also comparable to each other regarding their use of vaguely phrased provisions and low thresholds ('likely' damage) that allow governmental interventions and penal sanctions. They also share substantial differences to 'Western' counterparts that largely refrained from criminalisation. The oft-mentioned German 2017 Netzwerkdurchsetzungsgesetz (NetzDG) created monitoring and take-down duties for social media websites. The French 2018 law relating to the '*lutte contre la manipulation de l'information*' (law no 2018-1202) empowers courts to order the removal of false information during election campaigns. And the EU's 2022 Digital Services Act, again, focuses on social media's monitoring duties and transparency. The frequently repeated claim that

[49] Lasse Schuldt and Pudit Ovattananavakhun, 'Thailand's Law on Criminal Online Falsehoods: A Critical Discussion' (2021) 1 *Thai Legal Studies* 150, 162.

[50] ibid 170 ff; Section 14(1) of the Computer Crime Act stipulates a maximum penalty of imprisonment that is 60 times higher than the maximum provided in a comparable Criminal Code provision.

any of these jurisdictions criminalised the communication of falsehoods is, ironically, fake news.

D. Patterns of Law Enforcement

The localisation of the anti-fake news war is also defined by the enforcement of enacted rules: in which types of cases and against whom is the law mobilised? In Malaysia, only a single AFNA conviction was reported in the three weeks between the promulgation of the law and the 14th general election that swept Barisan Nasional out of power.[51] No further cases were pursued as incoming Pakatan Harapan honoured its pre-election commitment not to enforce the law. The COVID-19 pandemic led to a moderate revival of the rules after a newly composed government introduced the Emergency Ordinance in early 2021. While the Ordinance was in force between March and October 2021, police and prosecutors launched overall 30 investigations into pandemic-related fake news nationwide, half of which were classified as 'no further action'.[52] At the same time, however, other laws such as the Communications and Multimedia Act 1998 (Section 233) were enforced throughout the pandemic,[53] with some allegations of politicisation.[54]

The POFMA enforcement in Singapore has been noticeably more Janus-faced. The Government, on the one hand, restrained itself and focused largely on issuing Correction Directions. Between October 2019 and June 2024, the competent ministers issued 114 Correction Directions, 22 Targeted Correction Directions, and five General Correction Directions. Sixteen websites were marked as Declared Online Locations.[55] No criminal prosecution has been instituted under the Act.[56] The immediate run-up to the general election of 10 July 2020, on the other hand, saw an almost daily flurry of Correction Directions against opposition parties and

[51] 'Individu Pertama Dihukum Ikut Akta Antiberita Tidak Benar' ['First Individual Punished Under the Anti-Fake News Act'] BH Online (30 April 2018), www.bharian.com.my/berita/kes/2018/04/418998/individu-pertama-dihukum-ikut-akta-antiberita-tidak-benar#google_vignette.

[52] 'Dewan Rakyat Approves Motion to Revoke Emergency Ordinances' *New Straits Times* (25 October 2021), www.nst.com.my/news/nation/2021/10/739449/dewan-rakyat-approves-motion-revoke-emergency-ordinances-nsttv.

[53] 'Five More Probed for Spreading Fake News on Covid-19' *New Straits Times* (24 March 2020), www.nst.com.my/news/crime-courts/2020/03/577561/five-more-probed-spreading-fake-news-covid-19.

[54] 'Coronavirus: Malaysian Opposition MP Pleads Not Guilty to Spreading Fake News' *Straits Times* (30 April 2020), www.straitstimes.com/asia/se-asia/malaysian-opposition-mp-pleads-not-guilty-to-spreading-fake-news.

[55] POFMA Office, Tabulation of POFMA Cases and Actions, www.pofmaoffice.gov.sg/files/tabulation_of_pofma_cases_and_actions.pdf.

[56] It must also be noted, however, that ministers have successfully pursued civil damage claims for defamation after Correction Directions were ordered (and complied with) under POFMA; see, for instance, High Court of Singapore, *Shanmugam Kasiviswanathan v Lee Hsien Yang* and *Vivian Balakrishnan v Lee Hsien Yang* [2024] SGHC 136.

government critics.[57] Moreover, the Government's fact-checking outlet, Factually, also began disclosing the names of impugned social media and website operators, most of whom were critics of the PAP.[58] Over the course of the Act's enforcement, Correction Directions have been issued almost entirely to defend government agencies against claims of malfeasance or corruption.[59] Consequently, law enforcement clearly focused on protecting trust in the Government while other public interests listed in the Act proved practically unimportant.

Enforcement in Thailand strongly focuses on criminal prosecution with palpable indications of a politicised use. Initially, police and prosecutors also brought criminal defamation cases under the Computer Crime Act, until the 2017 revision ended this practice. But the Act's anti-falsehood provisions were nonetheless used against progressive politicians, activists and the media with rising frequency,[60] often in conjunction with charges for *lèse-majesté*.[61] There has been a remarkable growth in criminal cases since the July 2020 'Free Youth' student protests that dared to address the taboo subject of monarchy reform. Official statistics show an outright jump of the nationwide number of suspects facing computer crime charges, from 405 and 494 suspects in the years 2019 and 2020, to 3,296 and 4,093 suspects in 2021 and 2022, respectively – an almost tenfold increase that displays a manifestly changed enforcement policy.[62] The Government thus apparently combined the fight against fake news with the pursuit of political goals, mainly directed against individuals and parties who challenged the constitutional status quo. The instrumentalisation of criminal sanctions, which can amount to years or even decades of imprisonment, clearly distinguishes the Thai case from Singapore, where the Government largely limits its POFMA-related actions to correction orders.

Enforcement patterns across the three countries can thus be summarised as follows. In Malaysia, *temporary* enforcement occurred in the politicised run-up to the 14th general election, though on a negligible level, and for a limited time during the COVID-19 pandemic. Singapore pursues *calibrated* enforcement, with targeted correction orders repeatedly addressed at political opponents. And Thailand's *excessive* enforcement combines allegedly politicised prosecution with high levels of punishment.

[57] Lasse Schuldt, 'Shaping the Fake News Discourse: Laws, Electoral Arenas and the Emergence of Truth as a Public Interest' in James Gomez and Robin Ramcharan (eds), *Fake News and Elections in Southeast Asia: Impact on Democracy and Human Rights* (Routledge, 2022) 16, 34.

[58] Schuldt (n 46) 362.

[59] POFMA Office, Media Centre, www.pofmaoffice.gov.sg/media-centre.

[60] 'Does Govt Fear 'Fake News', or the Truth?' *Bangkok Post* (12 June 2021), www.bangkokpost.com/opinion/opinion/2131171/does-govt-fear-fake-news-or-the-truth-.

[61] 'Thai Police Charge Politician for Insulting King over Vaccine Remarks' Reuters (30 March 2021), www.reuters.com/article/us-thailand-politics-vaccine/thai-police-charge-politician-for-insulting-king-over-vaccine-remarks-idUSKBN2BM0UG.

[62] Data from the Statistical Office and the Digital Government Development Agency. The publicly available statistics do not distinguish between different types of computer crimes, but it appears highly likely that a large number of cases is based on Section 14 Computer Crime Act.

III. Conclusion

Andrew Harding alerted comparative lawyers to the significance of local particularities in global law diffusion: universal social problems invariably provoke local solutions. In this spirit, my chapter suggests engaging with the concept of norm localisation which focuses on the process of domestic norm adaptation and the roles of local actors and discourses. I illustrated the approach with a case study of the localised war on fake news where some scholars asserted the possibility of universal responses.

Evidence from Malaysia, Singapore and Thailand, however, cautions against global silver bullets. The legal-political settings, discursive framing, enacted laws and enforcement patterns in these jurisdictions rather suggest manifest variations within the Southeast Asia region. While the case studies revealed that anti-fake news discourses resembled each other across borders, the paths of localisation diverged on the legislation and enforcement stages, reflecting different approaches to governance: from heavy-handed criminalisation in Thailand to calibrated coercion in Singapore.

The respective Governments of the day were major stakeholders that influenced the content and application of the laws. Barisan Nasional under Najib Razak introduced AFNA and commenced its enforcement in Malaysia. But the anti-fake news foray was abruptly upended when the Pakatan Harapan coalition took over after the 2018 general election, only to be revived shortly during the pandemic. Singapore's PAP Government integrated POFMA into its existing web of laws and regulations that are mobilised whenever a minister considers it necessary or expedient. And Thailand was under military rule both in 2007 and in 2017 when the relevant anti-falsehood crimes were enacted and amended, respectively. Today, they are still enforced in frequent conjunction with *lèse-majesté* charges, which reflects another local particularity. The Thai case, in particular, shows that global calls to use the criminal law against fake news may, in fact, lead to additional harm locally.

The integration of localisation into comparative legal studies therefore promises an enhanced understanding of the processes and actors of norm diffusion. In addition, it provokes a critical-relativist distance as it induces us to examine the goals and discourses of relevant actors and the legislative outcomes and their implementation. The success of a norm transfer thus becomes an increasingly relative category that is measured against the aims initially pursued by key players, rather than against supposedly global standards. In this sense, a localised approach to comparative law also supports wider-reaching analyses of the connections between the legal and political dimensions of norm diffusion. But choosing anti-fake news laws to illustrate the value of the localisation concept for comparative legal studies provokes the question how representative this case study really is. The fake news topic clearly involves matters with close relation to power and politics. Does it offer sufficient insights for less political but more 'technical' types of norms?

The truth is that politicisation is a matter of degree. Law-making and enforcement is always political. As social problems are constructed and shaped by influential actors and their discourses, law inevitably becomes the outcome of these discourses, whether it is in civil and commercial law, administrative or criminal law.[63] Consequently, norm localisation is characterised by varying intensities of discourse, but never by none. Engaging more closely with local actors' agendas, as well as with the local processes of framing, legislating and enforcing, fruitfully expands comparative law.

[63] Law is discourse, too; see Rajah (n 20) 55–64.

12

The Centenary of Thailand's 1923 Civil and Commercial Code: Failure or Beta Test?

SURUTCHADA REEKIE AND ADAM REEKIE*

I. Introduction

The legal reform of Siam (or Thailand, as the country became known after 1939) in the early twentieth century has always drawn much academic attention, both as part of a wider modernisation discourse and as a topic worthy of academic pursuit its own right. A recent revival of interest may be attributable to a symposium on Thai legal history held at the Faculty of Law, Thammasat University in September 2019, which culminated in an edited volume by Andrew Harding and Munin Pongsapan.[1] In this chapter, the authors take the opportunity of the centenary of the 1923 Civil and Commercial Code ('1923 Code') to offer some new perspectives on this little-discussed code, in order to underline Professor Harding's (lesser-known) contribution to the field of legal history, drawing upon his much applauded contribution to Watsonian legal transplants discourse.

The 1923 Code was Thailand's first codified civil and commercial law, comprising two books on general principles (Book I) and obligations (Book II). It was promulgated and published in the *Government Gazette* (also known as the *Royal Gazette*) on 11 November 1923. Although it was intended to come into force on 1 January 1924, its starting date was postponed for one year – to 1 January 1925[2] – and in the end it was operational for a mere 10 months. The 1923 Code was swiftly replaced by the revised version of Books I and II of Civil and Commercial Code, promulgated on 1 November 1925 ('1925 Code'). In a rare piece of legislative

* The authors would like to thank the Honourable Justice Nikorn Tassaro for his valuable insights.

[1] See Andrew Harding and Munin Pongsapan (eds), *Thai Legal History: From Traditional to Modern Law* (Cambridge University Press, 2021).

[2] On promulgation, the two books were to come into force on 1 January 1924 (see section 2 of the 1923 Code). However, the Decree on the Promulgation of Book III, and the Postponement of Book I and II of the Civil and Commercial Code was promulgated on 1 January 1924, which postponed the coming into force of the 1923 Code to 1 January 1925.

manoeuvring, it was decreed that the 1925 Code was to take effect retrospectively, deeming itself to have been effective from 1 January 1925.[3] Thus, the 1923 Code was effectively 'erased' from legislative memory, even though it was in force for a short time between January and the end of October 1925.

The 1923 Code is generally considered a mere historical footnote; an abject failure, decades in the making, that was never genuinely adopted by the country. This chapter aims to challenge this narrative. It argues that the two Codes – 1923 and 1925 – should not be viewed as rivals in their sources of inspiration, legislative method or ideology; one a failure, the other a success. Instead, they should be seen as two contiguous phases of the same process. Indeed, we suggest that the 1923 Code may be thought of as – to use an analogy with software development – a 'beta test' to prepare the legal community for the reality of imminent legal change, subsequently achieved by the 1925 Code. As such, the 1923 Code should be remembered not as a failure, but as an indispensable part of the 'success' of the 1925 Code, attested by its longevity since, subject to amendments, it remains in force to this day.

In attempting this task, the chapter first addresses the legal transfer in the Southeast Asian context, as a conceptual framework for the ensuing discussion. Then it will examine the extensive drafting process and initial feedback from legal practitioners, to demonstrate that the 1923 Code should not be seen simply as a failure. In fact, all indications point to the conclusion that the old code was instrumental to the success of the second, longest-serving, civil and commercial code of Thailand.

Sources in Thai language that have received little international attention have been included and highlighted. In particular, the discussion will draw on the record of interviews of a key Siamese drafter of the 1925 Code, Phraya Manavarajasevi (the official title of Mr Plod Vichien Na Songkhla), which illuminates issues left out of official records and writings.

II. Legal Transplantation in the Southeast Asian Context

Just over two decades ago, Harding noted that in comparative law and its related fields, Southeast Asia had received little academic interest: 'Scholars in the field of law in South East Asia have therefore trodden a somewhat lonely path.'[4] Today,

[3] Section 2 of the Decree on the Promulgation of the Revised Books I and II of the Civil and Commercial Code (*Government Gazette* vol 42, 1 (11 November 1925)), which repealed the 1923 Code; and promulgated the new Books I and II of the 1925 Code (*Government Gazette* vol 42, 3 (11 November 1925)).

[4] Andrew Harding, "Comparative Law and Legal Transplantation in South East Asia: Making Sense of the "Nomic Din" in David Nelken and Jhannes Feest (eds), *Adapting Legal Cultures* (Hart, 2001) 199 (footnote omitted).

with a plethora of comparative and non-comparative academic works on the laws of Southeast Asia, Harding can be thanked as an inspiring pioneer in the field. He is credited with bringing Southeast Asia into the Watsonian legal transplantation debate, as a region that offers a rich variety of legal transplants, supporting Watson's thesis that legal transplants, even between countries which share few similarities, are not only possible but may be thriving.[5]

Thailand's experience of large-scale legal transplantation in the name of legal reform in the late nineteenth and early twentieth centuries may indeed be described as thriving. In less than a century, the country embraced legal and cultural pluralism, adaptation and evolution, albeit with difficulties at times. At the conclusion of the process, which the authors take to be the promulgation of the six main codes and the revocation of extraterritorial jurisdiction by Western colonial empires and Japan, it can be said with some confidence that the transplantation was, all things considered, successful, if we measure 'success' in the pragmatic terms of introducing to the country what was considered by those involved to be progress in a short period of time. The substantive law was transformed from traditional law based on the Three Seals Code[6] to codes and statutes modelled on those of Western nations and Japan. The traditional legal system also underwent wholesale changes, with the adoption of the civil law system, the establishment of similarly styled courts, a law school and other legal institutions.[7] The legal reform was part of a grand-scaled process of 'state-building' and 'nation-building', the terms adopted by a distinguished Thai scholar, Professor Kittisak Prokati.[8] The need to build a 'new' state and nation better captures the experience than the generally used term 'modernisation', as the 'old' Siam had to be transformed and emerged victorious, as an equal and free member of a global society of nation states and international trade, instead of a forced entry as a colony.[9]

During this period of transformation, Thai society managed to absorb a plethora of newness and otherness, and develop a Western-styled legal system that is still functioning today. This ability to adopt, as well as to adapt, might be attributable to Thai society's embracing nature. Harding argued that Southeast Asia, despite many obstacles, did very well in accommodating legal and cultural diversity,

[5] John W Cairns, 'Watson, Walton, and the History of Legal Transplants' (2013) 41 *Georgia Journal of International and Comparative Law* 637, 684–85.

[6] For a highly illuminating discussion of whether the Three Seals Code should be seen as 'law', see Chris Baker and Pasuk Phongpaichit, 'The Child is the Betel Tray: Making Law and Love in Ayutthaya Siam' (2021) 1 *Thai Legal Studies* 1.

[7] See, for example, Tamara Loos, *Subject Siam: Family, Law, and Colonial Modernity in Thailand* (Silkworm Books, 2002) 43–52; Andrew J Harding, 'The Eclipse of the Astrologers: King Mongkut, His Successors, and the Reformation of Law in Thailand' in P Nicholson and S Biddulph (eds), *Examining Practice, Interrogating Theory: Comparative Legal Studies in Asia* (Martinus Nijhoff, 2008) 319–28; and Harding and Pongsapan (n 1) Part II.

[8] Kittisak Prokati, *The Reform of Thai Legal System under European Influences* [การปฏิรูปกฎหมายไทยภายใต้อิทธิพลยุโรป), 4th edn (Winyuchon, 2013) 37 (Thai language).

[9] ibid, 43.

significantly due to the region's ability to absorb foreign influences into its psyche, without destroying its antecedent local wisdom.[10] This can truly be said about Thailand, which during the reign of King Mongkut (King Rama IV, 1851–1868) opened up its intellectual arena for a great variety of Western knowledge, ranging from law to religion and science – by way of preparation for the impending extensive reforms.[11]

Thailand's rich legal development, at times marked by the dynamic tension between internal and external influences,[12] fits Harding's description of the unique Southeast Asian legal landscape, which is comparable to overlaying geological strata whereby multiple layers are still visible but not perfectly distinguishable from each other.[13] The topic of discussion of this chapter, the 1923 Code, represents a stratum that was pushed to the surface of Thailand's legal landscape and remained visible for a time, due to the tectonic shifts that were political and legal willpower; and was shortly after overlain by a new layer that was the 1925 Code. However, it will be demonstrated that the lower layer of the 1923 Code remains 'visible' to keen eyes, as the new code absorbed the old's many basic elements and developed upon, rather than completely discarded, them. Thus, although different layers, they are part of the same legal landscape.

III. The Making of the 1923 Civil and Commercial Code

Many contemporary accounts of the drafting of Siam's new laws are congruent in their recognition of the immense scale of time, effort and preparation that went into the process. This alone was highly laudable.

A. The Timeframe

The process of codification in Siam spanned over half a century, and involved many stages. A preliminary stage may be said to be the promulgation of Western-styled statutes which marked a point of departure from traditional laws.[14] This resulted in a

[10] Harding (n 4) 216, Andrew Harding, 'Global Doctrine and Local Knowledge: law in South East Asia' (2002) 51 *International & Comparative Law Quarterly* 35, 41.

[11] See Harding (n 7).

[12] See Preedee Kasemsup, 'Reception of Law in Thailand – A Buddhist Society' in Masaji Chiba (ed), *Asian Indigenous Law: In Interaction with Received Law* (KIP Limited, 1986) 267.

[13] Harding (n 4) 205, 218.

[14] Of course, one may also take the initial stage to be the issuance of numerous edicts and decrees by King Mongkut in the mid-19th century.

number of important laws, for instance, the Evidence Act of 1895,[15] the Temporary Criminal Procedure Act of 1897[16] and the Civil Procedure Act of 1897.[17]

The starting point of the drafting process which culminated in the current six major codes of law may be considered to be the beginning of the twentieth century, growing out of the more piecemeal reform by Acts on individual topics at the end of the nineteenth century, as observed by René Guyon, a French lawyer who served in the drafting committee of the codes from 1908:

> In Siam, the plan to provide the country with a complete set of codified civil and criminal laws was decided upon only at the beginning of the 20th century. But, as early as 1892, the Government had undertaken a general reform of the administration of justice in the Kingdom ... The question of legislation naturally arose at the same time.[18]

Alternatively, the starting point may be taken to be the first formal stage of the drafting process, commencing in 1908, when the Commission of Codification was established, headed by MG Padoux, a French lawyer.[19]

The end point of the codification process may be taken to be the coming into force of the last of the six main codes – Books V and VI of the Civil and Commercial Code, the Civil Procedure Code, the Criminal Procedures Code, and also the Law for the Organisation of the Courts of Justice – all on 1 October 1935.

The work on the Civil and Commercial Code (CCC) started at the very beginning of the process, parallel to the work on the Criminal Code (referred to in many historical documents as the Penal Code[20]).[21] However, the introduction of the Penal Code was considered 'the core beginning of the legal reform' – a necessary first step to revoke extraterritorial jurisdiction of many powerful nations imposed by various treaties.[22] Therefore, the work on the CCC initially took a back seat. It was only after the completion of the first Penal Code in 1908 that the drafting committee was able to put resources to the CCC. Initially, Padoux anticipated that the entire remaining codification project would be completed in five years.[23] In

[15] *Government Gazette* vol 11 pt 47, 400 (16 February 1894).

[16] *Government Gazette* vol 13 pt 5, 56 (2 May 1896).

[17] *Government Gazette* vol 13 pt 13, 367 (14 November 1896).

[18] René Guyon, *The Work of Codification in Siam* (Imprimerie Nationale (published by the authority of the Code Commission), 1919) 4–5.

[19] ibid, 9.

[20] For further discussion of the drafting of the Penal Code, see Tokichi Masao, 'The New Penal Code of Siam' (1908–1909) 18 *Yale Law Journal* 85; Kanaphon Chanhom, 'The Modernisation of Thai Criminal Law: from the 1908 Penal Code to the 1956 Criminal Code' in Harding and Pongsapan (n 1) 138.

[21] Guyon noted that the general plan for the CCC was adopted by the Siamese Government in 1908, the year of the establishment of the Commission of Codification: Guyon (n 18) 13. However, the preliminary work on the Criminal Code started in 1906, before the formal establishment of the Commission of Codification (ibid, 26).

[22] Chanhom (n 20) 144.

[23] Communication from Mr Padoux, Legislative Adviser, to HRH Price Damron, Minister of Interior, dated 19 January 1908, Archive of the Council of State, Microfilm Roll 01-01,75.

reality, 15 years would elapse before the completion of the 1923 Code, containing only the first two books, on General Principles and Obligations. The gap between expectations and delivery may be explained by the numerous pressing legislative needs of the country and the limited resources of the drafting committee, which also undertook parallel work on other areas of law.

On the difficulty of the task of drafting the CCC, Guyon noted that the preparation of the code was:

> a rather long work and entailing some unavoidable interruptions, according as one part of the Code is more or less advanced than the other, the Commissioners had to consider the possibility of its promulgation in two separate Codes … The present state of the work, and the simultaneous completion of its principal Parts, will, however, probably allow the promulgation of one Code only, embodying all the civil and commercial provisions.[24]

Despite the difficult navigation, the first version of the CCC was promulgated on 11 November 1923, comprising Book I on general principles (sections 1–105) and Book II on obligations (sections 106–452). It offers the first codified substantive rules on wide range of topics: persons (natural and juristic), capabilities, things (chattels) and property, contracts, management of affairs without mandates, unjust enrichment and wrongful acts (torts), as well as methods on legal interpretation.

B. The Meticulous Task of Writing a Complete Set of New Laws for a Country

The meticulous manner in which the draftsmen approached the task of codification was matched by their lofty ambitions. In 1908 Padoux, in unambiguous terms, rejected the idea of codification achieved through the introduction of 'brand new codes taken from Western countries',[25] in the style of what, today, we may consider a Watsonian transplant: 'This is the very thing I would never advise to do. Siam is Siam, and the Siamese law must be a national law adopted to the wants of the country.'[26] Rather, Padoux envisaged putting the existing local law in a definitive form, removing any inconsistencies and obsolete legal rules, and condensing

> the matter of hundreds of volumes of regulations, case-law, and commentaries into the shape of some hundreds of sections so as to enable the man in the street to be easily aware of his duties and rights. This does not mean reference to any particular system

[24] Guyon (n 18) 13.
[25] Communication from Mr Padoux (n 23) 76.
[26] ibid.

of laws other than the system which the Siamese Government will consider the most suitable to the inhabitants.[27]

The difficulty of this task in the context of early-twentieth-century Siam may be illustrated by the ruminations of PW Thornely, a British national working as a foreign judge in the Bangkok courts, who wrote a detailed account of the development and workings of the courts which was published in 1923, prior to the 1923 Code's promulgation.[28] Anticipating the coming codification of civil and commercial law, after first declaring that 'no drastic change in the present law will be made'[29] by the codes, which he expected merely to add convenience of reference and gap-filling, Thornely turns directly to admit that codifying laws of inheritance and marriage in Siam is 'no easy matter',[30] given the pluralistic nature of society. Turning to the example of polygamy, he notes that contemporary Siamese law recognised polygamy, although the tendency in society was moving towards monogamy; however, the many Muslims in Siam were permitted to follow their own religious laws on the subject. Muslim law was treated by the courts as foreign law, the provisions of which were to be proved in court as evidence, which, in Thornely's words led to 'the most extraordinary and contradictory evidence being given by persons posing as religious teachers'[31] and those judges who could read English resorting to whatever textbooks were available for verification. Moreover, this also would lead to issues where, for example, a Buddhist Siamese woman would polygamously marry a Muslim man: would Muslim law apply to the marriage and to the inheritance of the children, for example? Thornely gave no opinion on the answer, but assumed that the coming Code would provide a satisfactory solution.[32]

However, over time, it seems that the already Herculean task of foreign legislative advisers gaining a sufficient understanding of Siamese civil and commercial law to condense it in such a manner developed into an even more distant objective. Rather than codifying Siamese law as it was, the committee attempted to impose an overarching structure and logic, adding doctrinal coherence, filling gaps and drawing inspiration from all quarters. As described by Guyon, a successor of Padoux, the commissioners saw the codification project as 'a good opportunity for the study, and the introduction into Siamese law, of entirely new matters which up to that time had remained untouched by the laws of the country'.[33] In particular, Guyon describes how a number of specific enactments had been made on topics such as marriage, divorce, inheritance and various types of contracts including sale,

[27] ibid.
[28] PW Thornely, *The History of a Transition* (Siam Observer Press Ltd, 1923).
[29] ibid, 282.
[30] ibid, 282.
[31] ibid.
[32] ibid.
[33] Guyon (n 18) 6.

loan, mortgage, etc, but 'the general principles determining the creation, existence and extinction of legal obligations'[34] and 'the conditions of real property'[35] had not been definitively determined.

The team of French commissioners undertook this momentous task in the meticulous manner described by Guyon:

> They have, for each Draft, pursued the same method: first, they have made a general study of the matter as it stands in the existing Siamese texts (laws or judgments) and in the principal foreign Codes. They have frequently referred to such valuable guides as the French Code, with its traditional lucidity, the English laws with which the Siamese lawyers are often better conversant, the practical and modern rules of the Swiss and Japanese Codes, the technical precisions of the German Codes, the improvements which recently have often been made in the legislations of Italy, Belgium, the Netherlands, America, etc.[36]

For the preliminary works for the book of Obligation in particular, Guyon noted that the Commission considered, understandably in addition to the above, the recently passed laws of Switzerland, Tunis and Morocco.[37]

Once a draft code was prepared, it was presented to a Revising Committee – appointed from senior Siamese officials and foreign advisors – along with preliminary reports, to enable further discussion between the Drafting Committee and the Revising Committee. Opinions were sought from relevant officials to enable further revision, 'then after all were in agreement, the actual drafting of the code may begin'.[38] This meticulous and careful process was further stymied by external events, including Padoux's resignation in 1914 and First World War in Europe. However, as early as 1914, the Commission, apparently, was sufficiently confident and the drafting sufficiently far progressed to publish an English version of the draft book on obligations, containing general provisions on obligations and provisions concerning specific types of contracts, including partnerships and companies, totalling almost 1400 sections.[39]

The 1923 Code, as eventually promulgated, coming into force in 1925 (as mentioned above), contained two books. The first contained general provisions on matters such as time periods, natural persons, juristic persons, and things. The second book covered the creation of obligations – contracts generally (incapacity, agreement, objectives), management of affairs without mandate, unjust enrichment and wrongful acts – specific kinds of obligations, transfer of obligations, effects of obligations, rights of creditors over debtors' property, and extinction of obligations.

[34] ibid.
[35] ibid.
[36] ibid, 11.
[37] ibid. 13.
[38] ibid, 10–12.
[39] Draft Civil and Commercial Code for the Kingdom of Siam: Book on Obligations (Bangkok Daily Mail, 1914).

C. The Professional Feedback on Siam's First Civil and Commercial Code

It is rare to find a study on the wider reception of a law after it is passed. Fortunately, an account of the public and professional perception of the drafting process and the resulting 1923 Code was provided in a series of interviews of one of Siamese members of the drafting committee, Phraya Manavarajasevi, conducted by professors from the Faculty of Law, Thammasat University in 1980–1981.[40] The interviews offer a very illuminating account into the actual reception and perception of the 1923 code, from the perspectives of the Siamese.

First, the earlier drafting of the Civil and Commercial Code was seen as a significantly lengthy process. Phraya Manavarajasevi alluded to the fact that the process started before he went to study law in England, and was not done by the time he came back.[41]

Second, and perhaps most important of all, the draft prepared by the French commissioners was seen as too complicated, both by officials and practitioners. This can be seen from many references by Phraya Manavajarasevi. He did not understand the draft code because the provisions did not fit well together, and, even after he translated it into Thai, those [presumably other officials] who read the Thai version also found it difficult to decipher.[42] The drafts were then submitted to the Revision Committee, who also did not understand them.[43] The Thai version was later distributed to judges and lawyers, and received overwhelmingly negative feedback.[44] As a result, Phraya Manavarajasevi said that he proposed that a new committee be appointed for the purpose of drafting a new version of the code.[45]

Third, on a personal level, it was clear that Phraya Manavarajasevi believed that the problem was mainly caused by two elements. The first was that the French commissioners tried to draft the new Siamese Civil and Commercial Code from scratch – as an original and novel system of civil and commercial law, unlike codes from other countries – resulting in a highly complicated legal scheme.[46]

[40] Department of Legal Studies in Society, Philosophy and History, *Record of an Interview with Phraya Manavarajasevi* (บันทึกคำสัมภาษณ์พระยามานวราชเสวี (ปลอด วิเชียร ณ สงขลา)) (Winyuchon, 2014) (Thai language).

[41] ibid, 18–19.

[42] ibid, 20 (Thai version: 'ฉันได้อ่านร่างกฎหมายแล้วก็รู้สึกว่าไม่เข้าใจ เขียนกฎหมายไม่กินเกลียวกัน ฉันจึงแปลกฎหมายเป็นภาษาไทยแล้ว … ใครต่อใครอ่านแล้วก็ไม่เข้าใจ อ่านยากมาก' – 'I read the Draft Code but did not understand it because the legal provisions were inconsistent with each other. I then translated it to Thai, yet those who read it still failed to understand it. It was a difficult read' (translation by the first author).

[43] ibid, 20–21.

[44] ibid, 28 (Thai version: 'พอแปลออกมาจากฉบับเดิมที่ร่างแล้ว ก็ดำเนินการแจกไปตามศาลต่างๆ แจกทนายความ ก็ปรากฏว่าบ่นกันมากว่าอ่านแล้วไม่เข้าใจ' – 'The translated version of the Draft Code was distributed to courts and also to lawyers. Much complaint was received about how it was difficult to understand' (translation by the first author).

[45] ibid, 21.

[46] ibid, 20 (Thai version: 'ฉันพิจารณาดูก็เห็นว่า พวกฝรั่งเศสนั้น จะเขียนกฎหมายไทยให้เป็นแบบออริจิแนล คือสร้างระบบของตัวเองขึ้นมาใหม่' – 'In my view, the French were trying to draft an original Thai Code, which was to establish our own system of law' (translation by the first author).

The second element was the lack of experience of the French drafters in taking on such monumental task.[47] The proposed solution was to follow Japan's experience of 'copying' from a successful foreign model, such as the German Code, which was perceived to be more systematic and thus easier to understand.[48]

Therefore, whilst it may be argued that the 1923 Code did not receive favourable feedback, Siam should be given due credit for making an informed choice after extensive research and consultation, to localise foreign legal rules in order to maximise the chance of success. The next section elaborates on this notion and argues that the 1923 Code is indispensable to the overall successful transplant of the country's CCC.

IV. Unpacking the Story of the 1923 Code

The journey of the 1932 Code will be examined from various perspectives, in order to support the claim that it was not merely an instance of a failed transplant. It should be given the recognition it deserves – not as a quiet footnote in legal history, but an instrumental part of the overall success of the country's civil and commercial law.

A. Modes of Transplantation

The first perspective of examination is from the legal transplant discourse. Our understanding of legal transfer between societies has been enriched since Watson. Harding recently suggested that we need more encompassing terminology: 'legal transplantation' should refer only to the imperial transplanting of law to colonies; 'legal mimesis' or 'legal copying' refers to legal transfers in the twenty-first-century law reforms, where a society looks externally for ideas; and 'legal reception' refers only to the Great Reception of Roman Law.[49] In Siam's case, the experience of the legal reform does not quite fit any of the above terms. This is important, as Siam was never colonised, and thus the transplantation process was distinctly different from the imperial transfer process that took place elsewhere in Southeast Asia where the legal transfer may be said to be coercive.[50] Nevertheless, the overall scheme of legal reform could not be said to be completely voluntary, as external

[47] ibid, 21 (Thai version: 'อันที่จริงแล้วคนที่มาเขียนกฎหมายเรานั้นมือยังไม่ถึงขั้น เวลาเขียนไป มันเลยไม่กินเกลียวกัน' – 'In fact, the capability of the drafters were not sufficient, resulting in inconsistencies in the drafting' (translation by the first author).

[48] ibid, 21–22, 31–32.

[49] Andrew Harding, 'The Legal Transplants Debate: Getting Beyond the Impasse?' in Vito Breda (ed), *Legal Transplants in East Asia and Oceania* (Cambridge University Press, 2019) 13, 27.

[50] See, eg, David P Dolowitz and David Marsh, 'Learning from Abroad: The Rule of Policy Transfer in Contemporary Policy-Making' (2000) 13 *Governance* 5.

pressures – mainly threats of colonisation – instigated the changes. Therefore, to borrow from the language of policy transfer, the process may be seen as an 'indirect imposition', where both voluntary and coercive elements exist;[51] in this case the exogenous threats incentivised Siam to voluntarily reform the whole legal system.

Given this overall nature of legal transfer, how should the 1923 Code in particular be viewed? A helpful suggestion to understand the process may be found in Stefan Vogenauer's categorisation of cross-border transfer of the legal rules in mapping contemporary contract laws of Asia: straightforward transfers (whereby rules were simply copied from the donor society and posited in the recipient); indirect or 'double' transfers (whereby the law is transferred to the first recipient system, and then onwards to a second); hybrid transfers (whereby the resulting rule, etc combines ingredients from different legal traditions); flexible transfers (which appears after the initial transfer, and charts the rise and fall of a legal rule, etc in the donor society); sticky transfers (where the law of the donor society moves on and the transferred law in the recipient society fails to follow suit); rejected transfers (where a body of law from the donor society is accepted, except for particular aspects); localised transfers (where the recipient society extensively modifies the original rule to accommodate local considerations); and irrepressible transfers (where the courts or other legal institutions later adopt the rules that were originally rejected, due to particular pressing needs).[52] Some of this terminology will be employed in the following discussion.

The first observation regarding legal transplants and the 1923 Code is that it was clear that the drafting of the 1923 Code was not a result of a single 'straightforward transfer'.[53] Instead, the work involved in the preparation of the 1923 Code was extensive and meticulous, including detailed research and comparison of many foreign and domestic sources as mentioned above, and encompassing numerous modes of legal transplants along the process. As mentioned above, this informed choice of foreign law to be adapted and localised leads to the receptivity of the legal transplant, meaning that the imported law is more likely to be effective in the new legal order and positively contribute to socio-economic growth.

It is also clear that, in combining elements from many foreign sources, the 1923 Code underwent a 'hybrid transfer',[54] leading to the final result which was a hybridised body of law, but the foreign sources of which were still recognisable – what Harding painted as a tectonic landscape. However, the resulting 1923 Code was not simply a combination of various foreign sources that were sewn together in pieces, but a more nuanced mixture of the global and the local. This is clear from Guyon's description

[51] ibid, 14.

[52] Stefan Vogenauer, 'Comparative Conclusions' in Mindy Chen-Wishart and Stefan Vogenauer (eds), *Studies in the Contract Laws of Asia III: Contents of Contracts and Unfair Terms* (Oxford University Press, 2020) 552–55.

[53] Given the scope and limitation of this chapter, the discussion here necessarily side-steps the issue of linguistic impossibility of legal transplants, as propounded by Legrand, a proper engagement with which is far from 'straightforward' and requires a separate piece.

[54] Vogenauer (n 52) 553.

of how foreign drafting commissioners incorporated local elements into the law. He explained that during the preliminary process before the actual drafting could begin, the commission sought opinions from Siamese officials:

> [T]o be supplied with competent opinions and to receive useful directions upon all the questions under consideration … As a result of these discussions … important precisions have been made and a good knowledge of the local needs has in turn enabled the Commissioners to submit drafts which do not consist only in theoretical scheme but are framed according to the actual and real requirements of the country.[55]

Given these multiple modes of legal transplants, the most important characteristic of the whole process, in the authors' view, is the localisation process that determined the appropriate interplay of all these transplanted pieces. It has been suggested that the localisation of foreign laws to meet local demands is vital to the success of the transplant.[56] This was the case for the 1923 Code, which was the embodiment of the foreign advisors' and drafters' genuine interest and dedication to develop the new law for the country. This can be seen from the way that these foreign lawyers worked on the draft laws and the subsequent efforts in educating the public. They adopted a drafting approach that embodied local requirements in an attempt to achieve a fitting transplanted law, evolved to account for diversity rather than simply imposing foreign laws into the local arena. To this end, Tamara Loos opined, in relation to the foreign advisors who oversaw the overall project of modernisation:

> Although it is tempting to dismiss them all as part of the homogenizing machinery of European capitalist modernity, the foreign advisers made enormous sacrifices that cannot be captured by evaluating them as purely self-interested imperialists.[57]

The sacrifices and the genuine interest in the well-being and progress of Siam, as observed in the case of the general advisors by Loos, are equally applicable to the foreign drafters.[58] The dedication of the drafters – Thai and foreign – was also evident from their efforts in preparing the country for the new law. As mentioned above, the drafters consulted various stakeholders for feedback in order to improve

[55] Guyon (n 18) 11.

[56] Daniel Berkowitz, Katharina Pistor and Jean-Francois Richard, 'The Transplant Effect' (2003) 51 *The American Journal of Comparative Law* 163. It should be noted that this study concluded that Thailand's legal transplant was 'unreceptive' (at 194); however, the study cited French law as the main source of legal reform (at 199), thus it appears that the conclusion is less applicable to the Civil and Commercial Code, which is widely acknowledged to have been received from many foreign codes, with German, Japanese and French laws being the main influences.

[57] Loos (n 7) 53.

[58] Loos mentioned the sacrifices by Gustave Rolin-Jaequemyns (Belgium) and Edword Strobel (USA), the first two general advisors, who died during their service in Siam, and also by Jens Westerngard (see Loos (n 7) 53). Beyond this, many foreign advisors have shown their genuine affinity for the country – consider, for example, Guyon, who served for over five decades, became a Siamese citizen with a Thai name Pichan Bulyong (พิชาญ บุลยง); Tokishi Masao who served as in the Ministry of Justice for nearly two decades, and later as an ambassador of Japan to Siam, and died in Siam (his death was recorded in the *Government Gazette* on 21 August BE 2464 (1921) vol 38, 1387).

the Code. In addition, after the promulgation, but before the Code was to come into force, the drafters published an annotated version of the 1923 Code, with explanation and examples accompanying every provision.[59] The preface, written by Phraya Manavarajasevi, stated the dual purpose of the publication: to be used in the law school and to provide legal understanding to the general public beyond the law school.[60]

The various efforts in preparing and familiarising the country with the new law made the drafting of Siam's major codes, in general, and the 1923 Code in particular, an attempted 'localized transfer' – where the transplanted rules have 'gone native' by being modified to fit local requirements.[61] This also serves another latent purpose of pre-empting or reducing any criticism or resistance that the new law might garner. To this end, the 1923 Code may be seen as the first attempt of localisation, which paved way for a more receptive second localisation that was the 1925 Code.

B. A Failure is a Gain: The 1923 Code as the 'Beta Test' for the Current Code

Frequently one's reasoning ability is limited by linguistic framework: if something is correctly labelled as a 'failed attempt', can it ever be a 'success'? To elaborate on this point, the authors respectfully borrow one of King Bhumibol's mottos, 'our loss is our gain', which encapsulates the notion that a loss, viewed from one perspective such as financial, may be a true long-term gain in public well-being.[62] Similarly, when viewed from one perspective, the 1923 Code was a genuine failure, evidenced by the resounding rejection by practitioners, followed by the swift introduction of the replacement 1925 Code. However, the authors argue that the 1923 Code served a very important purpose, without which the 1925 Code perhaps would never have been adopted successfully. This purpose was being the 'beta test' for the 1925 Code.

In software development, an 'alpha test' is an in-house test of a product in development before its release to the public. A 'beta test' is typically the first time that software is released outside the developer's organisation. At this stage, the software is usually complete in terms of its features, but will likely have several known or unknown bugs. A limited audience outside of the production team, known as 'beta testers' – usually invited from the pool of customers or potential customers of the developer – provide feedback on the product, which will eventually become the 'stable release' version that will go into production.

[59] The Law Drafting Department, *The Civil and Commercial Code B.E.2466 Books I and II and Examples* (Kong Lahutosa Press, 1924) (Thai language).

[60] ibid, 3.

[61] Vogenauer (n 52) 554.

[62] The National Identity Office, *King Bhumibol: Strength of the Land* (Amarin Printing and Publishing Co Ltd, 2009) 199–200.

We suggest that the 1923 Code may be seen as essentially a beta test of the 1925 Code: a version containing virtually all the essential features of the eventual 'stable release', but not intended to be put into actual usage. This is simply an opportunity for practitioners and stakeholders to peruse and experiment, so that the drafters may acquire important real-world feedback and uncover any problem or issue before the general release to the public. This contention is supported by a number of pieces of circumstantial evidence.

First, it was clear from Guyon's own account that the drafting committee had already adopted the practice of canvassing for real-world critiques from practitioners. This might have been a response to the rather adversarial local environment at the time, as alluded to by Phraya Manavarajasevi, on the basis that codified law was contradictory to the long-standing practice of the application of traditional law.[63] Therefore, as mentioned above, before the actual drafting could begin (but after the consultation and discussion with the Revising Committee), the drafters sent out a basic form of the draft code to government officials to gather their opinions, which were then used to further revise and develop the Code. This shows that the drafting committee was already 'beta testing' even at the initial process.

Second, the 1925 Code, despite being presented as a newly drafted version with a pivot of foreign sources away from French law towards German and Japanese law,[64] retained much of the content of 1923 Code, mainly in its conceptual framework. Indeed, the first book of the 1925 Code follows a similar structure to the 1923 Code: general provisions, followed by persons, divided into natural persons and juristic persons, followed by things (chattels) – the 1925 Code added additional sections on juristic acts and prescription, where were not found in Book I of the 1923 Code. Book II of the 1925 Code contains a very similar list of headings to Book II of the 1923 Code, albeit in a different order: the general provisions on obligations are promoted to the start of the Book rather than the end, with contracts, management of affairs without mandate, unjust enrichment and wrongful acts following. However, the topics covered by Books I and II are generally of a similar scope.

In terms of substance, a table of references containing comparative sources of the first five Books of the Civil and Commercial Code, compiled by Phraya Manavajarasevi, and published alongside his interviews, shows that approximately half of the provisions of 1925 Code[65] list provisions in the 'Old Text' – ie the 1923 Code – as one of the sources. However, it is important to heed a drafter's caveat here: Phraya Manavarajasevi explained that the drafters did not necessarily use or turn the old provisions into the new provisions, but the old provisions were listed there alongside other foreign sources 'to honour the original drafters and to not

[63] Preface by Phraya Manavarajasevi in The Law Drafting Department (n 59) 1.

[64] Phraya Manavarajasevi's account was that the direction of the code was changed from the French system to German Pandectist system, but also following the Japanese model (Department of Legal Studies in Society, Philosophy and History (n 40) 23, 77).

[65] 218 out of the original 452 sections. See 'References' section in Department of Legal Studies in Society, Philosophy and History (n 40) 143–64.

affect the goodwill'.[66] Nevertheless, it may still be said that the spirit of the Old Text lived on in the new. It may even bring to mind the famous 'ship of Theseus' philosophical paradox, over whether an object is the same object or loses its identity if all of the component parts are replaced.[67]

Third, many drafting committee members of the two codes overlapped; and the head of the committee during the transition period from the 1923 Code to the 1925 Code remained the same: Guyon. It can therefore be seen that there was a continuation in terms of the supervising member who oversaw the drafting of both codes.[68]

Fourth, there was a significant overlap in the sources of the two codes – the German and Japanese Codes, often quoted as the main source for the 1925 Code, were already considered in detail during the drafting process of the 1923 Code. Whilst there were other sources listed under 'Miscellaneous' in the table of references referred to above,[69] many of these were already considered by the French commissioners who drafted the 1923 Code.[70] As such, the major change was a pivot in terms of what the drafting committee presented to the public. A hypothesis may be made here that the decision to accentuate the German/Japan lineage was perhaps to allude to the general perception of those laws in Siam at the time, which Guyon himself referred to: 'the practical and modern rules of the Swiss and Japanese Codes, the technical precisions of the German Codes'.[71] This was also echoed by the opinion of Phraya Manavarajasevi, that the German Code was systematic and easy to understand.[72] This perception fits with the context of that time when the Government was pressed to swiftly introduce a CCC that was seen to be more pragmatic, to abate the criticisms of the practitioners. It would have been reasonable for them to use the German and Japanese Codes as flagship models for the 1925 version, to allude to their pragmatic side. Of course, the 1925 Code was well received and did not attract any significant pushback from practitioners, despite it being rather similar to the 1923 Code as discussed above.

Finally, common sense would suggest that, despite the brilliance and diligence of the new drafting committee, it would have been virtually impossible to devise a completely new code (containing two Books, and over 400 provisions) based on

[66] ibid. 26 (Thai version: 'แต่อันที่จริงเราไม่ได้เอามันมาหรอก แต่ก็เขียนเอาไว้ เพื่อจะได้เป็นเกียรติยศแก่ผู้ร่างเดิม และจะได้ไม่เสียไมตรีต่อกันด้วย' – 'Actually we did not use them, but it was recorded as such to honour the original drafters and to not affect the goodwill between the countries' (translation by the first author).

[67] See eg Thomas Hobbes, *Elements of Philosophy, the First Section Concerning Body* (R & W Leybourn, 1656) reprinted in Sir William Molesworth (ed), *The Collected Works of Thomas Hobbes* (Routledge 1992) 136.

[68] However, a Thai member of the later drafting committee, Phraya Manavarajasevi, commented that Guyon was retained in the later committee because he was a drafter of the old 1923 Code, and as such keeping him was due to the need to keep the goodwill, presumably with France (Department of Legal Studies in Society, Philosophy and History (n 40) 23).

[69] See 'References' section in Department of Legal Studies in Society, Philosophy and History (n 40) 143–64.

[70] Such as the civil codes of France, Switzerland and Italy.

[71] Guyon (n 18) 11.

[72] Department of Legal Studies in Society, Philosophy and History (n 40) 21–22, 31–32.

new sources, equipped with new theoretical direction and new substantive laws, in less than two years, without it being constructed on the foundation of the 1923 Code. To start anew and discard the works of the 1923 Code altogether would have been a waste of valuable time, manpower and capital. Code-drafting was a highly expensive project and required consultation with and feedback from various stakeholders. Indeed, much consultation had already been undertaken in the decades of drafting of the 1923 Code. Building a new code based on an old code, as all indications here point to, was clearly a more efficient process.

Therefore, we argue that what was presented as a new and drastically different Code was the stable release version, developed out of the beta test. The 1923 Code was not discarded; instead, it lives on in the 1925 Code, which, with amendments, is the code that Thailand uses today. They are part of a continuum that has proven to be a successful legal transplant.

V. Conclusion

The chapter presents different ways to contemplate the relationship between the 1923 Code and the 1925 Code. One narrative is a story of foreign hubris: an attempt to take existing Siamese law and impose a conceptual and doctrinal framework drawn from European jurisprudence. History exposes this as a flawed approach, since the delay resulting from the complicated, arguably overly intellectual drafting process undermined its successful reception. The success of the quick and practical process of the 1925 Code can be seen as a polar opposite, supporting Watsonian transplant theories, that simple transplantation is possible without necessary close connection between the donor and donee societies.

The chapter also proposes an alternative narrative. The 1923 Code could be seen as a 'beta test', and any difficulties, or 'bugs', that were uncovered were, at least in part, presentational regarding the goals, inspiration and method of drafting. The main difficulty was perhaps the *claim* that the new civil code could capture Siamese law as it was, but modernised through categorisation, definition and distillation of concepts. This bug was solved through presenting the 1925 Code as an imperfect import: a pragmatic solution to the needs of the country. This was a code based on those with a track record of success elsewhere, and any flaws and incompatibilities with Siamese society were easily explainable by the difference in context and excusable by the haste in drafting. The unsung role of the 1923 Code was in paving the way for the 1925 Code. It drew the criticism that the 1925 Code might otherwise have faced, allowing the latter to be what it is: a success.

13

Local Participatory Democracy Promotes Economic Development: Philippine People Power and the Schumpeterian Proviso

BRYAN DENNIS G TIOJANCO*

A few years ago Andrew Harding asked a fundamental question: is constitutionalism and development a mismatch or a dream team? If it is a dream team, how can constitutionalism assist development, and vice versa? I agree with Harding's conclusions that constitutionalism and development is a dream team and that 'The solution of the riddle of development and constitutionalism … lies in the empowerment of communities and individuals.'[1] Hence the thesis of this essay: local participatory democracy promotes economic development. I support this thesis with two arguments. The first is an approach Harding endorses: an argument from a constitutional ethnography of Philippine democracy. There is evidence from several Philippine case studies that constitutionally enforcing people empowerment boosts development and would therefore promote what Harding calls the developmental operativity of constitutionalism in the Philippines. This, I show, was both the original intent behind the 1987 Philippine Constitution and the legislative intent behind the country's 1991 Local Government Code.

The second is an argument from democratic theory. The predominant model of democracy today is Joseph Schumpeter's procedural definition, supplemented by liberal prescriptions of rights and the rule of law. This has led to the neglect or even disavowal of direct participatory democracy, based on a perceived lack of civic virtue among the citizenry. But while Schumpeter himself generally agreed with this position, he recognised that the local affairs of towns and other small

* I thank Andrew Harding, Maartje de Visser, Dan Puchniak, Benjamin Ong and Dean Dulay for their helpful comments on an early version of this chapter that I presented at a seminar organised by the Singapore Management University's Center for Commercial Law on 27 September 2023.

[1] Andrew Harding, 'Constitutionalism and Development: A Mismatch or a Dream-Team?' (2019) 12 *Law and Development Review* 647, 662.

communities could be safely managed by citizens. Call it the Schumpeterian proviso: the citizenry can be trusted to directly participate in democratic decision-making on local affairs.

I. Harding on Constitutionalism and Development

Comparative constitutional law studies in Southeast Asia owe several harvests to seeds Andrew Harding had sown. He is a pioneer in turning this once fallow frontier into fertile fields.[2] This chapter harvests one such field: constitutionalism and development in Asia. Recall that the dominant model in the region had long been the Asian developmental state. This state was decidedly illiberal; it had a very visible hand in the economy and was unconstrained by liberal democratic rights. This had to do with a narrow notion of development. Despite a longstanding international consensus that development includes promotion of the rule of law, in Asia development had historically meant nothing more than economic development. Constitutionalism was considered a hindrance to the pursuit of rising prosperity. Recently however the role of law in maintaining a strong, stable, prospering state has been increasingly recognised in the region. Law, in other words, promotes sustainable economic development. This has increased interest in constitutionalism and constitutional reforms in Asia.[3]

In his 2019 essay, 'Constitutionalism and Development: A Mismatch or a Dream-Team?', Harding raised a fundamental question relating to this increased interest: how can constitutionalism assist development, and vice versa?[4] His answer: by politically empowering communities and individuals.[5] This is in line with the United Nations Sustainable Development Goals (SDG) 2015, which emphasise good governance, accountability and the rule of law.[6] SDG Goal 16 is to 'Promote peaceful and inclusive societies for sustainable development, provide access to justice for all and build effective, accountable and inclusive institutions at all levels.'[7] A specific goal under this that Harding highlights is Goal 16.7: 'ensuring responsive, inclusive, participatory and representative decision-making at all levels'.[8] As Harding points out, these development goals are achieved by

[2] eg, Andrew Harding, 'Global Doctrine and Local Knowledge: Law in South East Asia' (2002) 51 *International & Comparative Law Quarterly* 35; Andrew Harding, 'The Constitutional Dimensions of Decentralisation and Local Self-Government in Asia' in Adriaan Bedner and Barbara Oomen (eds), *Real Legal Certainty and its Relevance: Essays in honour of Jan Michiel Otto* (Amsterdam University Press, 2018); Andrew Harding, *The Constitution of Malaysia: A Contextual Analysis*, 2nd edn (Hart Publishing, 2022).

[3] Harding (n 1) 651, 654–55, 661.

[4] ibid, 650.

[5] ibid, 662.

[6] ibid, 647.

[7] ibid, 662.

[8] ibid, 656.

constitutional means.[9] This chapter argues that the 1987 Philippine Constitution and the 1991 Local Government Code (LGC) give the self-same answer as Harding, and that this constitutional strategy has worked in the patches where it has been implemented. Filipinos have prospered in localities where they are politically empowered by law.

This chapter also follows the approach Harding recommended in his 2019 essay. He says that people empowerment can be sustained only 'under a rule of law that has the quality of developmental operativity'.[10] By developmental operativity he meant a practical constitutional strategy for maintaining the rule of law, political stability and justice.[11] This requires a strategy which fits the country's socio-political culture, which always features its own quirks. Scholars can help formulate this strategy by providing local knowledge of how law in the books works on a specific soil.[12] The scholarly approach Harding recommends in this effort is constitutional ethnography, which analyses how political, legal, social and economic practices interact under a given constitutional system.[13]

Harding's worry sadly remains timely in our age of democratic backsliding and anti-constitutional populism: voters will come to reject constitutional democracy if only the rich prosper in it. 'For too long development has been development for those who are already fortunate', wrote Harding, and constitutional democracies will come 'under threat globally if they do not deliver wide distribution of the benefits of development'.[14] The explanation for this is backed by extensive surveys from 72 societies, including 13 from East and Southeast Asia: people usually regard social justice and fairness as essential to any democracy (alongside good governance, free and fair elections, and liberal freedoms),[15] and those who feel good about their own or their country's economic fortunes tend to be satisfied with their government.[16] Naturally, during economically satisfying times, most citizens will esteem their democracy very highly and would seldom compromise its values even for clear personal gain.[17]

Nearly two decades of data comparing East Asian democracies support Harding's worry: democratic values predominate in prosperous Japan, Korea and Taiwan, while in the Philippines decades of insufficient and unequal economic development have helped spread and strengthen authoritarian values.[18] It is true that, given their country's decent economic performance of late, Filipinos

[9] ibid, 658–59.
[10] ibid, 662.
[11] ibid, 647 and 659.
[12] ibid, 659.
[13] ibid, 658 and 662.
[14] ibid, 659.
[15] Jie Lu and Yun-Han Chu, *Understandings of Democracy: Origins and Consequences Beyond Western Democracies* (Oxford University Press, 2022) 171.
[16] ibid, 123.
[17] ibid, 96.
[18] Larry Diamond, 'Trends in Support for Democracy in East Asian Democracies' in Yun-Han Chu et al (eds), *How Asians View Democratic Legitimacy* (National Taiwan University Press, 2023).

are presently satisfied with Philippine democracy. Nevertheless, when forced to choose, most of them would trade the freedoms of democracy for faster economic development and reduced wealth inequality.[19]

However, widespread prosperity will not come naturally from economic development, as the previous generation of economists, jurists and policymakers had formerly believed; it is a product of egalitarian law and policy.[20] The Philippine case studies below show that people empowerment leads to such a wide distribution of developmental benefits. They suggest a way in which constitutional law can counteract the tendency towards increasing wealth and income inequality under capitalist democracies.[21]

II. People Power in the Philippines

Harding's thesis – that constitutionalism can assist development by politically empowering communities and individuals – is supported by the Philippines' experience with local people empowerment. Statistically, there is still insufficient available data on Philippine local governments to strongly correlate economic development with people empowerment.[22] Nevertheless, in several documented cases the quality of local public services has remarkably improved where there is broad popular participation in local politics; conversely, in localities where public decision-making is not participatory, local governance tends to favour narrow interests, not the public good.[23] For example, a 2012 dataset shows a high incidence of political dynasties in the country's 10 poorest provinces, with the three poorest having the majority of political leadership posts held by dynasties.[24]

Eight case studies on Philippine local government collected in an edited volume, *Transforming Local Government*, give evidence for Harding's thesis.[25] The volume's second Foreword concludes that the 'most important' of the 'key transformative elements' that have remade the studied local governments into effective governance units is 'people involvement and empowerment': 'the participation of people in policy formulation and in the planning, implementation, monitoring, and evaluation of programs and projects'.[26] Such 'critical role of citizen engagement and

[19] Linda Luz Guerrero, Iremae Labucay and Steven Rood, 'Philippine Citizen Attitudes toward Democracy' in Chu et al (n 18) 286–88, 292.

[20] Thomas Piketty, *Capital in the Twenty-First Century* (Belknap Press, 2014) 11–15; Zachary Liscow, 'Is Efficiency Biased?' (2018) 85 *The University of Chicago Law Review* 1649, 1663–66.

[21] ibid, 25–27.

[22] Joseph Capuno, 'The Quality of Local Governance and Development under Decentralization in the Philippines' (University of the Philippines School of Economics, 2005) 3 and 11.

[23] ibid, 3–5.

[24] Jose Ramon Albert et al, 'Regulating Political Dynasties toward a More Inclusive Society' (2015) *Philippine Institute for Development Studies: Policy Notes* 3, table 1.

[25] Maria Regina Hechanova, Mendiola Teng-Calleja and Edna Franco (eds), *Transforming Local Government* (Bughaw, 2017).

[26] Eddie Dorotan, 'Foreword' in Hechanova, Teng-Calleja and Franco (n 25) viii–ix.

public-private partnerships', observed the editors, was a 'common thread across the transformation stories'.[27]

These transformation stories trumpet the astonishing success of people empowerment in bettering lives in the countryside. From 1998 to 2010, Naga City, 'a third-class city operating with a very limited budget', became 'a bustling first-class city' through its charismatic mayor Jesse Robredo's programme of enabling 'citizen participation in local governance [which] went beyond consultation to include concrete roles in making policies, implementing projects, as well as monitoring and evaluating LGU [ie, local government unit] projects'.[28] Naga City has become 'a model of local governance for cities and municipalities all over the Philippines'.[29] 'Having learned from … Jesse Robredo', for example, the mayor of the municipality of Upi 'organized the civil society groups [in his municipality] into the Upi People's Council and made them co-managers, helping the government plan, organize, implement, monitor, and evaluate all government programs and projects'; this helped transform Upi from 'a fourth-class municipality with badly damaged roads … and dilapidated infrastructure' into 'a first-class municipality' where 'roads are paved in concrete', there is 'a good water system' and 'streets are lit at night'.[30] Similarly, from 1995 to 2015, one of the country's poorest provinces, Bohol, more than halved its poverty rate through a programme where constituents were 'empowered thru a participatory and shared style of leadership'.[31]

The Philippines owes its return to democracy in 1986 to this radical democratic idea that all citizens, including the poor, have both the right and duty to participate in democratic politics. During the preceding dictatorship this idea, called people power, spread from parishes organising self-help Basic Christian Communities throughout the country, to the urban poor in street protests, then the labour movement in strikes, then to the political opposition in elections, to the peaceful 1986 People Power Revolution that catapulted Corazon Aquino to the presidency.[32] Wide-scale citizen participation at all levels of public decision-making was then enshrined as a structural principle in the 1987 Philippine Constitution and implemented in many statutes, including the LGC.[33]

[27] Maria Regina Hechanova, Mendiola Teng-Calleja and Edna P Franco, 'Preface' in Hechanova, Teng-Calleja and Franco (n 25) xii.

[28] Ramon Benedicto Alampay, 'Naga City: Governance for and by the People as a Way of Life' in Hechanova, Teng-Calleja and Franco (n 25) 87 and 94.

[29] ibid, 87.

[30] Marshaley Baquiano, 'Upi, Maguindanao: Left Behing No More' in Hechanova, Teng-Calleja and Franco (n 25) 121–23.

[31] Maria Ligaya Menguito and Ramon Benedicto Alampay, 'From Poverty to Sustainability: The Bohol Experience' in Hechanova, Teng-Calleja and Franco (n 25) 25 and 37.

[32] Bryan Dennis Tiojanco, '1987年フィリピン革命憲法のキリスト教的起源' '1987-Nen Firipin Kakumei Kenpô No Kirisuto-Kyô Teki Kigen' ['Christian Origins of the Philippine Revolutionary Constitution of 1987'] (2021) 37 論究ジュリスト [*Quarterly Jurist*] 140.

[33] Bryan Dennis Tiojanco, 'The Making of the 1987 Philippine Constitution' in Ngoc Son Bui and Mara Malagodi (eds), *Asian Comparative Constitutional Law: Constitution-making* (Hart, 2023).

The 1987 Constitution declares that 'The Philippines is a democratic and republican State.'[34] The word 'democratic' here goes beyond liberal representative democracy, which the word 'republican' already encompasses; it was added 'precisely to emphasize people power and the people's rights'.[35] The 1986 Constitutional Commission wanted to emphasise that Philippine democracy is a participatory democracy, where the citizenry can directly partake in politics through referendum, recall, people's initiative, etc.[36] There are at least 30 such people empowerment provisions in the Constitution, including 'Legislative bodies of local governments shall have sectoral representation as may be prescribed by law',[37] and 'The President shall provide for regional development councils or other similar bodies composed of [among others] representatives from non-governmental organizations [NGOs] within the regions'.[38] During the drafters' deliberations, a proposal to remove reserved seats for sectoral representatives in local legislative bodies was rejected on the reasoning that 'sectoral representation in local legislative bodies … is already an earned right' and 'already a working principle which has been proven by experience to be useful and to be desirable for a community'.[39]

The LGC builds on this constitutional principle. The principal author of the LGC, former Senator Aquilino 'Nene' Pimentel, Jr, explains that:

> The heart of the Local Government Code was already beating when the 1987 Constitution was written. The Code is a manifestation of how we envisioned our democracy when we reclaimed it from the dictatorship … The people must always be on top of the situation to monitor what is being done and to express their views regarding the way the government is being run in the localities … Local governance does not depend on the governors alone. The people must do their share.[40]

The LGC's overarching policies include periodic consultations with non-governmental and people's organisations, local communities and sectoral groups.[41] And, as Harding highlights in his 2025 book, *Territorial Governance in Southeast Asia*, the LGC features many provisions which 'seek to provide for genuine local democracy': sectoral or NGO representation in local legislative bodies (*sanggunians*), development councils, health boards, peace and order councils, prequalification bids and awards committees; and mechanisms of recall, local

[34] The Constitution of the Republic of the Philippines 1987, Art II, s 1.
[35] *Macalintal v COMELEC* [2023] GR No 263590.
[36] Record of the 1986 Constitutional Commission (18 September 1986) vol IV, no 86.
[37] The Constitution of the Republic of the Philippines 1987, Art X, s 9.
[38] The Constitution of the Republic of the Philippines 1987, Art X, s 14.
[39] Record of the 1986 Constitutional Commission (16 August 1986) vol III, no 58.
[40] Quoted in Czarina Medina-Guce and Ana Martha Galindes, 'A Review of Citizen Participation Issues, Responses, and Prospects for Reform in Local Development Councils' (2017) 61 *Philippine Journal of Public Administration* 43, 43–44.
[41] Republic Act No 7160 1991, s 2(c) (LGC).

initiative and referendum.[42] Its passage was intently backed by Cory, who regarded decentralisation as crucial to the success of democratisation.[43] When she signed it into law Cory called the LGC a 'high point in our effort as a people to strengthen democracy and attain a sustainable development'.[44] Pimentel adds that decentralisation is also 'the key to our country's development'.[45]

Robredo designed the Naga City governance model in 1989 'as a response to the calls of Pres. Corazon Aquino and her administration for people empowerment across the country'.[46] He was consciously championing people power. However, many Filipinos today, including Robredo's most influential admirers, have largely forgotten that this radical democratic idea was central to the revolution and enshrined in the Constitution.[47] This forgetting has thwarted the Constitution's people power principle. The Naga City model is the shining exception that proves the rule. Under this model accredited people's and non-government organisations are empowered to represent various sectors – the urban poor, the youth, business, labour, senior citizens, women, persons with disabilities, peasants, transportation, etc – in the city's legislative council and its committees.[48] The 1987 Philippine Constitution mandates a similar arrangement for all local governments: 'Legislative bodies of local governments shall have sectoral representation as may be prescribed by law.'[49] The LGC, in turn, reserves three seats for sectoral representatives in municipal, city and provincial *sanggunians*.[50] Though publicly celebrated and legally mandated, however, the Naga City model of local participatory democracy has not been widely imitated.[51] For every example of a local government successfully adopting the model there are several others where local politics has long been dominated by political dynasties.[52] Hence LGUs governed by progressive politicians like Robredo are

[42] Andrew Harding, *Territorial Governance in Southeast Asia* (Hart Publishing, 2025) 114, 114–15; LGC, ss 37, 98, 102, 107 and 116. See also Terrence George, 'Local Governance: People Power in the Provinces?' in G Sidney Silliman and Lela Garner Noble (eds), *Organizing for Democracy: NGOs, Civil Society, and the Philippine State* (Ateneo de Manila University Press, 1998) 223–53.

[43] Nathan Gilbert Quimpo, *Contested Democracy and the Left in the Philippines after Marcos* (Ateneo de Manila University Press, 2008) 173–74.

[44] Aquilino Pimentel, *Local Government Code Revisited* (Central Book Supply, Inc 2011) 1.

[45] ibid, 7.

[46] Gerardo Eusebio, 'Developmental Machinery in the Third District of Pangasinan and in Naga, Camarines Sur: An Exploratory Comparison' (2023) 44 *Philippine Political Science Journal* 85, 95.

[47] eg Francis Pangilinan, 'The Relevance of the 1986 People Power Revolution Today', School of Economics Auditorium, University of the Philippines Diliman, Quezon City, Philippines, 24 February 2017), www.rappler.com/nation/162426-relevance-edsa-people-power today (trumpeting Robredo's achievements yet interpreting it as an ideal, a 'new people power', instead of a fulfillment of an already enshrined constitutional principle).

[48] Eusebio (n 46) 95–96.

[49] Art X, s 9.

[50] LGC, Book III, Title 2, ch 3, Art 3, Sec 446; 3, ch 3, Art 3, Sec 457; and 4, ch 3, Art 3, Sec 467.

[51] Capuno (n 22) 14.

[52] ibid, 2.

still but small, scattered islands in a sprawling archipelago dominated by local political dynasties.[53]

It is quite understandable why the Naga City model has been scarcely adopted. Many Filipinos participate in politics as clients of one of a few wealthy patrons to whom they feel duty-bound to lifelong loyalty if not tethered to by threats, bribes and the like. Political parties are structured along these lines: personal followings link village leaders, mayors and governors to congressmen, senators and the President in a system of shifting coalitions where votes flow upward and patronage downward.[54] Patronage politics ensnares the poor in a vicious cycle by making them dependent on the support of their patrons from womb to tomb; they depend on the financial assistance of their mayors for childbirth, weddings, funerals, etc.[55] Political dynasts, in turn, have little incentive to implement the Constitution and the LGC's calls for more broad-based participation in local public decision-making, as that would weaken their decision-making monopolies.[56] Institutions needed to implement the people power principle would make public decision-making more transparent and accountable, which would expose the irregularities of personalistic, patronage-driven politics.[57] Even enlightened elites will likely hesitate before empowering the poor to push for radical social justice measures, as the privileged often harbour a 'cognitive bias favoring the political status quo when people conceptualize democracy'.[58]

If local participatory democracy is to spread widely in the country, therefore, the impetus must come from ordinary people. But this is also an uphill battle. Most Filipinos associate Philippine democracy with periodic elite competition for the people's vote, not – as the 1987 Constitution's enactment history might suggest – with people power.[59] As political scientists Jie Lu and Yun-Han Chu argue,

[53] Patricio N Abinales and Donna J Amoroso, *State and Society in the Philippines*, 2nd edn (Ateneo de Manila University Press, 2017) 301. In a 2015 nine-country comparison (Argentina, Greece, India, Ireland, Japan, Mexico, Philippines, Thailand, USA, the Philippines had the highest incidence of national legislators coming from political dynasties, which was at 75%, with Thailand, the second highest, only at 42% (Albert et al (n 24) 2, figure 2). This high incidence reflected the prevalence of political dynasties in key local government positions: governors (85%), vice-governors (75%), and mayors (66%) and vice mayors (50%) outside of the national capital region (ibid, figure 1); in the 2013 elections for provincial governors, 40% of the outcomes were dynasties beating other dynasties, 19% were dynasties beating non-dynasties, and in 9% the ruling dynasty ran uncontested; only 4% were non-dynasties beating dynasties, 5% non-dynasties beating other non-dynasties, and 3% with non-dynasties winning uncontested (ibid 5, figure 4).

[54] Bryan Dennis Tiojanco, 'The Philippine People Power Constitution: Social Cohesion through Integrated Diversity' in Jaclyn Neo and Bui Ngoc Son (eds), *Pluralist Constitutions in Southeast Asia* (Hart, 2019).

[55] Capuno (n 22) 29.

[56] Paul Gready, 'Rights-Based Approaches to Development: What Is the Value-Added?' (2008) 18 *Development in Practice* 735, 742.

[57] Weena Gera, 'Public Participation in Environmental Governance in the Philippines: The Challenge of Consolidation in Engaging the State' (2016) 52 *Land Use Policy* 501, 502.

[58] Lu and Chu (n 15) 82.

[59] Quimpo (n 43) 9–10.

> popular understandings of democracy provide the benchmark against which people assess their existing political regimes and evaluate possible alternatives, by shaping their expectations on what a 'good' regime should look like. Such understandings and related assessments may further shape how people participate in politics.[60]

Given how democracy is thought of and practised in the Philippines, Filipinos have sadly become instrumental about it. Most are willing to trade off a little democracy for overall or personal prosperity.[61] Such an attitude makes one less critical of their Government's undemocratic practices.[62] It also makes one less willing to partake in politics for expressive (as opposed to instrumental) reasons, including in election campaigns, demonstrations and protests aimed at implementing constitutional principles such as people power.[63]

The above considerations should be enough reason for courts to step in to enforce the people power principle. Constitutional law scholar John Hart Ely influentially argued that courts should protect legislatively underenforced constitutional rights '(1) that are essential to the democratic process and (2) whose dimensions cannot safely be left to our elected representatives, who have an obvious vested interest in the status quo.'[64] The discussion above shows that judicial enforcement of the people power principle would comply with both of Ely's requirements. Unfortunately, the Philippine Supreme Court has balked at enforcing this principle.

First, the LGC, alongside the 1991 Synchronized Elections Law, mandated the Commission on Elections (COMELEC) to promulgate the rules and regulations governing the election of three sectoral representatives in every municipal, city and provincial *sanggunian*: one for women; another for either agricultural or industrial workers; and the last from the urban poor, Indigenous cultural communities, disabled persons, or any other sector the sanggunian concerned may determine.[65] Despite this clear mandate, no election for local sectoral representatives was held in the 1992 elections, and none was scheduled for the 1995 elections. In 1994 the Supreme Court dismissed a petition to compel the COMELEC to call for the elections of local sectoral representatives, declaring

[60] Lu and Chu (n 15) 7.

[61] Guerrero, Labucay and Rood (n 19) 286; Marco Garrido, *The Patchwork City: Class, Space, and Politics in Metro Manila* (University of Chicago Press, 2019) 165–66.

[62] Lu and Chu (n 15) 19, 118–21.

[63] ibid, 20, 147–58.

[64] John Ely, *Democracy and Distrust: A Theory of Judicial Review* (Harvard University Press, 1980) 117; though Ely was discussing US constitutional law, his argument has been adopted (and, in fact, expanded) by comparative constitutional law scholars, who prescribe courts around the world to follow suit, eg, Stephen Gardbaum, 'Comparative Political Process Theory' (2020) 18 *International Journal of Constitutional Law* 1429; and Rosalind Dixon, *Responsive Judicial Review: Democracy and Dysfunction in the Modern Age* (Oxford University Press, 2023).

[65] LGC, Book I, Title 2, ch 1, s 41(c); Book III, Title 2, ch 3, Art 3, s 446, Book III, Title 3, ch 3, Art 3, s 457; and Book III, Title 4, ch 3, Art 3, s 467; Republic Act No 7166 (1991), s 3(d).

that there was no 'justiciable controversy'.[66] In 1995 the Synchronized Elections Law was amended so that the COMELEC would have to await a 'law which may hereafter be enacted providing for the election of sectoral representatives' before it could promulgate the pertinent rules and regulations.[67] No such law has yet been enacted, and so since 1991 no election for sectoral representatives in local legislative bodies has yet been held.[68]

Second, the LGC requires that local implementation of government projects must undergo prior and 'periodic consultations with appropriate local government units, non-governmental and people's organisations, and other concerned sectors of the community'.[69] The Supreme Court has severely narrowed the scope of this prior consultation requirement to government projects and programs that

> (1) may cause pollution; (2) may bring about climactic change; (3) may cause the depletion of non-renewable resources; (4) may result in loss of crop land, range-land, or forest cover; (5) may eradicate certain animal or plant species from the face of the planet; and (6) other projects or programs that may call for the eviction of a particular group of people residing in the locality where these will be implemented.[70]

These judicial doctrines, among others, have left the extent of democratic space for civil society groups to the vagaries of politics.[71]

III. The Schumpeterian Proviso

Political scientists Frances McCall Rosenbluth and Ian Shapiro argue that empowering citizens to directly influence public decision-making at the local level would be disastrous.[72] They say that 'voters' inability to weigh the relative costs and benefits of policies against other policies and over the long haul is a central market failure of politics'.[73] For them the better reform is to strengthen political parties, which they consider 'the core organs of democratic politics'.[74] To keep winning elections, political parties need to sell policies that appeal to different constituencies and balance short-term welfare gains for each with long-term consequences for all.[75] Because of this, 'they are more capable of delivering desired outcomes

[66] Alberto Agra, 'The Non-Passage of the 1993 Proposed Election Code of the Philippines' (1997) 13 *Kasarinlan: Philippine Journal of Third World Studies* 67, 72.
[67] Republic Act No 7887 (1995), s 1.
[68] Gera (n 57) 505.
[69] LGC, Title 1, ch 1, s 2(c).
[70] *Lina v Paño* (2001) GR No 129093; *Bangus Fry Fisherfolk Diwata Magbuhos v Lanzanas* (2003) GR No 131442, 453 Phil 479.
[71] Asian Development Bank, 'Civil Society Briefs: Philippines' (2013) 2.
[72] Frances McCall Rosenbluth and Ian Shapiro, *Responsible Parties: Saving Democracy from Itself* (Yale University Press, 2018) 3.
[73] ibid, 231.
[74] ibid, 4.
[75] ibid.

than any amount of direct democracy, and more trustworthy than even the most appealing individual politician'.[76] And since political parties rely on broad platforms to win, their electoral campaigns are cheaper than those who rely on personal favours; parties are therefore 'a bargain for voters' since they scarcely need to compromise with rich donors.[77]

As Rosenbluth and Shapiro recognise, however, parties work only when they are disciplined, meaning that party members obey their party leaders because they trust that whatever short-term individual costs they might incur would lead to their long-term collective good.[78] Philippine political parties are weak, not disciplined.[79] This is a consequence of Philippine patronage politics. Since political loyalties are to personal networks not parties, national and local elections are won mainly by patronage-powered local political machines led by the locality's leading politician or family.[80]

Like many political scientists, Rosenbluth and Shapiro follow Joseph Schumpeter's influential equation of democracy with periodic free and fair[81] elections for choosing a country's top political decision-makers.[82] This model of elite democracy remains an influential model in the Philippines and worldwide, though is now often supplemented by liberal constitutional guarantees such as the separation of powers and a Bill of Rights.[83]

The root of any political theory – from Herodotus to Machiavelli, Hobbes to Rawls – is an account of human nature, which is usually spelled out, but need not be so.[84] To fully understand Schumpeterian democracy, therefore, we need to examine Schumpeter's account of persons in their roles as political actors – that is, political person (*homo politicus*) – which he discusses in his seminal book, *Capitalism, Socialism and Democracy*, in a short section on 'Human Nature

[76] ibid, 230.
[77] ibid, 73.
[78] ibid, 13.
[79] Allen Hicken, 'The Political Party System' in Mark Thompson and Eric Vincent Batalla (eds), *Routledge Handbook of the Contemporary Philippines* (Routledge, 2018) 38–54; Ronald Holmes, 'The Myth of the Machine' in Allen Hicken, Edward Aspinall and Meredith Weiss (eds), *Electoral Dynamics in the Philippines: Money Politics, Patronage, and Clientelism at the Grassroots* (Singapore University Press, 2019) 48–50.
[80] Allen Hicken et al, 'Introduction: The Local Dynamics of the National Election in the Philippines' in Hicken, Aspinall and Weiss (n 78).
[81] Schumpeter himself did not exclude elections that many might consider unfair; Joseph Schumpeter, *Capitalism, Socialism and Democracy* (Harper Perennial, 2008) 271. His modern followers however require that elections are periodic, open, free, honest and fair, and feature universal adulthood suffrage; see eg, Samuel P Huntington, *The Third Wave: Democratization in the Late Twentieth Century* (University of Oklahoma Press, 1991) 7, 9 and 12.
[82] Schumpeter (n 81) 269.
[83] Quimpo (n 43) 6; eg, Tom Ginsburg and Aziz Huq, *How to Save a Constitutional Democracy* (Oxford University Press, 2019) 8–15; Rosenbluth and Shapiro (n 72) 3–4; Richard A Posner, *Law, Pragmatism, and Democracy* (Harvard University Press, 2003) 130–212; Huntington (n 81) 9–10.
[84] Isaiah Berlin, *The Proper Study of Mankind: An Anthology of Essays* (Henry Hardy and Roger Hausheer eds; Farrar, Straus and Giroux 1997) 79–88; See also Alan Ryan, *On Politics: A History of Political Thought from Herodotus to the Present* (W Norton & Company, 2012); and Wim Voermans, *The Story of Constitutions* (Cambridge University Press, 2023).

in Politics'.[85] And what we find there supports this chapter's thesis. Call it the *Schumpeterian proviso*.

Schumpeter disagreed with the notion, standard in his time, that the people elect their representatives to carry out their 'definite and rational opinion about every individual question'.[86] In 'Human Nature in Politics', Schumpeter argued that people act rationally only when it comes to daily decisions concerning 'the little field which the individual citizen's mind encompasses with a full sense of its reality'.[87] This zone of rationality comprises

> things that directly concern himself, his family, his business dealings, his hobbies, his friends and enemies, his township or ward, his class, church, trade union or any other social group of which he is an active member – the things under his personal observation, the things which are familiar to him independently of what his newspaper tells him, which he can directly influence or manage and for which he develops the kind of responsibility that is induced by a direct relation to the favorable or unfavorable effects of a course of action.[88]

There is no guarantee that people will act rationally in most of their daily decisions. Nevertheless, we can expect everyone to have some zone familiar to them, however small, where they are wont to act rationally and responsibly. Zonal boundaries change with the circumstances and differ from person to person and group to group. It is rare, however, for this zone to cover public affairs unrelated to one's private concerns. Citizens typically give their hobbies more attention than national and international issues which do not concern their family or business; for example, they would rather study chess openings than environmental policies. This includes successful entrepreneurs, engineers, doctors, and the like; they may be the best educated in their field, but despite readily available information they are often ignorant about domestic and foreign policy.[89]

Outside their tiny zones of rationality citizens are typically ignorant, prejudiced, impulsive, irrational. Worse, says Schumpeter, they would prove willing to relax moral standards which they staunchly uphold within their zones; or, just as easily, give in to harmful, knee-jerk policy responses to exaggerated moral indignation. Politicians, interest groups and ideologues routinely exploit these weaknesses – always trying to manufacture a public opinion congenial to their desires. Thus without strong, trustworthy political parties the citizenry can be manipulated into supporting policies that hurt their long-term welfare.[90]

Still there are two areas of public affairs that one's zone of responsibility will likely cover. The first are national issues related to one's private concerns. This is especially true when money is directly involved, for example agricultural tariffs

[85] Schumpeter (n 81) 256–64.
[86] ibid, 269.
[87] ibid, 258.
[88] ibid, 258–59.
[89] ibid, 259 and 261.
[90] ibid, 262–64.

and subsidies or additional taxes. On these, however, Schumpeter thought that voters would usually favour short-sighted policies that go against not just the national, but also their own long-term interests.

The second area of public affairs that citizens can reliably comprehend are local affairs of towns and other small communities – street cleaning or road construction, for example. It is not hard to draw on, say, managerial experience, to form a defensible view on these.[91] Since these local public affairs are typically within a citizen's zone of responsibility, they should be fair game for participatory democratic processes – even under a Schumpeterian model of democracy. Hence the Schumpeterian proviso: the citizenry can be trusted to directly participate in democratic decision-making on local affairs.

The Schumpeterian proviso offers a critical institutional design strategy for developing democracies like the Philippines. The main reason patronage politics thrives in a democracy is distrust. Political dynasties win election after election because they have shown that they can deliver quick, palpable gains – however meagre. As long as they can rely on piecemeal patronage to keep winning, they have no incentive to invest in credibility for delivering long-term developmental projects.[92] By contrast, it is hard for voters to trust that progressive upstarts would follow through on their promises of broad public policies such as universal education or access to information, which might be more beneficial in the long term; they need proof of concept.[93] This ensnares a flawed democracy in a 'political development trap'.[94]

Economists Philip Keefer and Razvan Vlaicu suggest three main reasons why voters in flawed democracies tend to put their faith in local patrons instead of national parties or politicians. The first is a trust advantage: mutual trust earned from repeated face-to-face encounters. The second is an informational advantage: it is easier for local patrons to learn about their clients' immediate preferences, such as jobs, roads or basketball courts. Third, is a transaction-cost advantage: it is also easier for clients to approach patrons for their emergency needs, such as helping pay for hospital expenses, weddings or funerals. Absent well-functioning democratic institutions, these three advantages would outweigh the drawbacks in the form of kickbacks and other personal gains which patrons extract in the process.[95]

It is a Herculean task for civil society groups, workers' federations, people's organisations, etc to contest a local political dynasty on its own turf without a supporting institutional framework. They need mechanisms for

[91] ibid, 260–61.

[92] Philip Keefer and Razvan Vlaicu, 'Democracy, Credibility, and Clientelism' (2007) 24 *The Journal of Law, Economics, & Organization* 371, 388.

[93] Philip Keefer, 'Clientelism, Credibility, and the Policy Choices of Young Democracies' (2007) 51 *American Journal of Political Science* 804, 804–05.

[94] Keefer and Vlaicu (n 92) 387.

[95] ibid, 385.

public accountability, transparency and democratic participation in public decision-making.[96] These are exactly what the people power provisions of the 1987 Constitution and the LGC provide. These institutions can help progressive challengers promising broad public goods (eg, universal healthcare and quality education) gain credibility, as they can point to independent mechanisms for garnering democratic support before elections and then holding them accountable afterwards.[97] The increased risk of exposure that transparency and accountability mechanisms present also raises the electoral costs of corruption and rent-seeking, which are the bread and butter of patronage politics.[98] Constituents who regularly participate in democratic decision-making and governance are also better situated to monitor the performance of incumbents.[99] Moreover, the pay and perks that come with a sectoral seat in the local council can also help finance the continued operations (including simply attending meetings) of usually underfunded civil society organisations representing marginalised sectors.[100]

IV. Conclusion

Preaching the idea of people power to the Philippine populace can be a persuasive strategy to promote local participatory democracy across the archipelago. It has worked before.[101] And the fact that it is now a constitutionally enshrined principle helps the argument not just in the public square but also in the courtroom.[102] There is also the general propensity of dissatisfied citizens in a democracy to embrace more robust democratic values.[103]

Recent success stories of people power offer hope. For example, when Arlene 'Kaka' Bag-ao was appointed caretaker of Dinagat Islands (to replace the incumbent, who had been convicted of graft and parricide),[104] she proudly established local mechanisms for, among others, 'participatory governance rooted in the principles of popular inclusion, empowerment, and democratic processes'.[105] She says that these mechanisms enabled her to 'ask them [local people] what's next, so they are aware that we decide based on needs, not political accommodation' and

[96] Gera (n 57) 502.
[97] Eusebio (n 46) 88.
[98] Keefer (n 93) 806.
[99] Capuno (n 22) 21.
[100] Medina-Guce and Galindes (n 40) 55.
[101] Tiojanco (n 32); Tiojanco (n 33).
[102] See Michael Walzer, *Interpretation and Social Criticism* (Harvard University Press, 1993).
[103] Chin-en Wu, 'Economic Performance, Regime Types, and Political Support' in Chu et al (n 18) 171.
[104] Angela Casauay, 'Party-list rep as district caretaker a first' Rappler (4 January 2013), www.rappler.com/philippines/19093-party-list-rep-as-district-caretaker-a-first.
[105] Kaka Bag-ao, 'Breaking down doors, walls, and ceilings' Rappler (15 November 2019), www.rappler.com/voices/thought-leaders/244892-opinion-kaka-bagao-breaking-down-doors-walls-ceilings.

then 'debate on this so people would understand'.[106] In time these mechanisms improved her constituency's political acumen and democratic ethos; as Bag-ao puts it, 'Their political awareness is growing little by little.'[107] Bag-ao won the lone district representative seat of Dinagat Islands in 2013 and 2016 against a powerful local dynast, earning her the monicker 'dragon slayer'.[108] In 2019 she became its governor, though she lost this post in 2022. She won the 2025 elections to again become district representative of the lone district of Dinagat Islands.[109]

[106] Quoted in Tamiki Hara, 'Beyond Personalistic Politics: A Progressive Congresswoman's Challenge to a Political Dynasty in Dinagat Islands, Philippines' (2021) *42 Philippine Political Science Journal* 30, 45.

[107] Quoted in ibid, 47.

[108] ibid, 49. '"Dragon slayer" Kaka Bag-ao wins as Dinagat Islands governor' Rappler (14 May 2019), www.rappler.com/philippines/elections/230644-dinagat-results-kaka-bag-ao-wins-as-governor.

[109] Hana Bordey, 'Ex-Dinagat gov Bag-Ao files COC for House comeback' GMA News Online (4 October 2024), www.gmanetwork.com/news/topstories/regions/922603/ex-dinagat-gov-bag-ao-files-coc-for-house-comeback/story/#goog_rewarded.

14

Local Lawmaking for Urban Development in Late-Colonial Bandung, Indonesia: Looking Back in Anger?

JAN MICHIEL OTTO*

> The reception of Netherlands Indies administrative law has been very smooth and gradual. The law was not so strange, it was not so much political but technical. It was aimed squarely at the conditions here.
>
> Syahrir SH, Head of Legal Department, Bandung Municipality
> (interview 16 February 1990)

I. Introduction: What Minutes of Local Council Meetings can Tell Us

Writing a chapter in honour of Andrew Harding has been a pleasure. First, because Andrew has been such wonderful inspirational scholar, colleague and friend for decades; and secondly, because the prospect of writing about a subject close to Andrew's heart made me feel like a child in a pastry shop: Andrew has been involved in so many fields, from administrative law and local government law to comparative constitutional law, from the laws of urban planning and environmental protection to legal transplants, from legal history to law and development.

Geographically, Andrew's work has covered law and governance in the UK, Singapore, Malaysia, Thailand and Myanmar. I thank him for leaving the study of Indonesia's law and governance largely to us, his friends and colleagues in Leiden.[1]

* I would like to thank the late Prof Dr Ateng Syafrudin, my counterpart in Bandung back in 1989–1990, for helping me to obtain research access to Bandung's town hall, and the late Prof Dr J Th de Smidt for his suggestion to examine the minutes of the local council.

[1] Adriaan Bedner, Leon Buskens, the late Albert Dekker, Laure d'Hondt, Ab Massier, Nicole Niessen, Sebastiaan Pompe, Gustaaf Reerink, Jacqueline Vel, and many others.

This chapter takes us back in time a century and more, to the late-colonial period, to examine a nascent practice of local lawmaking and urban planning. At the beginning of the twentieth century several Indonesian towns became municipalities, to be run by a mayor, a town council with considerable powers and a local civil service. When the council members were first appointed, most of them were Dutch and the Indonesian (*Inlandsche*) members remained in the background. From 1918 onwards the members were elected, the role of Indonesian members increased, and some became prominent co-producers of policy and law.

At Leiden University most of our work on Indonesia has been about the country's contemporary law and society. However, when I came to Bandung[2] 35 years ago for a socio-legal field research on the implementation of spatial planning and environmental law in and around Bandung, the Indonesian Government had decided, after a lengthy process of more than a year, to not grant me a research permit.[3] There I was in Bandung, with nine months of research leave obtained with difficulty from my dean, and a young family. Then, one morning in the office of Bandung municipality, in the legal department's library, I stumbled upon the minutes of Bandung's local council meetings, in its first two decades, from 1906 to 1926. This turned out to be a treasure.[4]

The verbatim minutes, all in Dutch, showed in great detail how this brand-new local government operated, how council members, the mayor and civil servants behaved, argued, agreed or disagreed, and how the positions of Indonesians, Dutch and Chinese matched or diverged. This material, which covered the bi-weekly council meetings over a long period, enabled me to reconstruct and understand several aspects of the genesis of local government, regulation and urban development in Indonesia's late-colonial period.

In a previous publication based on these minutes, I highlighted the impressive opposition by vocal Indonesian council members in the early 1920s, notably by the journalist Darna Koesoema and by Ratu Langi, who would become a national hero.[5] This chapter looks at the beginnings of the municipal council, the expansion of late-colonial Bandung, of its municipal policies and apparatus, the roles of mayor B Coops, and director of Public Works, H Heetjans, and in particular at the body of local regulations for urban development, notably for building and town planning.

[2] This chapter uses both the contemporary spelling of Bandung and the historical spelling of Bandoeng, depending on context.

[3] The permit finally arrived nine months later, when we were about to leave and return home.

[4] The credits for pointing out the potential of these minutes go to the late Professor J Thom de Smidt, professor of legal history, who together with Dr Heleen Gall joined me on a visit to the town hall.

[5] See JM Otto, 'Indonesian Opposition in the Colonial Municipality: a Minahasser in Bandung' 1 (2015) *Asian Journal of Law and Society* 169.

II. Colonialism and Colonial Law

Today, whoever writes about colonial law and governance enters a contested field. In Europe, colonialism has become a topical subject once again. For example, the 2023 election manifesto of what presently is The Netherlands' most successful political party, states:

> The PVV[6] loves the Netherlands. We are proud of our culture, identity and traditions. We must therefore preserve them. And not erase. The hatred of the left by which heroes of our history are reviled, is being ended. The apologies for slavery in the past and the 'politionele acties' [the military repression of Indonesia's independence struggle, jmo] as made by the King,[7] are to be withdrawn. Black Pete must stay.[8,9]

The PVV's pride in the 'heroes of our history' matches with traditional justifications of colonialism.[10] Proponents have long maintained that it was a civilising mission in the best interests of local peoples, replacing superstition and witchcraft with beneficial religious beliefs, disseminating technological knowledge, improving infrastructure, enhancing trade, and – last but not least – introducing modern legal systems, with individual rights.

Presently, in contrast, there is widespread acknowledgment of the negative effects of colonialism, including violent repression, systemic racism, economic inequity, environmental degradation, the loss of language and culture, and the imposition of colonial laws, to neatly regulate all of this.[11]

Indeed, colonial law is usually conceived as follows. First, as a European national legal system being imposed, with minor modifications, on a non-western society, in order to control and exploit it. Secondly, this implied unfair, differential treatment based on race or ethnicity. Thirdly, the law worked mainly for the benefit of the colonial power and to the detriment of the subjugated people. Fourth, most local people were oppressed by the colonial administrators, with the support of

[6] PVV stands for Partij voor de Vrijheid (Party for Freedom) and is led by Geert Wilders, a long-time right-wing parliamentarian who became known nationally and internationally for his radical anti-Islam views.

[7] On 10 March 2020, during his state visit to Indonesia, King Willem-Alexander offered an apology for the excessive violence committed by the Dutch during Indonesia's struggle for independence in 1945–1949.

[8] In the original text: 'De PVV houdt van Nederland. Wij zijn trots op onze cultuur, identiteit en tradities. Die moeten we dan ook behouden. Niet uitwissen. De linkse haat waarin helden uit onze geschiedenis worden beschimpt wordt beëindigd. De excuses voor het slavernijverleden en de politionele acties, zoals gedaan door de Koning, worden ingetrokken. Zwarte Piet blijft.'

[9] The PVV's rise to power, though, has not yet affected the recent Indonesian Dutch rapprochement concerning the restitution of thousands of pieces of what is often called 'looted' art. Deliberations about natural history collections, including the remains of the 'Java Man', presently kept in Leiden, are still ongoing at the time of writing (October 2024).

[10] See for example B Gilley, 'The Case for Colonisation' (2017) *Third World Quarterly*.

[11] See E Blakemore, 'What is Colonialism' (2023) *National Geographic* (6 October 2023) and J McQuade, 'Colonialism was a disaster and the facts prove it' (2017) *The Conversation* (27 September 2017), who states 'It takes a highly selective misreading of the evidence to claim that colonialism was anything other than a humanitarian disaster for most of the colonised.'

indigenous powerholders who acted on the basis of tradition, religion, custom and customary law. Five, colonial law was implemented top-down through direct or indirect rule by a colonial administration.

Accordingly, Robert Home[12] argues that Britain used the formation of towns and cities as an instrument of colonial expansion and control throughout the empire.

While such conceptions may be largely true, the findings presented in this chapter do not fit that fivefold image of colonial law very well.

Bandoeng town was of course part of a colonial system. The colonial constitution for the Netherlands-Indies (henceforth Indies) distinguished explicitly between two 'population groups', ie, '*Europeanen*' (Europeans) and '*Inlanders*' ('Indigenous', henceforth *Inlanders*, *Inlands* or Indonesian), later adding 'Foreign Orientals' (*Vreemde Oosterlingen*, notably Chinese) as the third population group. Whereas the Europeans, mostly Dutch, were subject to a 'European'-type 'Indies' legislation and administration, the *Inlanders* were, in many of their interactions, subject to their customary (*adat*) and religious norms as administered by their own authorities.

For the legal underpinning of the expansion of Indies towns like Bandoeng, the Dutch had no model of a national urban planning law of the Netherlands, which could be 'imposed'. While in the Indies an urban planning law would be issued in the 1930s, the first national spatial planning law in the Netherlands would be promulgated only in 1962.

Therefore, the local administrators in Bandoeng had to make their own regulations as much as possible, and when they borrowed from elsewhere, it was usually from other local governments in the Indies. While the colonial system remained based on principles of ethnic and racial discrimination, discussions and decisions by the local council on urban development and planning also transcended those principles. For example, the distinction between types of dwellings and buildings – irrespective of who lived in them – was leading in urban plans and regulations, and *in this context* diversity based on ethnicity or race, as laid down in the colony's constitution, became increasingly irrelevant. The fact that since 1918 Indonesian members were elected to the council, participated actively and called for equal treatment, may have furthered this development, as well as rising nationalism and activist political mobilisation of the masses.

The minutes of Bandoeng's municipal council are very detailed; therefore, they enable us to reconstruct not only the practice of law- and policymaking but also the roles and views of the main characters and the relations between them. Given the highly contested views about colonial governance and law, they enable us to follow in the footsteps of Alan Lester, who states that he, 'in what has become a politicised struggle over the legacies of the British Empire', aims 'to bring the evidence-based and curiosity-driven approach of academic historians to bear.'[13]

[12] See R Home, *Of Planting and Planning. The Making of British Colonial Cities* (Routledge, 1996).

[13] A Lester, 'The Debate on British Colonialism', Snapshots of Empire project website (2023), blogs.sussex.ac.uk/snapshotsofempire/2023/10/02/the-debate-on-british-colonialism.

III. Bandung's Steady Growth: 1811–1900

Bandung lies in a basin in the middle of Priangan, West Java's mountainland. North of the town rise three high mountains, the sometimes steep slopes of which run to the city and flatten out in Bandung's southern area.

There, since time immemorial, local Sundanese people lived in the vast plain in small villages (*desa*) and reclaimed parts of the forest to grow rice, cassava and fish. Their houses were made of light temporary materials, so that during flooding caused by heavy rainfall they could quickly move them out of danger. When in 1810 the Dutch Governor-General Daendels was overseeing the construction of Java's new main road, the *Grote Postweg*, from west to east, he ordered the establishment of a new locality in this basin along the road. Hence, Bandoeng was founded in 1811.

An 1825 map shows only a few buildings around a traditional central square, the *alun-alun*. We see a military post, a tavern, a mosque, the house of the local ruler, the *Regent* (*Bupati*) and the house of a coffee garden supervisor. Around 1840 the civil administration also opened an office for an *assistent-resident* (see below), and in 1864 even the *resident*, who oversaw several *assistent-residents* of Priangan regencies, moved his office from Cianjur to Bandoeng. Meanwhile more forest was cut down, and new villages arose in the area, and rice fields developed around them.

After 1870, when the colonial Government allowed free enterprise to lease land in Java, European entrepreneurs poured in to set up plantations for tea, coffee and quinine in the mountains to the south of Bandoeng. Both government and entrepreneurs began making serious efforts to develop the town. KA Bosscha, a successful tea-planter, became famous for his contributions to the flourishing of Bandoeng. Schools were built, public works carried out, and in 1884 a railway to Batavia was opened. In 1900 Bandoeng already had around 30.000 inhabitants.

While the great majority of the population of Indonesians lived south of the railway line, the northern part of town – less populated, cooler and popular among Europeans – was home to the offices of the colonial Government.

Until 1906, Bandoeng, like other towns in the Netherlands Indies, had no autonomy to manage its own affairs. In 1800, the Dutch Government had formally succeeded the East India Company and assumed full responsibility for governing the Netherlands-Indies. To do so it established a centralised, dual governance system. A Dutch Administration was led by a Governor-General, supported by his secretariat, departments and agencies, all with their head offices in Batavia. This 'European' Administration was represented in the regions by residents, and in the districts (*afdelingen*) by *assistent-residents*. They would oversee and try to coordinate the civil and military officials of the department and agency branches in the regions, districts and towns.

In parallel, from the regional level downwards, an *Inlandse* Administration was led by Indonesian Regents, having their own regency offices, overseeing lower indigenous administrators all the way down to the village (*desa*) level. The Dutch

Administration led, and cooperated with, the *Inlandse* Administration to govern the colony.

In Bandoeng district, the Dutch *assistent-resident* oversaw the Dutch *controleur* of Bandoeng town. The Indigenous Administration was led by the Regent (*Bupati*) of Bandoeng; below him the *wedana* of Bandoeng town, who oversaw the *assistent-wedanas* of its various quarters.

IV. Ethical Policy, 1903 Decentralisation Act, First Council Meeting

The establishment of local councils, like Bandoeng's, was a political novelty in the Netherlands-Indies, part of a new approach, the so-called Ethical Policy (*Ethische Politiek*). This policy, officially issued in 1901, was meant to be a clear departure from what had until then been a just-for-profit colonial policy. The Netherlands now professed to assume an ethical responsibility for the welfare of its colonial subjects. This included not only making more investments in infrastructure, public hygiene and education, but also devolving parts of its highly centralised Government to regional and local councils, which would enable political participation of both Dutch and Indonesians inhabitants.

To this end, the Dutch Government, led by Abraham Kuyper, and Parliament in The Hague amended the colonial constitution with three articles, constituting the 1903 Decentralisation Act (*Decentralisatiewet*).[14] To implement this act the Government issued the 1904 Decentralisation Decree (*Decentralisatiebesluit*). And to implement the Decree, Governor-General Alexander Idenburg issued the Local Councils Ordinance (*Locale Raden-Ordonnantie*) in 1905 as well as several Establishment Ordinances (*Instellingsordonnanties*) to create local councils in major towns. Batavia, for example, got its local council in 1905, and Bandoeng followed in 1906.

So, on Tuesday 17 April 1906, at 6pm, the *Regent*, the traditional ruler of Bandoeng regency, a gentleman of Sundanese aristocratic descent, hosted the first meeting of the local council of Bandoeng Municipality in his residence, at the *alun-alun*, the town's central square. Yet, according to the beautiful handwritten minutes, it was not the Regent who chaired the meeting. In fact, he did not speak a word. The chairman of the meeting was Mr EA Maurenbrecher, the *assistent-resident* of Bandoeng. This first council consisted of 11 members: eight Dutchmen, two Indonesians and one Chinese; all men, all appointed by the Government in Batavia. According to the minutes of the meeting, only Dutch members took the floor.

The main items on the meeting's agenda were the selection and the salary of its first civil servant, the secretary. The chairman, the *assistent-resident*, presented a list

[14] For the full text and explanation of Articles 68a, 68b and 68c, see Otto (n 5).

of seven candidates and proposed to appoint someone he knew personally 'as a very experienced civil servant, knowledgeable about financial affairs'. Several members raised objections, expressed preference for a more open and transparent procedure, and made suggestions, which were then put to vote, one after another. After a lengthy discussion, Mr Maurenbrecher, the chairman, got his way, and the council appointed the secretary he had proposed. Still, the members' objections showed that they, rather than simply following the colonial Government, impersonated by the chairman, planned to act in their new capacity as fully fledged citizens.

This was in line with the 1905 Local Councils Ordinance which had given the council quite some powers, including enacting its internal rules, appointing and dismissing local government staff, forming committees to develop policies for a certain domain, etc. In its first meeting the council established a finance committee.

V. Second and Third Meetings: Some Assertive Council Members

In its second meeting, on 16 May 1906, the council discussed its rules of procedure. The chairman proposed a draft Internal Regulation that had actually been prepared by the administration in Batavia. The council members went through it, article by article, seriously, carefully and accurately. Whereas the draft text proposed in Article 2 that convocations were to be sent to the members at least two days before the meeting, the members changed this to four days, so they could better prepare themselves for the meeting. While the draft proposed in Article 4 that the council's minutes were to contain concise references to the documents presented, formal statements and proposals made, etc.', the members decided to add 'and the course of deliberations about the latter'. They wanted not only the Government's documents and statements to be laid down, but also their own views.

A draft Article 5 stating that each member had the right to demand that his dissenting opinion is mentioned in the minutes was also agreed upon. Several provisions guaranteed that voting on appointments of persons would be done in writing. When a member during the discussion about the council's voting procedures pointed to some undesirable effects of an article of the 1905 Local Councils Ordinance itself, the council decided that this member, Mr Sieuwertsz, would submit a proposal for amendment of this article to the Indies Government. All in all, the minutes of this discussion show that from the beginning there was room for local council members to play active and independent roles.

According to the 1906 Establishment Ordinance, the local council of Bandoeng had four main tasks: management and construction of roads and bridges; garbage collection; fire brigade; and cemeteries. Furthermore, the municipality was also responsible for public health, public traffic and 'beautification'. The budget allocated for the first year was 47,500 guilders, just enough for improvement of some roads, some minor public works and a small staff.

But the council members' ambitions went beyond those limited tasks and budget. In the same second meeting, a member, the industrialist HW van Dalfsen, proposed to set up a permanent committee to advertise Bandoeng as a health and leisure resort, not only in the Netherlands and the Dutch East Indies, but also in various places in the east, such as Singapore, Penang, Bangkok, Hong Kong and Shanghai. 'We agree,' he said,

> that Bandoeng has developed rapidly in a short period of time and is now the fourth largest city in the Dutch East Indies … it is our task to bring Bandoeng to further development and prosperity and to do so by the shortest possible route.

His lengthy speech, though, focused exclusively on Europeans and other foreigners who, in his view, should settle in Bandoeng, without mentioning the Indonesian inhabitants.

Still, the word *Inlanders* was mentioned in this meeting's minutes when van Dalfsen proposed to set up a weekly or bi-weekly cattle market and to appoint a committee to regulate this. He argued that the livestock in the Priangan was inadequate and that the city's butchers had to obtain their livestock from far away:

> This is not good for the quality … and is an unpleasant circumstance for the citizens. … The Government is trying to get a livestock here, everyone sees the importance of it, and already many people, both Europeans and *Inlanders*, are devoting themselves to the breeding of livestock. But in Bandoeng there is no actual cattle market like those in Central and East Java.

The council agreed, and the following persons were appointed as members of the committee: the *Regent* of Bandoeng, Raden Toemenggoeng Aria Martanegara; the *Wedana Kota* Rangga Tirta Madja; and Mr Van Dalfsen.

At the third meeting of the council, on 19 June, member Dr Westhoff, a private physician, proposed to set up a committee to investigate the possibility and implementation of an artesic water pipeline system for the entire city: 'Soerabaja is already in possession of a drinking water pipeline system; here in Bandoeng we also need to have such an establishment.' 'In the five years that I lived here', Dr Westhoff said,

> I already heard about various plans for the construction of a drinking water system, but nothing has come of the implementation of those plans so far. Now that this matter has been brought under the authority of the municipal council, we need to ensure that it takes the responsibility for its realization.

Those plans had been the responsibility of the national department for Civil Public Works (*Burgerlijke Openbare Werken*,) and the decentralisation did not change this immediately. Some equipment was transferred by the Civil Public Works to become property of the municipality, such as a steamroller, a hand roller, spray carts and firefighting materials.[15] However, in the first few years most public properties,

[15] Minutes of council meeting 25 July 1906 (handwritten, p 1).

such as public roads, streets and adjacent verges, squares, parks, wells, bridges, etc, as well as the public slaughterhouse, remained the property of the central *Indies* Government, and were only given to the municipality for management or use.[16]

VI. Mayor Coops and the Expansion of Urban Government 1913–1928

Mr Maurenbrecher, the *assistent-resident* who chaired the council meetings in 1906 and 1907, had several successors in the following years, until in 1913 Bertus Coops took office as *assistent-resident* of Bandoeng.[17] In 1917 the offices of *assistent-resident* and council-chairman-cum-mayor were separated. When the council members were clear about their wish to keep Mr Coops in Bandoeng as their first mayor (*burgemeester*), Coops left his promising career with the Indies Government to assume the post. As such he was warmly welcomed by the eldest council member.[18] Coops would hold this office until his retirement in 1928.

At its meeting of 30 December 1910, the council had appointed its first director of the Municipal Public Works. After two short-lived predecessors,

[16] ibid.

[17] Bertus Coops was born in the Netherlands in 1874 in the small provincial town of Doesburg. His father was a baker. His parents died at a young age, leaving Bertus and his siblings as orphans. At school he was a good student, and he was lovingly taken care of by an intellectual family in Deventer, where he completed his secondary education (HBS). At the age of 17 he enrolled in an administrative training programme for future civil servants at the Indies Institution in Delft. Each year, the six best graduates were eligible for deployment to the East Indies at the Government's expense. Coops was one of them, and from 1895 to 1906 he worked as an administrative official, first with the central Government in Batavia and then in Sukabumi, West Java, where he married. In 1906 he went on leave with his young family to the Netherlands. Here Coops followed a two-year course at the Indies Public Administration Academy, which was established in 1907 in The Hague. It admitted each year 12 promising civil servants with at least six years of experience, to train them for higher offices. Here Coops was trained in colonial administration, acquiring more knowledge of the laws, administration, economics, society and culture of the Netherlands-Indies (see C Fasseur, 'Hemelse godin of melkgevende koe: de Leidse Universiteit en de Indische ambtenaarsopleiding 1825–1925' [Heavenly goddess or milk cow: Leiden University and the training of civil servants for the Indies] (1988) 103 *Bijdragen en mededelingen betreffende de geschiedenis der Nederlanden* 221). In 1909 Coops returned to the Indies, and after a few positions in Central and West Java, he was appointed *assistent-resident* of Bandoeng in 1913. The biographical information in this footnote is taken from R Coops, *Over wat moet ik je toch schrijven, Indische brieven van Bertus Coops 1896–1928* [About what should I write to you. Letters from the Indies by Bertus Coops 1896–1928] (TAO Publishers, 2023), a book written by his grandson, Robert Coops based on letters written by Bertus Coops to his sister in the Netherlands. See for more information also A Kurnia, *Bertus Coops, Walikota Bandung Pertama* [Bertus Coops, first mayor of Bandung] (2021) bandungbergerak.id/article/detail/693/bertus-coops-wali-kota-bandung-pertama.

[18] When, on 1 July 1917, the offices of *assistent-resident* of Bandoeng and mayor were separated, and Bertus Coops was appointed to the latter office, the following words were spoken by the oldest councillor, R Kartadikoesoema by way of congratulation: 'to a greater Bandoeng, that is the way to which he (mayor Coops, jmo) will lead us and to which we want to be led … On this issue there has been a happy consensus in recent years between all of us who sit at this green table, which gives us power. We want to move forward strongly towards a greater Bandoeng.'

Mr Heetjans, captain of engineers in the Indies Army, was appointed to this position in February 1914, just after Coops had taken up his role in Bandoeng. While many would contribute to the successful expansion of Bandoeng, Coops and Heetjans were definitely instrumental in the succesful urban planning and expansion of Bandoeng. During their term, many branches of municipal service were established. The following four are directly relevant here.

(1) Municipal Public Works – By 1909 the Municipal Public Works department had already started to improve and pave a number of roads every year, and several bridges were built. After 1914 Heetjans took on many more roads and improved the water drainage system through gutters along the roads and culverts under those roads. His department also built workshops for its own projects and equipment. Furthermore, works at the European cemetery were carried out, several large market halls were renovated and provided with concrete roofs, and a new slaughterhouse was built. In 1917, a sewerage plan was drawn up for the city, and two waste incineration plants were built.
(2) Municipal Building Control – From 1910, the municipality had a Building and Housing Control Department, which was to grant building permits, based on the 1910 General Regulation for Building Control in Bandoeng Municipality, to keep control of the construction and renovation of homes, shops, offices, warehouses and warongs in the rapidly growing city.
(3) Municipal Land Company – In 1915 the council decided to establish a municipal land company whose purpose was to guide urban expansion in the desired direction by acquiring land and making plots available to citizens with the obligation to build. Within a few years, hundreds of plots were issued, both for the benefit of private individuals and for buildings of public interest, such as a new general hospital, several military establishments, and the Pasteur Institute for vaccination research.
(4) Municipal Construction Company – since Bandoeng developed a reputation as an attractive place to live, the Indies Government in Batavia decided in 1918 after negotiations with the municipal council that an important government department from Batavia, the Department of Government Enterprises, would move to Bandoeng. The head office of the Indies State Railways also moved to Bandoeng. Hence, offices and residential houses for civil servants had to be built at a rapid pace. The municipality agreed to set up a municipal construction company for this purpose that would meet the need for housing and build the government offices and then rent them out to the Indies Government.

The need for a coherent view of Bandoeng's spatial development had become clear soon after Coops' appointment. The minutes of a council meeting on 21 January 1914 read as follows:

> Objections are raised as the Department of War wants to claim all sorts of attractive plots in a new town quarter (for army officers, jmo). But according to the chairman,

> the council has not yet chosen a firm direction for what itself actually wants. The new director of Public Works should begin to study the problem of Bandoeng's extension. In addition, it needs to be considered whether Bandoeng shall have a land policy and if so which policy. Speaker finds that the council should steer towards land acquisition and then issue parcels in ground lease. But financial means do not yet allow this. The chairman would like to ask the *Resident* to try achieve a delay of the Government's decision on the houses for army officers.

In April 1915, as we read in the minutes, director Heetjans pointed out to the council that 'in all countries so-called "expansion plans" (*uitbreidingsplannen*) are being adopted', allowing municipalities to lead the development of new quarters. 'The intention is to establish an expansion plan for the whole of Bandoeng.' Heetjans refered also to the Netherlands, 'where the government has now ordered larger municipalities to adopt such plans and to revise them periodically'.

Coops and Heetjans soon developed an ambitious land policy. For millions of borrowed guilders – a lot of money in those days – land north of the railway line was bought on a large scale, to prepare it for construction and then issue the plots in leasehold or ownership.

In September 1916, at the request of Mayor Coops, Heetjans submitted proposals to the council for the preparation of an expansion plan. He advocated to take 'a visionary and daring approach and assume the most favourable future of Bandoeng, Bandoeng as Seat of the Government in the broadest sense'.[19] He recommended compliance not only with utility requirements, but also with aesthetic requirements. Regarding the former, Heetjans deemed himself competent; for the latter, he preferred to recruit an expert, preferably a private urban planner. When the council agreed, Mayor Coops, in a letter dated 3 November 1916, commissioned the General Bureau of Engineering and Architects (GBEA) in Batavia.[20] GBEA's mandate was to draw up an expansion plan for the municipality, sufficient for an estimated need of 20–25 years, and the adaptation of the roads, buildings and infrastructure according to that plan. This work would be done in two parts: first, north of the *Grote Postweg* – now *Jalan Asia-Africa* – which ran parallel to the railway, for a maximum of 6,000 guilders; and next, 'the remaining part', for a maximum of 4,000 guilders.

[19] Bandoeng's local government hoped and expected for some time that the central Government would move entirely from Batavia to Bandoeng. Hence, big investments were made, but in the end the Indies Government stayed in Batavia. And it accused the administration of Bandoeng, which faced a financial crisis, of irresponsible financial management. Only a few central government institutions were moved to Bandoeng. After major cutbacks and austerity measures, Bandoeng and its mayor would put the city back on course.

[20] The GBEA was led by FJL Ghijsels and AF Aalbers. They were among the leading architects and urban planners of the Netherlands-Indies, together with Thomas Karsten, Henri Maclaine Pont and Charles Wolff Schoemaker. Maclaine Pont designed the Technical College (now Institut Teknologi Bandung, or ITB) which opened its doors in Bandoeng on 3 July 1920. Wolff Schoemaker became professor at this college in 1922.

Between 1915 and 1921 countless other municipal initiatives were taken; for example in the areas of education (primary, secondary and higher), healthcare, environmental sanitation, energy supply and rent protection. Unfortunately, there is no room to elaborate on them here.

VII. Bandoeng's Local Law-Making Picks Up Steam

Since Coops' arrival more attention was also paid to the production of municipal regulations. On 10 February 2014 the council decided to appoint a Legislative Committee of three members to advise the members and the chairman.[21] Draft regulations and elucidations, often prepared by the chairman personally, were circulated to the council members in advance. At council meetings Mayor Coops presented the draft and gave explanations. He often referred to similar regulations of the three biggest cities in the Netherlands-Indies ahead of Bandoeng, Semarang, Batavia and Soerabaja to see how Bandoeng could compete. If needed, the chairman also referred to developments and municipal regulations in the Netherlands, and to books and articles written by prominent Dutch legal scholars.

Several draft regulations in the field of Public Works were prepared by Director Heetjans, such as the 1917 Road Ordinance, discussed at the meeting of 7 August 1917. Sometimes individual council members were very active in drafting. For example, five regulations approved on 7 August 2017 (see Table 14.3 below) were drafted by JA Lagas, an accountant in the colonial administration.

The legislative activities of local councils were monitored, approved or disapproved by the Indies Government in Batavia. For example, the minutes of the meeting of 17 April 1917 mention under 'Documents received' a Circular of the First Government Secretary stating that 'several times the Governor-General has noticed that municipal regulations contain provisions on criminal procedure, which in so far as they repeat the Inlandsch Reglement[22] are redundant, and in so far as they contain more, are unlawful'. The council was 'requested to take this into account'.

In its first few years the council's legislative activity was minimal, as shown in Table 14.1.

[21] The chairman was Mr F Sieuwertsz, who was a lecturer in law at the Training Institute for *Inlandse* civil servants in Bandoeng; the other members were DP Kessler, a retired civil servant, and WC Moojen, a private citizen. This committee advised both Coops and Heetjans, and their fellow council members. In February 2017 Mr Sieuwertsz was succeeded as chairman by judge EEG Joakim, president of the District Court of Bandoeng (*voorzitter Landraad*).

[22] In 1848 the colonial Government had enacted the Regulation on Criminal Procedure for Indigenous People (*Reglement op de strafvordering voor Inlanders*) which also applied in principle to Foreign Orientals (*Vreemde Oosterlingen*); in short the '*Inlandsch Reglement*'.

Table 14.1 Regulations issued by the council of Bandoeng, 1907–1911

Year	Regulation	Number
1907	Fire Brigade Regulation	1
1908	–	0
1909	Traffic Regulation	1
1910	Building Control Regulation; Slaughter Regulation	2
1911	Entertainment Tax Regulation; Hotel Regulation; Water Regulation; Regulation on Public Order and Cleanliness	4

At a council meeting of 1 April 1916 Mayor Coops complained that 'notably in the field of legislation the council is lagging behind'. In the following two years the council worked hard to make up the deficit, as shown in Tables 14.2 and 14.3 below. In 1916 six regulations were enacted by the council, and in 1917 the council approved 21 municipal regulations.

Table 14.2 Regulations issued by the council of Bandoeng in 1916

7 March	Regulation declaring which of the penal regulations established by the municipal council and the head of the regional administration (*resident*) will still apply
25 May	Regulation on the management and use of the markets (*passers*) managed by the municipality of Bandoeng
28 June	Regulation on the levying and collection of a tax under the name of *Vergunningsrecht* (licence to sell liquor); Regulation on the supply of water from the municipal water supply in Bandoeng; Regulation laying down provisions regulating the sale of liquor in the municipality of Bandoeng (first part); Regulation referred to in Articles 4, 5 and 12 of the Regulation on the supply of water from the municipal water supply

Table 14.3 Regulations issued by the council of Bandoeng in 1917

7 February	Regulation concerning the construction other than according to an approved situation and concerning the construction of roads in the municipality of Bandoeng; Regulation establishing the municipal coat of arms; Amendment of the General Regulations for Building Control (1910)
16 February	Amendment of the Regulation on the levying and collection of a tax on the holding of public entertainments in the municipality of Bandoeng
26 February	Regulation levying a dog tax in the municipality of Bandoeng
9 May	Regulation on the closure of public houses of fornication (brothels); Regulation on street prostitution (first part)
15 June	Regulation on the numbering of buildings and plots in the application of nameplates in the municipality of Bandoeng

(continued)

Table 14.3 ***(Continued)***

24 July	Regulation designating the boundaries of the districts within which Chinese persons are obliged to reside
7 August	Regulation laying down detailed rules for the organisation of the municipal budget; Regulation on the use of and traffic on the roads in the municipality of Bandoeng (first part)
7 August	Regulation on the budget and accounts of municipal companies; Regulation establishing and regulating the management of the Municipal Land Company; Regulation designating the Service of the Municipal Markets as a municipal company; Ordinance designating the Municipal Drinking Water Supply Service as a municipal company; Regulation designating the Service of the Municipal Slaughterhouses as a municipal company
30 August	Civil Servants Regulation
22 October	Regulation on street prostitution (second part); Regulation on lodgings and coffee houses; Regulation to promote public order, and cleanliness (first part)
23 November	Regulation on the use of and traffic on the roads in the municipality of Bandoeng (second part); Regulation transferring to the mayor powers of the municipality pursuant to the Ordinance of 29 August 1917
27 December	Regulation on municipal taxes; Regulation on the sale of liquor in the municipality of Bandoeng (second part)

This legislative productivity shows how eager the council and its chairman were to conduct the municipal affairs on a legal basis. Council members also favoured providing input for lawmaking at the central level. For example, the council of Bandoeng decided to officially give its adhesion to a request by the council of Semarang to the Indies Government to provide input to the drafting process of a new Housing Ordinance.[23]

In the following sections we will take a closer look at two municipal regulations: the Building Regulation (*Bouwverordening*); and the Situation Regulation (*Situatieverordening*).

VIII. Building Regulation and Building Control

In 1910 the council had adopted a General Regulation for Building Control in Bandoeng municipality.[24] Like most building regulations it contained a general

[23] Minutes of council meeting of 30 March 1914, 15.

[24] See Burgemeester van Bandoeng, *Verslag aan den Gemeenteraad van den toestand der gemeente Bandoeng over de jaren 1906 tot 1918* [Report to the Municipal Council about the state of Bandoeng municipality over the years 1906 to 1918] (NV Boekhandel Visser & Co, 1919) 51. This regulation was adopted on 29 June 1910 and promulgated in the *Javasche Courant* of 11 November 1910, No 90. The

prohibition to build without a written permission by the competent official. Secondly, it obliged citizens to build and maintain their houses according to a set of technical rules, which could be monitored and enforced by officials of the building control department. The technical rules regarded both the physical infrastructure of a building – its foundation, walls, roof, chimneys, water, air, hygiene – and its position with respect to the building lines of the street and neighbouring buildings.

Building regulations were not new to the Indies. In Batavia, building regulations (*rooireglementen*) had already been issued in the seventeenth century, and a 'clerk of works' (*rooimeester*) would enforce compliance with the prescribed building lines. Later, building a house in central Batavia required a building licence, and when issuing such licence, the clerk of works would collect a building fee.

In the nineteenth century, when colonial rule was established across Java, regional administrators (*resident*), representing the central Government could issue similar building regulations (*Reglement voor de Bouwpolitie*) for their region. Such regulations differentiated between 'European housing' and '*Inlandsche* housing', and their 'permanent' or 'semi-permanent' materials. European housing had to comply with comprehensive building standards, but most of those rules did not apply to the '*Inlandsche* housing' in villages and urban *kampungs*. However, expanding towns like Bandoeng typically included a mix of *desas* or *kampungs* with mainly *Inlandse* housing and areas with predominantly, but not only, European housing.

A complicating factor was the legal principle of so-called *desa* autonomy. In parallel to the decentralisation laws of 1903–1906 the Indies Government had issued in 1906 an Ordinance on Indigenous Municipalities (*Inlandse Gemeente Ordonnantie*). This ordinance applied the idea of municipal autonomy also to *inlandse*, Indonesian communities, which on Java were usualy called *desa*. The stated goal of this *desa* autonomy was self-government of the *Inlandse* population in their *desas* (villages) according to their own local norms, or *adat*. A second important objective of the desa autonomy was to keep *inlands* land in the hands of local communities and protect them against land acquisition, speculation and development by eager entrepreneurs of mostly European, Chinese or Arab descent.

Therefore, the council of Bandoeng faced a complex situation. Upon the arrival of Coops and Heetjans in 1913/1914 both administators strongly advised the council to take an ambitious and strict approach to develop a comprehensive planning and regulation for all inhabitants.

An illustration of the new strictness was the statement of Heetjans, in a council meeting on 22 February 2015, that the Bragaweg, an important shopping street,

council would adopt amendments in 1911 and 1917. Several towns had already received a building regulation from the Indies Government, just before the decentralisation, namely Batavia and Makassar in 1899, and Blitar, Kediri, Padang and Palembang in 1901. In Bandoeng, the local council received in its third meeting on 19 June 1906 a circular, no 949 of 2 April 1906, from the Secretary of the Indies Government stating principles for adoption of a regulation on building control. This circular was probably one of the sources used when Bandoeng's first building regularion was drafted.

was now messed up due to a lack of supervision by the department for Building Control. Subsequently, he proposed to the council a Decision to Determine Building Lines along the Roads in the Municipality of Bandoeng, which it subsequently approved and issued.

In October 1915 the council discussed a proposal to appoint a third 'clerk of works' of *inlandse* descent for building control in the *kampungs*. The council deplored the lack of building control there, which led to poor hygienic conditions and diseases such as the plague. The council decided to appoint Mr Sjamsoedin as third 'clerk of works' (*rooimeester*) with the requirement that he would have to learn the Sundanese language.[25]

Meanwhile, it had become almost impossible to keep up with construction activities in the burgeoning town. In 1919 about 1,400 building applications a year were received: about 350 for stone houses; the rest for *Inlandse* houses made of wickerwork (*bilik*). The head of the department for Building Control kept requesting for more staff from the council, because control, especially in the *kampungs*, was, he said, almost impossible.

In 1920, control in the *kampungs* became tighter. While the council wanted to take responsibility for the development of the town in its entirety, the strict enforcement also gave rise to complaints, as it added to the already poor financial situation of the local population.

The ambitions of Bandoeng's municipal council to extend building control as well as public services like drinking water and sewerage to the *kampungs* was well in line with the Ethical Policy. Nevertheless, it faced objections from the Indies Government in Batavia. The latter disapproved, especially after the financial crisis of 1920, of Bandoeng's expansive financial management. The provision of full-blown public services to the *kampungs* in all municipalities would make the state's financial burden unacceptably high. In addition, the Government used the principle of *desa* autonomy to declare the municipality incompetent to extend its administration to the *kampungs*.

In December 1917 the mayor and council members agreed that they would request the Governor General to suspend the *desa* autonomy for a dozen of *desas* in the municipality. It would take the Indies Government six years to come up with an answer. In the meantime, the municipality's course of action was ambiguous. Its staff went into the *kampungs* for drainage work, but not for constructing roads or lighting. On the other hand, the planning of future water supply and sewerage systems took into account 'the upcoming abolition' of *desa* autonomy.

Meanwhile, another component was added to the building policy of Bandoeng municipality. Housing shortages and increased rent had caused difficulties for many less well-off people. As a result, they were forced to settle in *kampung* houses that were below par in terms of hygiene and comfort. As the private sector

[25] Minutes of council meeting 31 January 1915, item 14, 67. Mr Sjamsoedin was probably well qualified, but as he was from another region he was unable to speak Sundanese, the regional language of the largest population group of West-Java and the common language in Bandoeng.

appeared uninterested in building for those who had little money to spend, the council decided in 1919 that the municipality itself would build hundreds of 'small dwelling' houses (*kleinwoningbouw*) and rent them out. This had the desired effect of enticing private builders to build in the area.[26]

In March 1922[27] a new draft Regulation on Building and Housing was presented to the council. Mayor Coops wrote in his Elucidation that he preferred to first announce that the draft was available for inspection by interested persons for a period of two months; only afterwards would there be deliberations in the council. Drafting a building regulation was reportedly challenging. A previous draft had been presented to the council on 14 June 1921; subsequently, the council's Technical Committee and Legislative Committee had revised it. Mayor Coops warned that this time too the draft may still not be final, due to what he called 'the rapidly changing conditions in the expanding heterogeneous town'.[28] Finally, in 1929 the council would approve a new Building Regulation which was gazetted in 1931 and would remain in force for many years, even after Indonesia's independence.

Sixty years later, in February 1990, I conducted interviews in the secretariat of Bandung municipality. The head of the Legal Department told me that 'The reception of Netherlands-Indies administrative law had been very smooth and gradual. The law was not so strange to them.' He continued, 'it was not so much political but technical. It was law geared towards the circumstances here.'[29] The Head of the Department for Building Control spoke highly of the old municipal Building Regulation of 1931:[30]

> [T]he Dutch had thought it through and arranged it well. … At that time, the law was applied (*hukum berlaku*). Sometimes people now say that there should be a new building regulation; then I say: please! (*Silahkan*) as long as it is a good support for our work. But until now, the *Bouwverordening van Bandoeng* functions well. … Some provisions are not applied anymore … Like the concept of 'lingkungan' (sphere) in section 24 which distinguishes between six building areas or buildings spheres, such as 1) western building type, with separate construction, 2) oriental urban building type, with separate construction, 3) Village like kampung building type, with separate construction, 4)

[26] A Poldervaart, 'De Groei van Bandoeng – het Grond- en Woningbedrijf' [The Growth of Bandoeng – the Land and Housing Company], een Bandoeng nummer [a Bandoeng issue]. *D'Orient. Indië's Geïllustreerd Weekblad*, (27 June 1927) 16–17.

[27] Council meeting of 22 March 19, 2020, item 5, Gbl No 22.

[28] The minutes cite him as follows: 'Still, the possibility remains that soon certain provisions will turn out to be inadequate; the chances are even high that we will see continuous and frequent changes. The regulation is a particularly "living" law which should reflect the stage of development of a rapidly growing Indies town with heterogenerous population groups. Possibly, it will become desirable in the near future to draft a separate regulation for Indigenous Building (the so-called *Inlandsche bebouwing*) with its own colors, in which highly simplified formalities are prominent.'

[29] Interview with Syahrir SH, 16 February 1990.

[30] After independence in the 1950s the regulation (Bouwverordening van Bandoeng, 1931) was translated and officially issued in the Indonesian language. In 1974 a new draft was prepared but not adopted. Presently, Regulation no 6 of 2023 regarding Construction of Buildings is in force. It is based on the national Law no 6 of 2002 regarding Construction of Buildings.

building blocks for shopping, a- western model, b- oriental model, 5) commercial buildings, 6) other buildings. We do not apply this; we do not make a difference anymore between kampung and town.

IX. Spatial Planning and the Situation Regulation

From 1915 onwards, the city council began to work on expansion plans (see section VI) to accommodate the rapid growth of the city and to maintain good coordination between the various sectors – roads, bridges, rainwater drainage, sewerage, housing, construction of public facilities, facilitation of business, etc.

In order to provide a legal basis for these municipal expansion plans, director Heetjans drafted the so-called Situation Regulation (*Situatieverordening*), which was adopted by the municipal council on 7 February 1917.[31] It was mainly modelled after a similar regulation of the municipality of Semarang:

> According to Article 1 individual building plans can henceforth be rejected on the grounds of, among other things, 'conflict with the interests of traffic or future traffic, health, safety, fire hazard …, connection to the public road or because of failure to meet reasonable requirements of urban beauty.

According to Article 2, the municipal council may adopt expansion plans for the various parts of the municipality. In these plans, land could be reserved for public purposes, such as roads, squares and flushing pipes; in addition, the plans could indicate in which areas only specified types of buildings may be built. The latter was mainly intended to reserve land for *inlandse* or *kampung* housing in the new city districts.

Henceforth, applications for a building licence would have to satisfy not only the technical construction requirements but must also fit in the urban expansion plans. This Situation Regulation remained in force until 1931, when it was merged with the Building Regulation of Bandoeng.

On 25 September 1919, the first expansion plan, for the northern part of Bandoeng, was presented to the council, with an explanatory memorandum, a letter by Mayor Coops, and an advice from the council's Committee for the assessment of expansion plans, which had been set up by the council in June 1917.

The explanatory memorandum pointed out, among other things, that Bandoeng had grown more or less by chance, especially along the main roads:

> The more well-to-do appropriated the best morsels, and gradually forced natives … to settle in the kampungs behind their gardens … the general situation in these kampungs has deteriorated … so complexes have arisen that cannot be tolerated from a general urban planning point of view. In the formation of the city, guiding thoughts and

[31] Regulation on Building Other than according to an Approved Situation and on the Construction of Roads in the Municipality of Bandoeng (*Verordening betreffende het bouwen anders dan volgens een goedgekeurde situatie en betreffende het aanleggen van wegen in de gemeente Bandoeng*).

> foresight had been lacking. The central administration has started slowly and with little success. Now … it is high time to cut the knife in the sickest parts of the old city and to bring healing wherever this is still possible.

A description of general requirements indicated how traffic routes, buildings, squares and greenery, waste disposal and water supply should form a harmoniously coherent whole. With an eye to the future, it was argued that in the north of the city building blocks for European housing should arise, with smaller *kampungs* scattered in between. The buildings of the major public institutions were also to be located there, and that part was to have 'an explicit character of distinction'. Reservation of industrial sites in the south and south-west was advised. This plan was adopted by the council of Bandoeng on 12 May 1920, without any significant discussion.

The council also felt the need for an urban plan for the whole of Bandoeng. The council appointed a special committee and appointed municipal staff, who did a lot of work to fulfil this task in a coordinated way. The result did not disappoint. A 'framework expansion plan' for the whole of Bandoeng was submitted by the committee in April 1924. Subsequently, an additional report was drawn up under the chairmanship of councillor Professor CP Wolff Schoemaker in which the destination of municipal lands was further elaborated. The entire framework expansion plan was approved on 29 April 1925. It discussed in detail the question of what uses the municipal land should be given and how these uses could be achieved. Special attention was also paid to the housing of the less well-off in the *kampung* areas. With these first two plans, solid foundations were laid for the many city plans of Bandung that were to follow.

X. 'Law and development' in a Late-Colonial Town

Since this chapter sits within the part of the book on 'law and development',[32] one may wonder what it tells us about the role of law in socio-economic progress and nation-building, the twin goals of development.

In many ways the local council's lawmaking for the urban expansion and development of late-colonial Bandoeng was a precursor of what 50 years later would be called 'law and development'.

The colonial context was marked by principles of racial and ethnic discrimination laid down in a colonial constitution, and therefore, according to our standards of today, fundamentally unjust. The Ethical Policy of the Indies Government did not alter this, but it provided some extra space and support for those who

[32] Law and development' emerged as a 'movement' in international development assistance in the 1960s, and in its footsteps as a slightly amorphous interdisciplinary academic field. 'Development' was aptly characterised by MJ Esman as combining 'the twin goals of nation-building and socio-economic progress'.

genuinely wanted to improve the social and economic conditions and the political participation of the subjugated Indonesian people.

The verbatim minutes of Bandoeng's municipal council are a valuable source of knowledge about how the actors who made up this local government used this space, trying to make the best of a bad situation.

The minutes tell us that key actors in Bandoeng's local government were passionate in their commitment to urban planning for social and economic development. Mayor Coops and Director Heetjans of Public Works constantly studied, drafted and presented new policy proposals and regulations to the council. The role of Indonesian council members increased considerably after 1918 when they were elected and their number rose.

Bandoeng's local government drew inspiration from the worldwide movements aimed at improving the living conditions of the weaker classes. Meanwhile it felt the pressure from Indonesian activists and mass organisations, who strived for the political independence of Indonesia and no longer took the colonial structures for granted.

Against this backdrop, the Bandoeng council had to accommodate a rapidly growing population by improving the physical infrastructure and housing conditions. The regulations issued to this end by the council constituted a body of local administrative law which in part deviated from ethnic and racial discrimination as a basic principle of colonial law. The regulations for building and urban planning no longer distinguished between population groups, but rather between categories of housing and building, irrespective of which people were living there.

Accordingly, Bandoeng's council and its administrators wanted to extend their public services to all quarters of the town: European, Chinese and Indonesian. However, the Indies Government in Batavia delayed this. While the local government led by Coops spared no effort to obtain sufficient means from the Indies Government, in the end it lacked the budget to carry out the massive development projects that were needed.[33]

When I did field research in 1989–1990, during the heyday of Suharto's New Order, the 1931 Building Regulation of Bandoeng was still in force. The head of the municipal department for building control said he was quite happy with the regulation, calling it 'technical' rather than 'political'. The same applied to the colonial expansion plans and spatial planning legislation which also remained in force long after Indonesia's independence.

Colonial municipalities like Bandoeng may also have contributed, unintentionally, to Indonesia's nation-building. The minutes tell us that this local council was targeted by Indonesian activists and organisations as platforms to voice their concerns and ambitions. Meanwhile, the decentralisation provided the Indonesian council members with opportunities to join in with governing their town. And

[33] In the late 1920s and 1930s the colonial Government would carry out *kampung* improvement programmes which became a precursor to post-Independence development initiatives.

last but not least, these local administrations helped create a class of Indonesian administrative and technical officials who knew how to run a development-oriented local government. This would support Ricklefs' statement that 'In some senses, the Ethical Policy set patterns not for two decades, or three, or four, but for much of the rest of the century.'[34]

In sum, it is fair to say that the minutes of Bandoeng's local council tell us interesting stories of 'Law and development' – the likes of which may deserve a modest place in today's debates about the legacies of colonialism and colonial law.

[34] See MC Ricklefs, 'A New Colonial Age' in MC Ricklefs, '*A History of Modern Indonesia since c.1300*' (Palgrave, 1993) 151–62.

PART IV

Comparative Law and Society

15

Religion and the Semi-Autonomous World of Constitutional Law

BENJAMIN L BERGER*

> A court or legislature can make custom law.
>
> A semi-autonomous social field can make law its custom.[1]

I. Introduction

The comparative study of religion's role and treatment in constitutional systems offers various insights. Some such studies have deepened our understanding of secularism as a protean concept, though with certain stable structural features worthy of our attention.[2] Pursuing religion as an axis of comparative constitutional analysis has led to recognition of new categories of political and legal formations found in the family of constitutional systems.[3] But religion is equally powerful as a subject of study if one's goal is to better understand already recognised, even dominant, constitutional formations like liberal constitutionalism, including by helping to surface latent instabilities and fissures in those systems.[4] It is also the case that, owing to religion's particularistic nature, comparatively tracing the status and treatment of religion in a country or region's constitutional history commonly exposes the unique character of constitutional orders that may otherwise tend, at least on paper, to blend together in their shared commitment to more universalist

* Sincere thanks to Eli Remington for the superb research assistance that he provided during the development of this chapter. Thanks also to Grace Lang for her keen editorial eye. The author is deeply grateful to Professor Andrew Harding for his important scholarly contributions, but most of all for his mentorship and friendship over the years.

[1] Sally Falk Moore, 'Law and Social Change: The Semi-Autonomous Social Field as an Appropriate Subject of Study' (1973) 7 *Law & Society Review* 719, 744.

[2] Ahmet T Kuru, *Secularism and State Policies Toward Religion: The United States, France, and Turkey* (Cambridge University Press, 2009).

[3] Ran Hirschl, *Constitutional Theocracy* (Harvard University Press, 2010).

[4] Benjamin L Berger, 'Liberal Constitutionalism and the Unsettling of the Secular' in Rex Ahdar (ed), *Research Handbook on Law and Religion* (Edward Elgar, 2018).

features.[5] And so we stand to learn a great many things from serious engagement with religion in comparative constitutional study. But is there a way of generalising the conceptual contributions and importance of the study of religion in comparative constitutional law? Is there some overriding thing that religion teaches us about constitutionalism?

My growing intuition has been to respond affirmatively, but I have struggled to find a way of capturing the larger point. And, of course, this *festschrift* is an occasion not just to think generally about issues in comparative constitutional law but, rather, to reflect on Professor Andrew Harding's scholarly leadership in the field, particularly in Asian comparative law. Professor Harding's scholarship in this area has never been centrally concerned with the study of religion. It has, for Harding, always been something of interest given religion's role in the societies and, therefore, constitutional histories that concern him, but he has not tended to step away and reflect more broadly and theoretically on religion in the comparative study of constitutional orders. Yet it turns out that returning to Harding's work that discusses religion has helped me with that larger question about what religion offers to our understanding of comparative constitutional law. And so I want to take this occasion to tackle that larger question with Harding's work as a guide, in part because I think that the answer to that larger question also points to a feature characteristic of Harding's general posture to comparative constitutional study.

My discussion will be anchored by a classic piece in the legal pluralism literature: Sally Falk Moore's 1973 article, 'Law and Social Change: The Semi-Autonomous Social Field as an Appropriate Subject of Study'.[6] Moore's insights in hand, my claim is that the overriding lesson of the study of religion in comparative constitutionalism is that constitutional systems must be understood as movers amidst a variety of semi-autonomous social fields – this is their nature and also their burden. Moore generated the concept of semi-autonomous social fields in an anthropological register and intended it to guide the study of non-state normative communities. Nevertheless, the concept, and Moore's pluralist insights attached to it, shed significant light on what we see through the sensitive comparative study of religion's treatment and role in state constitutional orders. And as one of the finest comparative constitutional scholars of Southeast Asia, it should perhaps come as little surprise that one can find these pluralist insights reflected in Professor Harding's own sensitive treatment of religion in the constitutional orders he has most closely studied.

The organisation of this chapter is simple enough. I will begin with a review of Sally Falk Moore's 1973 article, outlining the key features of the concept of the semi-autonomous social field and what it appears to offer for comparative constitutional study. After a brief detour to address a methodological question about

[5] See Benjamin L Berger, 'Children of Two Logics: A Way into Canadian Constitutional Culture' (2013) 11 *International Journal of Constitutional Law* 319.

[6] Moore (n 1).

the treatment of religion (as process rather than fact), I put the concept of semi-autonomous social fields in play by looking at Harding's treatment of religion in his scholarship on the constitutional systems of Malaysia and Thailand. We see his tacit insistence on this pluralist way of understanding the interaction of religion and constitutional systems in the uses to which he puts constitutional history, his treatment of 'secularism' and his approach to legitimacy in constitutional orders. I conclude by suggesting – with Harding, I believe – that we might do well to think of constitutional law itself as a (merely) semi-autonomous social field.

II. 'Semi-Autonomous Social Fields'

I am reaching for Moore's piece and her concept of semi-autonomous social fields because of its lessons about the way that state law interacts with non-state normativities, lessons that have slipped from view in much of the contemporary legal pluralism literature. It is certainly the case that comparative constitutional law has been influenced by legal pluralist thinking, and Professor Harding's work has been among the most emphatic and persuasive in calling for attention to the fact of multiple legal orders at work in any given social setting. This recognition of the existence of many layers of law – what we might call the 'raw' pluralist insight – is terribly important, particularly for anyone studying comparative law. But Moore's contribution to legal pluralism represented in this piece pushes past this raw descriptive insight, focussing our attention on dynamics of dependence and mutual influence.[7]

Moore's starting point is the fact of the centralised state and the strong temptation that it nurtures to view state law as more important to, and effective in, the social world than an anthropological view would justify. This temptation translates swiftly into what she calls the 'social engineering view' of law, which is governed by 'the assumption that social arrangements are susceptible to conscious human control, and that the instrument by means of which this control is to be achieved is the law'.[8] 'Law', here, is state law; it is the complex aggregate of the elements that contribute to governance, including principles, rules, norms, practices and activities of the various agencies involved in legislation, administration and adjudication. All the elements of this aggregate are 'backed by political power and legitimacy'.[9] The social engineering view makes two moves: it imaginatively

[7] For brief but helpful accounts of the intellectual context for Moore's article, as well as its contributions to what Roberts calls the 'new anthropology of law' that took shape in the 1970s and 1980s, see Simon Roberts, 'Law and Dispute Processes' in Tim Ingold (ed), *Companion Encyclopedia of Anthropology: Humanity, Culture and Social Life* (Routledge, 1994) 976–79; Paul Schiff Berman, 'Federalism and International Law Through the Lens of Legal Pluralism' (2008) 73 *Missouri Law Review* 1149, 1156.

[8] Moore (n 1) 719.

[9] ibid.

separates this complex –'law' – from its surrounding social context and then it asserts its mastery over that context. That is the essence of the view, and Moore's account of it still serves as a workable description of much scholarship that takes place in comparative constitutional spaces. A reader might object that it is common, even normative, to find authors acknowledging the interrelationship between law and social context; but even here Moore offers a useful caution, noting that this acknowledgment is often only rhetorical and abstract. In 1973, she felt that the implications of this interrelationship seldom carried through into the way that law is analysed and treated, and that diagnosis not wholly inapt today.

One way of disrupting this social engineering view is simply to pluralise the category of 'law' – the raw pluralist insight: some norms are legitimated and enforced by the institutions and power of the state, others by more diffuse social forces or quite different structures of belief and authority, but all are law. Crucially, though, Moore counsels against comfort about this move, whereby one simply gathers all binding rules under the umbrella of 'law'. This is a too-easy invocation of pluralism and is apt to mislead. The worry, she says, is that this approach can direct our attention away from 'occasions when, though recognizing the existence of and common character of binding rules at all levels, it may be of importance to distinguish the sources of the rules and the sources of effective inducement and coercion'.[10] This is the key to her piece: rather than abandoning the idea of state law as importantly unique, the focus ought to be on how state law is made effective, how it goes about binding those subject to it. This is the puzzle that she seeks to address: the mystery of how state law works in a normatively rich universe. As she observes, 'an emphasis on the capacity of the modern state to threaten to use physical force should not distract us from the other agencies and modes of inducing compliance'.[11] The pluralist's focus should be on the pattern of mutual influence and the dynamics of mutual dependency among normative orders.

The 'semi-autonomous social field' is the concept she offers to generate that focus. Speaking of the normal object of anthropological study, the 'small field observable to an anthropologist',[12] Moore suggests that it is useful to think of it as semi-autonomous to emphasise not only 'the fact that it can generate rules and customs and symbols internally'[13] (the basic pluralist point), 'but that it is also vulnerable to rules and decisions and other forces emanating from the larger world by which it is surrounded'.[14] These social fields make rules and induce compliance, but are also set within 'a larger social matrix which can, and does, affect and invade it, sometimes at the invitation of person inside it, sometimes at its own instance'.[15] Though briefly stated, this picture is a complex one, involving powers of coercion

[10] ibid, 745.
[11] ibid, 721.
[12] ibid, 720.
[13] ibid.
[14] ibid.
[15] ibid.

at multiple levels, awareness and attention between these levels, and the movement of norms and influence between each, perhaps forcefully imposed, but sometimes invited. Tracing the resulting patterns of mutual influence is the stuff of the rest of the article; the fundamental utility of the concept of the semi-autonomous social field is simply put, though: it 'puts emphasis on the issues of autonomy and isolation, or rather, the absence of autonomy and isolation'.[16]

What does this focus yield that might be of use for comparative constitutional law, particularly as it interacts with religion? Moore suggests that the central insight to be gained from studying the semi-autonomous nature of social fields is that the forces and mechanisms that lead to compliance with internal norms are also the conditions of effectiveness for state law. As Moore explains, 'the various processes that make internally generated rules effective are often also the immediate forces that dictate the mode of compliance or noncompliance to state-made legal rules'.[17] Otherwise put, the success of state law turns on the same enforcement and persuasion mechanisms that determine compliance with the norms of these sub-state social fields. This explains why state legal innovations often fail or produce unintended consequences when they do partially succeed: 'new laws are thrust upon going social arrangements in which there are complexes of binding obligations already in existence'.[18] This is a first form of dependency or non-autonomy: these social fields and state law significantly share the systems and forces that lead to compliance.

But the normative world of a semi-autonomous social field does not merely limit the law, it is also relied upon by it; this is a second yield from the concept of semi-autonomous social fields for comparative constitutional analysis. Moore notes that far from inviting a bare competition of legal orders, state legislation is often best seen as seeking to affect or influence outcomes within and through these social fields. 'Socially significant legislative enactments', she explains, 'frequently are attempts to shift the relative bargaining positions of persons in their dealings with one another within these social fields', while 'The subject of the dealing and much else about the composition and character of the social field and the transactions in it are not necessarily tampered with.'[19] Viewed from within the social field, we see that, in general, state law 'only partially invades the ongoing arrangements'[20] in these fields. State law, here, acknowledges the importance of these fields – the relationships they create, the collaboration and cooperation they enable – as regulators of action. The largely piecemeal disruption of these semi-autonomous social fields by state legal orders is a measure of their interdependence.

In pointing to these aspects of the semi-autonomy of social fields – the way that they are subject to but also impose limits upon the normative force of the state,

[16] ibid, 722.
[17] ibid, 721.
[18] ibid, 723.
[19] ibid, 743.
[20] ibid.

the way they are both invaded and respected by state law – Moore's idea teaches a third, ancillary lesson of importance to how we might approach comparative constitutional analysis. Moore explains that the concept of the semi-autonomous social field 'draws attention to the connection between the internal workings of an observable social field and its points of articulation with a larger setting'.[21] This concept of the *points of articulation* with the larger state setting is a compelling methodological offering. Recognising the internal integrity and richness of non-state legal orders, but mindful of the fact that they are also implicated in and invaded by state law, we ought to go searching for the places where these interactions tend to take place. Sometimes these locations will be institutional, sometimes topical. But with this idea of the semi-autonomous social field, she counsels us to look for these sites of interaction, translation or communication between the social field and the state. It is here, we have reason to believe, we will find the richest information about the nature and workings of both.

III. Detour: Religion as a Social Field

This account of Moore's article in hand, my purpose in the remainder of this chapter is to show that religion is particularly valuable in demonstrating that constitutional law lives its life and does its work in relationship with semi-autonomous social fields, and to use Professor Harding's work on religion in Southeast Asian constitutionalism as demonstrative. Before making that case, however, I want to briefly pause to address a conceptual precondition.

It has become something of an old saw in the critical law and religion literature that one way in which constitutional systems tend to misapprehend religion is by construing it primarily as a system of beliefs, forgetting or supressing its nature as an activity.[22] Rituals, traditions and systems of authority are at least as important as ideas and beliefs; indeed, some have held that rituals and practices are the real stuff of religion, beliefs playing a much more contingent, secondary role.[23] And it

[21] ibid, 742.

[22] This is a channelling of the critique in the critical religious studies literature of 'belief' as the controlling category for understanding religion. For a now-classic articulation of this position, see Talal Asad, *Genealogies of Religion: Discipline and Reasons of Power in Christianity and Islam* (Johns Hopkins University Press, 1993) 43–48. See also, eg, Webb Keane, *Christian Moderns: Freedom and Fetish in the Mission Encounter* (University of California Press, 2007); Saba Mahmood, *Politics of Piety: The Islamic Revival and the Feminist Subject*, rev edn (Princeton University Press, 2011); Talal Asad, 'Thinking about Religion, Belief, and Politics' in Robert A Orsi (ed), *The Cambridge Companion to Religious Studies* (Cambridge University Press, 2012).

[23] Famous among those who advanced this view in the history of the study of religion, of course, is Durkheim. Emile Durkheim, *The Elementary Forms of Religious Life* (Karen E Fields tr, The Free Press, 1995). Writing from interpretive anthropology, Geertz made the point about the necessary mutual involvement of belief and practice in Clifford Geertz, 'Ethos, Worldview, and the Analysis of Sacred Symbols' in Clifford Geertz, *The Interpretation of Cultures: Selected Essays* (Basic Books, 1973).

is indisputably religious behaviour and activity, not beliefs themselves, that pose the true challenges for constitutional law. So, for constitutional law to approach religion as a system of beliefs that are sometimes in conflict with public norms is to strip away what is essential and difficult about religion as a constitutional matter.

Yet this kind of error is reproduced in the scholarly literature when religion is framed as salient for constitutional orders owing to the (constitutionally heterodox) ideas or beliefs to which individuals and communities might adhere. Even literature that seeks to channel pluralist insights falls into this error when it acknowledges religion as a normative order alongside the state, but sees it principally as an order of rules. That is a misleading and partial view that obscures all that sits behind that body of rules and makes religion a *legal order*: the background social relations, affective and aesthetic dispositions, and structures of authority and decision-making, to gesture to just a few of these deeper dimensions. My sense is that this is a habit into which too much comparative constitutional scholarship falls, treating religion as a social fact to be managed, rather than a matrix of institutions, relationships, powers and behaviours.

And so I pause at this juncture in to emphasise that the lessons and ideas at work in this chapter only obtain when we think of religion in this much thicker (and, with this, more realistic) pluralist mode, viewing things as an anthropologist might (and Moore, as an anthropologist did): sensitive to the webs of social relations; practices of authority, interpretation, and enforcement; and daily behaviours that generate and sustain the normative substance of religion. Otherwise put, in offering it as a semi-autonomous social field *par excellence*, I am both assuming and insisting upon an understanding of religion in procedural, rather than propositional, terms.

IV. Religion and Semi-Autonomous Social Fields in Comparative Constitutionalism

The burden I have assumed for this chapter is to demonstrate that sensitively, thoughtfully tracing the movement of religion in constitutional systems is an exercise in the study of the semi-autonomous ecosystem of constitutional law. In what follows, I seek to discharge that burden, in part by using Professor Harding's treatment of religion in his scholarship on constitutionalism in Southeast Asia. Though not the centre of his work, his attention to religion – in at least three dimensions – has precisely the sensitive and thoughtful character capable of surfacing the key aspects of Moore's claims about the nature and importance of semi-autonomous social fields in our legal lives.

For a more contemporary argument for the priority of practice in understanding religion, see Nancy T Ammerman, 'Rethinking Religion: Toward a Practice Approach' (2020) 126 *American Journal of Sociology* 6.

A. Religion and the Uses of Constitutional History

How does constitutional history appear – what is its function and value – viewed through the lens of Moore's concept of semi-autonomous social fields? It looks somewhat different with this picture of the operation and limits of state law firmly in mind. Constitutional history becomes, importantly, a description of the importance and durability of social fields that state law mistakenly imagines itself displacing. To map the social and political world that pre-existed a modern constitution, charting the social forces that prevailed therein, and to trace the efforts – sometimes successive efforts – to rule that world with modern law is to tell a story about non-autonomy and non-isolation, in Moore's terms. In such a history, the special features of the constitutional order, most ably identified by the comparativist, can only be accounted for in relation to a kind of background normative and historical architecture. The constitutional historian is, thus, always sketching the shape and operation of these fields, while simultaneously showing state law's use of and beholdenness to them. As 'new laws are thrust upon going social arrangements in which there are complexes of binding obligations already in existence',[24] some succeed, whereas others give way to the force and importance of those pre-existing arrangements. As Moore imagines it, constitutional law attempts to shift and influence dealings within these fields (what a fine definition of law, generally!) but much is (and must be) left intact. An account of change and stability at the constitutional level thus requires an account of the social world behind it; in this, history of constitutional change is an object lesson in the workings of these semi-autonomous fields.

Professor Harding's work on the constitutional systems of Southeast Asia is distinctively rich, particularly for a constitutional lawyer. But for the purposes of this chapter, a more specific feature of his histories stands out, namely the significance and regard given to religion, religious communities and religious systems. In his accounts of the history of Malaysian constitutional law, Islam is a crucial player, always present as the state order sought to give regard to the special position of Malays in that constitutional order.[25] This is not simply the demographic fact of Islam, but its status as an operative normative order with which the constitution must contend (Harding honours the point about the procedural, not just or principally propositional, character of religion). Religion is, in his hands, 'involved in the contract'.[26] His telling of the complexities surrounding the constitutional authority given to civil courts to decide matters of shari'a law is exemplary: it is simultaneously

[24] Moore (n 1) 723.

[25] See Andrew J Harding, 'Constitution-Making and Autochthony: The Constitution of The Federation of Malaya 1957' in NS Bui and M Malagodi (eds), *Asian Comparative Constitutional Law, Volume 1: Constitution-Making* (Bloomsbury Publishing, 2023). For Harding's telling of the religious and constitutional history of Malaysia, see also Andrew J Harding, 'Malaysia: Religious Pluralism and the Constitution in a Contested Polity' (2012) 4 *Middle East Law and Governance* 356.

[26] Harding (2023) (n 25) 184.

a study in the non-autonomy of Islam as a social field, and the dependence of state law on the legal structures of that social field.[27] Though it is far from my substantive area of expertise, informed by his telling of things, I am inclined to read his history of the evolving interpretation of Article 3 (recognising Islam as the religion of the Federation) and its relationship with Article 11 (providing for freedom of religion) as, similarly, a negotiation between state law and the force of this social field. Both issues – the status of shari'a law and the interpretation of Article 3 – are 'points of articulation' of the sort that Moore encourages us to seek.

I see this historical sensitivity to these dynamics of non-autonomy, and their core place in the contextual constitutional analysis that Harding has championed, in his treatment of monarchies in the region. Reviewing the long arc of influence of monarchies in Asian constitutional orders, he sounds very much like Moore when he observes the validating, legitimating role that religion has played in respect of those orders of state authority,[28] and one need not be a Schmittian to anticipate the migration of these dynamics into a modern constitutional register. Out of their historical telling, he and his co-author describe monarchies as occasions for 'braiding' of indigenous context, religion, local legal culture and state legal orders, such that views of monarchy and royal constitutional guardianship are 'more likely to be mediated by context, such as social norms, rather than settled in the text or "interpreted" by judicial bodies'.[29] In Moore's terms, their history is showing the monarchy as a point of articulation between state and religion; 'braiding' is a fine metaphor for this relation of non-autonomy.

The most express demonstration, in Harding's work, of the capacity of religion to surface the complex dynamics of constitutional semi-autonomy comes in his 2002 article, 'The Keris, the Crescent, and the Blind Goddess'.[30] In what should be regarded as a model of legal pluralist constitutional analysis, he offers a detailed account of the role and status of religion in Malaysian constitutional life. There is much of interest in, and much to learn from, this article, but for present purposes it stands as a sterling example of how following religion – done well – can transform the function of constitutional history in the vein I am imagining here. For Harding, the lesson of Malaysian constitutional history lies in the way that Westminster constitutionalism 'has had to engage with Islam both legally, as an important topic to be dealt with as an aspect of the constitutional order, and philosophically, *as an alternative conception of what the constitutional order might be*'.[31] With this, Harding is describing the way that religion is not just an object of concern for constitutional law, but a normative competitor that

[27] ibid, 191.
[28] Maartje De Visser and Andrew J Harding, 'Monarchical Constitutional Guardianship and Legal Métissage in Asia' (2022) 9 *Asian Journal of Law and Society* 345, 355.
[29] Andrew J Harding and Harshan Kumarasingham, 'The Malay Monarchies in Constitutional and Social Conception' (2023) 9 *Asian Journal of Law and Society* 399, 360.
[30] Andrew J Harding, 'The Keris, the Crescent, and the Blind Goddess: The State, Islam, and the Constitution in Malaysia' (2002) 6 *Singapore Journal of International and Comparative Law* 154.
[31] ibid, 160 (emphasis added).

shapes constitutional possibilities. We see, here – through religion – the way that social fields work as imaginative indexes for the state legal order. And we are miles away from the kind of isolated, grandiose view of state law that so troubled Moore. But in good pluralist form, Harding is also keenly alive to the risks of state law – through its invasions, co-optations, and uses of religion – to these semi-autonomous fields. And so, in this sensitive history of religion and state law in Malaysia, he also finds a kind of duty of constitutional care: 'the most important function of constitutional law, apart from the function of making general provision for governance', he concludes, 'is to ensure that the potentially fragile social fabric is kept intact'.[32]

B. The Ambiguities of Secularism

The question of the nature and meaning of secularism as a component of the overall structure of constitutionalism has, over the last 10–15 years, become a common matter for legal and scholarly debate. Litigation surrounding the term and its implications has sprung up in many countries,[33] as has scholarly interest in the term, often by way of exposing – in triumphal 'aha' moments – what are thought to be its internal contradictions. It is rightly observed, for example, that a state that is insistent on a form of secularism that seeks to bar religion from public matters is also, and by dint of that commitment, focused on and intimately involved in questions of religion.[34]

Comparative constitutional literature, for its part, has been very much interested in understanding the range and variations that attach to that concept. This latter contribution has been particularly valuable in that it has exposed that there is no common core to what the term means, apart perhaps from precluding theocracy as a form of government. Beyond that 'secularism', as a structural commitment about the relationship between public law and religion, can coherently bear a remarkable variety of meanings, ranging from an anti-religious *laicité* to a committed pluralism. In the result, I have elsewhere argued that is best to think of the term simply as identifying a repertoire moves available in managing the relationship between religion and the state.[35]

[32] ibid, 164.

[33] In Canada, for example, see *Mouvement laïque québécois v Saguenay (City)*, 2015 SCC 16. For examples from the American, UK and European case law, see, eg, *Town of Greece v Galloway*, 134 S Ct 1811 (2014); *Elk Grove Unified School District v Newdow*, 542 US 1 (2004); *R(E) v Governing Body of JFS* [2009] UKSC 15; *Lautsi v Italy* (2011) 54 EHRR 3; *Leyla Sahin v Turkey* (2005) 44 EHRR 5.

[34] Asad was one of the first to make this now common observation. See Talal Asad, 'French Secularism and the "Islamic Veil Affair"' (2003) 8 *The Hedgehog Review* 93; Talal Asad, *Formations of the Secular: Christianity, Islam, Modernity* (Stanford University Press, 2003).

[35] Benjamin L Berger, 'Belonging to Law: Religious Difference, Secularism, and the Conditions of Civic Inclusion' (2015) 24 *Social & Legal Studies* 47.

Viewing things through the lens of semi-autonomous social fields, the claim might be somewhat different yet, and this might be a rather attractive revision. Perhaps secularism is even better thought of as a domain-specific gesture toward the relationships of mutual influence and non-autonomy between religion and the state. Here, secularism is less of a state and more of a process, one that decouples religion from the state, thus positioning it as a social field, but that also then acknowledges both its salience and the vulnerability. Otherwise put, using Moore's language, 'secularism' is itself a point of articulation between the semi-autonomous social field of religion and state law. Conceived of in this way, secularism is an inherently indeterminate concept; to channel Moore more directly, the variety of secularisms is a function of the ineluctable salience of the pre-existing and ongoing social arrangements onto which law is thrust. Its apparent contradictions might simply be how secularism works: the tensions endemic to a complex normative configuration in which the orders cannot be isolated even as each seeks its autonomy. On this view, the fact that states concerned with establishing secularism are also deeply involved in monitoring religion practice and behaviour is a fine reflection of the interdependent character of both state law and religion.

The question of secularism arises vividly in Harding's discussion of constitutionalism in Southeast Asia through his discussion of Article 3 of the Malaysian Constitution. In tracing the tensions between understanding Article 3 as an act of mere demographic symbolism and the inclination in Malaysian constitutional life to transform it into an effective provision that grants Islamic law special constitutional status,[36] Harding identifies, at the origin of the provision, a concern about the 'logical tension between espousing a secular state and having an official religion'.[37] And yet his own analysis of this interpretive tension within Malaysian constitutionalism does not opt for the language contradiction or hypocrisy. To be clear, it is not that there is no tension or conflict here; rather, what matters is seeing that this tension surrounding secularism is a feature, not a bug. Harding takes a much more anthropological view of things, finding in this story about secularism evidence of a 'perpetual pluralist conflict' that he ultimately accepts as 'a kind of conflictual equilibrium'.[38] Indeed, beyond acceptance, he ennobles these dynamics with perceptive claim that very much participates in Moore's structural picture: 'in such a highly polarised society as Malaysia, pluralist "conflict" may actually contain stabilising elements'.[39] The idea of semi-autonomous social fields is precisely aimed at the manner in which social fields depend on and sometimes benefit from the invasion (sometimes invited, as Moore notes) of a larger social matrix, even as these social fields are conditions for the success of the state legal

[36] Harding develops this dynamic most fully in Andrew J Harding, 'Constitutional Trajectory in Malaysia: Constitutionalism Without Consensus?' in Michael W Dowdle and Michael A Wilkinson (eds), *Constitutionalism beyond Liberalism* (Cambridge University Press, 2017). See also Harding (2012) (n 25).

[37] Harding (2023) (n 25) 189.

[38] Harding (n 36) 254.

[39] ibid.

order, lending invaluable resources in the coin of assent, belonging and legitimacy. Each are 'stabilised', one might say, through mutual influence, and secularism is best seen as a point of articulation for that influence.

There are moments in his scholarship in which Harding's handling of the term 'secularism' has a somewhat thinner and less provocative feel. In his earlier article on Buddhism and human rights in Thailand,[40] for example, secularism tracks in a more conventional way – as a simple commitment about the non-relevance of religion. Here, Harding falls into the register of contradiction and hypocrisy, asserting for example that the special position accorded to Buddhism in Thailand is 'paradoxical' given constitutional commitments to secularism and equality.[41] Yet even in this piece, his clear emphasis is on drawing our attention to the relations of non-isolation and non-autonomy that take place beneath the abstract concept of the secular. And his conclusion in that piece, about which I will say much more in the next section, is that, if only we can move below the level of constitutional abstractions, we can see that religion as a social field has crucial resources to offer the state in its own legal projects.

C. Legitimacy, Authority and the Success of State Law

This idea is, indeed, central to the picture painted by Moore's account of semi-autonomous social fields: that an important part of these social fields' non-autonomy from the state inheres in the fact that they are often the very conditions and means of success for state law. The thought is that the same tools of enforcement and persuasion that make the norms of these sub-state social fields effective are the tools that determine whether state law will be effective. This is attributable to the fact that law is, as Moore puts it, 'thrust upon going social arrangements',[42] and the networks of obligation that these arrangements involve, it does not replace them. And when it seeks to create new social outcomes, state law must do so by working on the ideas, relationships and social positions of those within these fields. This is, ultimately, a way of understanding how the legitimacy and authority of state law is secured, a perpetual concern of legal theory. But it is a way of so doing that focuses on the lived interaction of normative orders. This claim about legitimacy and effectiveness works in the register of realism, not ideal theory. If accepted, it offers a picture of the authority of constitutional law as emergent from the way that it manages, uses and intervenes in this background matrix of social fields.

Harding's article on Buddhism and human rights in Thailand tells this story through the relationship between religion and the state's liberal human rights project.[43] In many ways the idea that religion is a resource used by the modern

[40] Andrew J Harding, 'Buddhism, Human Rights and Constitutional Reform in Thailand' (2007) 2 *Asian Journal of Comparative Law* 1.

[41] ibid, 8.

[42] Moore (n 1) 723.

[43] Harding (n 40).

state to attract fidelity and asset is a familiar one. Harding makes this point through a compelling and perceptive case study, one that does not simply gesture to religion as a repository of ideas to be picked up and instrumentalised by the state, but regards it as something on which state law is deeply dependent. He therefore works with it as an historically rich cultural field – with institutional, organisational and rhetorical components – that must be carefully engaged with for state legal projects to succeed. Consider his account of the historical role that Buddhism has played in statecraft in Thailand:

> In Thailand, Buddhism represents a national ideology of such importance that each successive regime since the establishment of the Chakri dynasty in 1782 has found it of great importance to ensure that its political programme was supported by the sangha, even to the extent that it has if necessary reorganized the sangha and suppressed dissent from official interpretations of religion to bring about this result, making quite overt use of legal and administrative controls …[44]

Religion, in this account, is a social field whose normative importance persists while the form of the centralised state shifts and evolves profoundly over time. Though he describes Buddhism as an 'ideology', it is clear that the institutional organisations and relations within the social field matter enough to warrant state interventions in its core organisation (the *sangha*) and in its internal interpretive practices. Harding is overt about the fact that the state 'has used Buddhism to create legitimacy, and has sometimes molded Buddhism itself, in its official positions and organisation, to suit the purposes of the state'.[45] These are attempts by the state to shift or use relations within the social field, in Moore's terms, and this use is the state's acknowledgment of the importance of these fields as regulators of action.

Harding's defence of official resort to Buddhism and Buddhist ideas to explain and justify human rights in Thailand is informed by a similar appreciation for religion as a regulator of action. We see here, again, Harding's willingness to recognise and even cultivate a certain intimacy between state and religion, combined with a principled toleration of the friction that this creates with simpler claims about Thailand as a secular state. It is principled precisely because it is based on a realist view of the matrix of semi-autonomous social fields that subsist in Thailand and the need for the state to acknowledge and interact with them if it is to succeed. 'Such an attempt to bridge the gap between culture and aspiration', Harding concludes, 'seems to me entirely sensible'.[46] The point here is that the source and means of legitimacy and assent in any given constitutional context will vary with the social fields in play; and, after all, when it comes to human rights norms, the reasons for agreement matter far less than the fact of agreement.[47]

[44] ibid 3.
[45] ibid, 4.
[46] ibid, 20.
[47] As Harding puts it, 'we do better to try and agree on the contents of human rights rather than on the justification for their observance': ibid, 21.

V. Conclusion: Constitutional Law as (Merely) Semi-Autonomous

I have sought here to defend a claim about the overriding lesson of attending to religion in the study of constitutional orders. Subtending all that we learn about such things as the workings of bills of rights, the nature of secularism, the varieties of constitutional formations, and the instabilities of modern liberalism, is religion's insistence in instructing us to be mindful that constitutional law lives its life within a matrix of semi-autonomous social fields, with all the burdens and realities that this entails. Returning to Moore's classic pluralist article that introduces this concept, I have argued that religion, the semi-autonomous social field *par excellence*, has a special capacity to point us to the patterns of mutual influence and dependence – of non-isolation – that characterise the relation between these normative orders and the state. The lessons of constitutional history, the nature of secularism, the legitimacy and authority of state law, and much else look different and richer when we attend to these dynamics. In short, by pointing us to the workings of semi-autonomous social fields, religion is uniquely helpful in shedding light on the mystery of how constitutional law works in a normatively rich universe.

As I see it, Andrew Harding's scholarship on religion and constitutionalism carries this lesson. But there is another point to be made here, by way of conclusion. True to her anthropological perspective, Moore's discussion of semi-autonomous social fields is focused on sub-state normative orders – the 'small field[s] observable to an anthropologist'.[48] Her message is that these must be 'studied in terms of [their] non-autonomy'.[49] In this chapter, I have largely followed her in that focus, looking to the internal workings of religion as it is touched by constitutional law. But I have also slipped from time to time, into speaking about the non-autonomy of constitutional law itself. This, I think, is because though she was not describing the centralised legal order (apart from critiquing the common over-estimation of its importance) the necessary implication of her claims is that state law – constitutional law – is itself best regarded as a (merely) semi-autonomous social field. Non-isolated, dependent upon, used and invaded by the broader social matrix, constitutional law, too, we may then conclude, must also be studied in terms of its non-autonomy. And this, of course, is one of the great lessons of the larger body of Andrew's work: in teaching and showing us what the contextual analysis of constitutional systems ought to look like, he has always been making just this point.

[48] Moore (n 1) 720.
[49] ibid.

16

Relational Law and Transplanted Law in Village Thailand

DAVID M ENGEL

Everything is change, he said, and everything is connected.
Also everything returns, but what returns is not
what went away—

Louise Glück[1]

I. Introduction

Andrew Harding's scholarship has enriched the study of comparative law in many ways, and one of his most influential contributions has been his work on legal transplants. Andrew reminds us – particularly those of us who conduct our research in the countries of Southeast Asia – not to confine our attention to imported legal texts and institutions, but to broaden our research to consider 'the lived reality of law.' In Andrew's words:

> [W]hat we should be paying attention to is not law as set out in the books, but the lived reality of law, which especially in legal-transplant areas like SE Asia will differ very much from law in the books.[2]

Mindful of Andrew's admonition that we must look to the social and cultural context in order to understand how transplanted legal systems actually function, this chapter will shift attention away from the courts, law texts and legal professionals of Bangkok and examine ordinary people's perceptions of law and justice in Northern Thailand. It will draw on years of informal conversations with the residents of one village I will call Ban Sai, located several hours' drive from the city

[1] Louise Glück, 'The Denial of Death' in *Winter Recipes from the Collective: Poems* (Farrar, Straus and Giroux, 2021) 6.

[2] Andrew Harding, 'The Legal Transplants Debate: Getting Beyond the Impasse?' in Vito Breda (ed), *Legal Transplants in East Asia and Oceania* (Cambridge University Press, 2019) 17.

of Chiangmai.[3] In Ban Sai, as in most Thai villages, the 'lived reality of law' can be fully appreciated only by considering customary practices for resolving disputes and achieving justice, practices that were grounded in Buddhism and the propitiation of ghosts and spirits.

I will suggest that customary village law in Ban Sai, as in many other Thai villages, is relational in contrast to the individualistic framework of Thailand's official – transplanted – laws and legal institutions. In village legality, as in the quote from Louise Glück's haunting poem that serves as an epigraph for this chapter, 'everything is connected'. However, Ban Sai in recent years has undergone radical social and economic transformations that have rendered these customary practices unstable. Thus, transplanted law in village Thailand grows in a cultural soil that is inhospitable in many ways yet is also experiencing shifts and stress. As social changes weaken the relational underpinnings of village law, villagers struggle to maintain the customary norms and practices but find that they have taken on new forms. To quote Glück again, 'Everything returns, but what returns is not what went away.'

II. 'Everything is Connected'

The defining quality of the 'lived reality of law' in Ban Sai is its relationality. Village-level legality is relational in several senses. This section will highlight three aspects of Ban Sai's customary law that sustain and reinforce its relational quality: legal personhood; legal institutions; and legal norms.

A. Legal Personhood

Although the law of the Thai state generally emphasises people's individual and separate existence as rights-bearing citizens, village law views them primarily in terms of their connectedness to the community. The interconnections linking Ban Sai villagers to one another are forged and maintained in a number of ways. When babies are born, they are presented to the shrine of *pho ban* (village father), who is the most important and powerful locality spirit for the entire village, and their relationship to the community is thereby established from a very early age. The same notification procedure must be followed if a resident of Ban Sai marries someone from outside the village. In both cases, identity is anchored in the community as a whole.

[3] Ban Sai is the fictitious name for a real village in northern Thailand that Jaruwan Engel and I have visited for many years. This chapter draws on casual, unsystematic observations and conversations during that time with a number of friends and acquaintances who live there and with a few former residents who now live in Chiangmai.

According to the Thai Civil and Commercial Code (TCC), legal personhood begins with birth and ends with death.[4] In Ban Sai, however, personhood does not begin with birth, since each newborn is thought to have existed in previous lives and arrives in the village bearing the physical and psychological marks of previous incarnations and the burden of karma from acts committed in prior lifetimes. Each villager is enmeshed in relationships – sometimes fraught – that stretch back in time over numerous rebirths. Nor does death extinguish a person's connection to the community, since the ghostly presence of deceased persons is frequently experienced. State law's temporally truncated and individualistic demarcation of the beginning and end of life, a conceptualisation transplanted from abroad,[5] denies the relational premise of personhood that is the very foundation of villagers' law.

The spiritual essence known as *khwan* resides in each villager and also in the fields, forests and mountains that surround them; and the *khwan* are connected rather than individually distinct and independent. Numerous ceremonies and celebrations reinforce the relational qualities of the *khwan* of Ban Sai villagers. The annual *suep chata* ceremony, for example, brings the entire community together in the temple to participate in a ritual that strengthens the congregation's fate and fortune. The monks' hypnotic chanting connects all the congregants at a physical as well as a spiritual level as the resonant sound waves vibrate in their bodies. High above the seated villagers is a net fashioned from sacred string, which symbolises the village society as a whole. Individual threads drop down and are tied around the heads and hands of all the villagers, linking each of them to the net. And the sacred string extends outward through the doors of the temple, reaching every house in the village, joining them all to one another and to the temple like an electrical grid. This ceremony connects the villagers' bodies, their minds and their *khwan*-souls. They are all part of a family-like community of humans, ghosts, spirits and nature. They are dependent on one another, they flourish together and, when harm occurs, they are all diminished.

B. Legal Institutions

When Ban Sai residents discuss village-level legality, they refer to three key institutions. First is the spirit medium. Eight or 10 villagers have the power to channel dead people or other powerful spirits – including *pho ban* – and they can speak in their voices. People go to the spirit mediums for help when they are involved

[4] TCC, Section 15, reads in relevant part: 'Personality begins with the full completion of birth as a living child and ends with death.'

[5] The entire TCC may be regarded as transplanted law. See Munin Pongsapan, 'The Fundamental Misconception in the Drafting of the Thai Civil and Commercial Code of 1925' in Andrew Harding and Munin Pongsapan (eds), *Thai Legal History: From Traditional to Modern*, (Cambridge University Press, 2021) 123 ('Thai private law … was entirely founded on foreign private law, mainly German and Japanese law').

in injury cases, disputes and even unexplained illnesses. The spirit mediums can determine the true causes of injuries or other disturbances in the village and can obtain advice from the spirits on how to remedy these issues. By communicating with ancestors or locality spirits or with *pho ban* himself, the spirit medium resolves disputes that might theoretically lead to litigation in the form of tort cases or lawsuits concerning real or personal property or family matters.

The importance of spirit possession rituals in Ban Sai is highlighted by an annual gathering of mediums from the surrounding area, who come to the village in large numbers to engage in a flamboyant all-day ceremony marked by music, dance at the shrine for *pho ban*, and sword play. The participants speak in strange voices as they dance, and they slash one another and themselves with sharp blades yet miraculously show no wounds. People who do not ordinarily smoke or drink will ostentatiously puff on cigarettes and drink whiskey when they become possessed.

The second key institution of village law is the abbot of Ban Sai's Buddhist temple, a man who is known to be wise, holy and learned. In keeping with northern Thai Buddhism, the abbot combines his teachings on compassion, forgiveness and selflessness with animist practices that predate the arrival of Buddhism in northern Thailand. This form of syncretism has been well documented, as in Shalardchai Ramitanon's description of 'villagers' Buddhism' in Chiangmai and John Holt's account of Buddhism and the spirit cults in neighboring Laos.[6] For the villagers, then, the abbot serves as another spokesperson for village legality when troubles arise or disputes threaten to disrupt the community. Indeed, maintenance of Ban Sai's relational web is one of the abbot's most important functions.

A third institution of village legality is the village chief, known as *pho luang* (great father) or, in the case of a woman, as *mae luang* (great mother). The very title signifies a relational and familial connection between leader and followers. Ban Sai residents hold their *mae luang* in high regard and frequently take their disputes and other troubles to her for resolution. Drawing on appeals to social harmony as well as Buddhist and animist concepts, she counsels moderation, compassion, forgiveness, empathy and compromise in contract or property disputes, in family matters, and in other threats to social harmony. By reminding villagers that they are all related as members of the same extended family, she encourages them to avoid what she characterises as the selfish assertion of individual interests and instead to consider the views of the other party and the welfare of the entire community.[7]

[6] Shalardchai Ramitanon, *Phi Jao Nai [Spirits of the Nobility]*, 2nd edn (Ming Müang Press, 2002); John Clifford Holt, *Spirits of the Place: Buddhism and Lao Religious Culture* (University of Hawai'i Press, 2009).

[7] Villagers occasionally mention the police as a resource to resolve disputes when the abbot or village chief fails. However, they offered no examples of such appeals, and there was a shared recognition that the police could not necessarily be trusted and might demand a payoff to ensure their intervention on behalf of one of the parties. Similarly, no one mentioned recourse to courts and lawyers for resolving disputes, handling injury cases, enforcing contracts, or hearing complaints about family conflict or domestic violence.

C. Legal Norms

Dispute resolution through the use of village law produces win-win outcomes. After the village chief, the spirit medium or the Buddhist monk have resolved a dispute, the relationship between the parties is even stronger where the break has mended. That is because village law, unlike the win-lose model of litigation in the courts, requires the two parties to understand one another and respectfully acknowledge their adversary's point of view – perhaps for the first time. Our friends in Ban Sai told us that village law differed greatly from state law. When disputants take part in a village mediation, both sides take a step back, they listen to the other side, and they reach an agreement. Neither party ends up in the wrong, and neither has to give in to the other. In the end, they simply understand one another and the problem is resolved.

In Ban Sai's village law, maintaining one's place in the group, rather than vindicating one's rights, remains the highest priority. Villagers' decisions when involved in injury cases or other disputes do not aim to maximise their individual legal interests but rather to reinforce the relational net. Their primary goal in this system of village legality is to remain a member of the community in good standing. Individual rights claims generate bad karma for the claimant and threaten village harmony. The well-being of everyone in the community depends on preservation of the interconnections that are the foundation of village customary law.

What then does justice mean in Ban Sai? Care must be taken in posing this question. There is no Thai language equivalent for the Anglo-European term 'justice', with its root in the Latin term *justitia*. The term approximating 'justice' in Ban Sai is *khwam pen tham*, literally 'things according to *dhamma*', an expression much broader than its English or Latin counterpart. *Dhamma* refers to a concept of cosmic order, truth and righteousness – not just correct conduct but the totality of the Buddha's teachings.[8] Indeed, in colloquial Thai, when people say they are studying the *dhamma*, they mean that they are studying Buddhism and not law in the narrow – or transplanted – sense of the word.

Not surprisingly, then, when asked for examples of justice (*khwam pen tham*) and injustice, villagers almost never refer to individual rights and never allude to Thai law or the Thai legal system. Justice to them means comity, mutual recognition and respect, acceptance, and more broadly social and economic balance and order. Their examples of justice breaches do not map readily onto the provisions of the Thai law codes. For example, some villagers cited the rude and condescending

[8] Robert Lingat provided the following influential description of *dharma*, which is the Sanskrit equivalent of the Pali term *dhamma*: '*dharma* is the action which, provided it is conformable to the order of things, permits man to realise his destiny to the full, sustains him in this life, and assures his well-being after death. By its own virtue that act produces a spiritual benefit for him who has performed it, which will necessarily bear fruit in the other world. Conversely, an act contrary to *dharma*, called *adharma*, necessarily involves a sanction, a 'fall' for the one who does it, which will strike him in his future existence if not actually in his present life.' Robert Lingat, *The Classical Law of India*, trans J Duncan M Derrett (University of California Press, 1973) 4.

attitudes of doctors in a large hospital who regarded them as socially inferior, or their unpleasant encounters with government officials who demanded bribes in response to simple requests for services.

Villagers express an understanding of justice that rests on equality, mutuality, honesty and respect. They do not speak the language of rights, which the law codes identify as the essence of legal personhood. Indeed, the word for rights – *sit* or *sithi* – is notably absence from villagers' discourse. A rights-based outcome in a dispute sounds to them more like injustice or even an unmeritorious form of behaviour by the winning party that could bring bad karma to their entire family. For them, transplanted Thai law and *khwam pen tham* operate on different scales and different moral maps entirely.

III. 'Everything is Change'

The 'lived reality of law' in Ban Sai is characterised by relational norms and practices and by longstanding beliefs about the nature of justice as *khwam pen tham*. Yet it would be a mistake to regard village legality as fixed and unchanging. Certainly the basic tenets of village law reach back to the time that western law codes first arrived in Thailand and, indeed, long before that; but very extensive changes in village society have occurred in the late twentieth and early twenty-first centuries. Those social, economic and demographic changes have transformed the lived realities of transplanted law in Thailand.

The two most important changes in Ban Sai have been the loss of population and the diminished role of rice farming as a way of life. In recent years, much to the displeasure of longtime residents, the village school was closed and the children are now bused each day to neighbouring towns and cities. As the children's horizons have expanded, so have the economic vistas of their parents. The physically exhausting work of rice farming and vegetable gardening has become financially precarious, since the price of crops often falls to a level that provides insufficient return on the investment in seeds, fertiliser and labour. Instead, many villagers have turned to salaried work in a nearby industrial park, while others have migrated to jobs in the cities of Chiangmai or Bangkok. The longan orchards of Ban Sai are not entirely abandoned, since they require little attention while the fruit ripens on the trees, but the exodus of students, young adults and even those in middle age, is striking. And as they leave, the disused gardens and rice fields are bought up by agricultural corporations and by real estate developers. As the population shrinks, the rhythms and rituals associated with cultivation and harvest have begun to disappear.

What happens to the legal practices associated with a relational net when it begins to stretch and fray? Among those who still remain in Ban Sai, the connection to one another and to *pho ban*, the temple, and the village chief remain strong. Among the many who have left the village, the situation is more difficult. Some do attempt to retain their place in the community. When a spirit medium or the abbot must be consulted about an injury, for example, the absent victim might ask a parent or a grandparent who still resides in Ban Sai to go in their place. During the annual *suep chata* ceremony, a few absent residents leave their government ID cards in the village as proxies for their physical presence, and the sacred string is wrapped around the cards to include them symbolically in the relational net. In this way, some former residents can remain a part of the community of souls and spirits even when they no longer live in Ban Sai.

But other villagers who have left Ban Sai to study or work elsewhere have begun to lose their connection to the relational net. Personhood defined in terms of group membership has become problematic and uncertain for those who rarely interact with the group, and practices associated with the community of humans and spirits have become inefficacious. For example, a college student who now lives and studies in Chiangmai frequently asked for guidance and protection from the local spirits while she was growing up in Ban Sai. Now she is staying far from home in a student dormitory known to be haunted by dangerous and totally unfamiliar ghosts, but where can she turn for protection? Just to be safe, she has followed a classmate's advice and placed a coin under her bed, requesting whatever ghosts live in the dormitory not to harm her. When she looks more closely, she can see piles of coins under each bed, heaps of prayers to unknown spectres offered by generation after generation of uprooted and fearful young people.

Among Ban Sai villagers who have left the community of their childhood, social alienation has replaced the connectedness they remember in Ban Sai. For example, a 47-year-old noodle seller, who is the son of Ban Sai rice farmers, left the village at the age of 19 to work, first in Bangkok and then in Chiangmai. Few of his childhood friends remain in Ban Sai; they have all migrated to the cities or to tourist centres in the south of Thailand. He regrets the loss of community in a city where people live their own lives and do not have what he calls 'true friendships'. He feels he cannot fully trust anyone in Chiangmai.

Similarly, a young university student observes that most of her friends and classmates now study elsewhere, and they seldom see each other. The old feelings of mutuality and trust have disappeared. In Ban Sai, if her household had extra rice they would give some to the neighbours, who would reciprocate if they had extra vegetables. In Chiangmai, however, she has not experienced that kind of exchange, and she feels that people tend not to know one another even if their homes are close together.

To the extent village law is rooted in feelings of connection, trust, mutuality and the rituals associated with a relational net, the loss of community leaves former residents feeling detached from any well-functioning normative system. As the potency of village legality weakens with distance, so does the capacity of village authorities to resolve injury or contract disputes, property claims, or other issues. Those Ban Sai villagers who now live far from home face an existential crisis: if I am no longer part of the relational net, if I rarely connect with the community of humans and spirits who sustain village legality and offer protection and support to its members, then who am I? How do I deal with the problems that inevitably arise in my life? Some scholars of law and social change might predict that the villagers in exile will turn to state law as they once turned to village law, that they will become the rights-bearing legal subjects envisioned by the Thai law codes. Yet conversations with Ban Sai villagers – both those who have left and those who have stayed – provide little support for the proposition that the 'lived reality of law' in northern Thailand has increasingly assimilated the forms and practices of transplanted law.

IV. 'What Returns is not what Went Away'

A. Substitute Practices

Absence from the relational net connecting the villagers of Ban Sai entails a loss of access to the institutions of village law – notably the spirit mediums, the Buddhist abbot and the village chief – who resolve disputes and maintain local norms and traditions. Ban Sai emigrants have sought to preserve some of these same customary practices in new ways. When it is difficult, for example, to return to Ban Sai, they may seek the services of a spirit medium who resides elsewhere, someone who has no roots in any particular locality but can connect people to mythical figures, gods or nobility rather than Ban Sai ancestral spirits or *pho ban*. In fact, spirit mediums today are more popular than ever in Thailand, and some have even become media stars.[9] They can perform some of the same tasks as those who are rooted in village culture, but they operate independently of any broader relational net. Consulting them does nothing to connect former villagers to Ban Sai or to any other community.

Similarly, those who can no longer visit the village abbot in Ban Sai may attend other temples, follow other religious leaders and make merit in new ways. For example, Wat Doi Kham atop a hill outside the city of Chiangmai attracts throngs of visitors from all over Thailand, who believe that the Buddha statue there (*pho luang than jai*) can instantly gratify their wishes. The crowds of worshippers promise the Buddha image that they will offer repayment (*kae bon*) if their prayers are fulfilled, and they pay thousands of baht daily for huge mounds of jasmine garlands to present in gratitude at the shrine. Similar temples and shrines are popular in Chiangmai and elsewhere in Thailand for worshippers who want supernatural help to deal with their misfortunes, to have children, to find spouses, to cure injuries or illnesses, or to obtain material wealth. But the

[9] Bénédicte Brac de la Perrière and Peter A Jackson (eds), *Spirit Possession in Buddhist Southeast Asia: Worlds Ever More Enchanted* (NIAS Press, 2022); Peter A Jackson and Benjamin Baumann (eds), *Deities and Divas: Queer Ritual Specialists in Myanmar, Thailand and Beyond* (NIAS Press, 2022).

form of spirituality such religious institutions offer differs greatly from mediation in the centuries-old Ban Sai temple with its deep roots in the local community of familiar spirits and humans.

Even a traditional ritual to ward off misfortune, known as *sado khro*, can be performed by Ban Sai villagers who have moved away. One popular practice is *long sop*, in which an individual wearing a white robe lies down in a coffin while a monk chants over the 'corpse'. Upon arising from the coffin, the person has symbolically died and been reborn, reducing her karmic burden so she can make a fresh start. Although *Long sop* has been practised in Ban Sai for centuries, its current popularity in Thailand is nevertheless well suited to the social changes that have transformed the village and its inhabitants. The *long sop* ceremony has no connection to any specific community – it is attended only by the subject, the presiding monk and a few family members. Since it is not relational in character, it can be performed anywhere and benefits the individual – such as an accident victim – without connecting her to a relational net.

The same could be said of the so-called blowing rituals that are perhaps the most common practices of injured persons. They offer immediate healing, but not a community-based connection and certainly not a legal remedy. Nearly every injury narrative contained an account of an officiant – usually a former monk in Ban Sai – blowing vigorously on the injury site. He wipes the injured limb with a leaf and with rice wine and then proceeds to symbolically 'chop' with a metal instrument dipped in medicine. This practice is considered even more efficacious than modern medicine to promote healing and hasten recovery. The ritual in Ban Sai is understood to restore injury victims to health and enable them to function once again as fully capable members of the community. This practice has continued despite the social changes and the loss of community in Ban Sai, but qualified officiants can be found anywhere. Nowadays, the treatment outside the village is performed by strangers and is not understood to sustain the relational net. The practice has lost its roots in the community.

In short, social, economic and demographic changes in Ban Sai have profoundly changed village law and disrupted its relational character, leaving the superficial forms of some practices associated with injuries or other misfortunes – such as the use of spirit mediums, supplication in Buddhist temples, performance of life extension ceremonies, and blowing rituals – while stripping away their community-based aspects. In the words of Louise Glück's poem, 'What returns is not what went away.'

B. Lumping, not Litigation

Ban Sai villagers seldom mention Thai courts, lawyers or law codes when they refer to the problems they encounter in life. In part, this is because transplanted law remains unfamiliar, even though an entire century has elapsed since its arrival in Thailand. The language of village law is immediately understandable to them, but the language, concepts and procedures of state law are written in an inscrutable code that only lawyers can decipher. Lawyers are expensive and, like other strangers, cannot be fully trusted; they can, in the words of one villager, 'turn a case upside down' and make the victim appear the wrongdoer. Moreover, the workings of Thai law are slow and highly unpredictable. Villagers fear that they could end up much worse than they started if they try to make use of it.

Villagers believe that the richer party almost always wins in court. In support of this view, they cite highly publicised criminal cases in which the children of wealthy parents commit crimes and receive only a slap on the wrist. They say that Thai law is unfair and unequal: if it involves a rich person, the case goes away quickly and nobody faces punishment. At worst, the wrongdoer can become a monk, and the case goes silent. In a true democracy, wrongdoers should face punishment whether they are rich or poor, kings or commoners. Unfortunately, Ban Sai villagers conclude, that is not the case in Thailand.

Although a few villagers reported instances in which a particular judge helped them, such positive statements about the institutions and agents of state law are exceedingly rare. Far more typical are the frustrated views of current and former villagers who never associate the Thai justice system with their understanding of *khwam pen tham*. They do not turn to Thai law even after socio-economic changes have disrupted and transformed their traditional community and its customary legal practices. They believe that no remedy at all exists for the legal issues they face; they have little faith in the Thai legal system and find it is hard nowadays to get justice (*khwam pen tham*). Too much depends on how government officials choose to apply the law, and ordinary people who are honest stand no chance. As one villager observed, written laws can be fixed, but not the people who apply them.

When they suffer injuries or other misfortunes, villagers who can no longer turn to Ban Sai's village legality see state law as a highly unattractive alternative, and instead they tend to lump their losses.[10] Lumping is partly consistent with their understanding of Buddhist teachings of forgiveness and compassion, but it falls far short of justice in the sense of *khwam pen tham*, which was formerly delivered by Ban Sai's village chief, abbot or spirit mediums. Traditional village legality never required unilateral capitulation. Lumping can hardly be considered 'things according to *dhamma*'; it feels more like disrespect, inequality, unfairness and even class-based discrimination. Lumping does not produce mutual understanding and satisfaction, nor does it mend the breach. But in the absence of a viable system of customary law, what choice do they have? Injury victims and other potential claimants do not believe state law offers any viable solution. In their minds, courts

[10] The term 'lumping' is used by law and society scholars to refer to behaviour by potential claimants who choose not to take any action against those who have wronged them. Instead they simply absorb their loss or the infringement of their rights without confronting the other party. See generally, David M Engel, *The Myth of the Litigious Society: Why We Don't Sue* (University of Chicago Press, 2016).

and judges can't be trusted, since they are thought to favour the haves over the have-nots. They appear to facilitate injustice and not to correct it.

Of course, there are times when direct contact with the Thai legal system is unavoidable, for example when registering marriages, divorces, or land sales and purchases. As we have seen, however, these contacts are often unpleasant, and villagers feel that, state officials treat them rudely unless they have connections or offer bribes. Although we heard elsewhere that the behaviour of civil servants has greatly improved in recent years, and we ourselves know judges of outstanding ability and character, Ban Sai villagers do not agree with this positive view. They have little good to say about the institutions, agents or procedures of legal transplants in Thailand.

V. Conclusion

Relational law for Ban Sai villagers has not been replaced by transplanted law, but by a legal vacuum in which rights are seldom invoked, disputes are seldom resolved, injuries and contractual breaches go without remedies, and suspicion of the Thai legal system runs high. One might conclude that legal transplantation has failed to flourish because it took place in barren soil, but the villagers of Ban Sai tell a different story. From their perspective, a rich and highly effective system of village law predated the arrival of western courts and law codes, and continued to serve the villagers quite well until the recent fraying of a relational net that bound members of the community together. As relational law grew more attenuated, the question became whether state law could gain enough acceptance to replace it. The answer provided by Ban Sai villagers is that they believe justice as they define it has no place in the modern Thai legal system, and consequently achieving it today is more difficult than ever. That is their 'lived reality of law'.

17

'Dual State', Authoritarian Rule of Law and the Case of China

ALBERT HY CHEN

In the early twenty-first century, the rule of law has been universally and internationally recognised as a human and social good or virtue. The rule of law may be used as a conceptual tool in comparative law to study different legal systems, and to assess the extent to which a particular legal system adheres to its requirements.

States whose legal systems fall short of such requirements are sometimes described as practising 'rule by law' rather than 'rule of law'.[1] In recent decades, the concepts of the 'dual state' – with a duality of rule of law and lawlessness in different domains of the operation of the state and society – and 'authoritarian rule of law' have been developed and used to study such legal systems as those of Nazi Germany[2] and South Africa.[3] More recently, the concept of the 'dual state' has also been applied to study the legal system of the People's Republic of China.[4]

This chapter critically reviews the existing scholarship in this regard, and assesses the validity and utility of concept of the 'dual state' or 'authoritarian rule of law' in the study of comparative law, with particular reference to the case of China. The chapter consists of two main sections. Section I begins by exploring the distinction between rule of law and rule by law as it is commonly understood. It then discusses the literature on authoritarian legality, dual state and authoritarian rule of law. Section II reviews the writings of several leading scholars who

[1] See eg Jeremy Waldron, *Thoughtfulness and the Rule of Law* (Harvard University Press, 2023) ch 10; Tom Ginsburg and Tamir Moustafa (eds), *Rule by Law: The Politics of Courts in Authoritarian Regimes* (Cambridge University Press, 2008).

[2] Ernst Fraenkel, *The Dual State: A Contribution to the Theory of Dictatorship* ([1941] Oxford University Press, 2017); Jens Meierhenrich, *The Remnants of the Rechtsstaat: An Ethnography of Nazi Law* (Oxford University Press, 2018).

[3] Jens Meierhenrich, *The Legacies of Law: Long-Run Consequences of Legal Development in South Africa, 1652–2000* (Cambridge University Press, 2008).

[4] See section II of this chapter. For the possible application of the 'dual state' concept to the Hong Kong Special Administrative Region after the introduction of the National Security Law, see Cora Chan, 'From Legal Pluralism to Dual State: Evolution of the Relationship between the Chinese and Hong Kong Legal Orders' (2022) 16 *Law & Ethics of Human Rights* 99.

have sought to apply the concept of the dual state to the study of the legal system of contemporary China. It examines to what extent the 'dual state' concept has been correctly or appropriately applied to the case of China, and identifies relevant issues arising from the existing scholarship that deserve further research. Finally, the concluding section reflects on the question of to what extent is the concept of 'dual state' or 'authoritarian rule of law' useful in the study of comparative law and the case of China.

I. Rule of Law, Rule by Law and 'Dual States'

In contemporary discourse of concepts of law, the concept of the rule of law exists side by side with the concept of rule by law. Many scholars are of the opinion that in many authoritarian states today, even though the government claims that there is the rule of law in the state, what is actually practised is not rule of law, but rule by law which, in Jeremy Waldron's words, is regarded as 'a debased version of the rule of law'.[5] In the study of law in authoritarian states today, the term 'authoritarian legality' has also been used.[6] Recently, Meierhenrich[7] has drawn on Fraenkel's concept of the 'dual state'[8] to introduced the concept of authoritarian rule of law (AROL) which, according to his threefold classification of the role of law in society, stands as a halfway house between the rule of law and rule by law. In this section, we will first explore the distinction between rule of law and rule by law as it is commonly understood. We will then discuss the literature on authoritarian legality. Finally, we will discuss Meierhenrich's concept of 'dual state' or 'authoritarian rule of law' and consider to what extent it enriches our conceptual framework for the study of rule of law, rule by law and authoritarian legality.

Let us start with the distinction between the rule of law and rule by law. As Waldron points out, the contrast between the two terms is always intended to be to the detriment of rule by law, which is seen as a debased version of the rule of law.[9] So we should start our discussion with the rule of law. In this regard and as a preliminary point, a distinction should be drawn between the 'thin' conception and the 'thick' conception of the rule of law.[10] Whereas the thick conception of the rule of law incorporates human rights and justice as its essential ingredients, the thin conception of the rule of law is often associated with Lon Fuller's theory of the eight principles of legality, or what he calls the 'internal morality of law',[11]

[5] Waldron (n 1) 236–37.
[6] See eg Weitseng Chen and Hualing Fu (eds), *Authoritarian Legality in Asia: Formation, Development and Transition* (Cambridge University Press, 2020).
[7] Meierhenrich (n 2).
[8] Fraenkel (n 2).
[9] See n 5 above.
[10] Randall Peerenboom, *China's Long March Toward Rule of Law* (Cambridge University Press, 2022) 130–41.
[11] Lon L Fuller, *The Morality of Law*, rev edn (Yale University Press, 1969) 4.

which is largely concerned with the formal and procedural aspects of the law and its enforcement rather than whether the substantive content of the law recognises and protects human rights. According to Fuller, the rule of law is in essence the enterprise of subjecting human conduct to the governance of rules, and in order to achieve this, laws should be general, publicised, non-retroactive, clear, consistent, capable of being followed, stable and actually enforced.[12]

The last point about enforcement or implementation of the law is particularly important. Law should not be simply law on the books, but actively implemented by officials and judges. To use HLA Hart's terminology, officials and judges should adopt an 'internal point of view' towards legal rules,[13] and genuinely believe in them, comply with them, act in accordance with them and enforce them. In such a situation, there is, as Fuller points out,[14] a kind of reciprocity between the ruler and the subjects. Subjects can reasonably foresee and predict how power will be exercised by the ruler, and what are the legal consequences of people's actions, and subjects can therefore adjust their behaviour and plan their lives accordingly. This at least means a minimum level of respect for human dignity, autonomy, freedom of choice and responsibility.

In his oft-cited article on the rule of law and its virtue,[15] Raz expresses his support for this thin conception of the rule of law. Raz himself develops an eightfold conception of the rule of law. Some of his criteria are similar to Fuller's. However, he also introduces some criteria which concern the legal machinery for the enforcement of the law, such as judicial independence, natural justice, the power of judicial review and access to the courts. In Raz's view, the principles of the rule of law can be derived from the central idea of the rule of law, which is that the law should be capable of guiding human behaviour. Thus this is similar to Fuller's view that the project of the rule of law is to regulate human behaviour by means of legal rules.

Fuller describes his theory as a theory of the morality of law, which in his view is a kind of 'morality of aspiration'.[16] This means that the morality is concerned with the striving to achieve a particular good that can be realised in different degrees. The higher the degree to which the good is achieved, the more successful is the moral project. Similarly, Raz considers that conformity to the rule of law is a matter of degree.[17] Thus it is clear that even if the rule of law is conceived in its thin version, it is still a demanding ideal that can only be realised to different degrees. It is not a question of 'either black or white', or of whether a country practises or does not practise the rule of law. That the rule of law is a matter of degree is part

[12] ibid, ch 2.
[13] HLA Hart, *The Concept of Law*, ELBS edn (Oxford University Press, 1970) 86–88, 99.
[14] Fuller (n 11) 39–40, 61.
[15] Joseph Raz, 'The Rule of Law and its Virtue' in Joseph Raz, *The Authority of Law* (Oxford University Press, 1979) ch 11 (the article was originally published in *The Law Quarterly Review* in 1977).
[16] Fuller (n 11) 4, 104.
[17] Raz (n 15) 222.

of the premise on which indices of the rule of law in different countries have been developed by various institutions in the contemporary world.[18]

We now turn to the distinction between rule of law and rule by law. As commonly understood,[19] the distinction between these two concepts hinges on whether the state or the government is subject to, bound by and constrained by law. Whereas the rule of law requires a government of laws instead of a government of men, or a political system in which both citizens and officials are equally subject to and constrained by the law, rule by law is often regarded as a situation in which the government uses the law to govern the people, but the government is not itself subject to, bound by or constrained by law. The concept of rule by law may therefore be applied to traditional political systems in which the top ruler or some members of the ruling elite were not bound by the law. For example, in traditional China, the Emperor as the supreme ruler and Son of Heaven was not bound by the law which he had made.[20] And as pointed out by Waldron,[21] Hobbes's theory of state power was such that the sovereign was above the law.

But the application of the concept of rule by law to modern or contemporary legal systems is not unproblematic. For example, even in authoritarian states, most officials are subject to and bound by the law, and can be prosecuted for violations of the criminal law. Many authoritarian states also have systems of judicial review of administrative action so that official actions can be challenged before the courts.[22] So even authoritarian states will not claim that, or promote a legal theory which says that, the government or its officials are not bound by the law and can violate it with impunity. Then the question becomes an empirical question of whether, in practice, officials who are in theory bound by the law will in practice be subject to legal sanctions for violations of it.

There is a growing literature on authoritarian legality, which investigates how authoritarian states use law as a tool or instrument for governance.[23] As pointed out by Chen and Fu,[24] 'legalized authoritarianism' may bolster the legitimacy of the regime. Some authoritarian regimes may actually promote state-led rule of law developments and seek to cultivate 'a feeling of "lawfulness" among the people',[25] while using the law to restrict human rights and to confer broad discretions on the authorities. This phenomenon may be explained with reference to Weber's idea of the three sources of authority and legitimacy – traditional authority, charismatic

[18] See eg the Rule of Law Index of the World Justice Project, worldjusticeproject.org/rule-of-law-index.

[19] Waldron (n 1), Peerenboom (n 10).

[20] See eg Wejen Chang, *In Search of the Way: Legal Philosophy of the Classic Chinese Thinkers* (Edinburgh University Press, 2016) 469–521.

[21] Waldron (n 1) 237.

[22] Qianfan Zhang, 'From Administrative Rule of Law to Constitutionalism? The Changing Perspectives of the Chinese Public Law' (2006) 3 *Asia Law Review* 47, reprinted in Albert HY Chen and Tom Ginsburg (eds), *Public Law in Asia* (Ashgate, 2013) 95.

[23] See eg Ginsburg and Moustafa (n 1); Chen and Fu (n 6).

[24] Chen and Fu (n 6) 5.

[25] Shucheng Wang, 'Varieties of Authoritarian Legality' (2024) 32 *Asia Pacific Law Review* 293, 302.

authority and rational-legal authority.[26] Weber's insight is that in conditions of modernity, legality can itself be a source of legitimacy. For example, in the case of China, the provisions in the Constitution that expressly affirm the leadership of the Chinese Communist Party and require officials to swear the oath of allegiance to the Constitution,[27] and the Government's 'legal educational propaganda' relating to the annual celebration of the National Constitution Day and the promotion of the authority of the Constitution, actually serve to enhance the legitimacy of Communist Party rule.[28]

Then the question arises as to how should we understand the nature and operation of authoritarian legality. Is it a form of the rule of law in its thin sense, or is it rule by law? In my view, authoritarian legality is built upon a form of rule by law, in the sense that laws, legal institutions and the ideology of legality, legalism or rule of law are used as tools of governance. Furthermore, in some domains of life within the authoritarian state, the ideal of the rule of law may be achieved to a significant extent. As mentioned above, the rule of law even in its thin sense consists of a set of fairly demanding requirements, and may be regarded as an ideal that can be realised to varying extents. In my previous writings,[29] I have suggested that the rule of law can be realised or complied with in varying degrees in different domains of socio-economic and socio-political life within a state. Thus the concept of differential degrees of compliance with the rule of law in different domains and contexts of a particular state would be a useful conceptual tool for studying authoritarian legality. As some have suggested,[30] in an authoritarian state such as China, the rule of law is realised to a higher degree in the domains of private law governing the market economy, property rights and other rights in civil law, but the rule of law has not been realised to any significant extent in domains and cases that are regarded by the regime as politically sensitive and that more directly touch upon the important interests of the party-state in maintaining its monopoly of power and securing social order and national security.

We now turn to the topic of the 'dual state' and 'authoritarian rule of law'. The concept of the 'dual state' was first developed by Fraenkel in his study of the operation of the legal system in Nazi Germany.[31] According to his analysis, there existed a duality of the 'normative state' in which the rule of law was well adhered to, and the 'prerogative state', which was a realm of lawlessness, arbitrariness and violence.[32] The normative state was a remnant of the Rechtsstaat that existed before the rise

[26] Max Weber, *Economy and Society, vol 1* (edited by Guenther Roth and Claus Wittich) (University of California Press, 1978) pt 1, ch III.

[27] See Arts 1 and 27 of the PRC Constitution as amended in 2018.

[28] See generally Albert HY Chen, 'China: Constitutions and Constitutionalism' in David Law (ed), *Constitutionalism in Context* (Cambridge University Press, 2022) 61.

[29] Albert HY Chen, *The Changing Legal Orders in Hong Kong and Mainland China* (City University of Hong Kong Press, 2021) 397–407.

[30] See eg Yuhua Wang, *Tying the Autocrat's Hands: The Rise of the Rule of Law in China* (Cambridge University Press, 2015), and section II of this chapter.

[31] Fraenkel (n 2).

[32] ibid, pt I.

of Nazism. The normative state existed at the sufferance of the prerogative state, in the sense that the Nazis could intervene at any time and in any context so as to take a matter or a case out of the hands of the normative state.

The concept of the dual state has provided the theoretical basis for the development of a new theory of 'authoritarian rule of law' (AROL) by Jens Meierhenrich.[33] According to Meierhenrich, AROL stands in the grey zone between the rule of law on the one hand and rule by law on the other hand. Borrowing from the political science literature on hybrid regimes such as 'electoral authoritarianism' and 'competitive authoritarianism',[34] Meierhenrich regards AROL or the dual state as another form of hybrid regime.[35] He refers to South Africa under apartheid[36] and contemporary Russia[37] as prime examples of AROL.

Meierhenrich defines AROL as a hybrid regime in which the normative state and the prerogative state are in tension with, but also mutually reinforce, each other.[38] The existence of a normative state in AROL means that a 'non-trivial portion of everyday life is governed by legal rules'[39] that are reasonably effective and reliable, and that are within people's common knowledge. 'Legal reasoning' and 'legal disputing' are prevalent in this portion of social life.[40]

This concept of AROL is useful for the purpose of analysing and understanding the operation of authoritarian legality. However, I would suggest that the concept of the prerogative state needs to be further refined. Fraenkel defines the prerogative state as 'a vacuum as far as law is concerned'.[41] It is a realm of 'lawlessness and arbitrariness',[42] and there is 'no legal regulation of the official bodies'.[43] There is 'unlimited arbitrariness and violence unchecked by any legal guarantees'.[44] The same laws that are complied with in the normative state are violated in the prerogative state.[45] According to Meierhenrich, the prerogative state is 'a form of institutionalized lawlessness, or wanton rule'.[46] Whereas there is a legal way of doing things in the normative state, the prerogative state is characterised by 'a *violent* way of doing things'.[47]

It is arguable that the above definition of the prerogative state is too narrow, and should be expanded to cover situations other than complete lawlessness, arbitrariness, violence or wanton rule. The better view is to define the prerogative state

[33] Meierhenrich (n 2) 245.
[34] ibid, 234.
[35] ibid, 236.
[36] ibid, 232, 238, 242.
[37] ibid, 238–39, 243–44.
[38] ibid, 236.
[39] ibid, 239.
[40] ibid, 239–45.
[41] Fraenkel (n 2) 3.
[42] ibid, 25.
[43] ibid, 3.
[44] ibid, xiii (introduction to the 1941 edition).
[45] ibid, xv (preface to the 1974 German edition).
[46] Meierhenrich (n 2) 237.
[47] ibid, 236; emphasis in original.

as a domain of social and political life in an authoritarian state in which the rule of law is largely or almost completely absent, and the mode of governance is a way of doing things *other than* the rule of law. It may be rule by law (including law that confers arbitrary power), or rule by arbitrary decrees and commands, or there may be frequent and serious violations of legality and the exercise of power in disregard of legal rules, or it may be a realm of lawlessness in which officials act without any legal basis, or it can be a realm of rule by violence and terror. For example, the prerogative state can be a realm of rule by law that fails to comply with the requirements of rule of law: for instance, there may exist laws that authorise actions by officials, but the laws are extremely vague and confer almost unlimited discretion on officials. This kind of rule by law uses law to confer arbitrary power on government.

Take the example of a preventive detention law that exists as part of the national security law of some jurisdictions, which authorises detention for unlimited periods without trial of people who are suspected of being a threat to national security.[48] Or take the example of the German Reichstag's enabling act of 28 February 1933[49] which conferred unlimited lawmaking power on the Nazi-led executive. Another possible form of the prerogative state is what Fu Hualing calls 'extra-law' or 'extra-extra-law', whereby the authorities act without any legal basis, without any legal authorisation or in complete disregard of existing legal rules.[50]

To conclude this section, the concept of the 'dual state' or 'authoritarian rule of law' (as modified in the ways suggested above as regards the definition of the prerogative state) can be a useful concept for the comparative study of legal systems, particularly authoritarian legal systems. Optimistically, it may be considered a useful concept for the study of legal evolution in the sense of a transition from rule by law to rule of law. The possibility of such a transition is sometimes discussed in the literature on authoritarian legality and also by writers on rule by law and its relationship to rule of law. As Peerenboom writes with reference to the case of China:

> The establishment of rule of law is a long-term process. No legal system can transform itself from rule by law into a fully implemented rule of law overnight. All countries now known for rule of law initially went through a period, in some cases lasting for centuries, in which legal institutions were weak and rule of law only imperfectly implemented at best.[51]

Peerenboom himself has not developed any concept that represents a halfway house between rule of law and rule by law. In my view, Meierhenrich's contribution

[48] An example is the Malaysian Internal Security Act 1960 which Singapore has also adopted as part of its laws.

[49] This is the Emergency Decree of 28 February 1933 described by Fraenkel as the 'constitutional charter' of the Third Reich: Fraenkel (n 2) 3.

[50] Hualing Fu, 'The Varieties of Law in China' (2011) 1–2 *China Rights Forum* 56–63; see the discussion of Fu's views in Chen (n 29) 101–05.

[51] Peerenboom (n 10) 139.

is precisely the development of such a concept, which is the 'authoritarian rule of law' based on Fraenkel's concept of the 'dual state'. However, whereas the normative state in Nazi Germany was a remnant of the Rechtsstaat that previously prevailed in Germany, in developing legal systems like that of China, the normative state – insofar as it actually exists – would have been the result of state-led efforts to develop authoritarian legality.[52] If China is now a 'dual state' that practises 'authoritarian rule of law', it is possible to conceive optimistically of a scenario in which the normative state gradually expands, and the prerogative state (as defined in the modified way suggested above) would dwindle in size and intensity as legal and political reforms unfold. We will therefore turn to the case of China in the next section.

II. Is China a 'Dual State'?

In recent years, there has emerged a body of scholarship on the possible application of the concept of the dual state (or Meierhenrich's 'authoritarian rule of law') to the study of the case of China. There is not yet any book-length treatment of the subject, but a number of articles have been published in this regard. This section will review and evaluate what the author considers to be the most significant contributions to the discussion of the subject in the works of Eva Pils, Fu Hualing, Zhang Xianchu and Donald Clarke.

Eva Pils has in her works applied the concept of the dual state to discuss the Chinese legal system. What is most directly relevant to our present purposes is her article,'China's dual state revival under Xi Jinping'.[53] In this article, she argues that there exist important features of a 'dual state' in China, which may even be 'contributing to new Dual State formations at a global level'.[54] Pils points out that whereas little attention was paid to legality in China's Maoist era, since Deng Xiaoping initiated the era of 'reform and opening' in the late 1970s, there has been a genuine attempt to embark on legal reform and to construct a normative state (using the terms 'normative state' and 'prerogative state' in the theory of the dual state) which has in practice competed with the pre-existing prerogative state.

Pils points out that China in the reform era has been a dual state rather than a rule-of-law state, because the developing legal system has not constrained the use of repressive 'prerogative' measures by the party-state.[55] She argues that there has always been an assumption that in domains that are regarded as politically sensitive, ordinary legal rules may always be suspended and extra-legal state-centred violence such as enforced disappearances may always be resorted to. Nevertheless,

[52] See section II of this chapter.

[53] Eva Pils, 'China's Dual State Revival under Xi Jinping' (2023) 46 *Fordham International Law Journal* 339.

[54] ibid, 341.

[55] ibid, 351.

in the pre-Xi Jinping era, there had been a hope among intellectuals and the legal community that the prerogative state may be gradually brought under control and its domains would gradually shrink, so that the dual state will transition towards a rule of law state. Such hope, however, has been dashed in the Xi era.

Pils believes that in the Xi era there has been a 'concurrent growth' of the normative state and the prerogative state.[56] On the one hand, the party-state has strengthened the legal system and relied on some legal means to achieve its goals of enhancing the domination of the party-state and repressing civil society. On the other hand, the party-state has resorted to extra-legal means in instances such as the crackdown against human rights lawyers (the '709 crackdown')[57] and the repression of the Uighurs in Xinjiang (in the form of mass detention in vocational training or education centres).

Pils emphasises that the main feature of the 'Dual State dictatorship' is 'its merely conditional subjection to the law, and its willingness to scorn legality whenever this seemed opportune'.[58] This in her view is a rejection of the rule of law. She also argues that the concept of the dual state is useful in challenging the 'simplistic belief' that the rule of law in the commercial domain may eventually promote the rule of law in other areas.[59] Pils also cautions against the use of the term 'authoritarian legality', which may be misleading because it seems to suggest that legality is valuable, 'authoritarian governance reliant on law is per se valuable, and that pursuit of the ideal of rule of law (*fazhi*) is possible in authoritarian systems'.[60]

In my view, Pils has used the concept of the dual state to establish a very useful framework for studying the developing legal system in China. The concept of the normative state as applied to the development of legal norms and institutions in the reform era can be used to acknowledge the progress towards the rule of law in post-Mao China. This proposition of course needs to be substantiated by research on both the legal rules, doctrines and principles introduced in the reform era, the enforcement and implementation of the legal norms, and the operation of the legal institutions in question.[61]

At the same time, the concept of the prerogative state that still forms part of the Chinese legal system can provide a foundation for researchers to identify the exact scope of the prerogative state in China and what actually happens in those political or politically sensitive domains that are subject to the control or interventions of the prerogative state. This would require research both as regards the

[56] ibid, 360.

[57] Eva Pils, 'The Party's Turn to Public Repression: An Analysis of the "709" Crackdown on Human Rights Lawyers in China' (2018) 3 *China Law and Society Review* 1; Fu Hualing, 'The July 9th (709) Crackdown on Human Rights Lawyers: Legal Advocacy in an Authoritarian State' (2018) 27 *Journal of Contemporary China* 554.

[58] Pils (n 53) 374.

[59] ibid, 348.

[60] ibid, 374.

[61] See eg Albert HY Chen, 'Legal Thought and Legal Development in the People's Republic of China' in John Gillespie and Albert HY Chen (eds), *Legal Reforms in China and Vietnam: A Comparison of Asian Communist Regimes* (Routledge, 2010) ch 3.

rules (if any) employed by the prerogative state (particularly where these rules are inconsistent with the legal rules of the normative state), as well as more arbitrary exercise of power (by the prerogative state) that is not governed by general and transparent rules.

We now turn to a series of three articles (including two by Fu Hualing and one co-authored by Fu Hualing and Zhang Xianchu) that also apply the concept of the dual state to the study of the Chinese legal system. By studying the three articles as a whole, we can observe how the authors apply the concept of the dual state to the case of China, and compare and contrast their approach with that of Pils.

In the first of the three articles, Fu Hualing uses dual state theory and its concepts of the normative state and the prerogative state in discussing the case of China.[62] He highlights the considerable degree of autonomy in the operation of private law in the Chinese legal system. He also points out that there is a duality in the Chinese legal system in the sense that the private law system exists side-by-side with a prerogative state that handles politically sensitive matters using 'substantively extra-legal methods'[63] according to considerations of political expediency rather than the law. In particular, he identifies the specific domains of political concern that are subject to such extraordinary treatment. These include media governance, religious and ethnic affairs such as Xinjiang affairs, collective or mass disputes, terrorism, national security and major cases of corruption. In these matters, 'ordinary legal rules are shoved aside, legal institutions are displaced, and rule of law is openly trumped by political considerations'.[64]

On the other hand, Fu points out that China has in the reform era developed a system of private law that can be considered a 'normal legal system'[65] operating with predictability and certainty. It is a system that he describes as 'professionalised, institutionalised, and semi-autonomous'.[66] He explains that this system has developed in response to the popular demand for rights and for fairness. It exists in a 'symbiotic relationship' with the prerogative state.[67] He also points out that despite the continued existence of the prerogative state in the Xi era, the Xi regime has increasingly resorted to formal legal rules and procedure – or what can be called authoritarian legality. In his view, the Chinese Communist Party has actually 'discovered the empowering aspect of legality'.[68] Thus some formerly extra-legal practices have now been written into the law and so legalised. And the status of the rules and regulations operating within the Party has been enhanced.

The views expressed by Fu in this article converge with Pils' analysis, as discussed above. Fu goes into more detail than Pils in identifying what are the 'politically

[62] Hualing Fu, 'Duality and China's Struggle for Legal Autonomy' (2019] 1 *China Perspectives* 3.
[63] ibid, 3.
[64] ibid, 4.
[65] ibid, 6.
[66] ibid, 6.
[67] ibid, 4.
[68] ibid, 5.

sensitive' domains that may fall within the scope of the prerogative state. He also underscores the fact that it is in matters of private law such as contract and property rights that the normative state largely operates. However, if this is the case, then the question arises as to the extent to which private law rights of contract and property are securely protected by law and legal institutions in contemporary China, and whether or to what extent, or what are the circumstances in which, the prerogative state will intervene in private law matters. This is a major research question opened up by Fu's article.

Whereas Fu in this article suggests that private law governing interpersonal relationships is largely the domain of the normative state in China, he has not discussed directly the extent to which the prerogative state prevails in domains of public law. Given the development of the law and institutions of administrative litigation and judicial review of administrative actions in China since the enactment of the Law of Administrative Litigation in 1989,[69] it is not unreasonable to suggest that there may be areas of public law in China that also largely fall within the scope of the normative state. If (which is to be established by empirical research) judicial review of administrative actions are largely dealt with in accordance with the law by the courts, what, if any, are the circumstances in which the prerogative state will intervene in public law cases, and what are the precise modes of intervention? These are the further research questions raised by Fu's article.

In his second article, Fu applies the concept of the dual state to the study of the Chinese party-state's power to detain suspected offenders in China.[70] His point of departure is what he calls the 'liberal detention mode',[71] the ingredients of which include the equal application of relevant detention law to different categories of offenders irrespective of their status, judicial control over the process of detention, and access to lawyers on the part of the detainees. Fu points out that China's dual state departs from this liberal detention model. The article studies three detention regimes in contemporary China: (1) administrative detention by the police (other than in the course of criminal law proceedings); (2) detention in the course of the criminal process; and (3) detention in the course of anti-corruption investigation. The article reviews the changes in the law and practice in these three domains in the course of the PRC's legal history, particularly in recent decades.

It is pointed out that in the Maoist era, the practice of detention was essentially lawless, in the sense that the police exercised the power to detain suspects on the basis of considerations of political expediency in the absence of detailed legal rules.[72] The article points out that in the reform era, legal rules and institutions have been developed that effectively regulate the police power of detention, even

[69] See Zhang (n 22).

[70] Hualing Fu, 'Between the Prerogative and the Normative States: The Evolving Power to Detain in China's Political-Legal System' (2022) 16 *Law & Ethics of Human Rights* 61.

[71] ibid, 62.

[72] ibid, 65, 67.

though legal rules and judicial oversight are still of little relevance in '[p]olitically significant matters'.[73]

As far as the police power of administrative detention is concerned, the article discusses the State Council's rules on re-education through labour (*laodong jiaoyang*) and the Public Order Punishment Law (*Zhi'an guanli chufa tiaoli*, alternatively translated as the Security Administration Punishment Law), and points out that with the abolition of the former, and the reform and gradual improvement of the latter, police administrative power to detain persons has been successfully subject to legal control.

As regards detention in the criminal process, the article discusses the rules on 'shelter for investigation' (*shourong shencha*)[74] and the reform introduced by the amendment of the Criminal Procedure Law of 1996. However, it is pointed out in politically sensitive cases where longer periods of detention were needed, the police distorted the legal rules on 'residential surveillance' and practised detention in designated locations for a six-month period (a period longer than the normal period of detention under the Criminal Procedure Law).[75] Such residential surveillance at a designated place was formalised by the amendment of the Criminal Procedure Law in 2012, and since then the scope of offences to which this practice applied has been significantly expanded.[76] Fu also points out that during the 'Jasmine Revolution' in 2011, extra-legal detention and enforced disappearances were practised, apparently on the basis that there was an emergency that necessitated extra-legal measures.[77]

Thirdly, as regards detention in anti-corruption investigations, the article discusses the *shuanggui* mechanism in the Chinese Communist Party's disciplinary rules.[78] *Shuanggui*, a mode of detention which was widely practised by the party-state, was not provided in state law but only in Party rules. However, since 2018, with the establishment of the national and local supervisory commissions and enactment of the new Law on Supervision, the Party's disciplinary procedures have been incorporated into state law and administered by state organs – the supervisory commissions. Yet according to Fu's analysis, this new system is of a political nature and not subject to constitutional or legal accountability and judicial oversight.[79]

How the concept of the dual state applies to the state's power of detention of suspected offenders is indeed a most important practical issue in dual state theory. The freedom of the person is a core human rights, and the practice of arbitrary arrest and imprisonment would be a hallmark of a prerogative state. Fu's article chronicles the gradual growth of the normative state in China as far as the state's

[73] ibid, 66.
[74] ibid, 79.
[75] ibid, 86.
[76] ibid, 88.
[77] ibid, 86–87.
[78] ibid, 91.
[79] ibid, 92–95.

power of detention of citizens is concerned, and thus also the relative diminution of the scope of the prerogative state. In this respect, the article has demonstrated how each of the three regimes of detention covered by the article has in the course of the last few decades increasingly come under legal regulation. However, the article does not present an explicit conclusion as regards the extent to which the prerogative state still exists in China at present with regard to the state's power of detention.

Neither does the article provide a full answer to the questions of what is the exact meaning of the term 'prerogative state' in the context of the state's power of detention, and under what conditions should an exercise of state power to detain be characterised as belonging to the prerogative state rather than the normative state. Take the example of the practice of *shuanggui* under the Party's regulations before the legal reform of 2018, when this *shuanggui* power was subsumed by the *liuzhi* power under the new Law of Supervision. This is apparently a feature of what Fu calls the 'prerogative state' which is however not the 'prerogative state' in the narrow sense of lawlessness and arbitrary power as discussed in section I of this chapter.

As Fu himself points out, the 'Prerogative state mechanisms' he refers to are 'not without rules',[80] and there may actually be detailed rules governing the operation of mechanisms such as the Party's disciplinary procedures of investigations, detention (*shuanggui*) and imposition of sanctions. This raises a theoretical question of whether measures governed by rules (such as Party-made rules) other than legal rules that are largely complied with by the party-state authorities administering them should be considered part of the prerogative state rather than the normative state.

It seems that Fu considers the exercise of the power to detain under the Party's disciplinary proceedings part of the prerogative state (even after the legal reform of 2018) because it does not conform to what Fu calls the 'liberal detention mode' as discussed above. This suggests the possibility that there may be different domains in the prerogatives state (if Fu's expansive concept of the prerogative state is to be adopted) in which different degrees of legality may be practised. On the one extreme is the exercise of arbitrary power in the absence of rules or in total disregard of rules that exist. On the other end of the spectrum is the exercise of power (detention power in this context) in accordance with rules that are not legal rules (such as Party regulations), or rules that do not comply with what Fu considers to be just and reasonable standards of detention law. This perspective is actually consistent with what was proposed in section I of this chapter regarding a broader understanding of what is the prerogative state within a dual state or under an authoritarian rule of law. According to this broader understanding, official actions that fail to meet the rule of law requirements of the normative state may be regarded as falling within the prerogative state.

[80] ibid, 69.

We now turn to the third article in the series, co-authored by Fu Hualing and Zhang Xianchu.[81] This article applies the concept of the dual state to the study of civil litigation in China that involves a Party organ or the application of Party rules. The study covers a number of judicial decisions in cases in which a citizen sought to enforce his private law rights, and the applicable law includes contract law, labour law and company law.

Some of the cases involved employment disputes between a worker and a Party organ, which was the worker's employer. The article demonstrates that, in these cases, the courts had no problem in enforcing the law relating to employment contracts against a Party organ.[82] On the other hand, there were also cases in which the employer was a state-owned enterprise, and the employee was a Party cadre. In these cases, the Party cadre's interest was adversely affected by actions taken in accordance with the Party's disciplinary rules, but not in accordance with the Law of Labour Contracts. The Party cadre failed to obtain remedies from the court.[83]

There was also another case in which an employee of a state-owned company was denied certain benefits which he would be entitled to enjoy under an incentive scheme established by the company. The scheme had been found to be in violation of relevant Party rules and was declared invalid by the Party authorities. The court held that even though the decision of the Party authorities was not based on or consistent with company law, it was still to be respected and the employee failed in his claim.[84]

The authors of the article suggest that such case law testifies to the operation of the dual state in China and the superior position of the prerogative state. In my view, it is arguable whether the case law discussed in the article illustrates the operation of a 'prerogative state' as part of the dual state in China. As the article itself points out, although Party rules are not law, 'the Party's operation is neither normless nor irrational', and the 'prerogative system' in China 'has increasingly been formalized, regularized, and institutionalized to an extent that can even create the appearance of legalism'.[85] The case law discussed in the article demonstrates the operation of a legal system in which state laws and Party regulations exist side-by-side. In such a system, occasional tension, conflict and interactions are inevitable as between the rules established by law and the rules established by Party regulations. It is doubtful whether all actions and decisions taken in accordance with Party regulations (that otherwise have no formal legal basis) should be described as part of the prerogative state. The better view is to understand the case law discussed in the article as the development of

[81] Hualing Fu and Xianchu Zhang, 'Judging the Party: Public Law Wrongs and Private Law Remedies' (2022) 10 *Chinese Journal of Comparative Law* 97.
[82] ibid, 105–07.
[83] ibid, 107–11.
[84] ibid, 111–14.
[85] ibid, 100.

jurisprudence by the courts to tackle the relationship and interaction between state law and Party regulations. It is perfectly conceivable that in the course of time, a set of legal rules can be developed to deal with situations of conflict between state law and Party regulations.

The above-mentioned articles on the dual state in China have only been published in recent years, and there is not yet much debate on whether the concept of the dual state can be appropriately applied to the case of China. A most noteworthy work in this regard is Donald Clarke's article on 'Is China a Dual State',[86] which contains the weightiest criticism to date of the application of the concept of the dual state to contemporary China.

Clarke agrees that 'certainly there can be no doubt as to the existence of the prerogative state' in contemporary China,[87] but he takes issue with the proposition that there is a normative state existing alongside the prerogative state. He questions the existence of the normative state in China on several grounds. First, he points out that in Fraenkel's dual state, the normative state was a remnant of the pre-existing legal culture in Germany where law and legality were already embedded in society in the sense that there was a legal consciousness in society that took law seriously.[88] Clark points out that this 'prior embeddedness' of a normative state is absent in the case of modern China.[89] 'What was established in China in 1949 looks very much like a prerogative State. … A normative state as theorized by Fraenkel is simply not something that can be constructed within the womb of a prerogative state.'[90]

Secondly, Clarke relies on a passage in Meierhenrich's book which refers to the existence of 'a space for legal contestation' in a dual state for 'dissenters, insurgents, or other opponents of dictatorship';[91] Clarke argues that China is not a dual state because 'Dissenters and opponents of the Party cannot take legal norms and institutions seriously as swords or shields', and 'the state seems uninterested in maintaining even a façade of fairness in its legal institutions'.[92]

Thirdly, Clarke compares the case of China with Nazi Germany, where the Nazis took control of the pre-existing police and new courts were created as instruments of the prerogative state. Clarke argues that in the case of China, the dual state model is unconvincing because 'there is no institutional or human basis for such a duality. It is the same officials, selected in the same way, that we may observe sometimes acting in a law-like way and sometimes in an arbitrary way'.[93]

[86] Donald C Clarke, 'Is China a Dual State?' GWU Legal Studies Research Paper No 2022-74 (15 December 2022), ssrn.com/abstract=4317126.
[87] ibid, 4.
[88] ibid, 6.
[89] ibid, 6.
[90] ibid, 6–7.
[91] Meierhenrich (n 2) 246.
[92] Clarke (n 86) 7.
[93] ibid, 10.

Fourthly, Clarke argues that even if there is a considerable degree of regularity and predictability in the operation of that part of China's legal system other than the prerogative state (which Clarke calls the 'non-prerogative state'),[94] official acts that appear to be law-compliant in this non-prerogative state may be more a matter of 'statistical probability' rather than being based on a 'legal motivation'.[95] Clarke suggests that this non-prerogative state may be governed by 'the general principles of order maintenance',[96] but it does not amount to a normative state in which officials are bound by and behave in accordance with principles of law that are 'sacrosanct'.[97]

Clarke has indeed raised important and fundamental issues that deserve further reflections and research, though I am not convinced by his arguments, each of which may be responded to as follows. Firstly, whereas it is true that the normative state studied by Fraenkel was a remnant of a fairly highly developed pre-existing legal system and legal culture in Germany, this does not mean that the concept of the normative state cannot be applied to a country with a different legal history and culture. There is nothing in the concept of the normative state itself that is tied to the existence of a pre-existing legal system and legal culture that is already fairly highly developed before the dual state emerges. As other scholars (including Pils and Fu mentioned above) have demonstrated in their research, even though Maoist China was largely a lawless prerogative state, the efforts made since Deng Xiaoping inaugurated the era of 'reform and opening' in the late 1970s were genuine efforts to establish a normative state in China, and a considerable degree of success has been achieved. So whether a normative state can be 'constructed within the womb of a prerogative state'[98] is a question of fact that can be resolved by empirical research.

Secondly, as regards whether there is sufficient space for legal contestation in China to enable it to qualify as a dual state, Clarke (and Meierhenrich in the passage cited by Clarke) seem to have focused their attention on whether dissenters and opponents of the party-state can meaningfully engage in legal contestation against it. With respect, the better view is that the test of whether there exists a space for legal contestation – for the purpose of determining whether a dual state exists – should be applied to those domains of social life that arguably or potentially fall within the scope of the normative state, as it is not surprising that there is no space for meaningful legal contestation in the domains of the prerogative state. If scholars such as Fu Hualing are correct in suggesting that there is considerable autonomy and legality in the legal system as far as the operation of private law is concerned, then there does exist space for legal contestation among litigants in private law, and a normative state has come into existence that forms part of a dual state in contemporary China.

[94] ibid, 8.
[95] ibid, 10.
[96] ibid, 8.
[97] ibid, 11.
[98] ibid, 7.

Thirdly, although Clarke has used the case of Nazi Germany to illustrate that a prerogative state may be operated by specialist personnel such as the Nazi SS and the special courts established by the Nazis, this does not necessarily mean that the operation of the normative state and the prerogative state within a dual state must be carried out by separate personnel and institutions. It is perfectly possible to conceive of a system in which officials and judges operate within a normative state except in situations considered to be politically significant in which it is accepted that party authorities may intervene and political considerations may override considerations of legality.

Fourthly, whether the regularity and predictability in that part of China's legal system that Clarke calls the 'non-prerogative state' is the outcome of officials and judges adopting what HLA Hart calls an 'internal point of view'[99] towards legal principles and norms is a question of fact that can only be resolved by empirical or anthropological research. Clarke's point in this regard is a positive and constructive one, in that it invites scholars to engage in research in comparative legal cultures so as to discover the extent of officials' commitment to or fidelity to law in different jurisdictions with different histories, traditions and cultures.

III. Conclusion

This chapter has considered concepts relating to the rule of law, such as rule by law, authoritarian legality, dual state and authoritarian rule of law; it has also reviewed a body of recent literature on the application of the concept of the dual state to the case of China. Section I consists of conceptual explorations while section II focuses on the application of relevant concepts to contemporary China.

Section I begins by exploring the distinction between the 'thin' sense and the 'thick' sense of the rule of law. It points out that Fuller's theory of the eight principles of legality largely coincides with the thin sense of the rule of law. Even this thin sense of the rule of law involves a set of fairly demanding requirements, and can be associated with what Fuller calls a 'morality of aspiration', in the sense that it is an ideal that may be realised to varying degrees.

On the other hand, rule by law may be regarded, in Waldron's words, as a 'debased version' of the rule of law. It connotes an instrumental conception of law as a tool to rule over subjects, and is associated with the notion that the ruler or government is not subject to the law. Section I of the chapter also points out that what has been called 'authoritarian legality' is based on the notion of rule by law. However, it is possible for the rule of law (at least in its thin sense) to be realised to a significant degree in some domains of life in an authoritarian state but not in other domains.

[99] See n 13 above.

Section I then introduces the theory of the dual state and authoritarian rule of law. These concepts are used to describe the co-existence of a 'normative state' governed by law and a 'prerogative state' within the same country or society. The concept of the dual state is useful insofar as it enables us to understand that the rule of law may be realised to different degrees in different domains of life within a state or society. As originally theorised by Fraenkel and Meierhenrich, the 'prerogative state' within a 'dual state' is a realm of lawlessness, arbitrariness, wanton rule or violence. Section I suggests that this definition of the prerogative state should be modified and expanded to refer to those domains of the dual state that are not governed by the rule of law. In those domains, what exists may be lawlessness or violations of legality, but the situation may also be some form of rule by law, rule by arbitrary decrees and commands, or by legal rules that confer arbitrary power on government.

By reviewing a body of existing literature on China and the dual state, section II of this chapter demonstrates how the concept of the dual state or the related concept of authoritarian rule of law may be usefully employed in studying the legal system in contemporary China. The application of dual state theory to the case of China acknowledges the progress and achievements of post-Mao legal reform in building what may be called a normative state in at least a significant portion of people's lives. It also points out that China is not yet a rule of law state but is only a dual state, because the prerogative state which predominated in the Maoist era is still in existence and active.

Dual state theory invites scholars of Chinese law in their future research to explore the boundaries and interactions between the normative state and the prerogative state in China. For example, insofar as the normative state largely prevails in domains of private law, what are the circumstances in which the prerogative state would intervene in the operation of private law and the enforcement of private law rights, and what are the modes of intervention? The same question may be raised as regards domains of public law such as judicial review of administrative action, an area in which legal rules apparently have a reasonably significant role to play.

New research questions have also been raised, for example, as regards how the prerogative state should be understood in the case of China. Section II of this chapter shows that the broadened definition of the prerogative state proposed in section I can be realistically applied to what may be called the prerogative state in China. The broadened definition understands the prerogative state as operating in those domains in the dual state in which official actions do not fully or largely conform with the requirements of the rule of law at least in the thin sense.

The case of the Chinese prerogative state raises the particularly interesting and important theoretical issue of how the nature and operation of rules made by the Party (the Chinese Communist Party) should be understood in dual state theory. Section II of this chapter suggests that insofar as such Party-made rules (even though they are not legal rules enacted by state organs) are genuine general rules and are largely complied with by the party-state authorities administering them, it is doubtful whether the relevant official actions should be regarded as part of the prerogative state. It is also suggested that the relationship, possible tension and interaction between legal rules enacted by state organs and Party rules enacted by Party authorities in China deserve further investigation. In this way, the model of the dual state as applied to the case of China can be refined, the nature of the party-state in China can be better understood, and the application of dual state theory to such a party-state can be better explored.

Finally, the question arises as to whether a possible transition from the dual state to a rule of law state such as that suggested by Peerenboom in the quotation at the end of section I of this chapter may materialise sometime in the future. Further research on dual state theory and its application to country studies may assist in answering this question. What, for example, were the cases of success in other countries of transition from dual state to rule of law state? What were the conditions for such a transition, and what were the dynamics of such transition? This kind of comparative law research may throw light on this big question of China's possible transition from dual state to rule of law state.

INDEX

www.ingramcontent.com/pod-product-compliance
Ingram Content Group UK Ltd.
Pitfield, Milton Keynes, MK11 3LW, UK
UKHW020242290926
15470UKWH00002B/685